RED RIVER™

vol.11

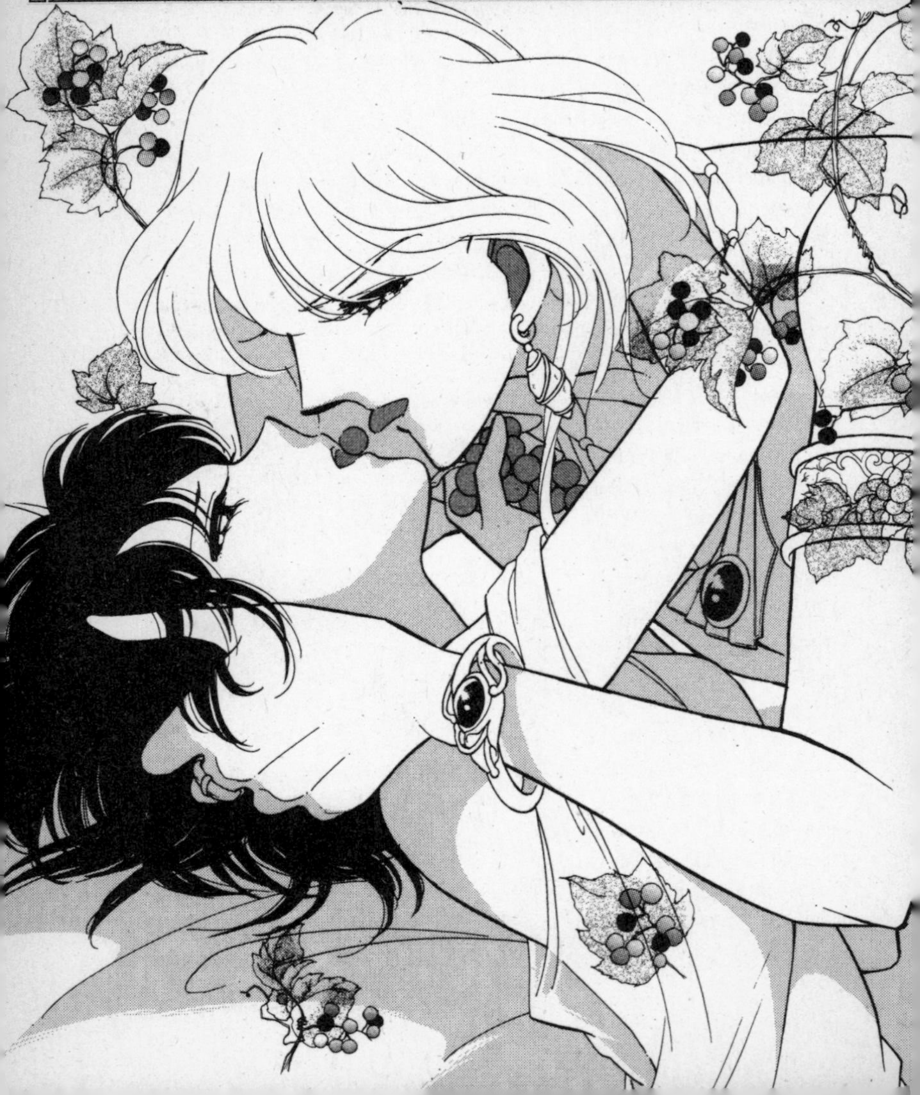

Yuri is a typical junior high student until she's sucked into a puddle and emerges in the ancient Hittite Empire! Evil Queen Nakia has drawn Yuri across time and space to be a sacrifice to her god, Teshub. Rescued by the handsome but arrogant Prince Kail, who wishes to have her as his concubine, Yuri soon learns that returning home requires three things: the help of a sorcerer equal to the queen—which Prince Kail happens to be; Hattusa's seven springs must all fill with water; and she must be in the clothes she wore when she was kidnapped.

In an attempt to recover her clothes, Yuri makes her way into the queen's palace with Kail's young servant Tito at her side. But they walk into a trap, and Tito is killed after saving Yuri's life. When the opportunity finally arrives for Yuri to go home, she refuses, vowing to stay until she has seen Tito avenged. Meanwhile, the Hittites have come to adore Yuri as the incarnation of the goddess Ishtar, and Yuri becomes aware of Prince Kail's dream of creating an empire of justice.

With the passing of the aged Hittite king, Kail's older brother assumes the throne. Though both Prince Kail and Queen Nakia's son, Juda, are nominated to become the crown prince, Kail attains the office through the overwhelming acclaim and support of the people of the Hittite Empire.

Queen Nakia orders her aide, Urhi, to assassinate the new Hittite king. Urhi succeeds, and Nakia accuses Yuri of the crime. To the queen's surprise, Juda bears witness to Yuri's innocence, so Nakia takes magical control of her son and directs him to give false testimony before the senate. To protect Yuri, Kail sends her to Alinna, home of the tribe of Yuri's loyal maidservants. Queen Nakia is not about to let that stop her, and soon her private army is on its way to Alinna to capture Yuri.

Story Thus Far:

Prince Kail
A Hittite royal prince, general, and priest-sorcerer.

Yuri
A Japanese schoolgirl magically transported to the ancient Hittite Empire.

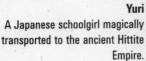

Queen Nakia
Kail's stepmother, an evil sorceress determined to see her own son on the Hittite throne.

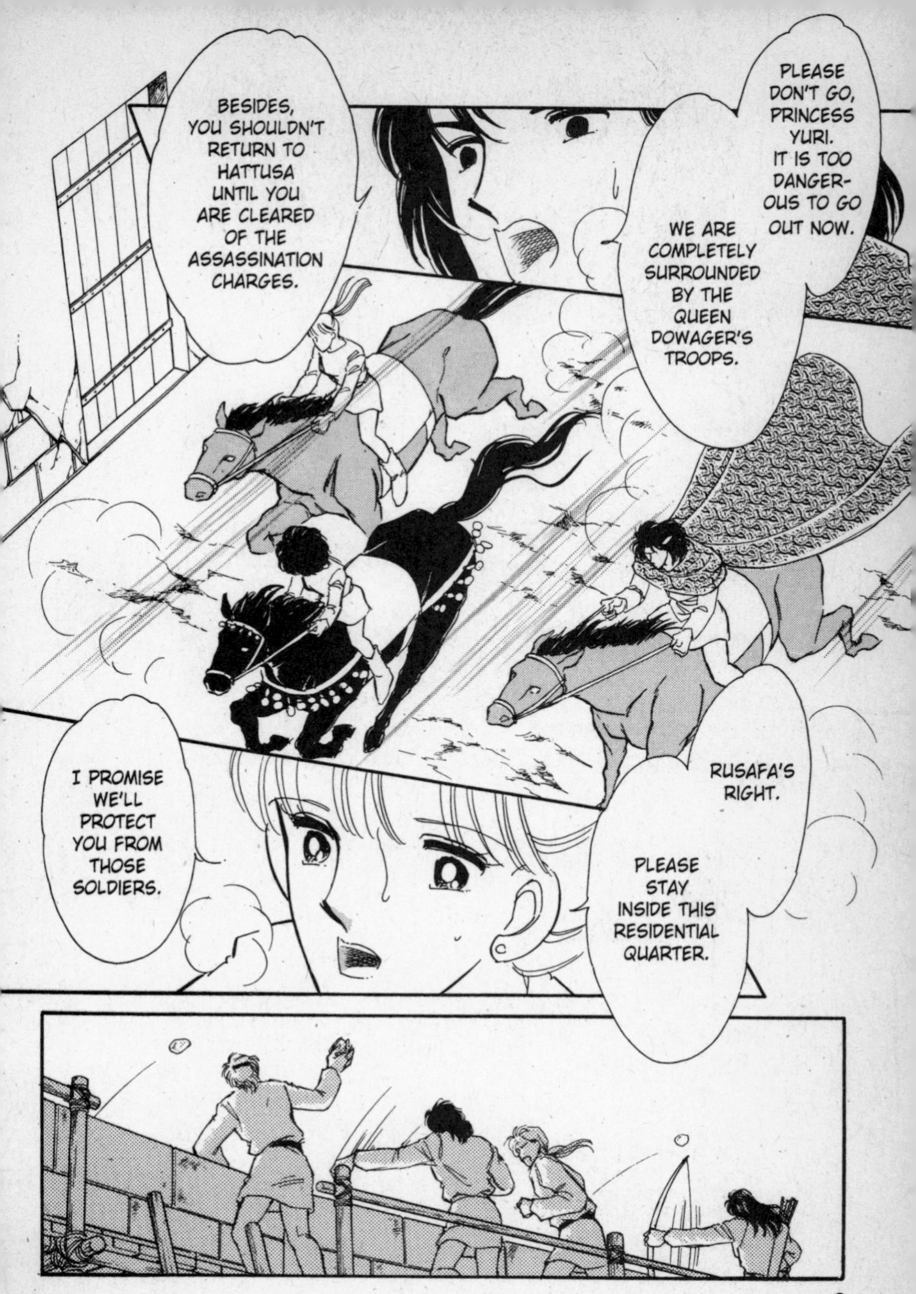
PLEASE DON'T GO, PRINCESS YURI. IT IS TOO DANGEROUS TO GO OUT NOW.
WE ARE COMPLETELY SURROUNDED BY THE QUEEN DOWAGER'S TROOPS.
BESIDES, YOU SHOULDN'T RETURN TO HATTUSA UNTIL YOU ARE CLEARED OF THE ASSASSINATION CHARGES.
RUSAFA'S RIGHT.
PLEASE STAY INSIDE THIS RESIDENTIAL QUARTER.
I PROMISE WE'LL PROTECT YOU FROM THOSE SOLDIERS.

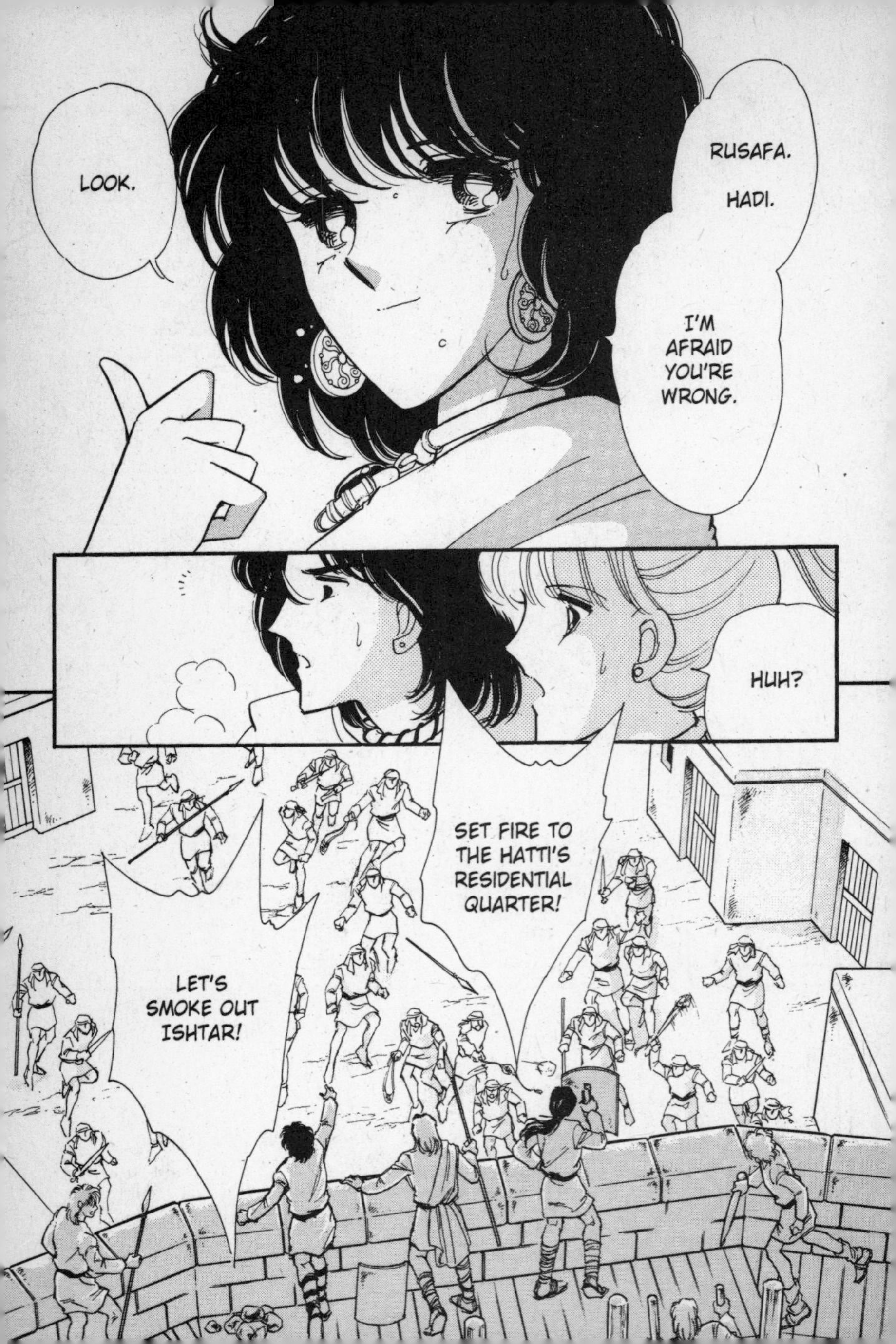
RUSAFA.
HADI.
I'M AFRAID YOU'RE WRONG.
LOOK.
HUH?
SET FIRE TO THE HATTI'S RESIDENTIAL QUARTER!
LET'S SMOKE OUT ISHTAR!

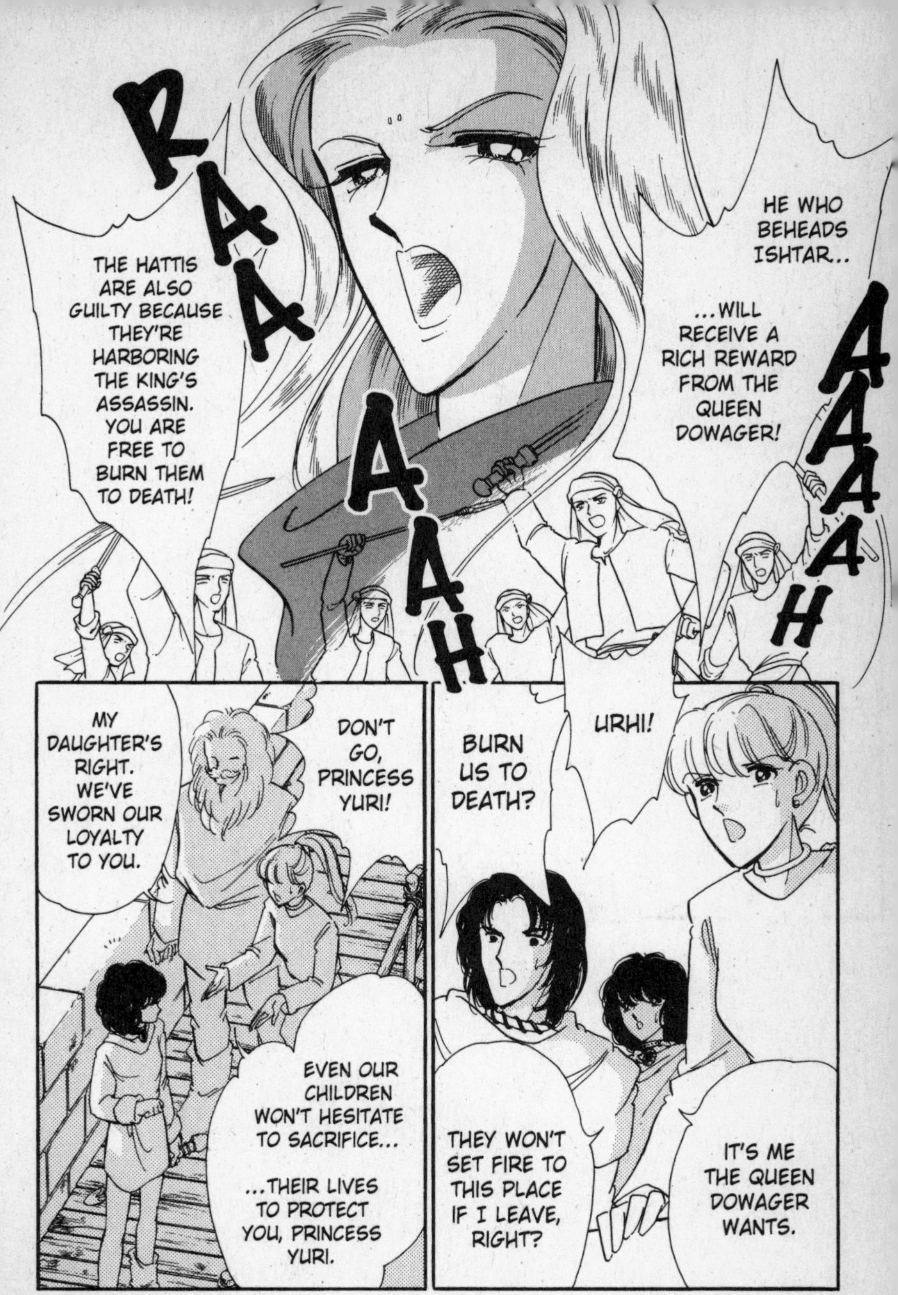
HE WHO BEHEADS ISHTAR...
...WILL RECEIVE A RICH REWARD FROM THE QUEEN DOWAGER!
AAAAH
RAAAAH
THE HATTIS ARE ALSO GUILTY BECAUSE THEY'RE HARBORING THE KING'S ASSASSIN. YOU ARE FREE TO BURN THEM TO DEATH!
URHI!
BURN US TO DEATH?
IT'S ME THE QUEEN DOWAGER WANTS.
THEY WON'T SET FIRE TO THIS PLACE IF I LEAVE, RIGHT?
DON'T GO, PRINCESS YURI!
MY DAUGHTER'S RIGHT. WE'VE SWORN OUR LOYALTY TO YOU.
EVEN OUR CHILDREN WON'T HESITATE TO SACRIFICE...
...THEIR LIVES TO PROTECT YOU, PRINCESS YURI.

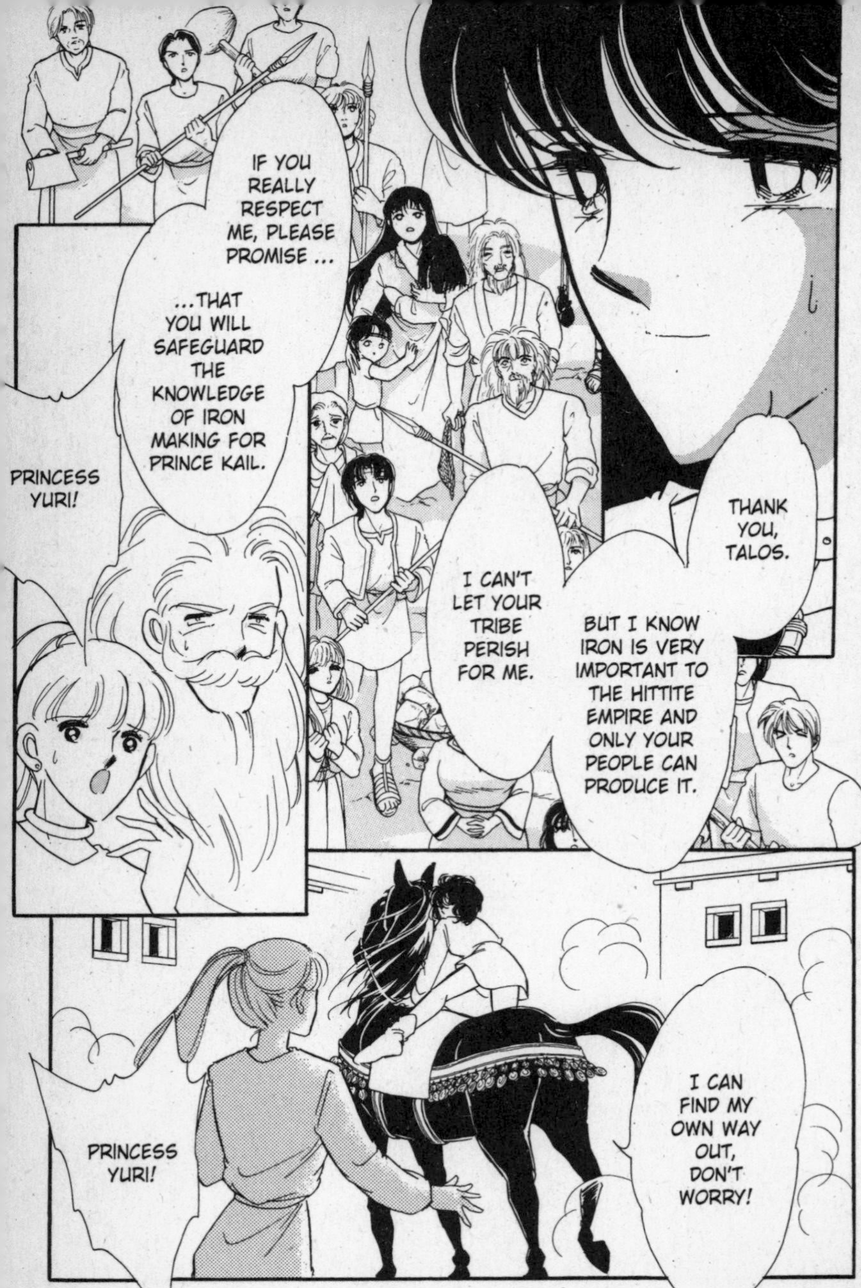
THANK YOU, TALOS.
I CAN'T LET YOUR TRIBE PERISH FOR ME.
BUT I KNOW IRON IS VERY IMPORTANT TO THE HITTITE EMPIRE AND ONLY YOUR PEOPLE CAN PRODUCE IT.
IF YOU REALLY RESPECT ME, PLEASE PROMISE ...
...THAT YOU WILL SAFEGUARD THE KNOWLEDGE OF IRON MAKING FOR PRINCE KAIL.
PRINCESS YURI!
I CAN FIND MY OWN WAY OUT, DON'T WORRY!
PRINCESS YURI!

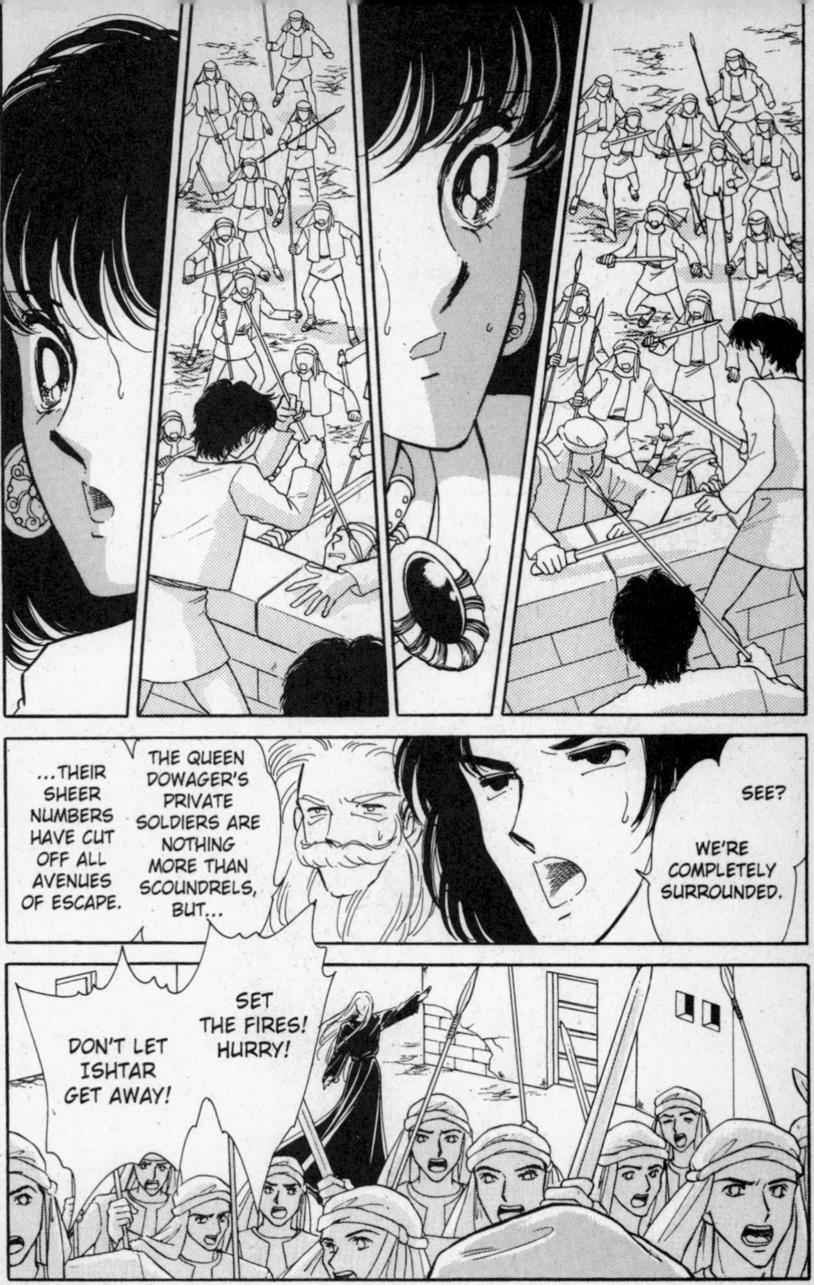
SEE?
WE'RE COMPLETELY SURROUNDED.
THE QUEEN DOWAGER'S PRIVATE SOLDIERS ARE NOTHING MORE THAN SCOUNDRELS, BUT...
...THEIR SHEER NUMBERS HAVE CUT OFF ALL AVENUES OF ESCAPE.
SET THE FIRES! HURRY!
DON'T LET ISHTAR GET AWAY!

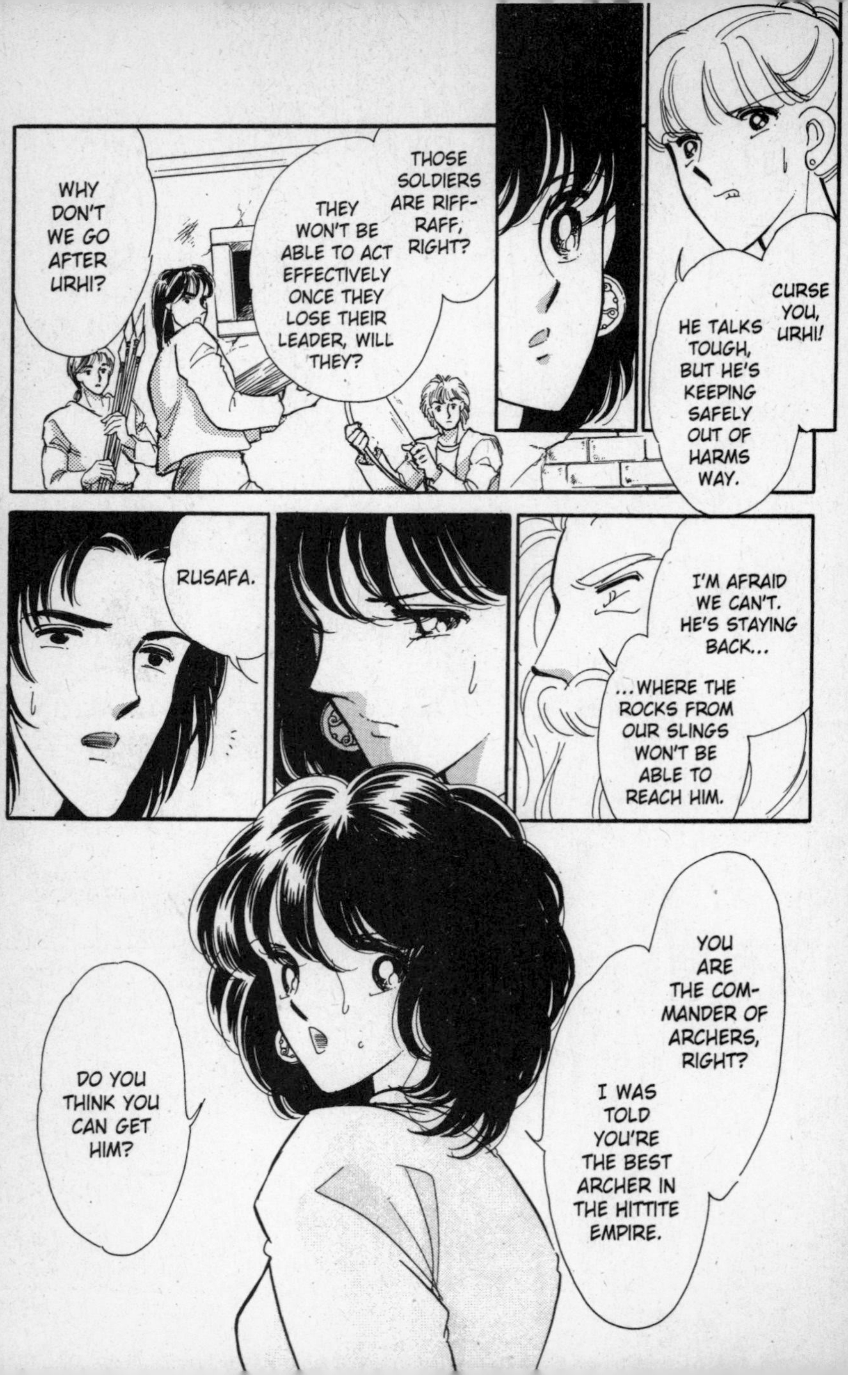
CURSE YOU, URHI!
HE TALKS TOUGH, BUT HE'S KEEPING SAFELY OUT OF HARMS WAY.
THOSE SOLDIERS ARE RIFF-RAFF, RIGHT?
THEY WON'T BE ABLE TO ACT EFFECTIVELY ONCE THEY LOSE THEIR LEADER, WILL THEY?
WHY DON'T WE GO AFTER URHI?
I'M AFRAID WE CAN'T. HE'S STAYING BACK...
...WHERE THE ROCKS FROM OUR SLINGS WON'T BE ABLE TO REACH HIM.
RUSAFA.
YOU ARE THE COM-MANDER OF ARCHERS, RIGHT?
I WAS TOLD YOU'RE THE BEST ARCHER IN THE HITTITE EMPIRE.
DO YOU THINK YOU CAN GET HIM?

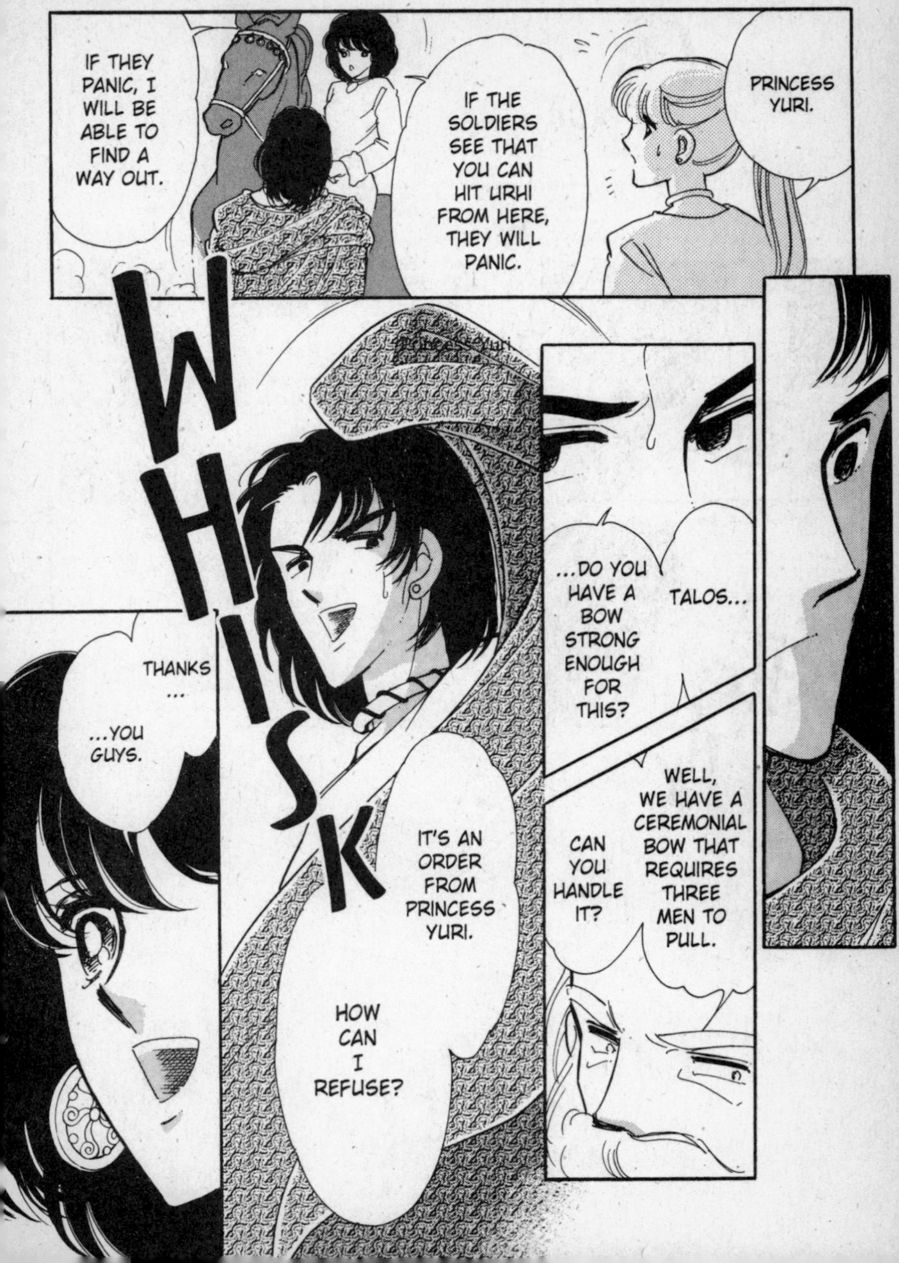
PRINCESS YURI.
IF THE SOLDIERS SEE THAT YOU CAN HIT URHI FROM HERE, THEY WILL PANIC.
IF THEY PANIC, I WILL BE ABLE TO FIND A WAY OUT.
TALOS...
...DO YOU HAVE A BOW STRONG ENOUGH FOR THIS?
WELL, WE HAVE A CEREMONIAL BOW THAT REQUIRES THREE MEN TO PULL.
CAN YOU HANDLE IT?
WHISK
IT'S AN ORDER FROM PRINCESS YURI.
HOW CAN I REFUSE?
THANKS...
...YOU GUYS.

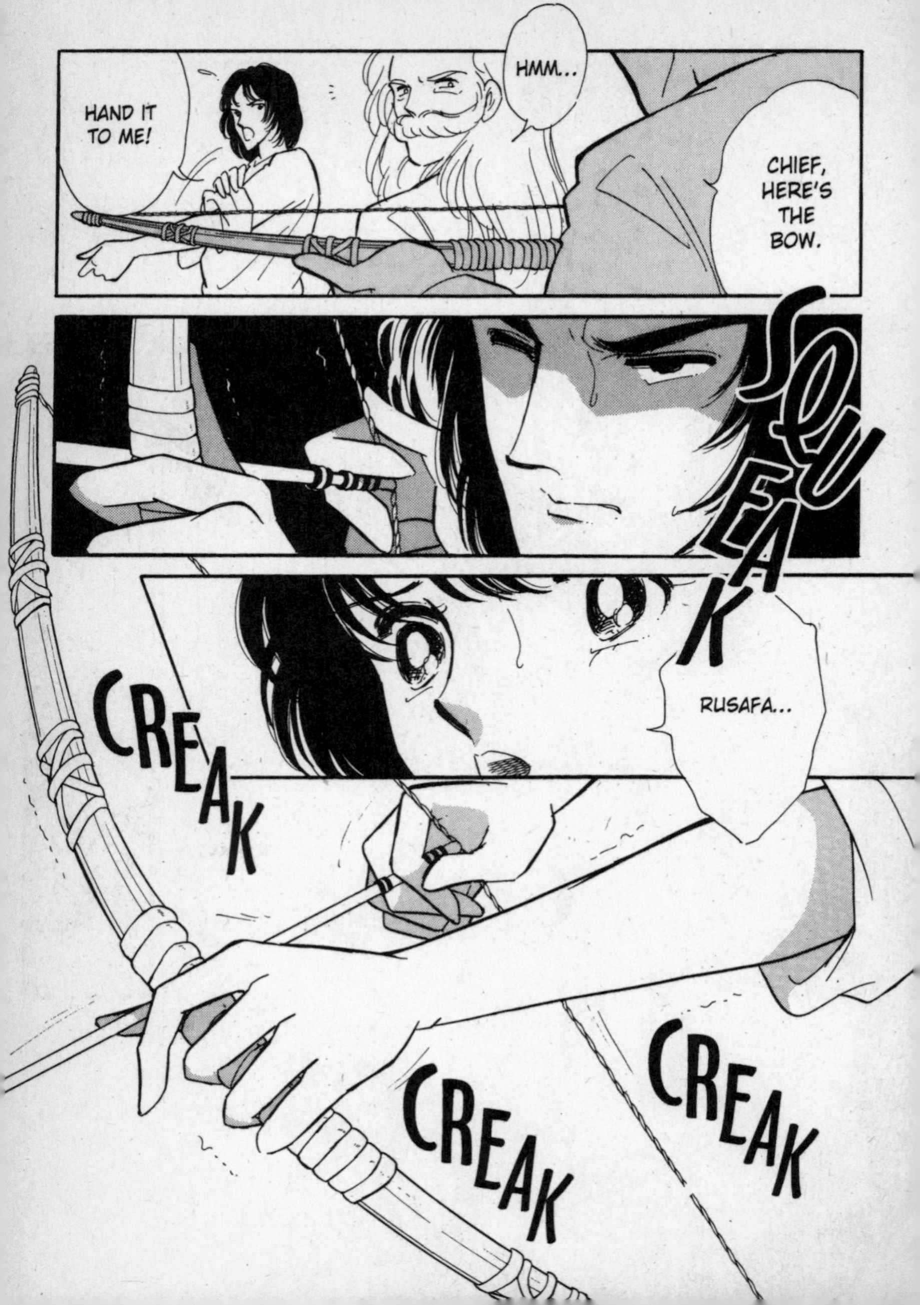
CHIEF, HERE'S THE BOW.
HMM...
HAND IT TO ME!
SQUEAK
RUSAFA...
CREAK
CREAK
CREAK

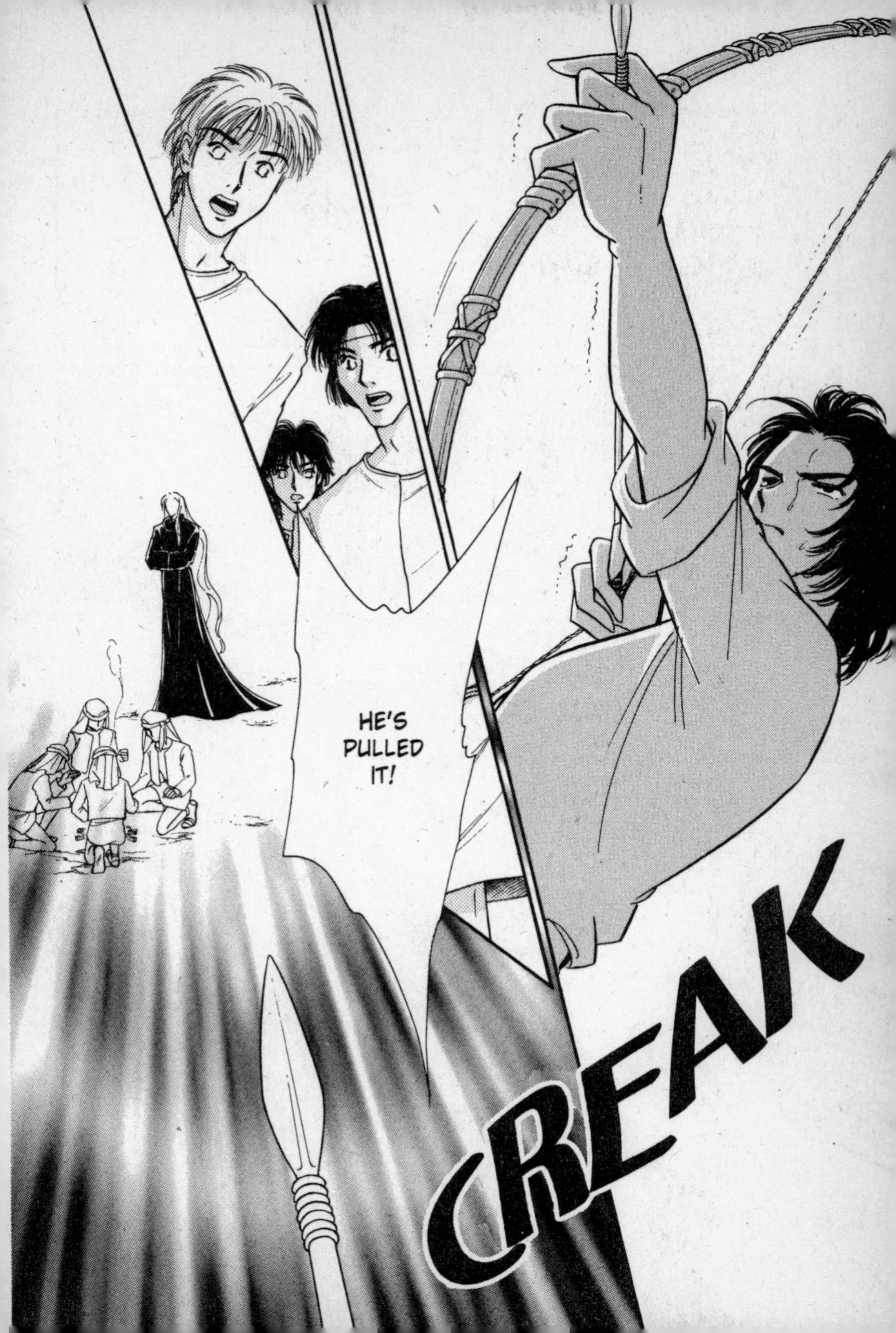
HE'S PULLED IT!
CREAK

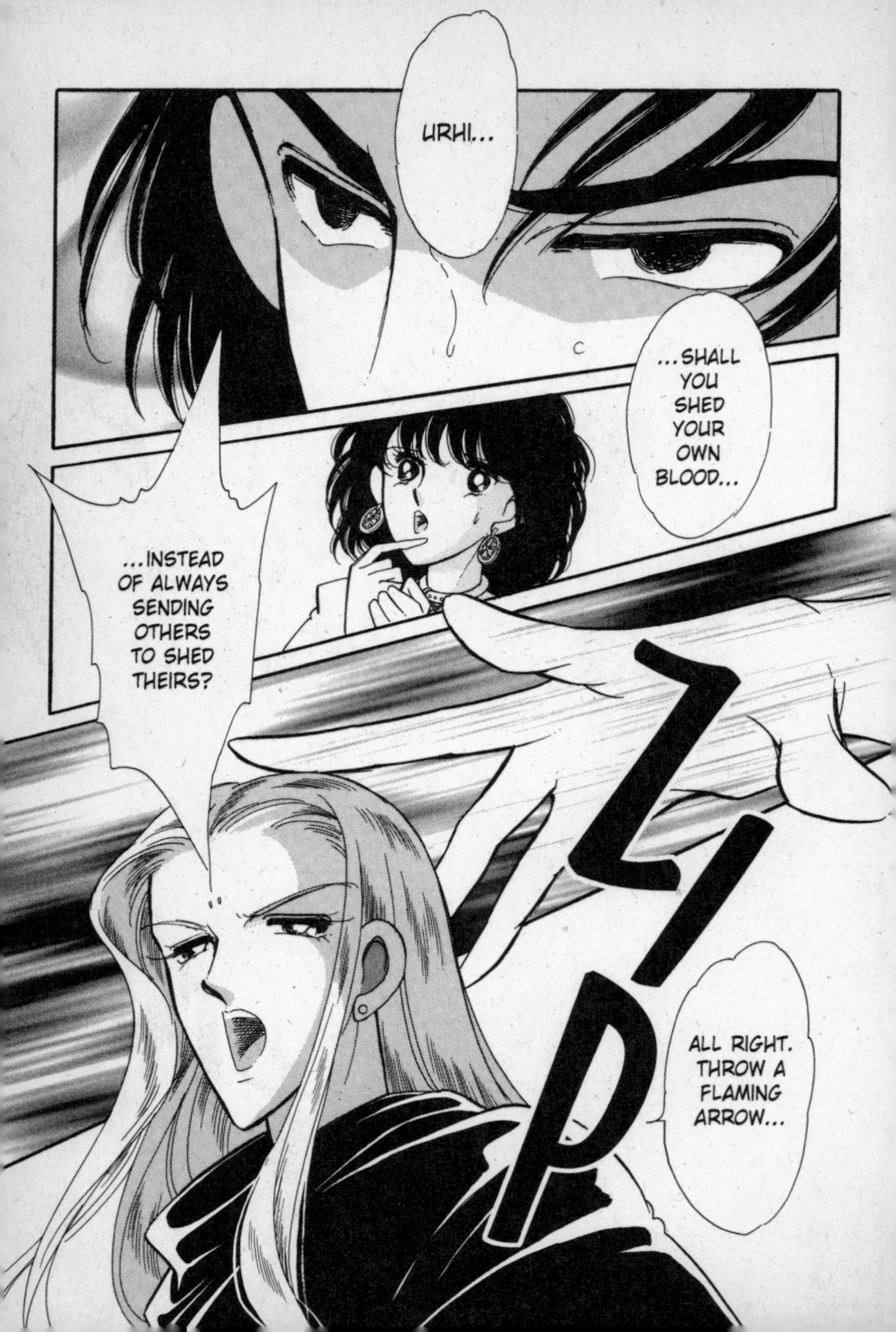
URHI...
...SHALL YOU SHED YOUR OWN BLOOD...
...INSTEAD OF ALWAYS SENDING OTHERS TO SHED THEIRS?
ZIP
ALL RIGHT. THROW A FLAMING ARROW...

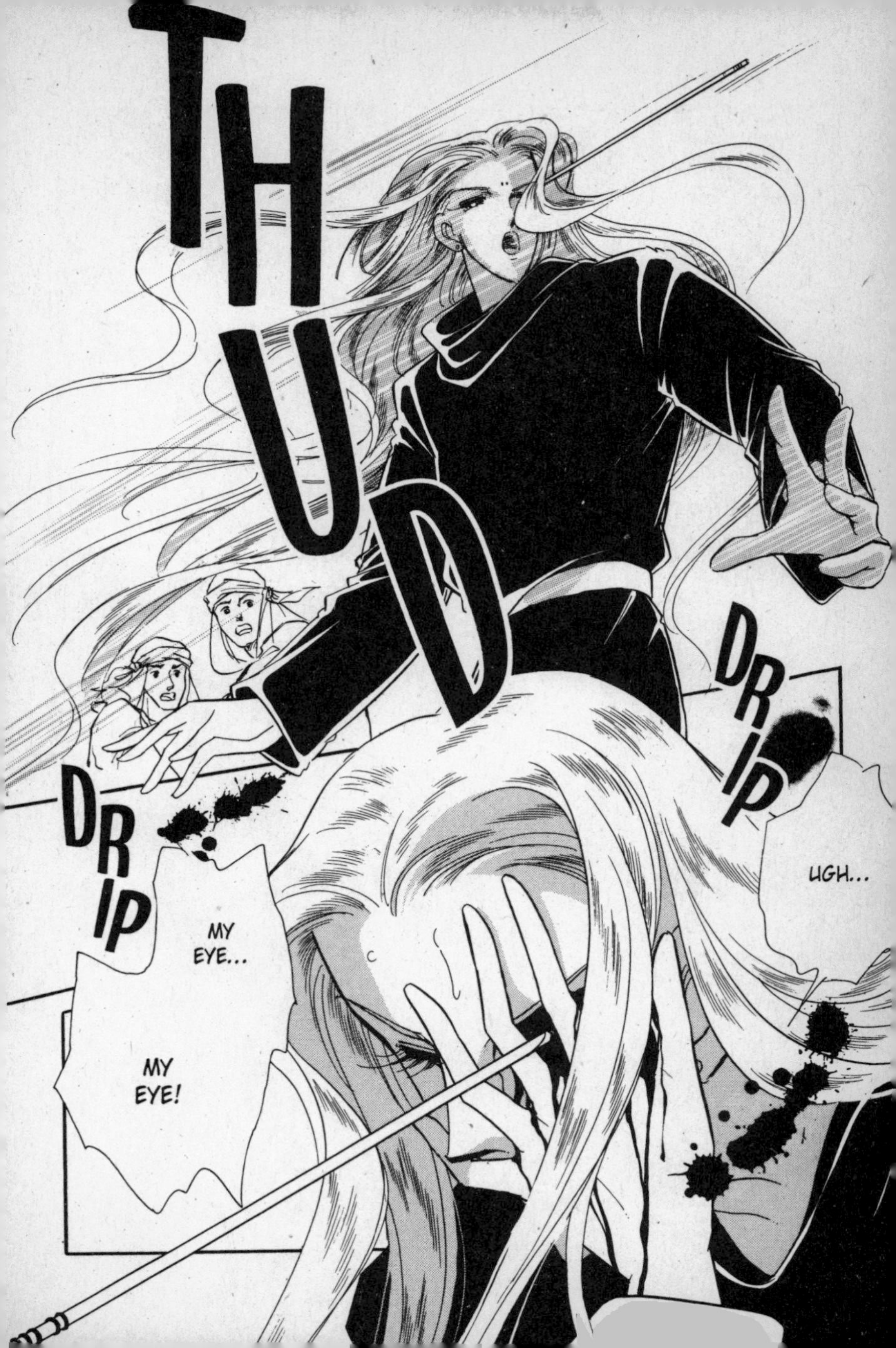
THUD
DRIP
UGH...
DRIP
MY EYE...
MY EYE!

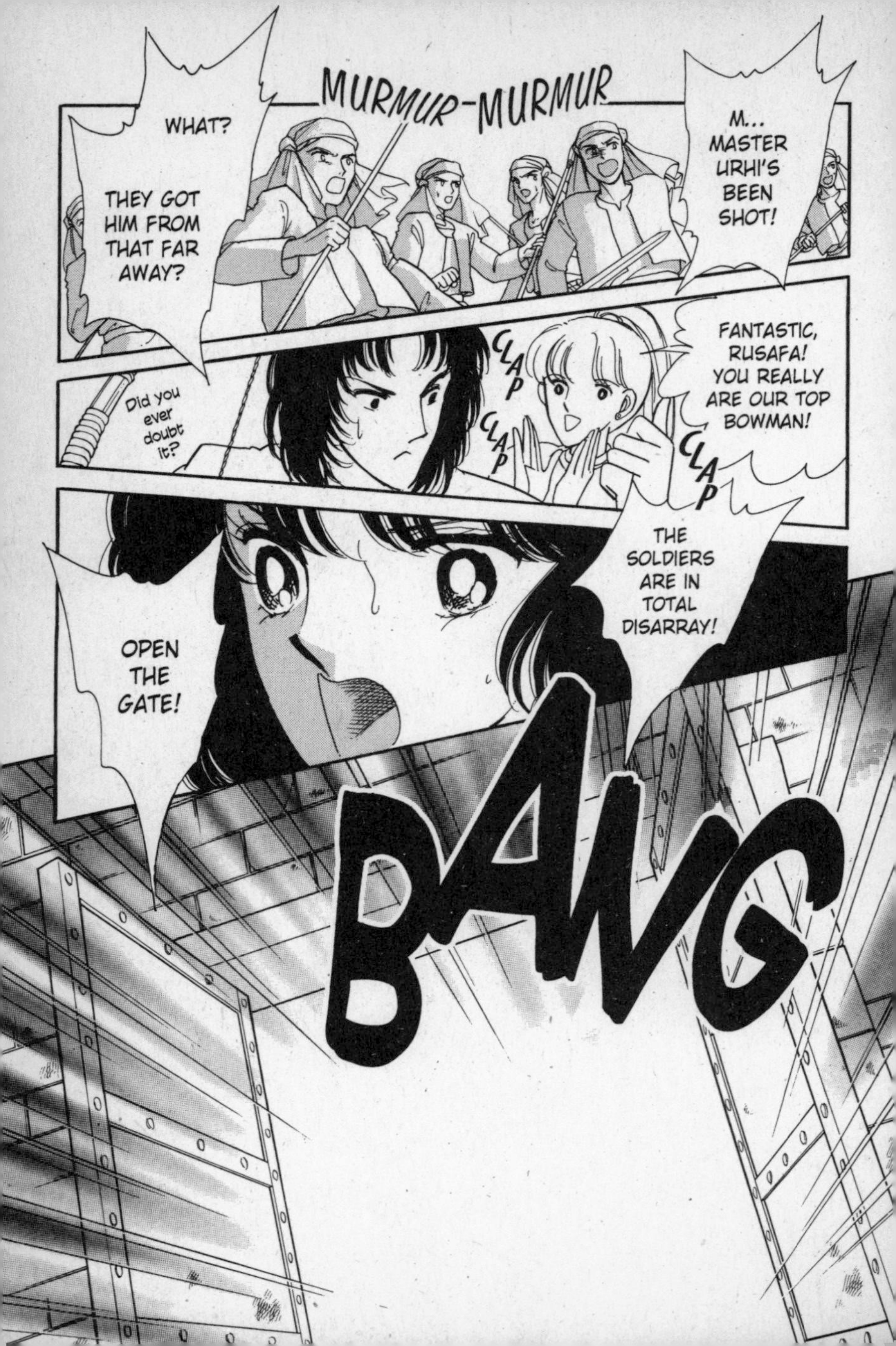
M... MASTER URHI'S BEEN SHOT!
MURMUR-MURMUR
WHAT?
THEY GOT HIM FROM THAT FAR AWAY?
FANTASTIC, RUSAFA! YOU REALLY ARE OUR TOP BOWMAN!
CLAP
CLAP
CLAP
Did you ever doubt it?
THE SOLDIERS ARE IN TOTAL DISARRAY!
OPEN THE GATE!
BANG

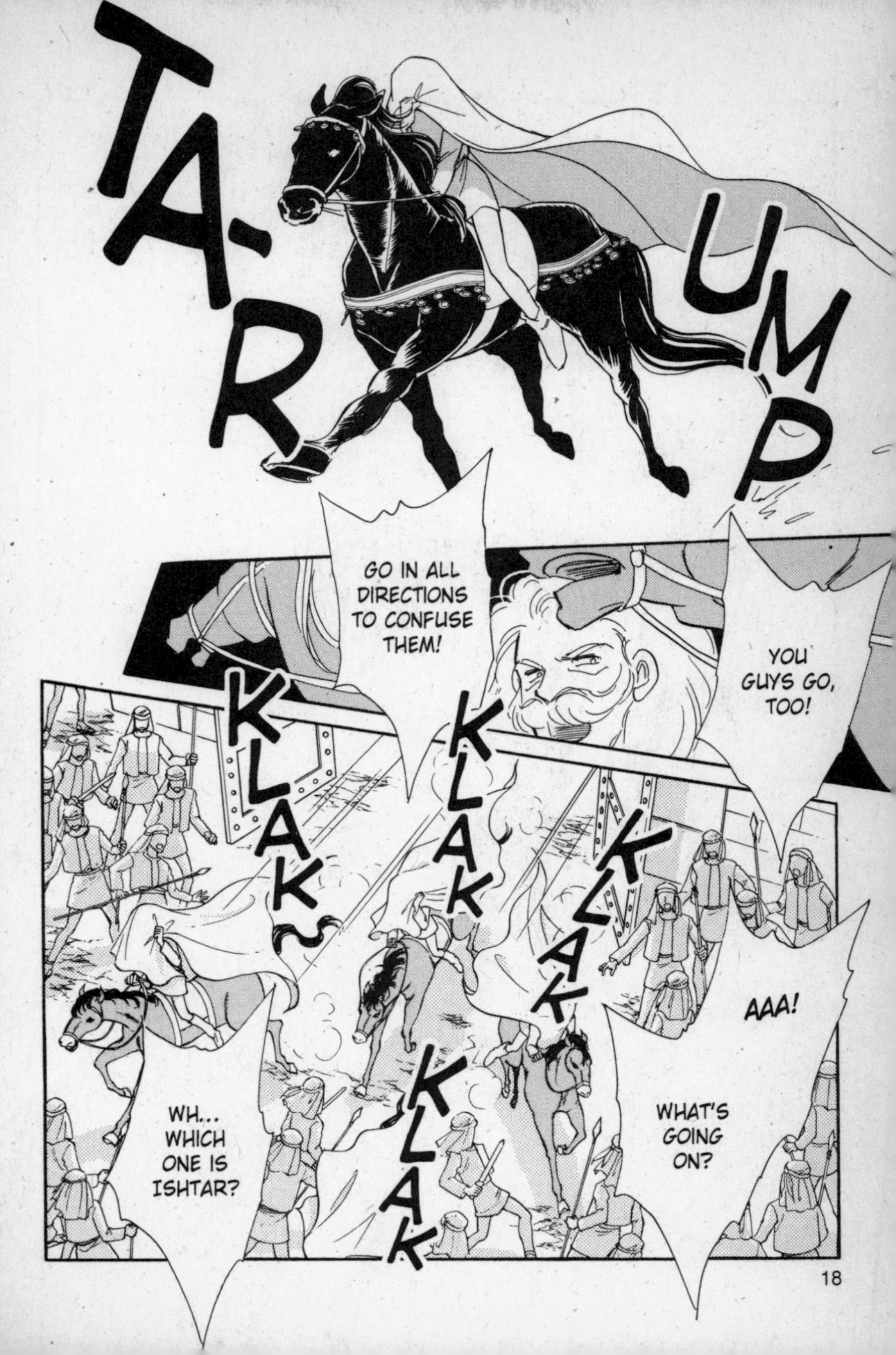
TA-RUMP
YOU GUYS GO, TOO!
GO IN ALL DIRECTIONS TO CONFUSE THEM!
AAA!
WHAT'S GOING ON?
KLAK KLAK KLAK KLAK
KLAK KLAK
WH... WHICH ONE IS ISHTAR?

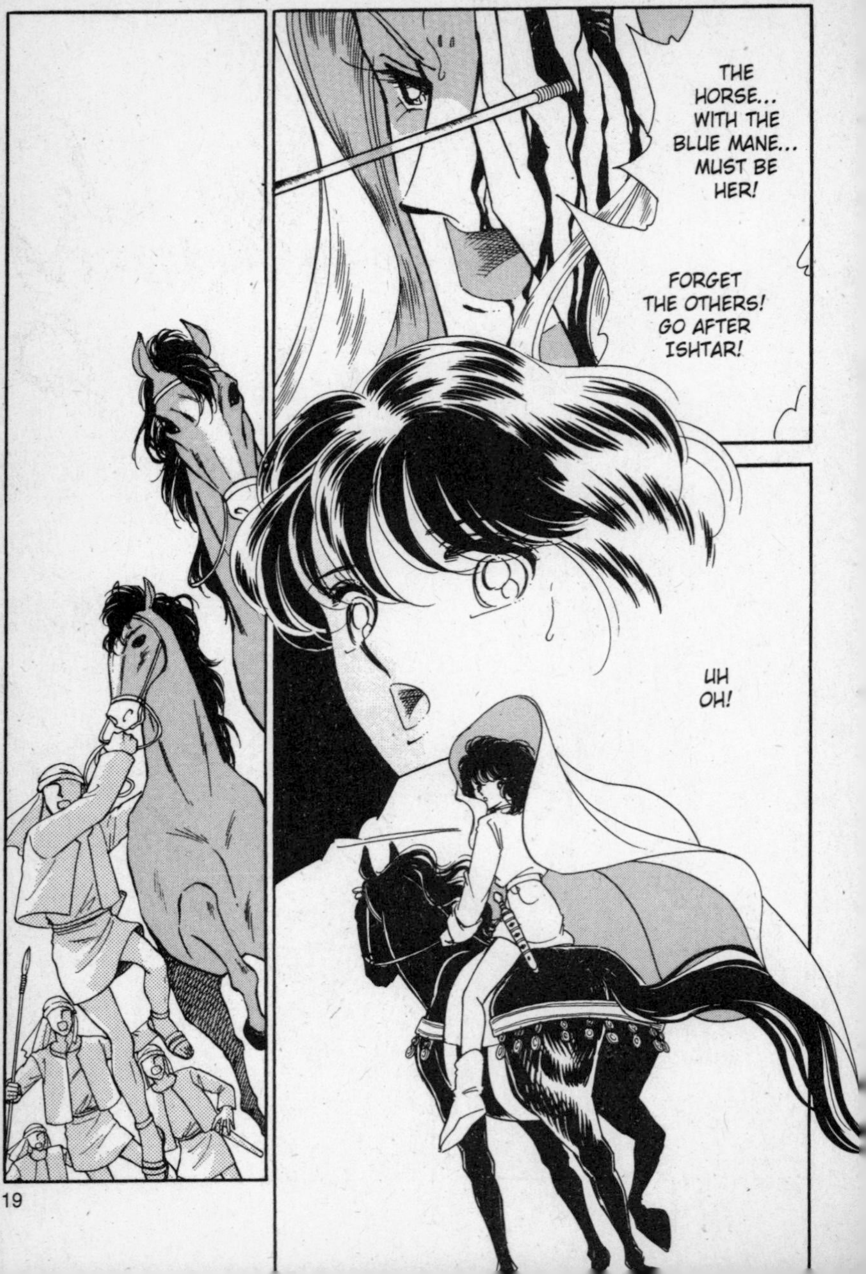
THE HORSE... WITH THE BLUE MANE... MUST BE HER!
FORGET THE OTHERS! GO AFTER ISHTAR!
UH OH!

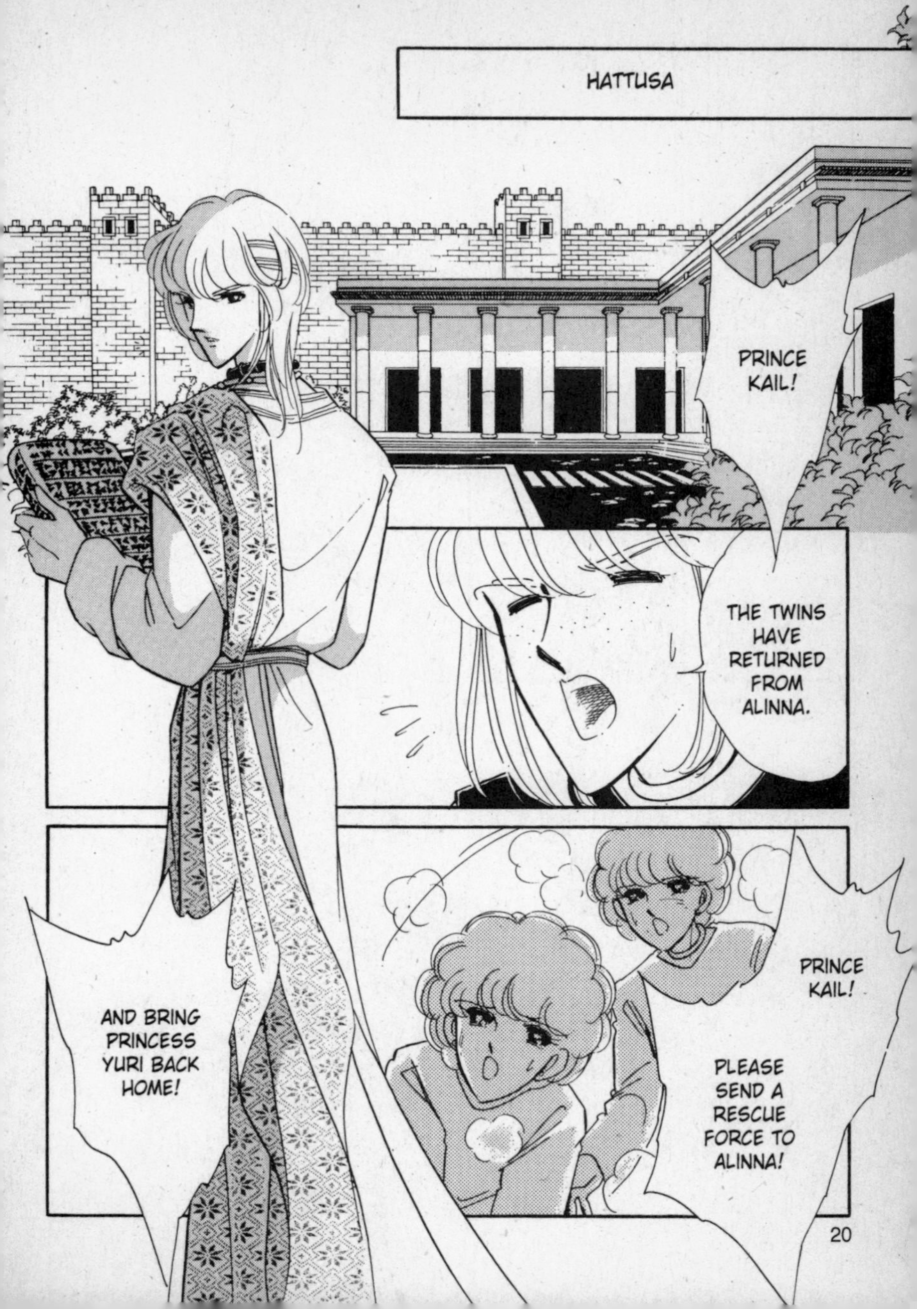
HATTUSA
PRINCE KAIL!
THE TWINS HAVE RETURNED FROM ALINNA.
PRINCE KAIL!
PLEASE SEND A RESCUE FORCE TO ALINNA!
AND BRING PRINCESS YURI BACK HOME!

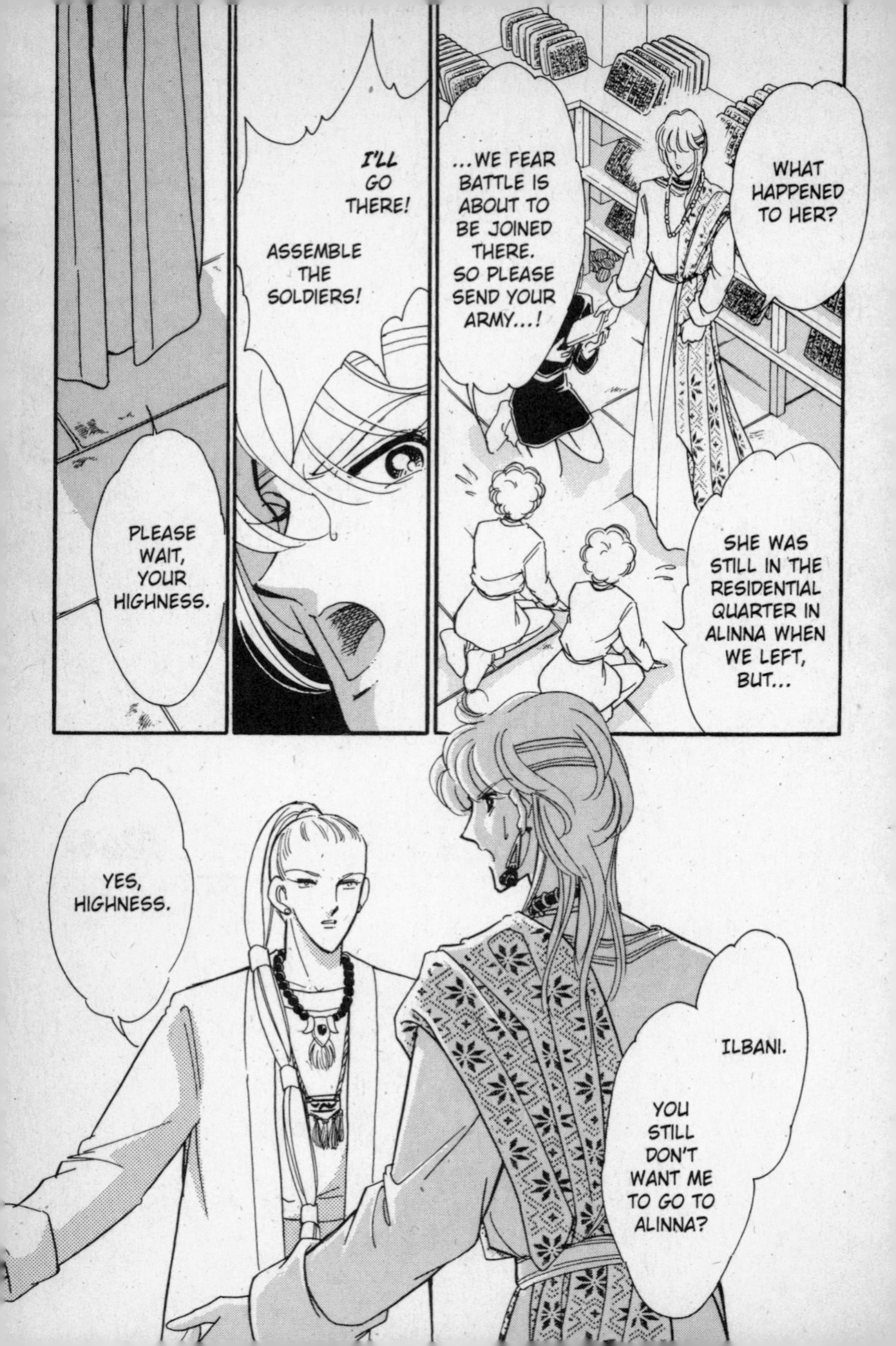
...WE FEAR BATTLE IS ABOUT TO BE JOINED THERE. SO PLEASE SEND YOUR ARMY...!
WHAT HAPPENED TO HER?
SHE WAS STILL IN THE RESIDENTIAL QUARTER IN ALINNA WHEN WE LEFT, BUT...
I'LL GO THERE!
ASSEMBLE THE SOLDIERS!
PLEASE WAIT, YOUR HIGHNESS.
ILBANI.
YOU STILL DON'T WANT ME TO GO TO ALINNA?
YES, HIGHNESS.

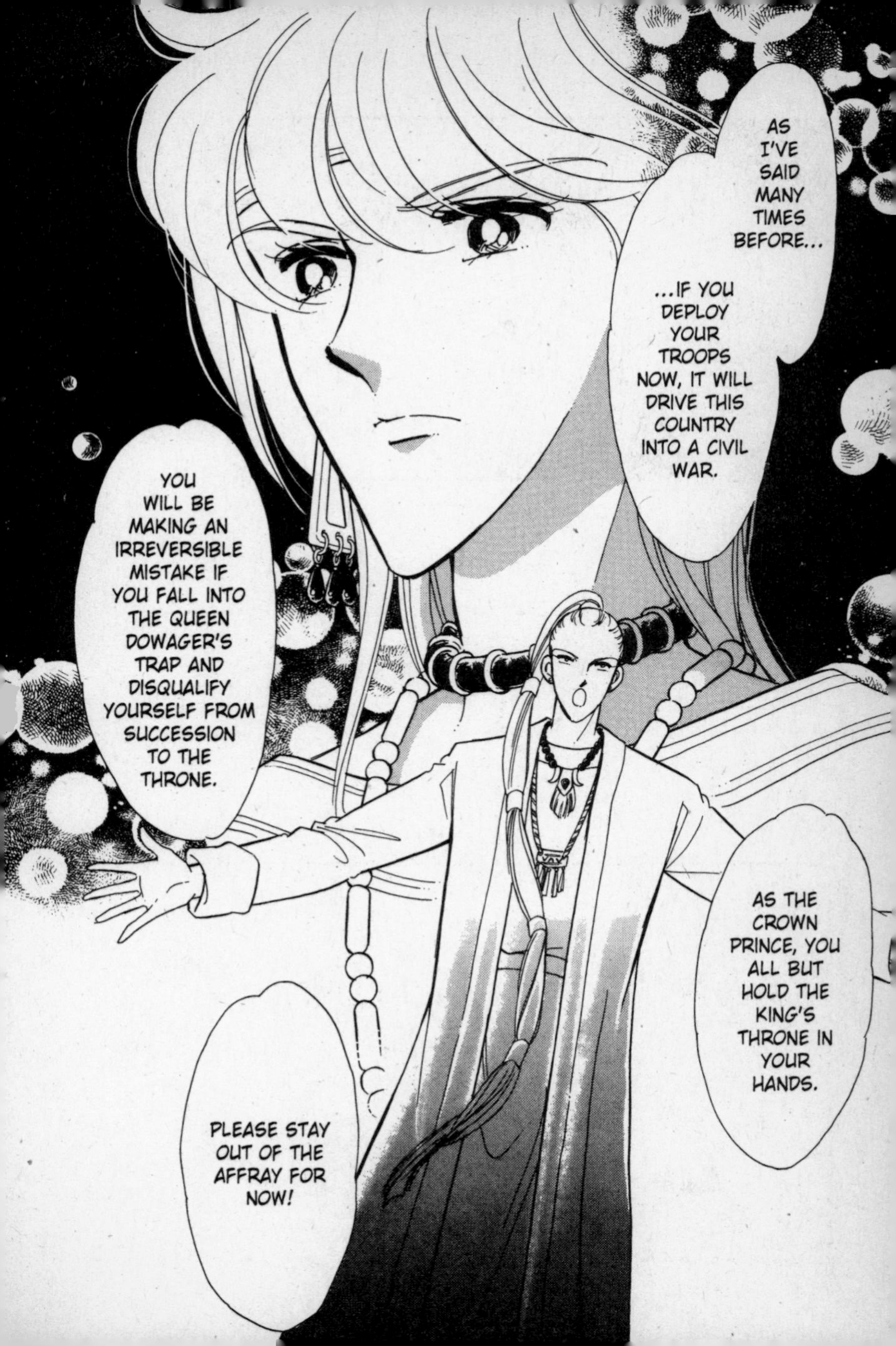
AS I'VE SAID MANY TIMES BEFORE...
...IF YOU DEPLOY YOUR TROOPS NOW, IT WILL DRIVE THIS COUNTRY INTO A CIVIL WAR.
YOU WILL BE MAKING AN IRREVERSIBLE MISTAKE IF YOU FALL INTO THE QUEEN DOWAGER'S TRAP AND DISQUALIFY YOURSELF FROM SUCCESSION TO THE THRONE.
AS THE CROWN PRINCE, YOU ALL BUT HOLD THE KING'S THRONE IN YOUR HANDS.
PLEASE STAY OUT OF THE AFFRAY FOR NOW!

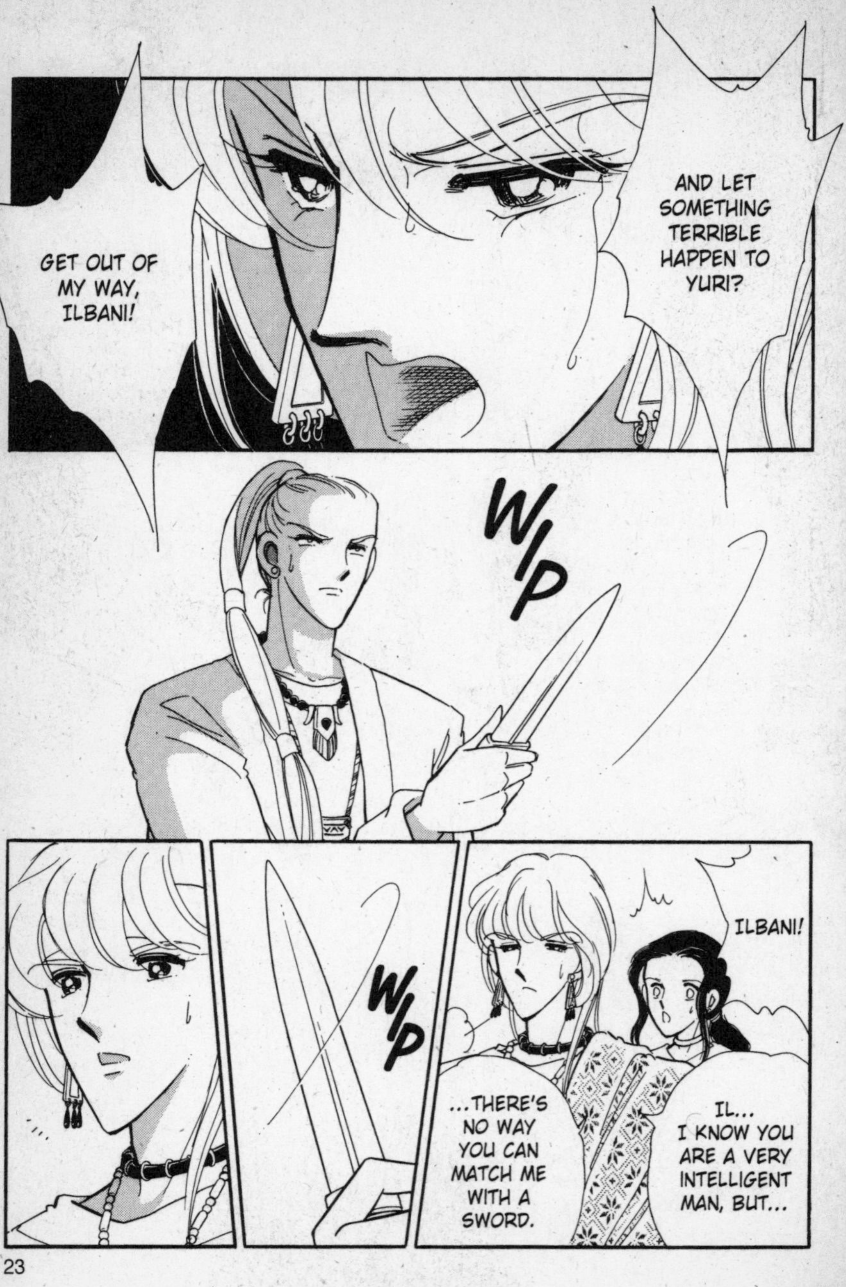
AND LET SOMETHING TERRIBLE HAPPEN TO YURI?
GET OUT OF MY WAY, ILBANI!
WIP
ILBANI!
IL... I KNOW YOU ARE A VERY INTELLIGENT MAN, BUT...
...THERE'S NO WAY YOU CAN MATCH ME WITH A SWORD.
WIP
...

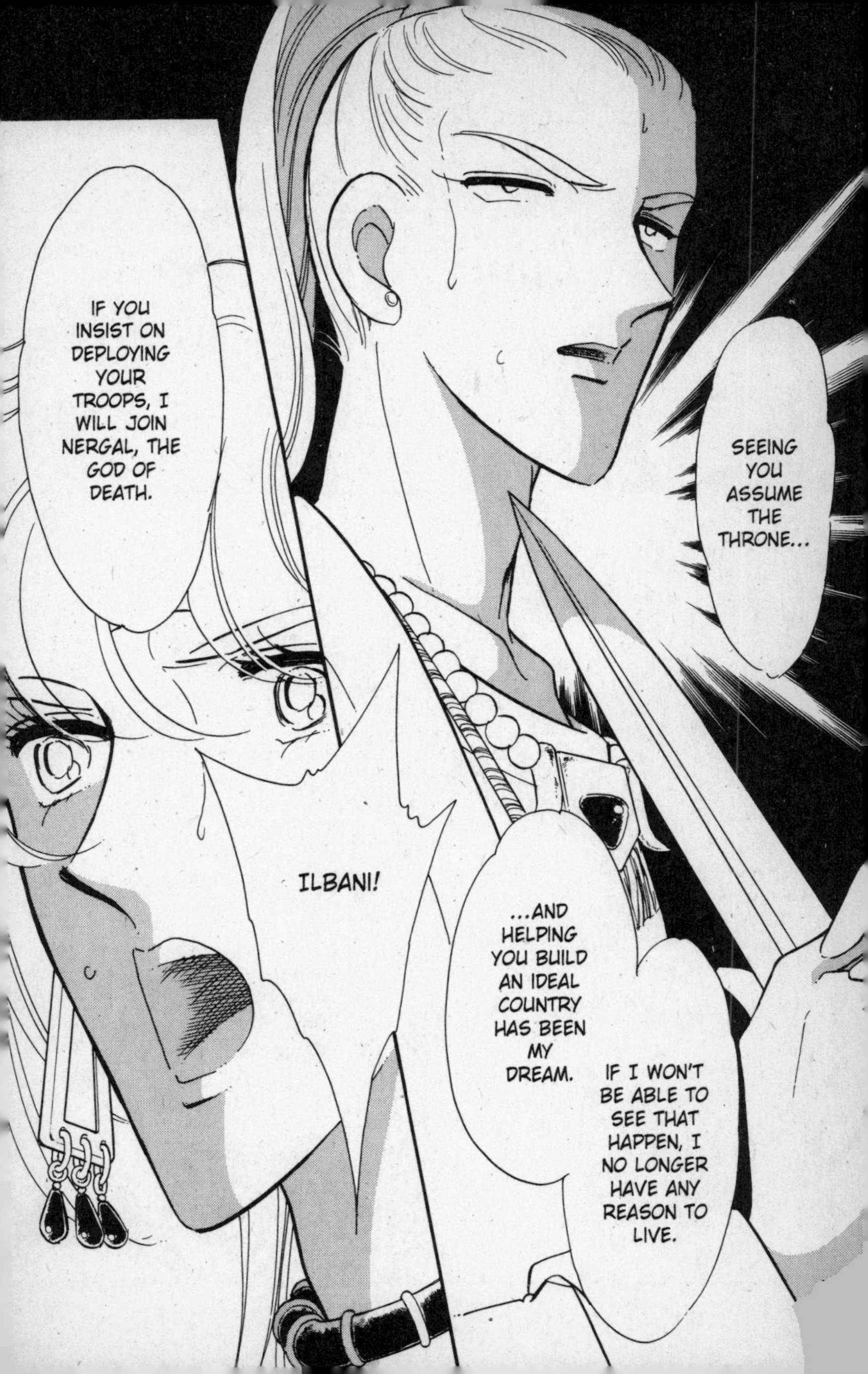
SEEING YOU ASSUME THE THRONE...
...AND HELPING YOU BUILD AN IDEAL COUNTRY HAS BEEN MY DREAM.
IF I WON'T BE ABLE TO SEE THAT HAPPEN, I NO LONGER HAVE ANY REASON TO LIVE.
IF YOU INSIST ON DEPLOYING YOUR TROOPS, I WILL JOIN NERGAL, THE GOD OF DEATH.
ILBANI!

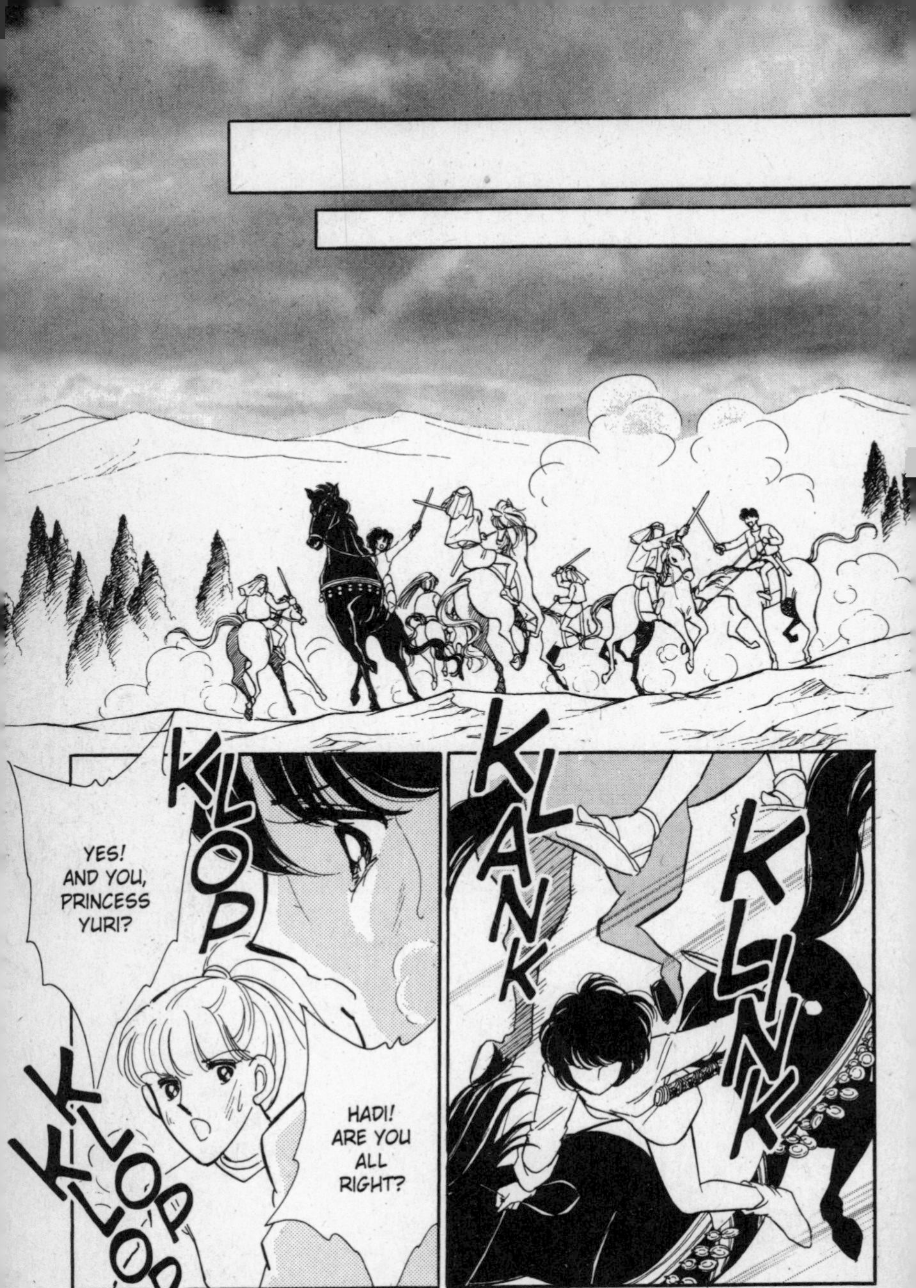
KLANK
KLLINK
KLOP
HADI! ARE YOU ALL RIGHT?
YES! AND YOU, PRINCESS YURI?
KLOP
KLOP

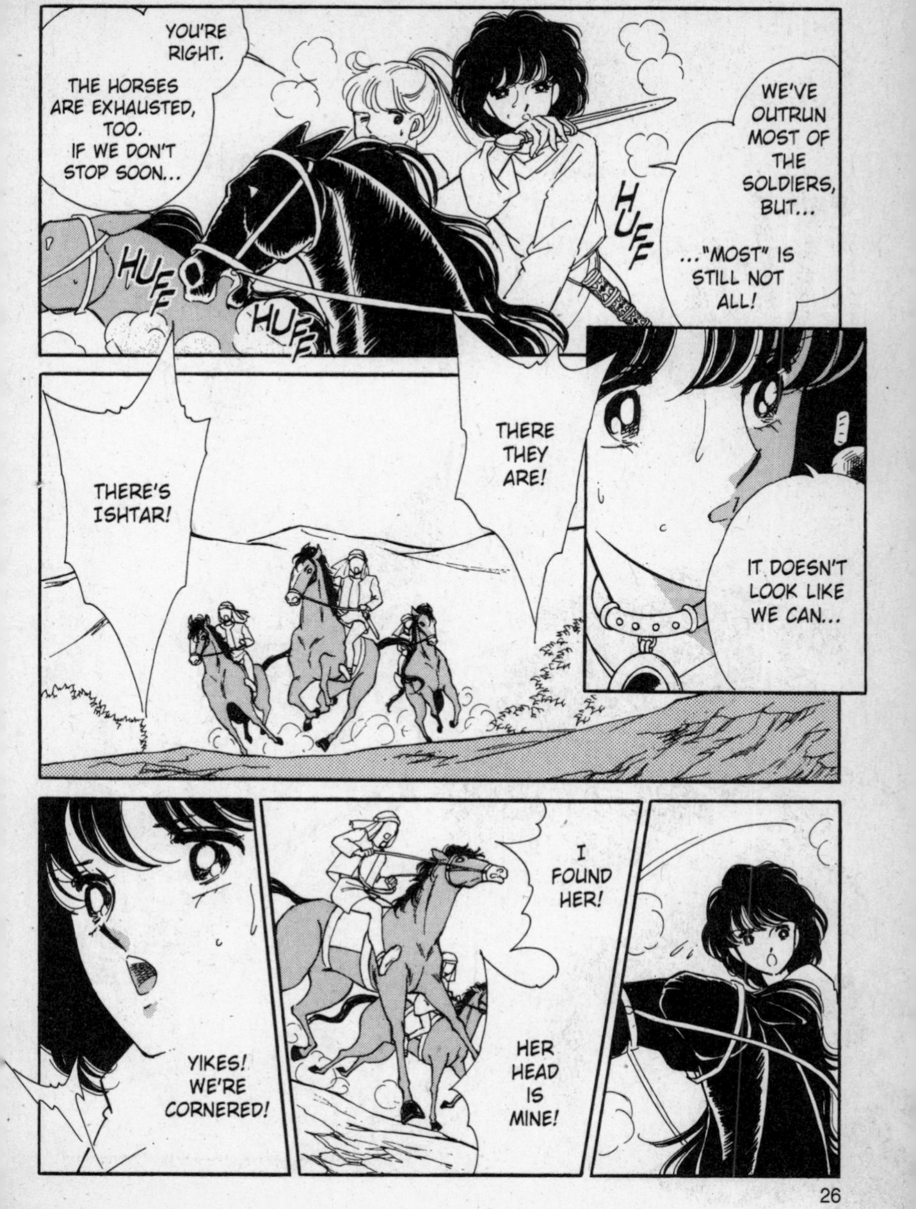
WE'VE OUTRUN MOST OF THE SOLDIERS, BUT...
..."MOST" IS STILL NOT ALL!
HUFF
YOU'RE RIGHT.
THE HORSES ARE EXHAUSTED, TOO. IF WE DON'T STOP SOON...
HUFF
HUFF
IT DOESN'T LOOK LIKE WE CAN...
THERE THEY ARE!
THERE'S ISHTAR!
I FOUND HER!
HER HEAD IS MINE!
YIKES! WE'RE CORNERED!

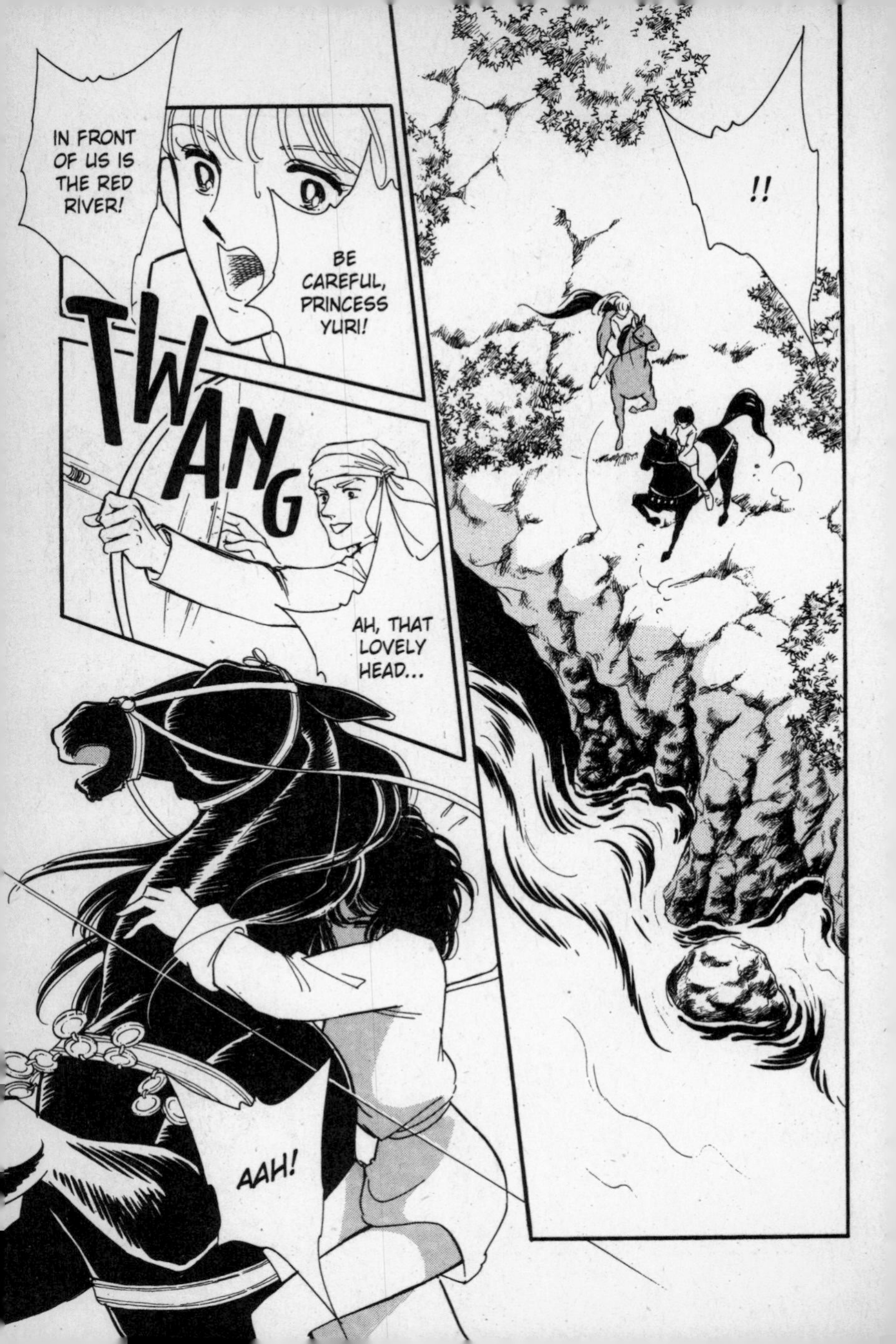
!!
IN FRONT OF US IS THE RED RIVER!
BE CAREFUL, PRINCESS YURI!
TWANG
AH, THAT LOVELY HEAD...
AAH!

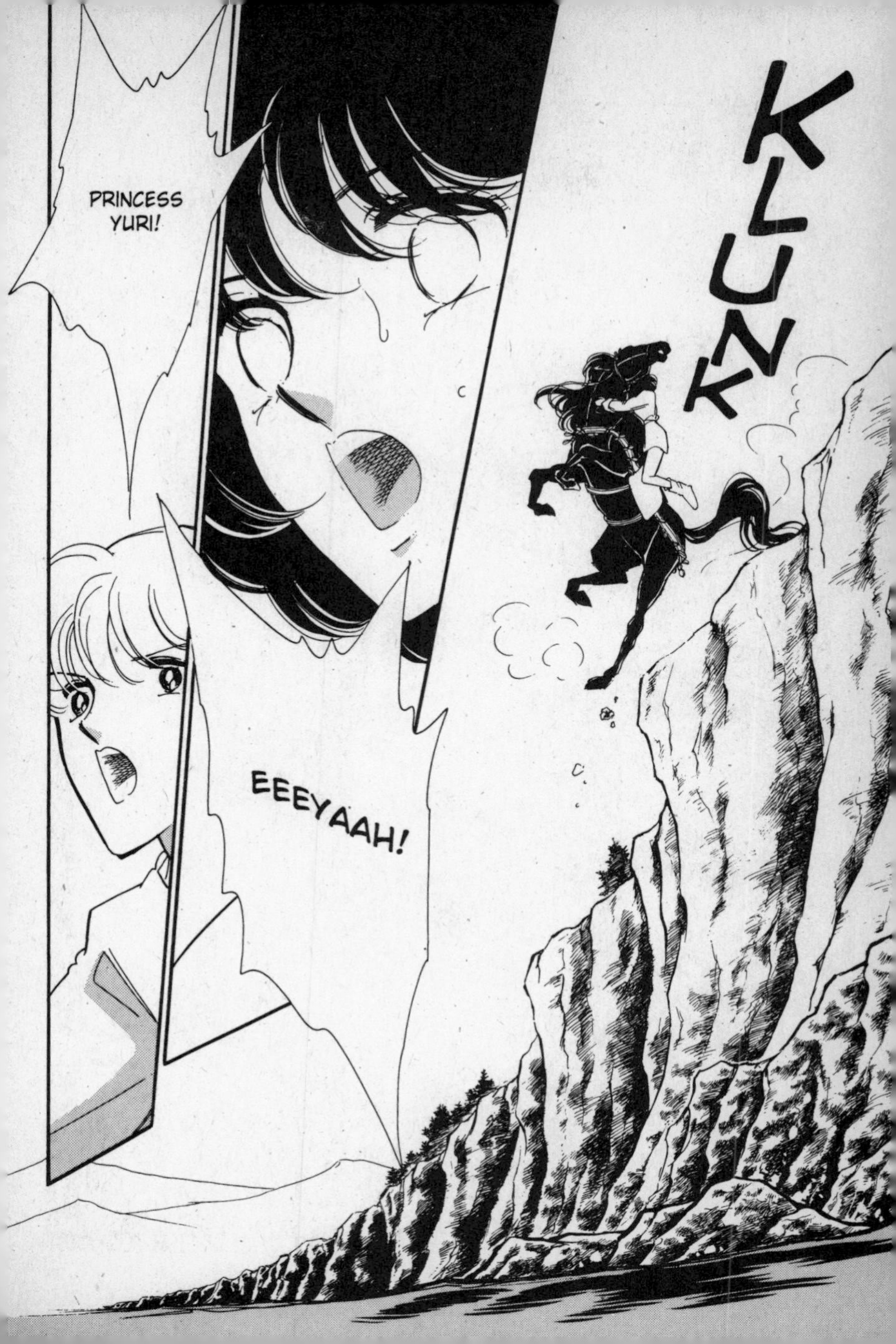
KLUNK
EEEYAAH!
PRINCESS YURI!

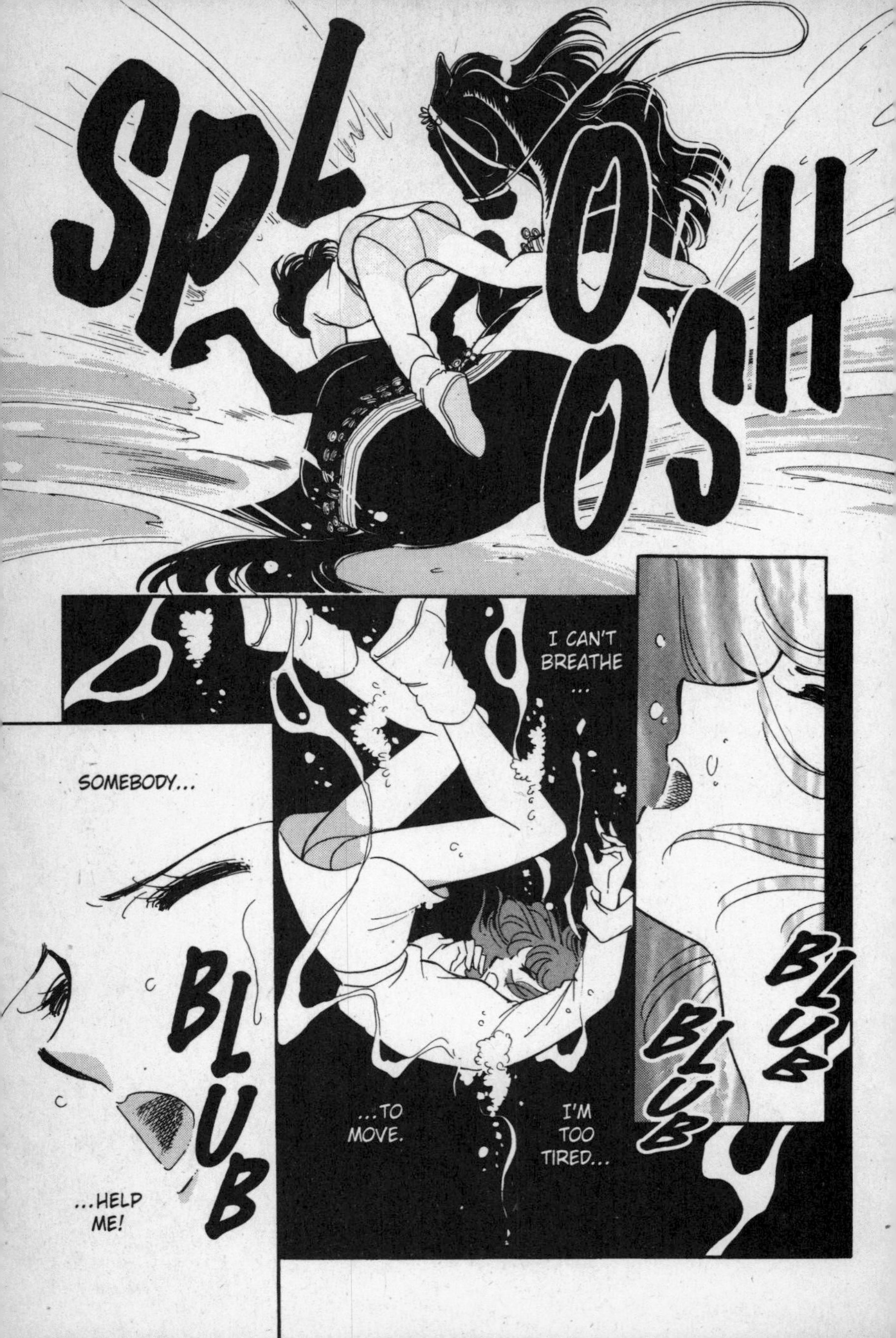
SPLOOSH
BLUB
BLUB
I CAN'T BREATHE ...
I'M TOO TIRED...
...TO MOVE.
SOMEBODY...
BLUB
...HELP ME!

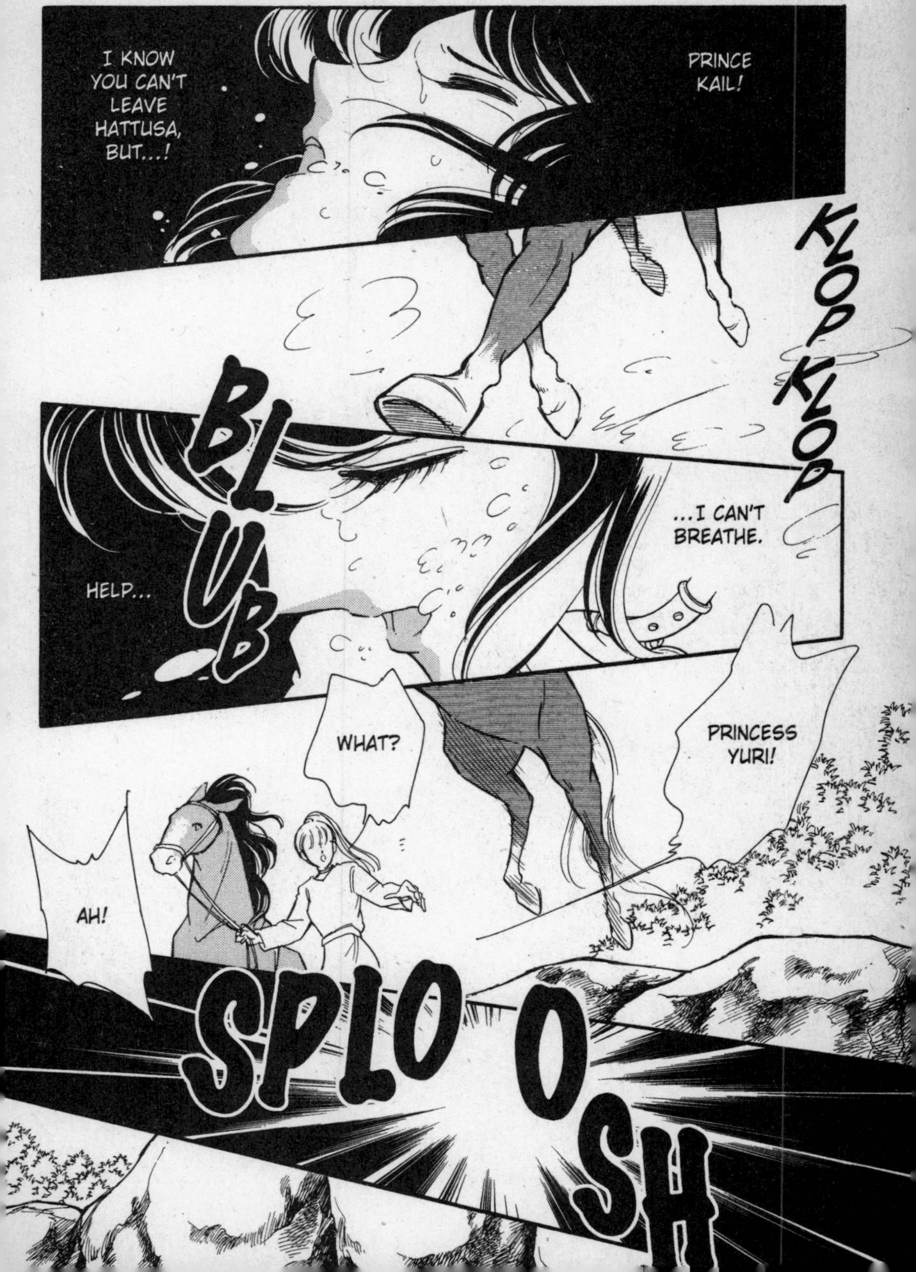
PRINCE KAIL!
I KNOW YOU CAN'T LEAVE HATTUSA, BUT...!
KLOP KLOP KLOP
...I CAN'T BREATHE.
HELP...
BLUB
PRINCESS YURI!
WHAT?
AH!
SPLOOOSH

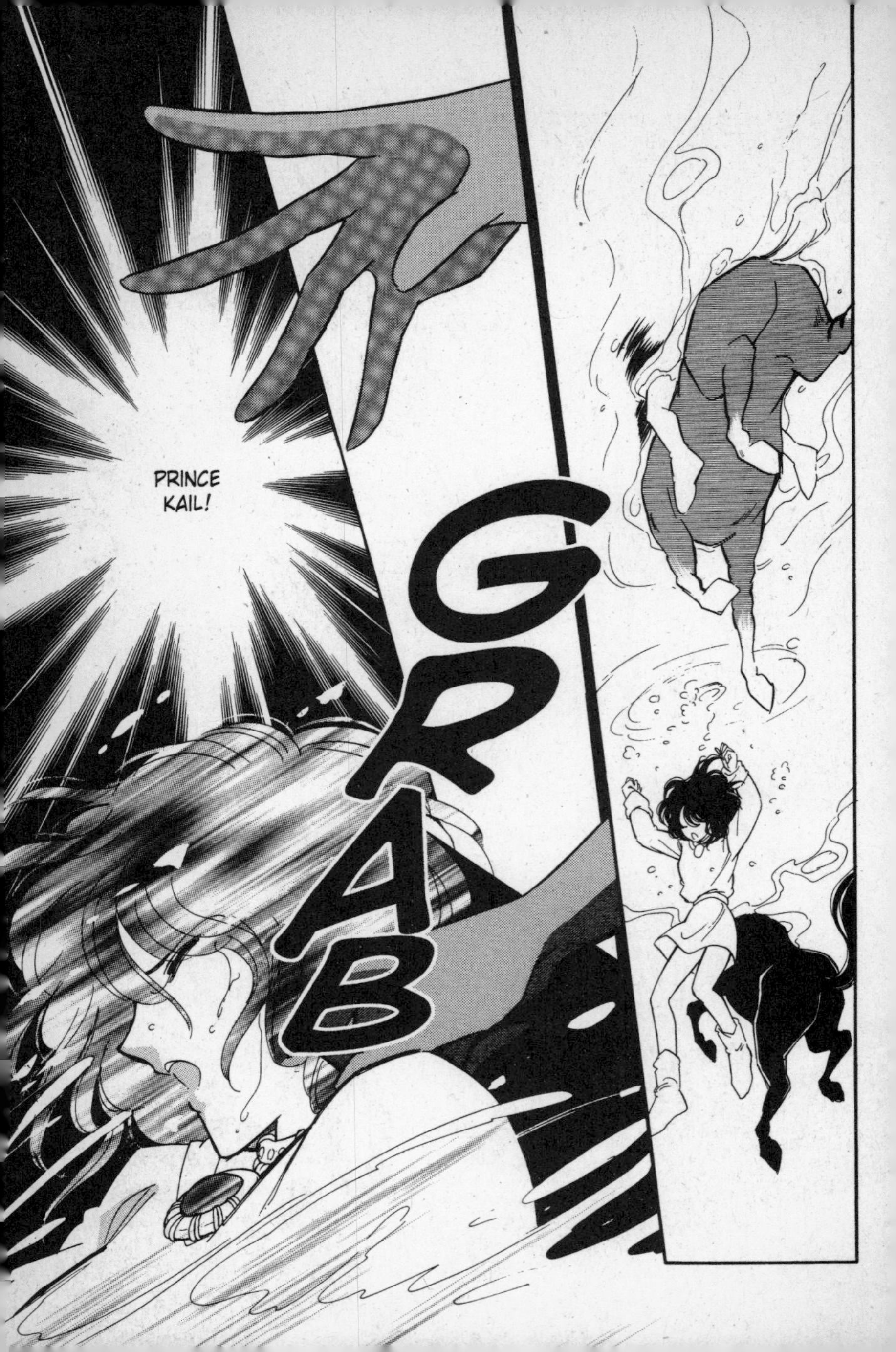
GRAB
PRINCE KAIL!

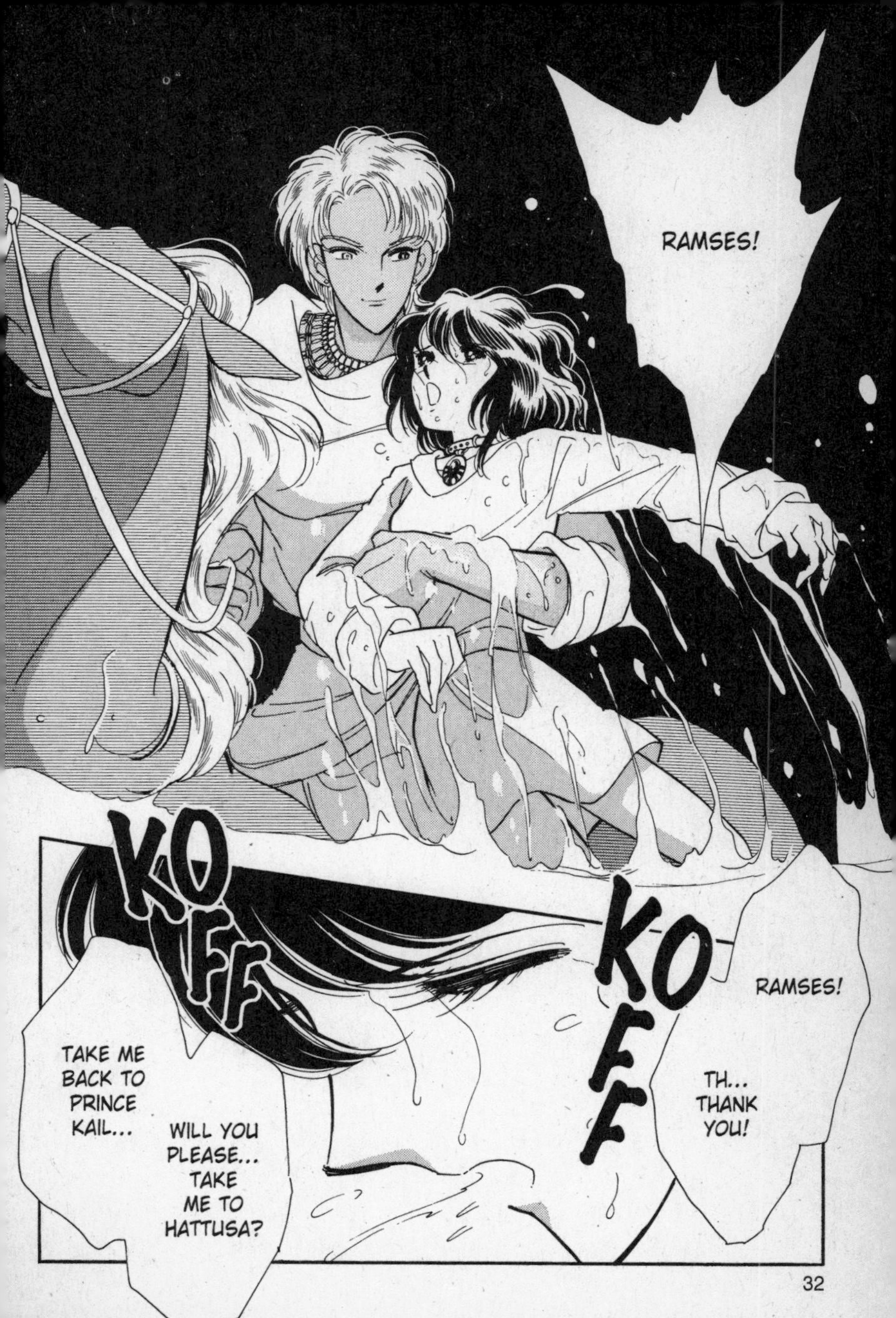
RAMSES!
RAMSES!
TH... THANK YOU!
KOFF
KOFF
WILL YOU PLEASE... TAKE ME TO HATTUSA?
TAKE ME BACK TO PRINCE KAIL...

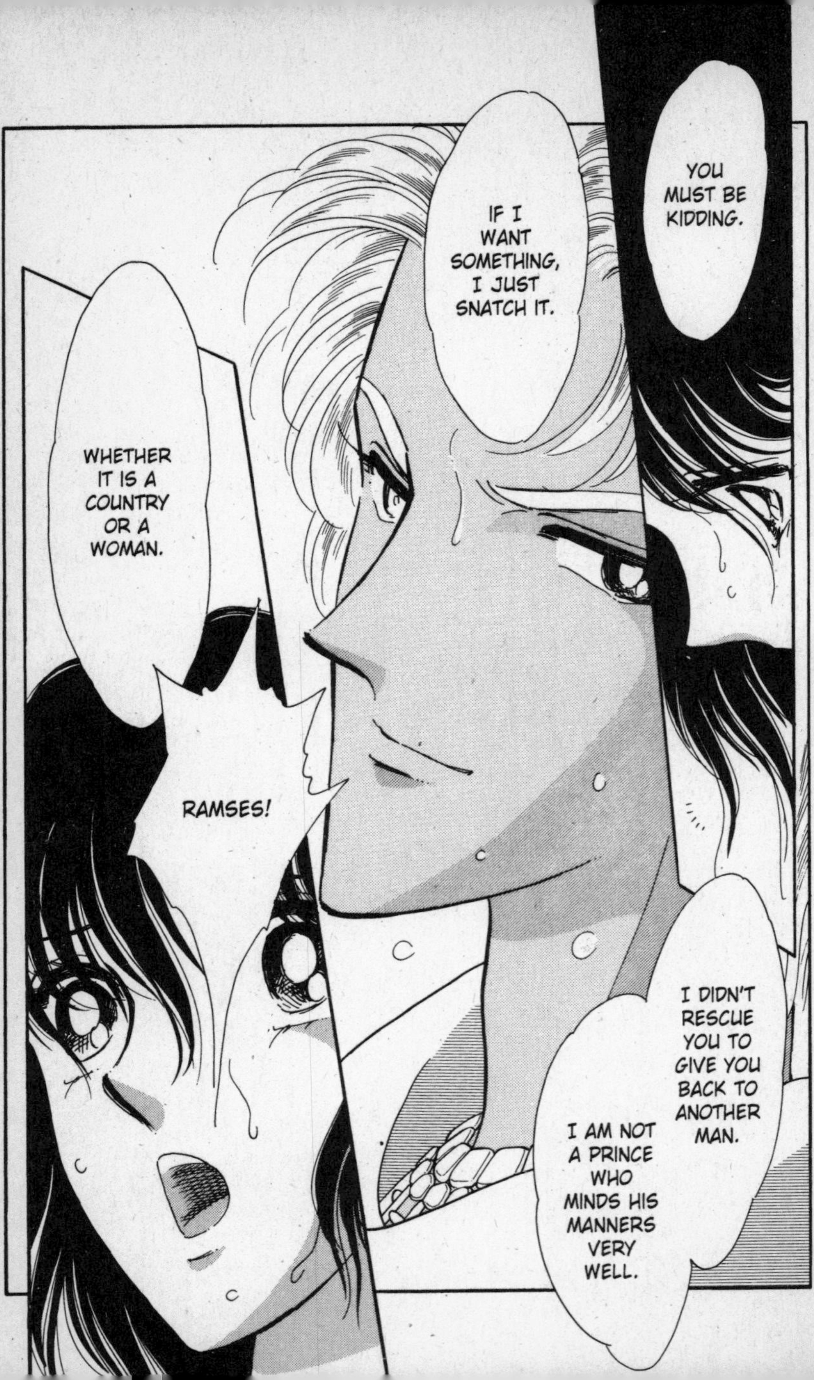
YOU MUST BE KIDDING.
IF I WANT SOMETHING, I JUST SNATCH IT.
WHETHER IT IS A COUNTRY OR A WOMAN.
RAMSES!
I DIDN'T RESCUE YOU TO GIVE YOU BACK TO ANOTHER MAN.
I AM NOT A PRINCE WHO MINDS HIS MANNERS VERY WELL.

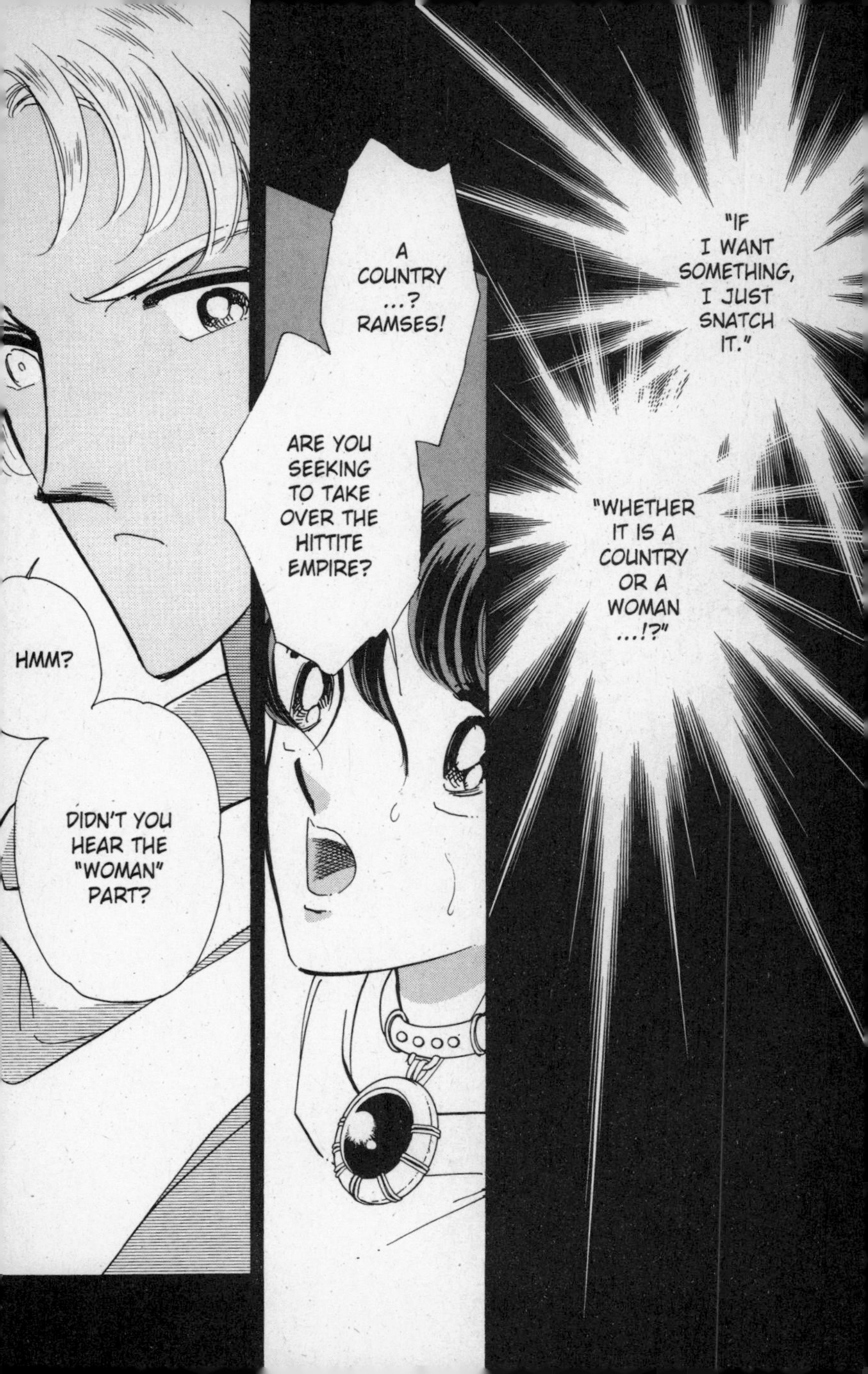
"IF I WANT SOMETHING, I JUST SNATCH IT."
"WHETHER IT IS A COUNTRY OR A WOMAN ...!?"
A COUNTRY ...? RAMSES!
ARE YOU SEEKING TO TAKE OVER THE HITTITE EMPIRE?
HMM?
DIDN'T YOU HEAR THE "WOMAN" PART?

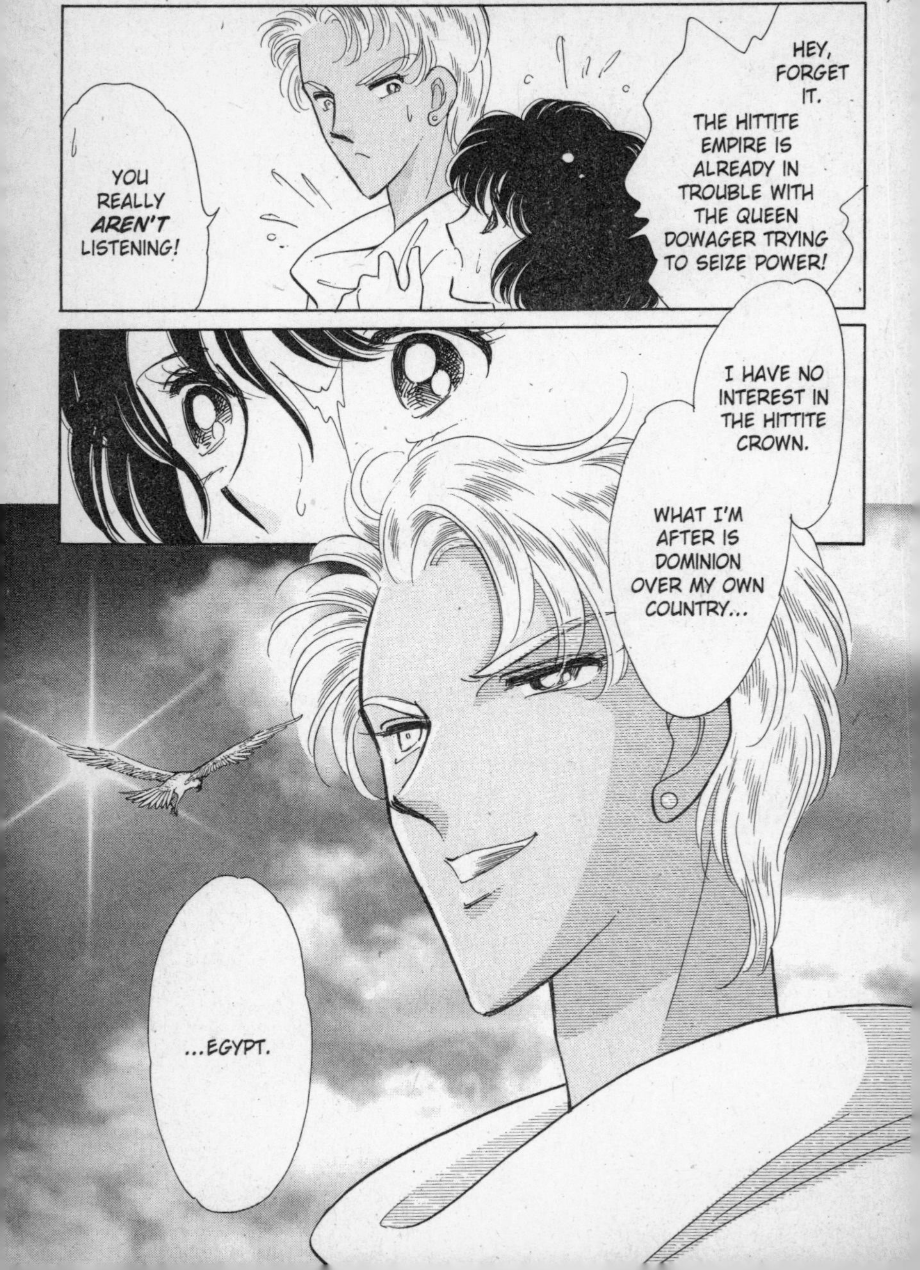
HEY, FORGET IT. THE HITTITE EMPIRE IS ALREADY IN TROUBLE WITH THE QUEEN DOWAGER TRYING TO SEIZE POWER!
YOU REALLY **AREN'T** LISTENING!
I HAVE NO INTEREST IN THE HITTITE CROWN.
WHAT I'M AFTER IS DOMINION OVER MY OWN COUNTRY...
...EGYPT.

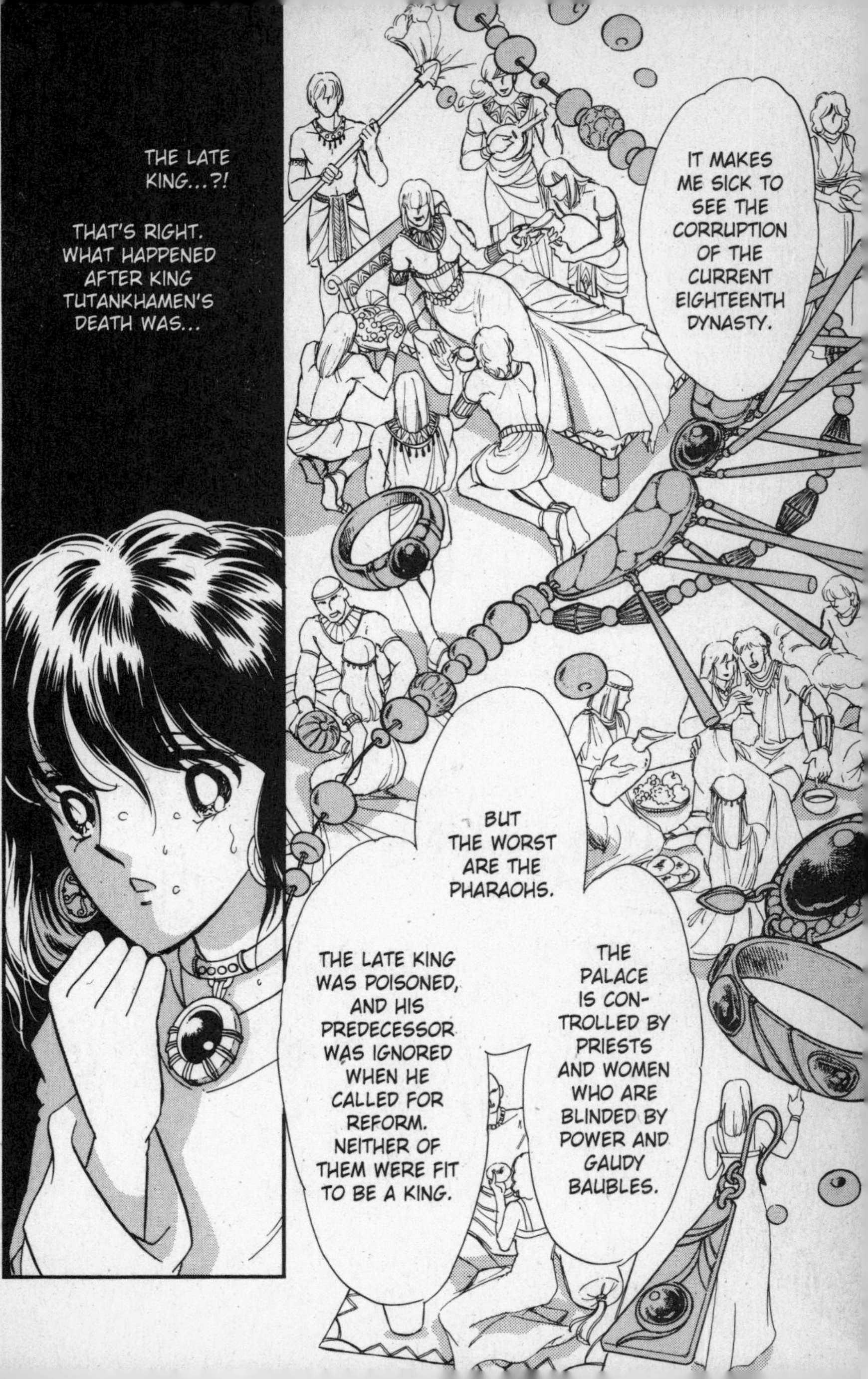
IT MAKES ME SICK TO SEE THE CORRUPTION OF THE CURRENT EIGHTEENTH DYNASTY.
BUT THE WORST ARE THE PHARAOHS.
THE PALACE IS CON-TROLLED BY PRIESTS AND WOMEN WHO ARE BLINDED BY POWER AND GAUDY BAUBLES.
THE LATE KING WAS POISONED, AND HIS PREDECESSOR WAS IGNORED WHEN HE CALLED FOR REFORM. NEITHER OF THEM WERE FIT TO BE A KING.
THE LATE KING...?!
THAT'S RIGHT. WHAT HAPPENED AFTER KING TUTANKHAMEN'S DEATH WAS...

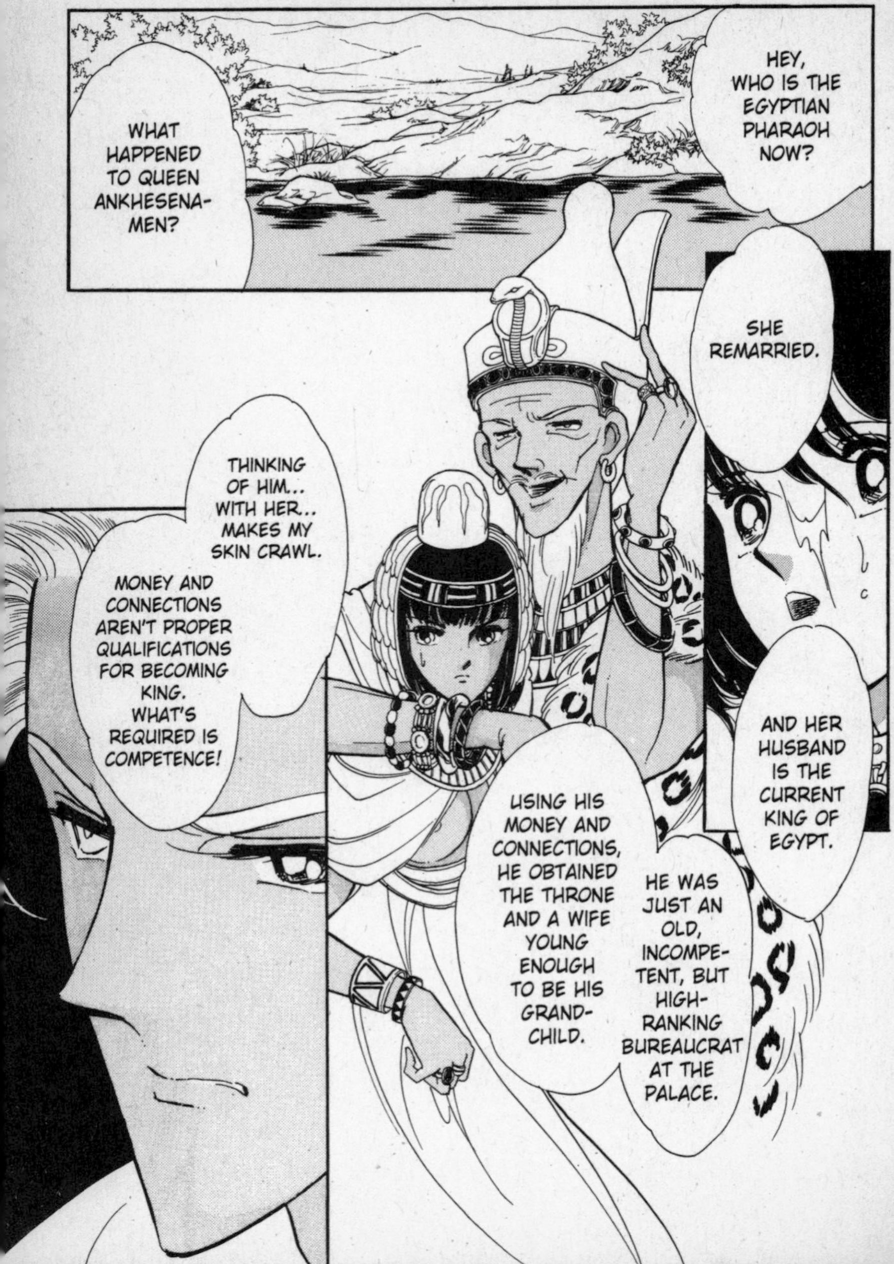
HEY, WHO IS THE EGYPTIAN PHARAOH NOW?
WHAT HAPPENED TO QUEEN ANKHESENAMEN?
SHE REMARRIED.
AND HER HUSBAND IS THE CURRENT KING OF EGYPT.
HE WAS JUST AN OLD, INCOMPETENT, BUT HIGH-RANKING BUREAUCRAT AT THE PALACE.
USING HIS MONEY AND CONNECTIONS, HE OBTAINED THE THRONE AND A WIFE YOUNG ENOUGH TO BE HIS GRANDCHILD.
THINKING OF HIM... WITH HER... MAKES MY SKIN CRAWL.
MONEY AND CONNECTIONS AREN'T PROPER QUALIFICATIONS FOR BECOMING KING. WHAT'S REQUIRED IS COMPETENCE!

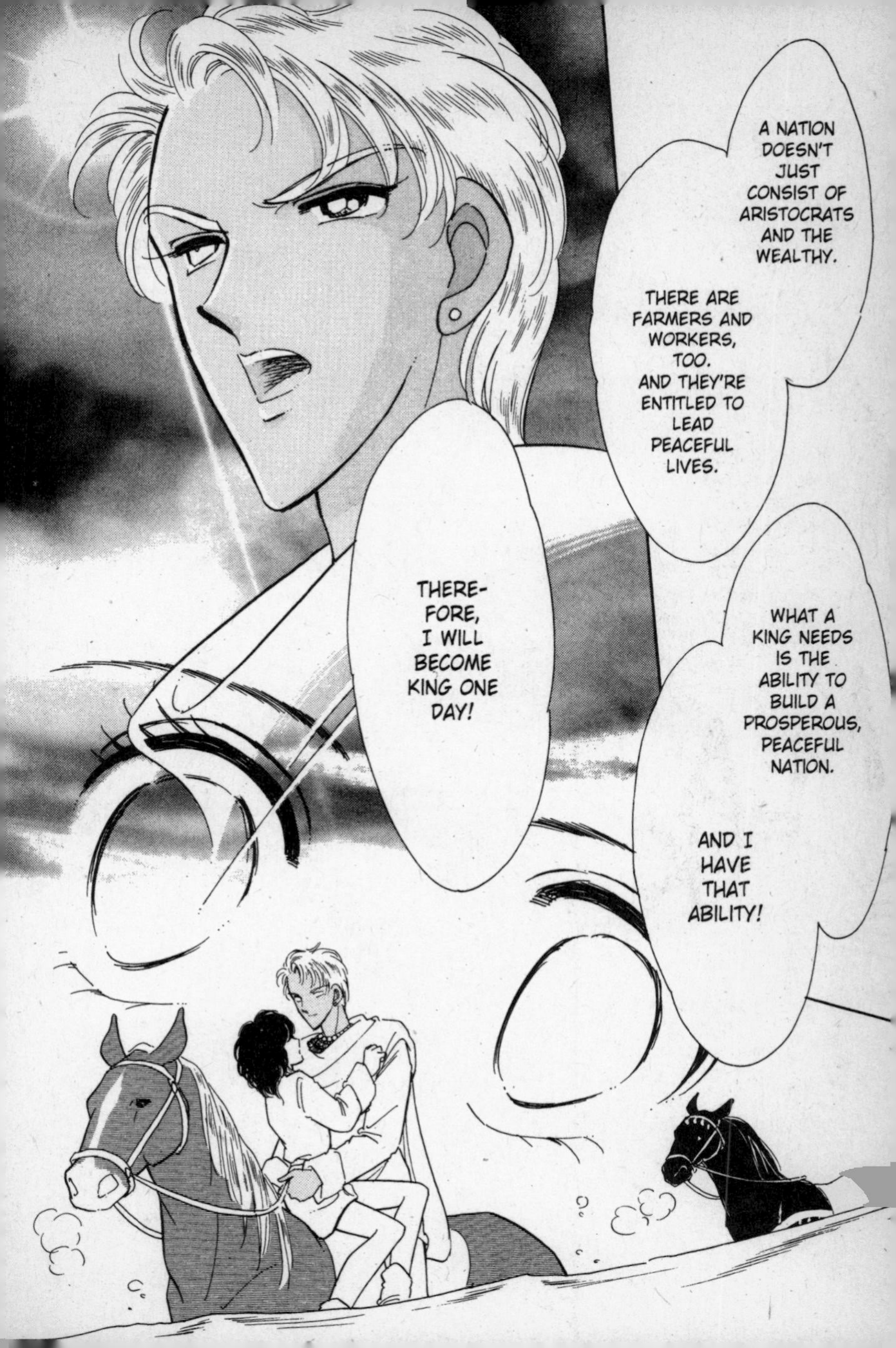
A NATION DOESN'T JUST CONSIST OF ARISTOCRATS AND THE WEALTHY.
THERE ARE FARMERS AND WORKERS, TOO. AND THEY'RE ENTITLED TO LEAD PEACEFUL LIVES.
WHAT A KING NEEDS IS THE ABILITY TO BUILD A PROSPEROUS, PEACEFUL NATION.
AND I HAVE THAT ABILITY!
THERE-FORE, I WILL BECOME KING ONE DAY!

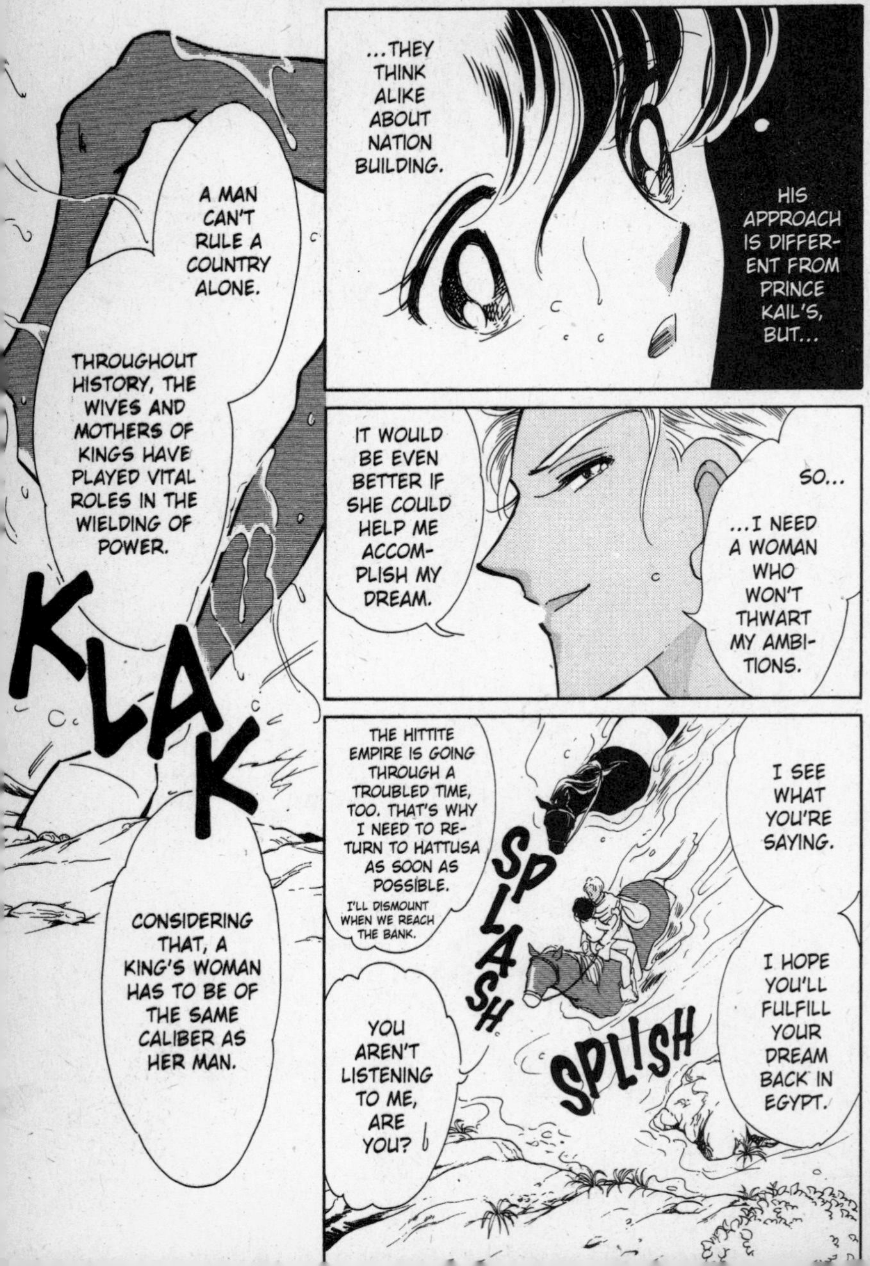
HIS APPROACH IS DIFFERENT FROM PRINCE KAIL'S, BUT...
...THEY THINK ALIKE ABOUT NATION BUILDING.
SO...
...I NEED A WOMAN WHO WON'T THWART MY AMBITIONS.
IT WOULD BE EVEN BETTER IF SHE COULD HELP ME ACCOMPLISH MY DREAM.
I SEE WHAT YOU'RE SAYING.
THE HITTITE EMPIRE IS GOING THROUGH A TROUBLED TIME, TOO. THAT'S WHY I NEED TO RETURN TO HATTUSA AS SOON AS POSSIBLE.
I'LL DISMOUNT WHEN WE REACH THE BANK.
I HOPE YOU'LL FULFILL YOUR DREAM BACK IN EGYPT.
SPLASH
SPLISH
YOU AREN'T LISTENING TO ME, ARE YOU?
A MAN CAN'T RULE A COUNTRY ALONE.
THROUGHOUT HISTORY, THE WIVES AND MOTHERS OF KINGS HAVE PLAYED VITAL ROLES IN THE WIELDING OF POWER.
KLAK
CONSIDERING THAT, A KING'S WOMAN HAS TO BE OF THE SAME CALIBER AS HER MAN.

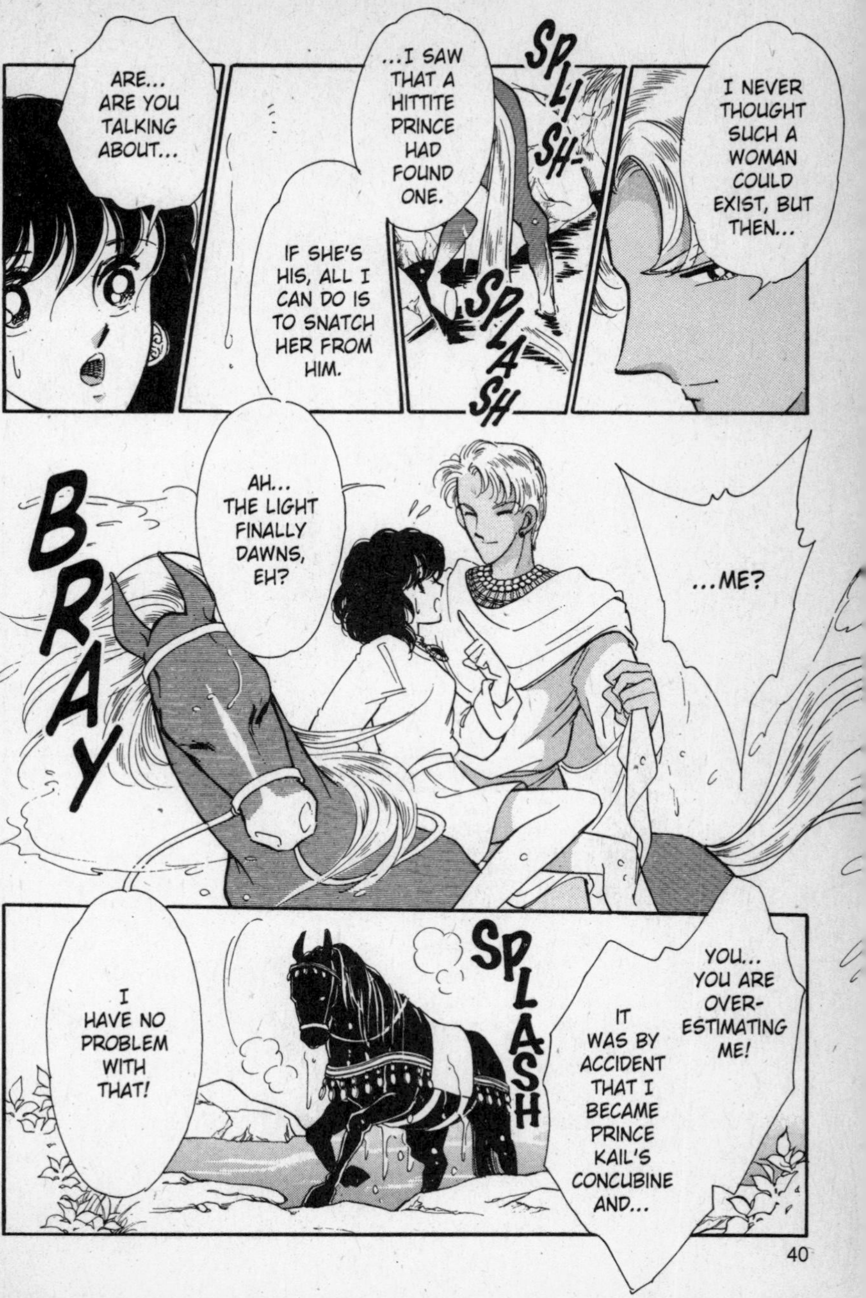
I NEVER THOUGHT SUCH A WOMAN COULD EXIST, BUT THEN...
SPLISH-
SPLASH
...I SAW THAT A HITTITE PRINCE HAD FOUND ONE.
IF SHE'S HIS, ALL I CAN DO IS TO SNATCH HER FROM HIM.
ARE... ARE YOU TALKING ABOUT...
...ME?
AH... THE LIGHT FINALLY DAWNS, EH?
BRAY
YOU... YOU ARE OVER-ESTIMATING ME!
IT WAS BY ACCIDENT THAT I BECAME PRINCE KAIL'S CONCUBINE AND...
SPLASH
I HAVE NO PROBLEM WITH THAT!

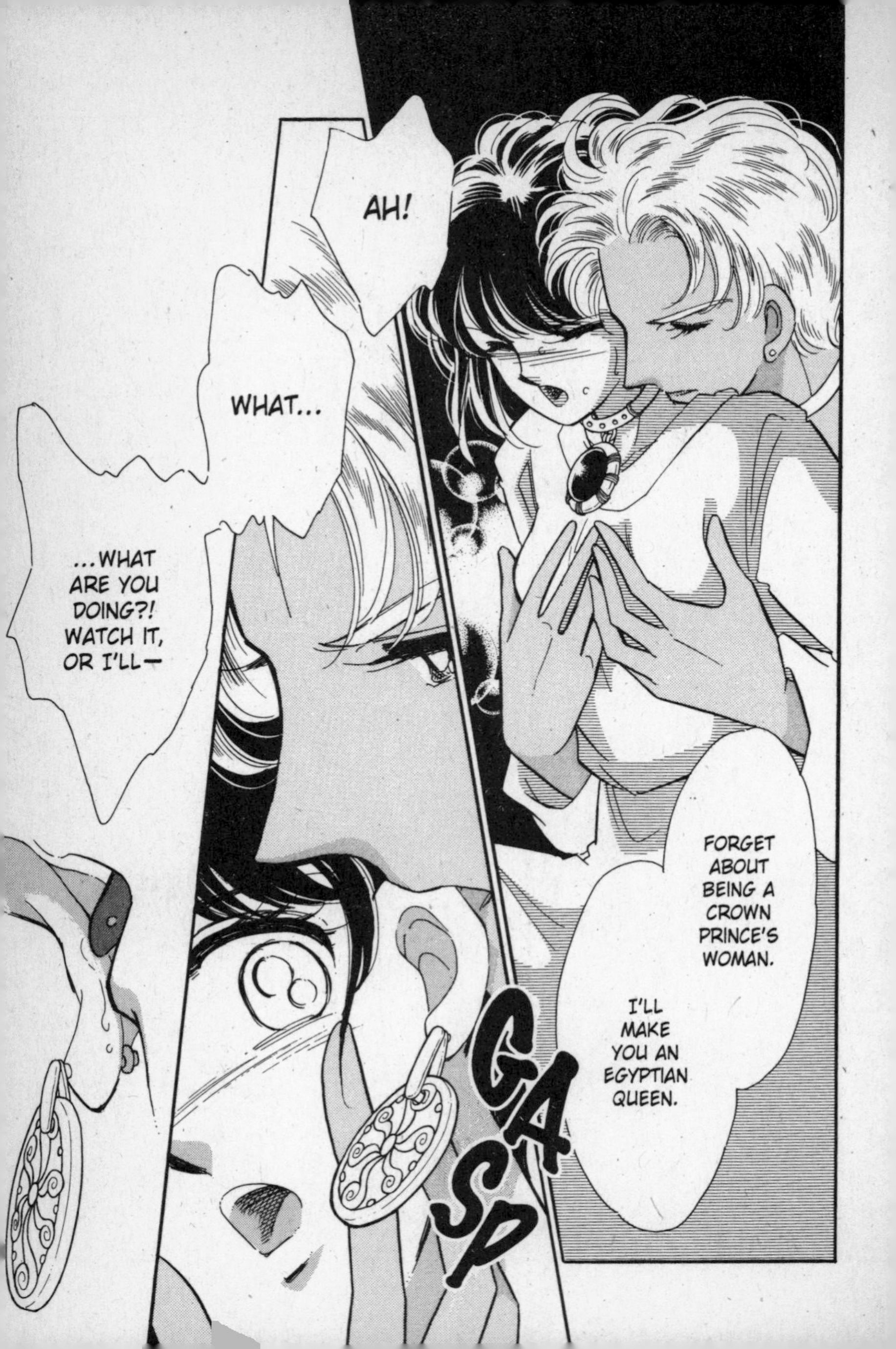
AH!
FORGET ABOUT BEING A CROWN PRINCE'S WOMAN.
I'LL MAKE YOU AN EGYPTIAN QUEEN.
GASP
WHAT...
...WHAT ARE YOU DOING?! WATCH IT, OR I'LL—

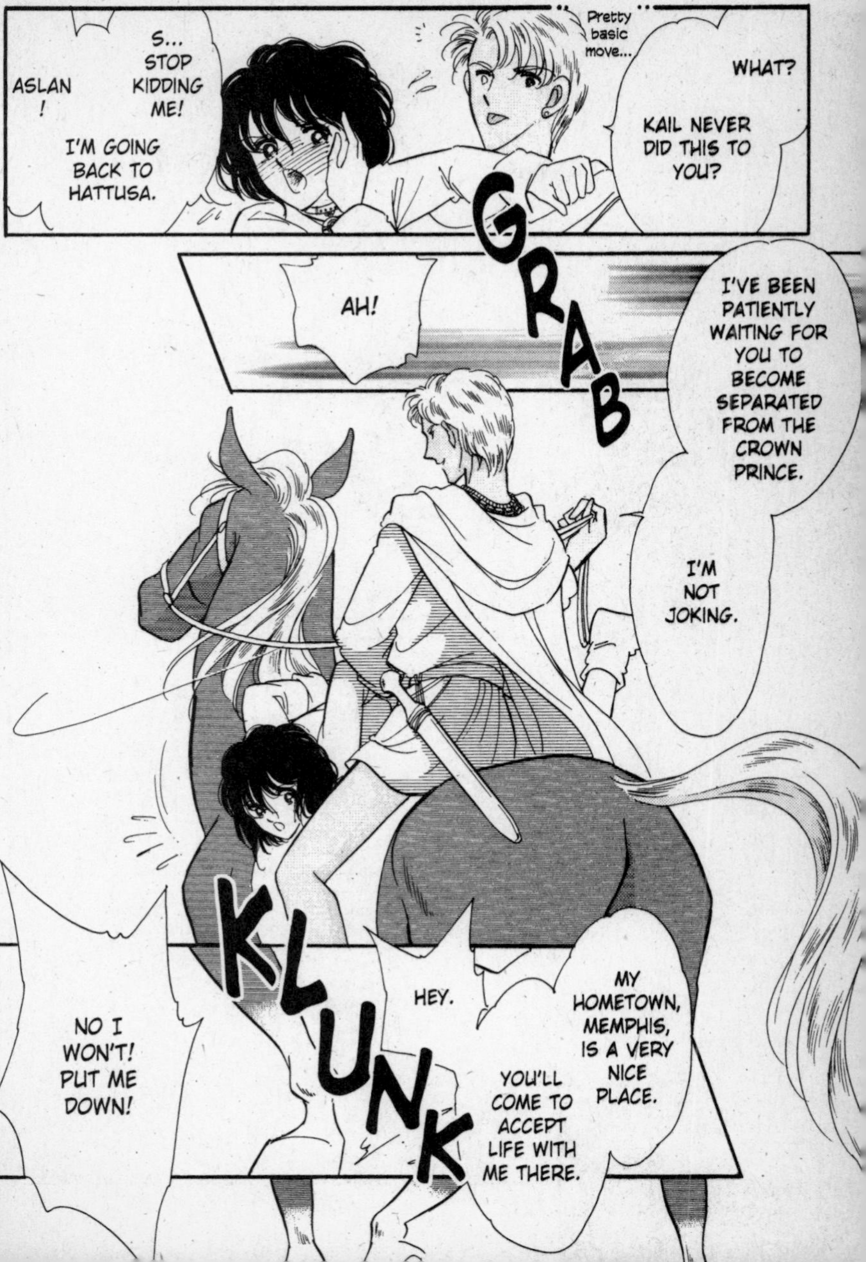
WHAT?
KAIL NEVER DID THIS TO YOU?
...Pretty basic move...
S... STOP KIDDING ME!
ASLAN!
I'M GOING BACK TO HATTUSA.
I'VE BEEN PATIENTLY WAITING FOR YOU TO BECOME SEPARATED FROM THE CROWN PRINCE.
GRAB
AH!
I'M NOT JOKING.
MY HOMETOWN, MEMPHIS, IS A VERY NICE PLACE.
YOU'LL COME TO ACCEPT LIFE WITH ME THERE.
HEY.
KLUNK
NO I WON'T! PUT ME DOWN!

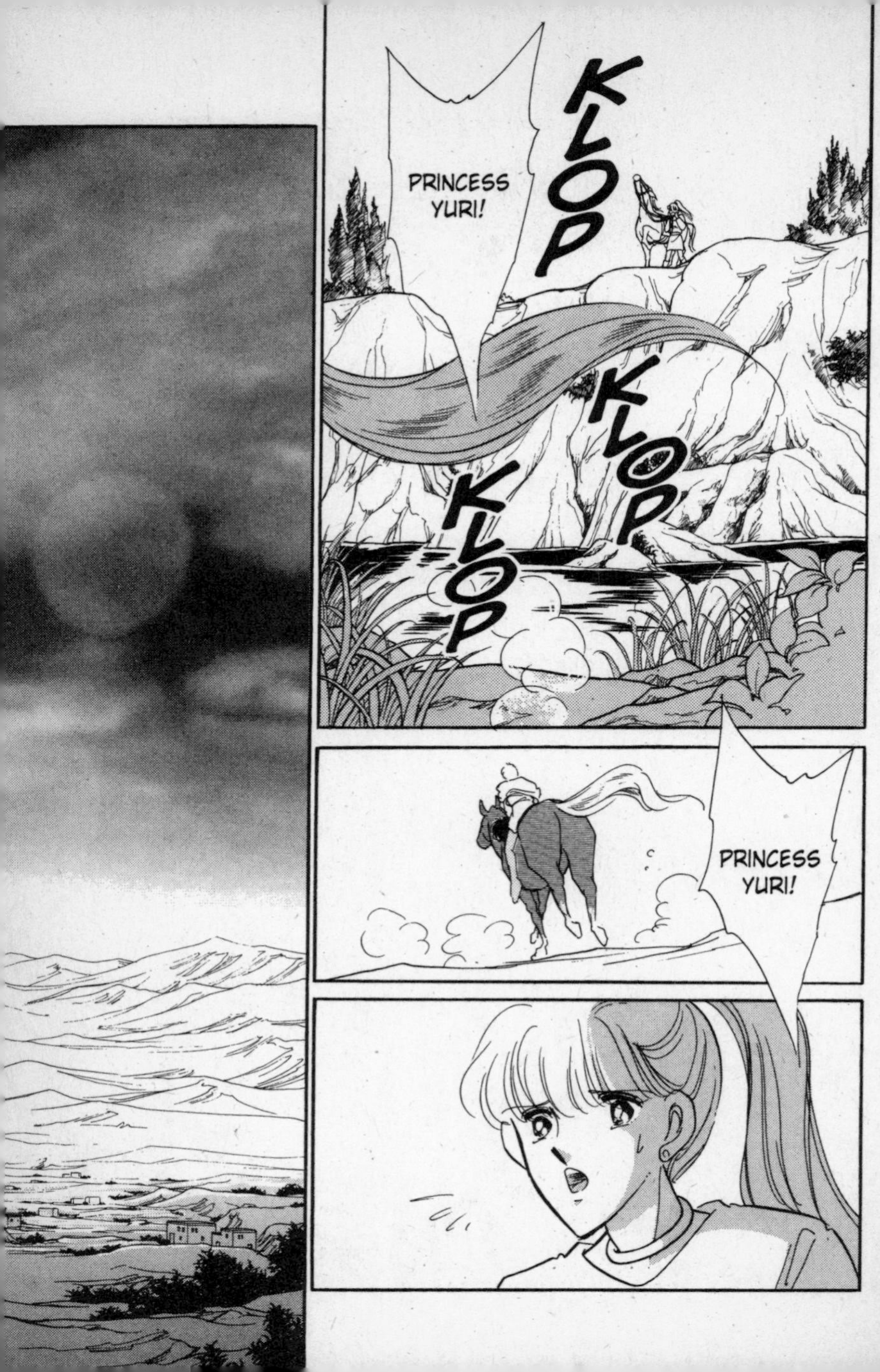
PRINCESS YURI!
KLOP
KLOP
KLOP
PRINCESS YURI!

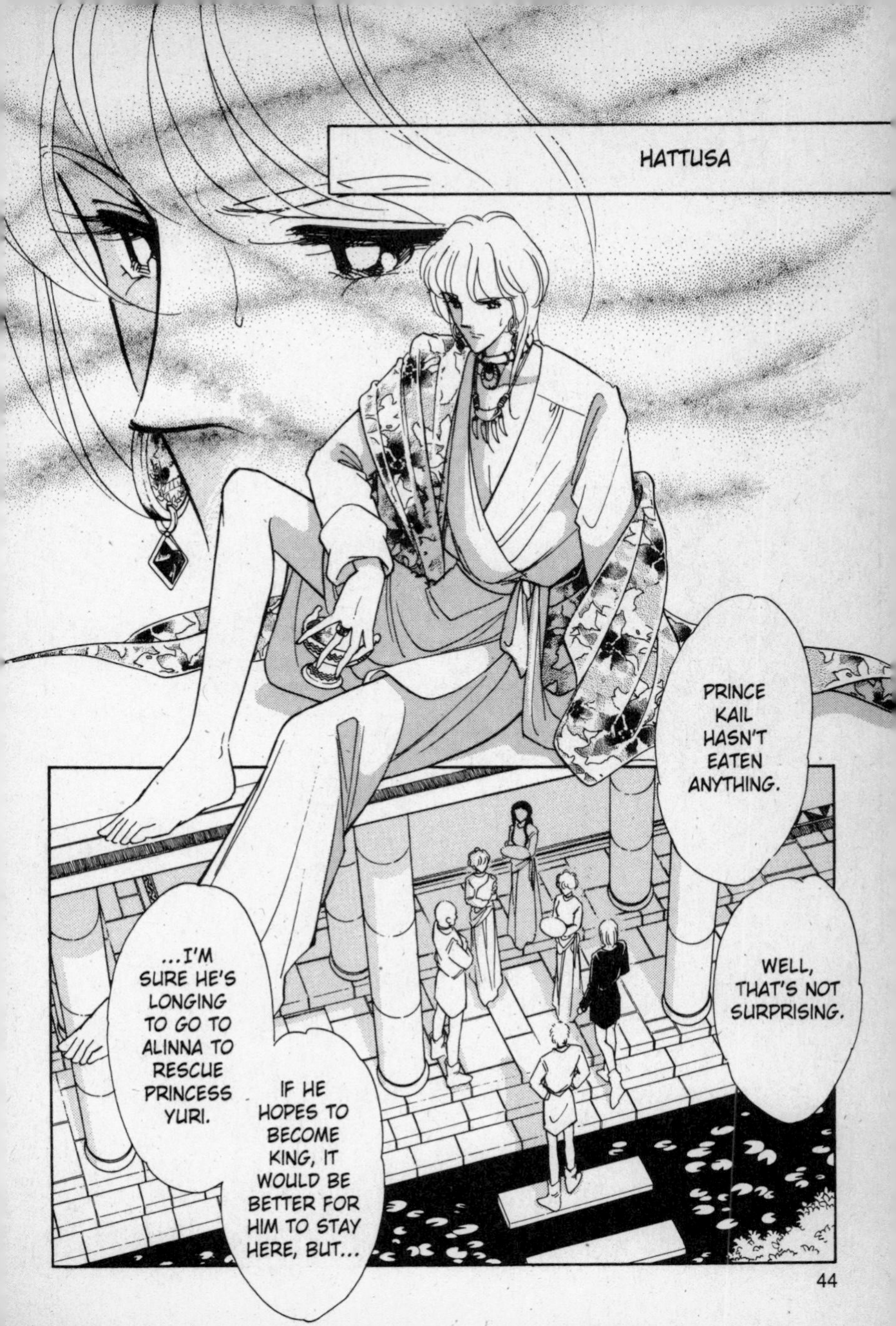
HATTUSA
PRINCE KAIL HASN'T EATEN ANYTHING.
WELL, THAT'S NOT SURPRISING.
...I'M SURE HE'S LONGING TO GO TO ALINNA TO RESCUE PRINCESS YURI.
IF HE HOPES TO BECOME KING, IT WOULD BE BETTER FOR HIM TO STAY HERE, BUT...

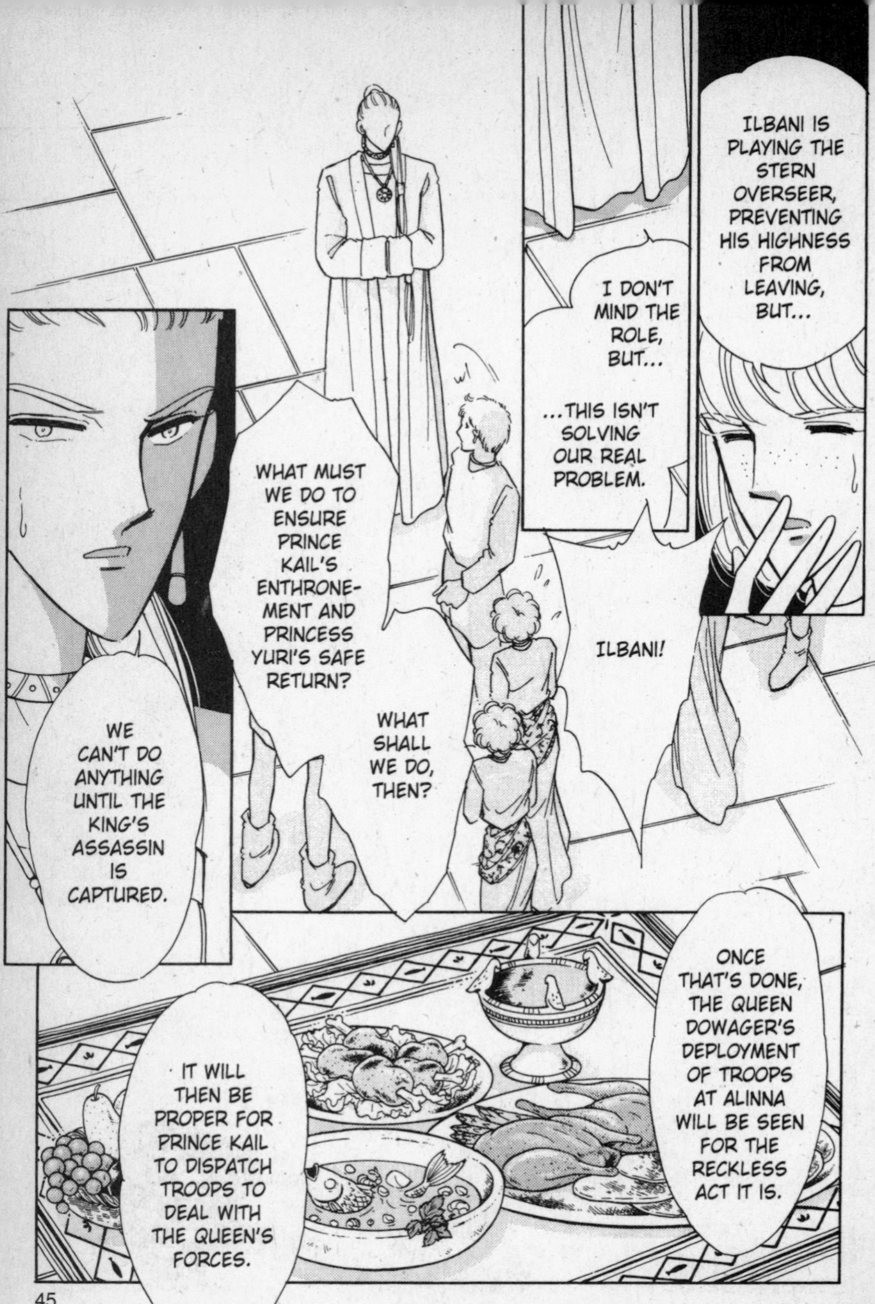
ILBANI IS PLAYING THE STERN OVERSEER, PREVENTING HIS HIGHNESS FROM LEAVING, BUT...
I DON'T MIND THE ROLE, BUT...
...THIS ISN'T SOLVING OUR REAL PROBLEM.
ILBANI!
WHAT SHALL WE DO, THEN?
WHAT MUST WE DO TO ENSURE PRINCE KAIL'S ENTHRONE-MENT AND PRINCESS YURI'S SAFE RETURN?
WE CAN'T DO ANYTHING UNTIL THE KING'S ASSASSIN IS CAPTURED.
ONCE THAT'S DONE, THE QUEEN DOWAGER'S DEPLOYMENT OF TROOPS AT ALINNA WILL BE SEEN FOR THE RECKLESS ACT IT IS.
IT WILL THEN BE PROPER FOR PRINCE KAIL TO DISPATCH TROOPS TO DEAL WITH THE QUEEN'S FORCES.

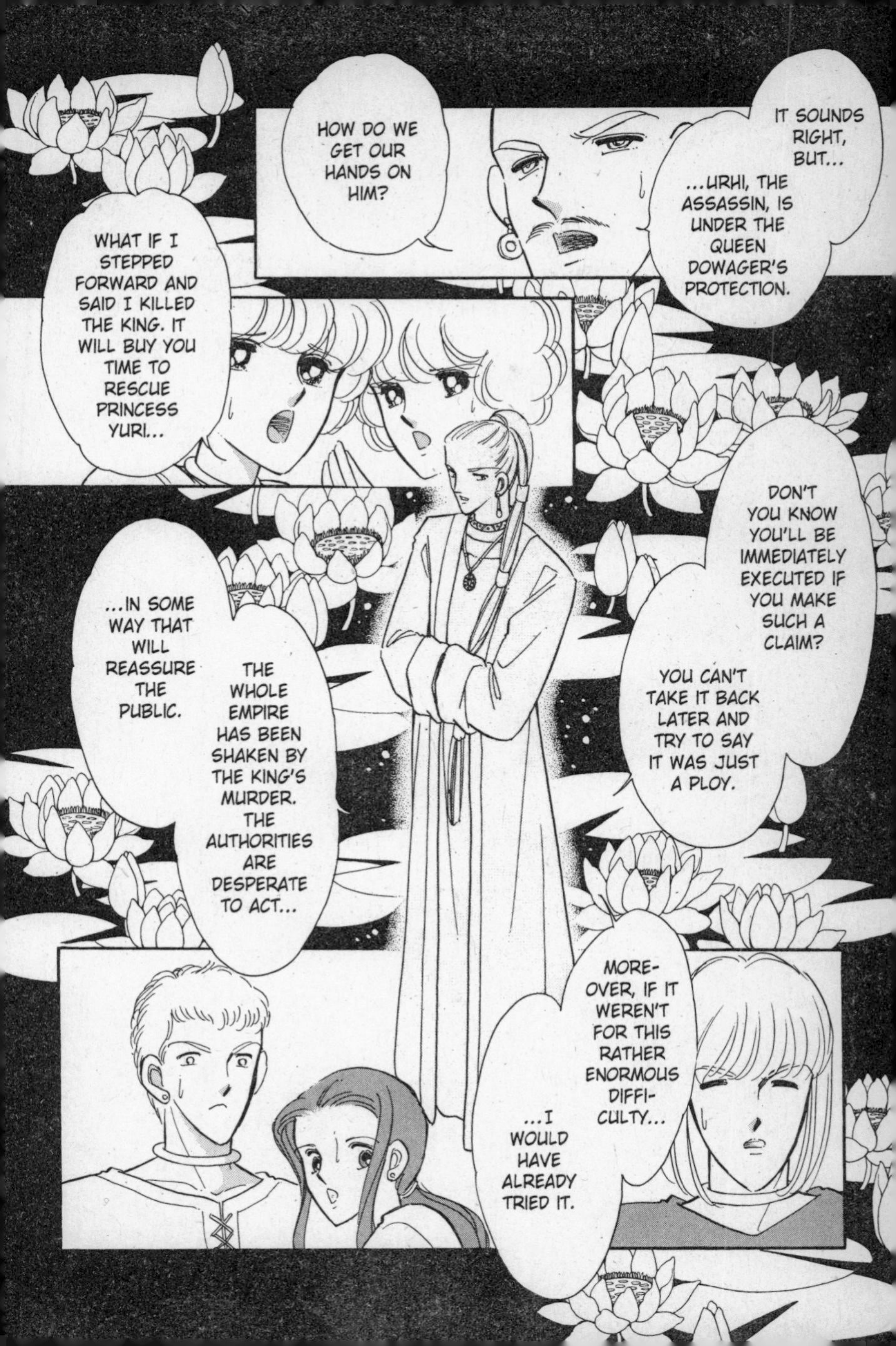

IT SOUNDS RIGHT, BUT...
...URHI, THE ASSASSIN, IS UNDER THE QUEEN DOWAGER'S PROTECTION.
HOW DO WE GET OUR HANDS ON HIM?
WHAT IF I STEPPED FORWARD AND SAID I KILLED THE KING. IT WILL BUY YOU TIME TO RESCUE PRINCESS YURI...
DON'T YOU KNOW YOU'LL BE IMMEDIATELY EXECUTED IF YOU MAKE SUCH A CLAIM?
YOU CAN'T TAKE IT BACK LATER AND TRY TO SAY IT WAS JUST A PLOY.
THE WHOLE EMPIRE HAS BEEN SHAKEN BY THE KING'S MURDER. THE AUTHORITIES ARE DESPERATE TO ACT...
...IN SOME WAY THAT WILL REASSURE THE PUBLIC.
MORE-OVER, IF IT WEREN'T FOR THIS RATHER ENORMOUS DIFFI-CULTY...
...I WOULD HAVE ALREADY TRIED IT.

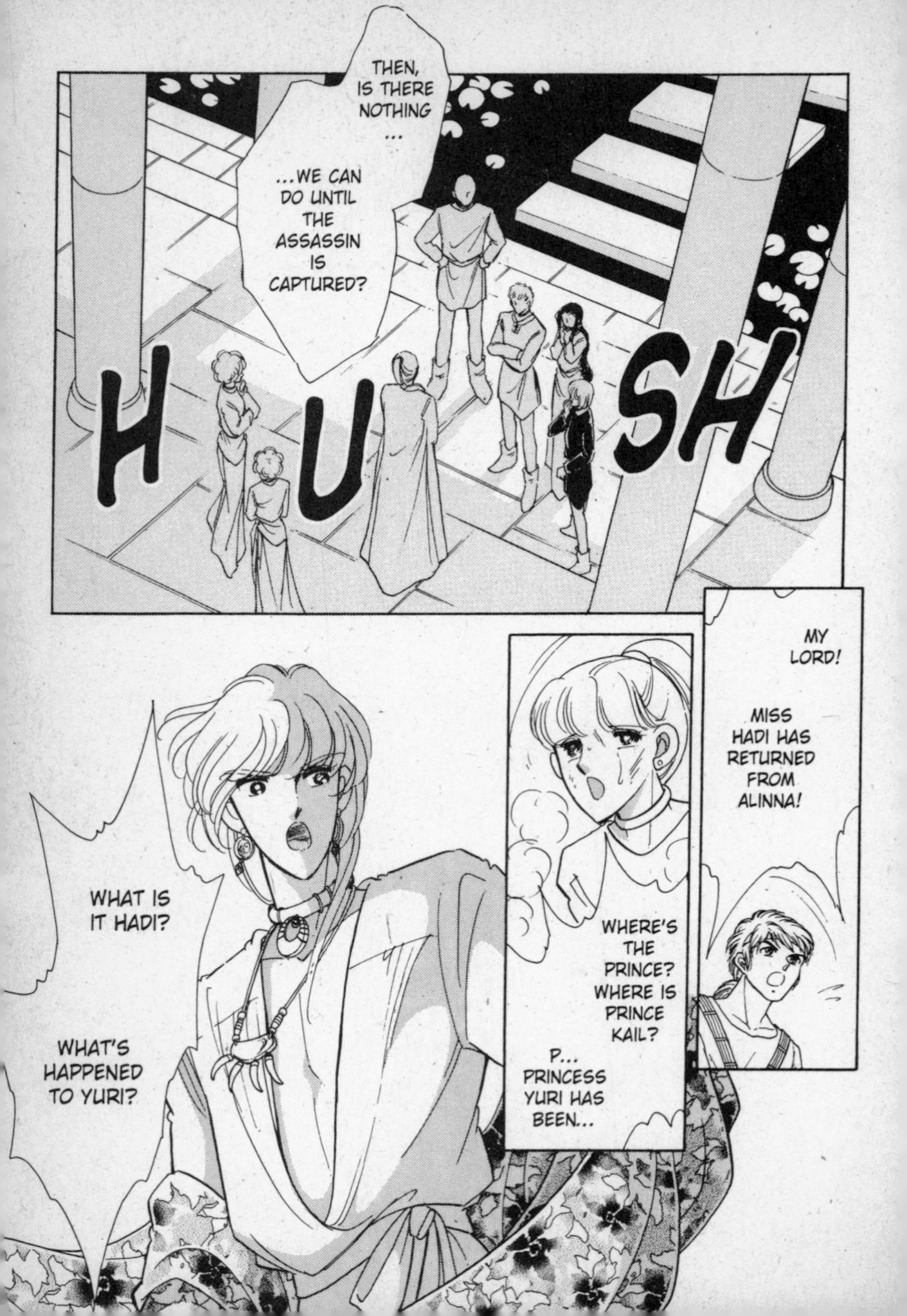
THEN, IS THERE NOTHING ...
...WE CAN DO UNTIL THE ASSASSIN IS CAPTURED?
HUSH
MY LORD!
MISS HADI HAS RETURNED FROM ALINNA!
WHERE'S THE PRINCE? WHERE IS PRINCE KAIL?
P... PRINCESS YURI HAS BEEN...
WHAT IS IT HADI?
WHAT'S HAPPENED TO YURI?

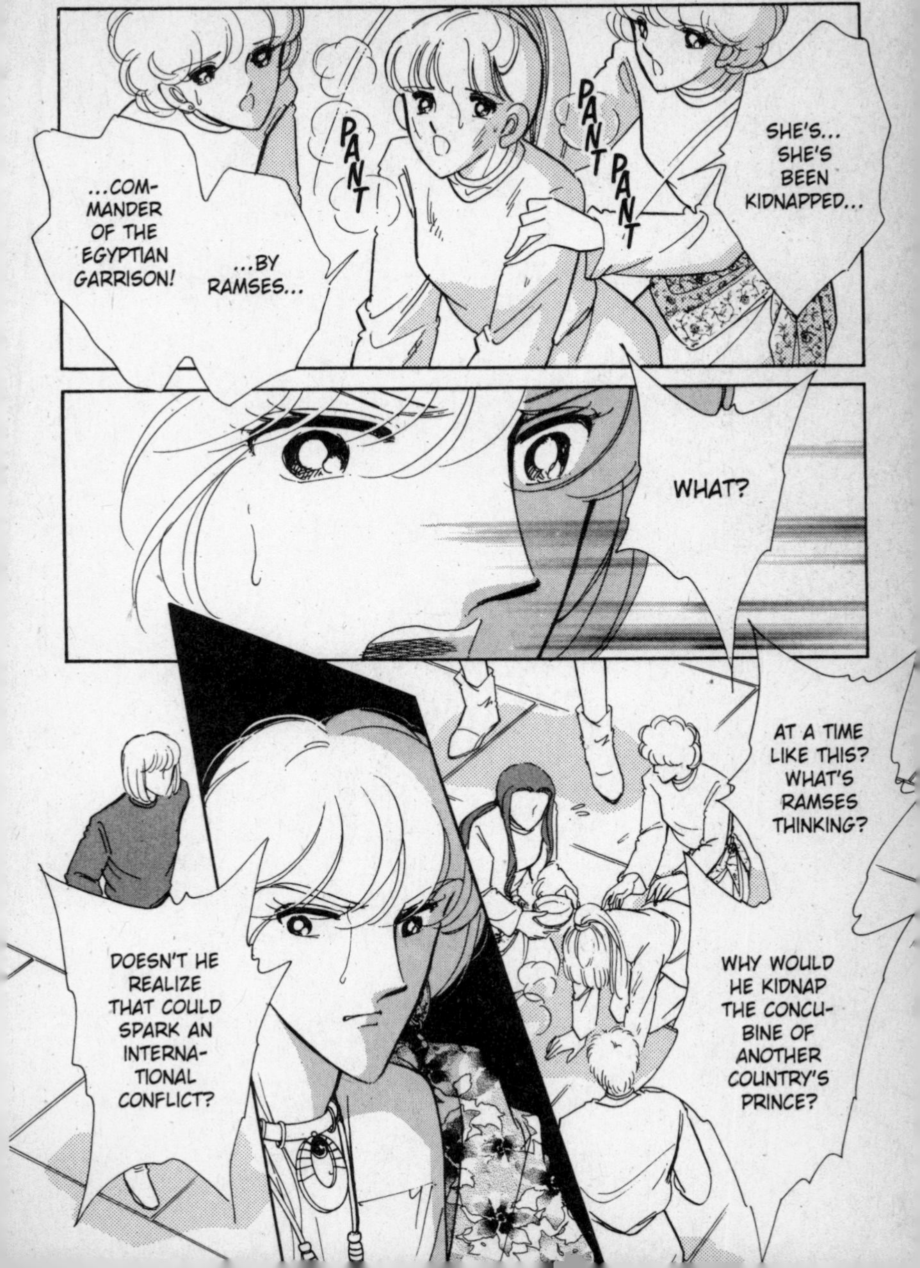
SHE'S... SHE'S BEEN KIDNAPPED...
PANT PANT
PANT
...BY RAMSES...
...COMMANDER OF THE EGYPTIAN GARRISON!
WHAT?
AT A TIME LIKE THIS? WHAT'S RAMSES THINKING?
WHY WOULD HE KIDNAP THE CONCUBINE OF ANOTHER COUNTRY'S PRINCE?
DOESN'T HE REALIZE THAT COULD SPARK AN INTERNATIONAL CONFLICT?

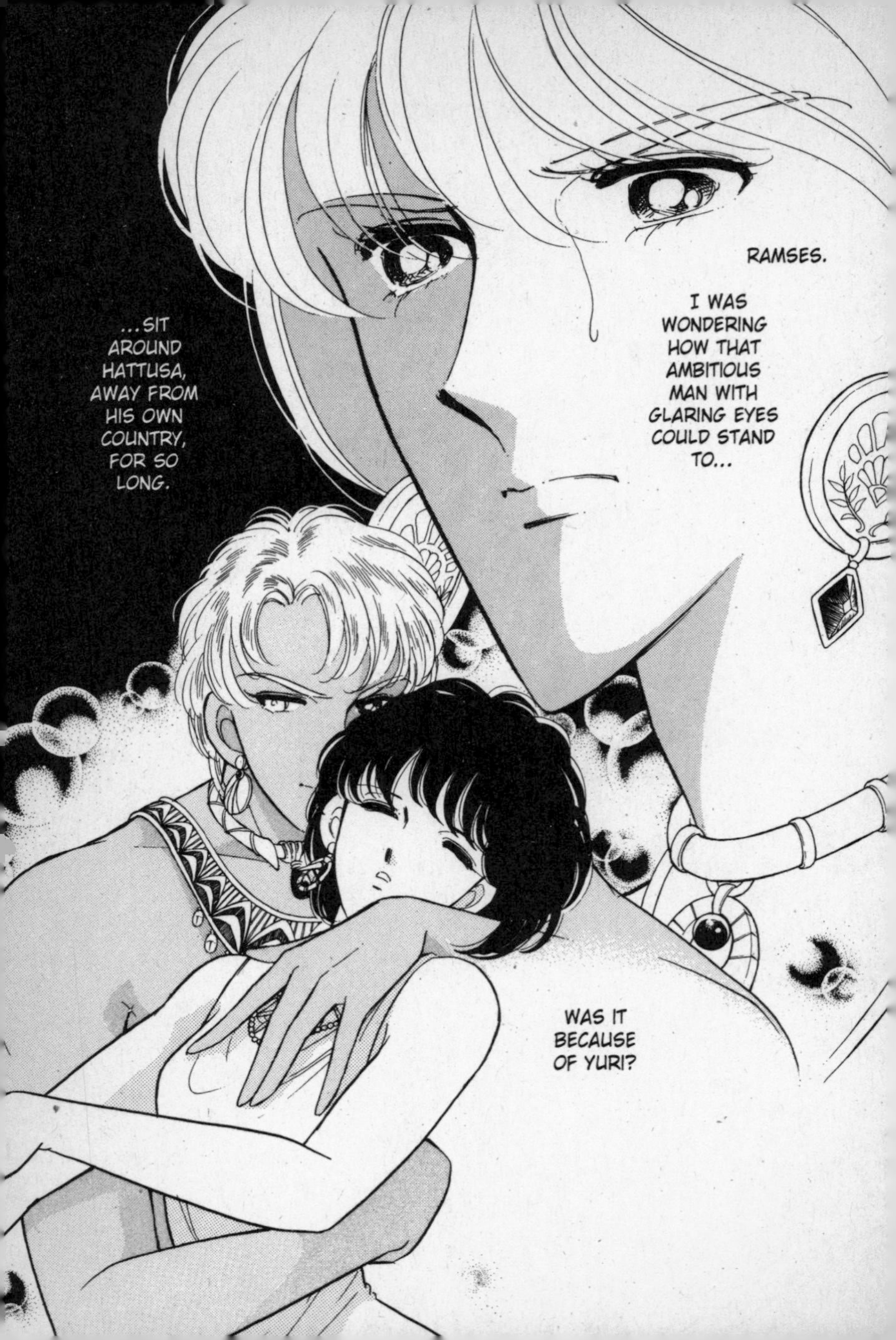
RAMSES.
I WAS WONDERING HOW THAT AMBITIOUS MAN WITH GLARING EYES COULD STAND TO...
...SIT AROUND HATTUSA, AWAY FROM HIS OWN COUNTRY, FOR SO LONG.
WAS IT BECAUSE OF YURI?

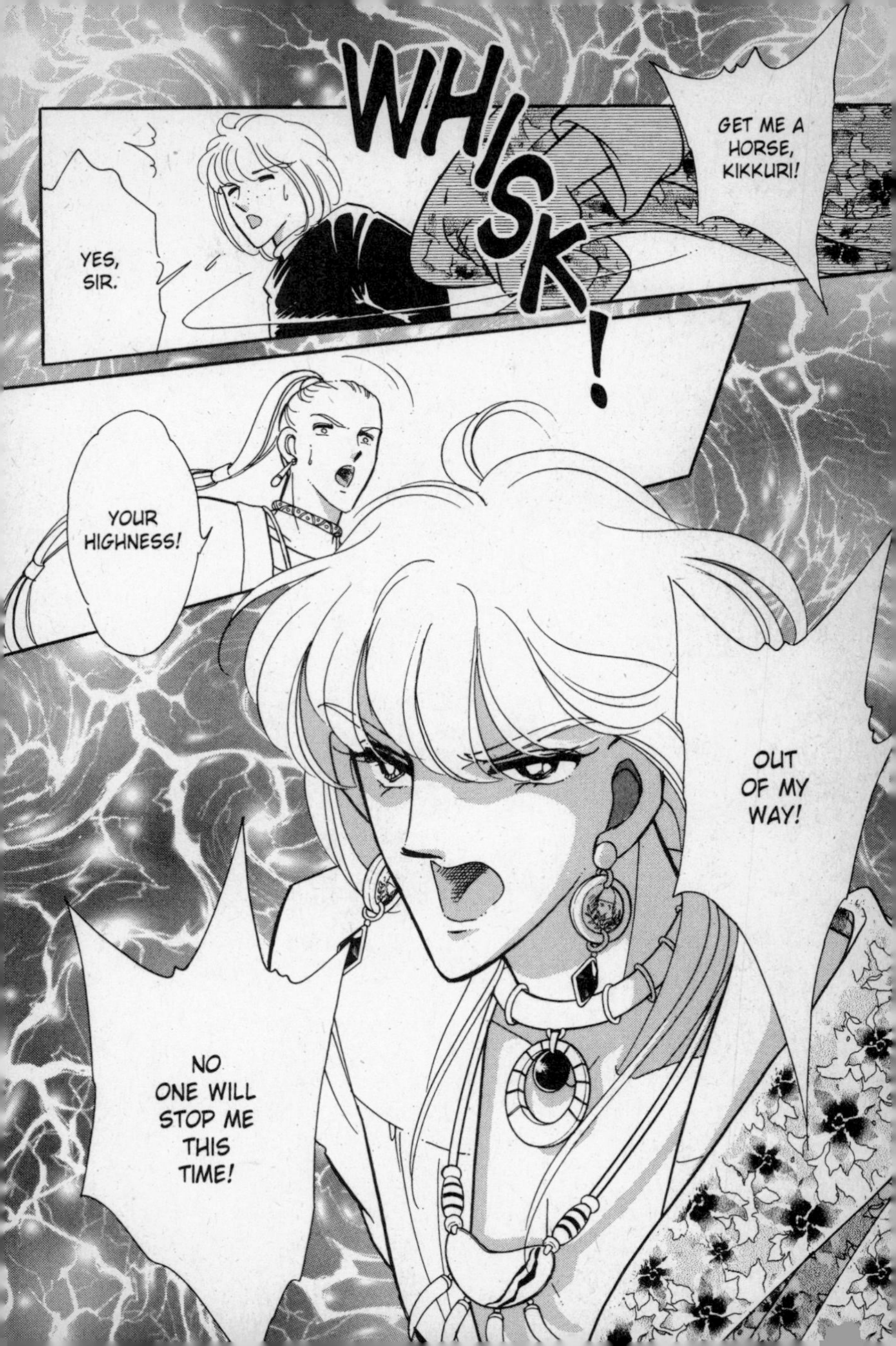
GET ME A HORSE, KIKKURI!
WHISK!
YES, SIR.
YOUR HIGHNESS!
OUT OF MY WAY!
NO ONE WILL STOP ME THIS TIME!

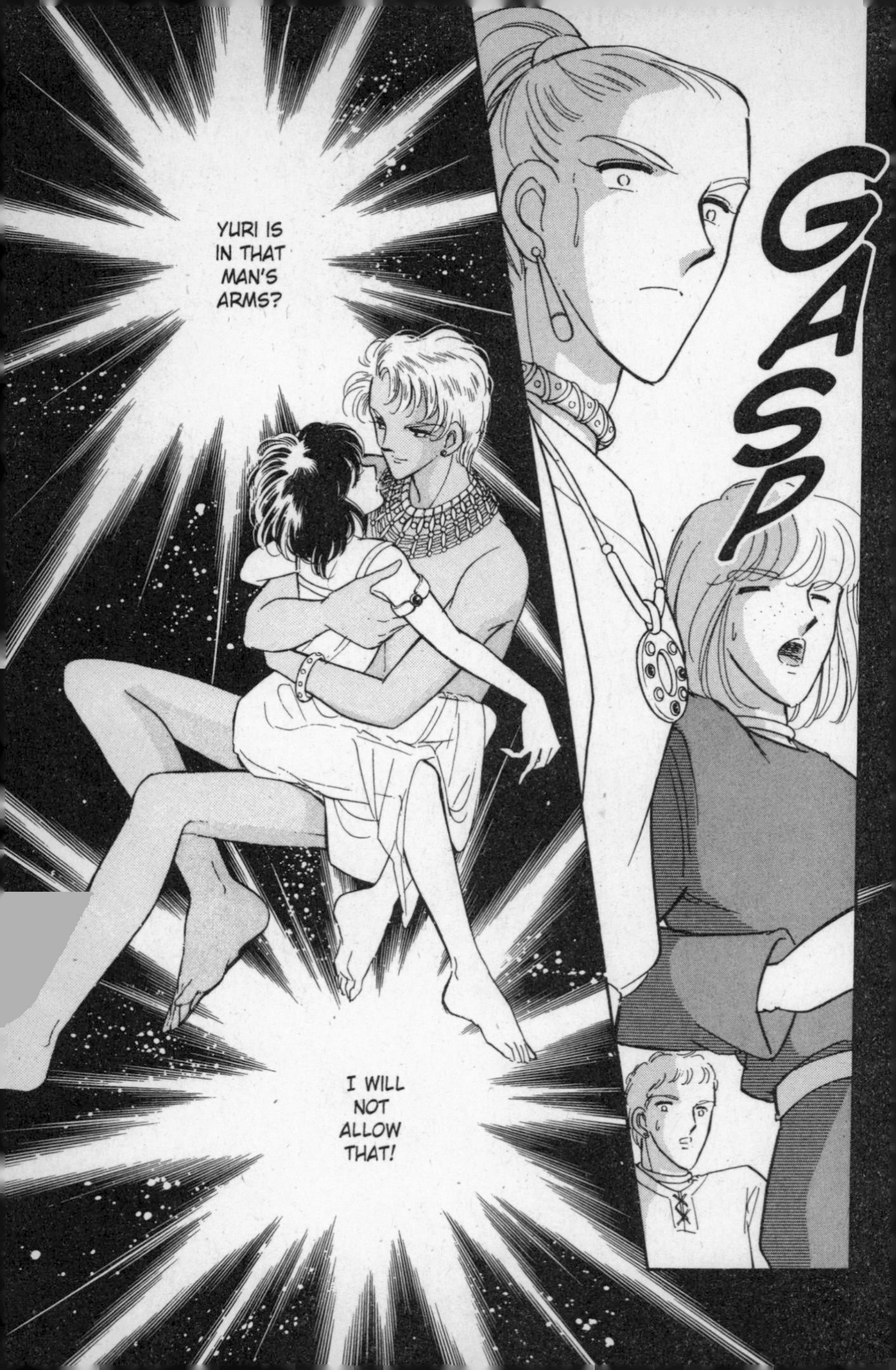
GASP
YURI IS IN THAT MAN'S ARMS?
I WILL NOT ALLOW THAT!

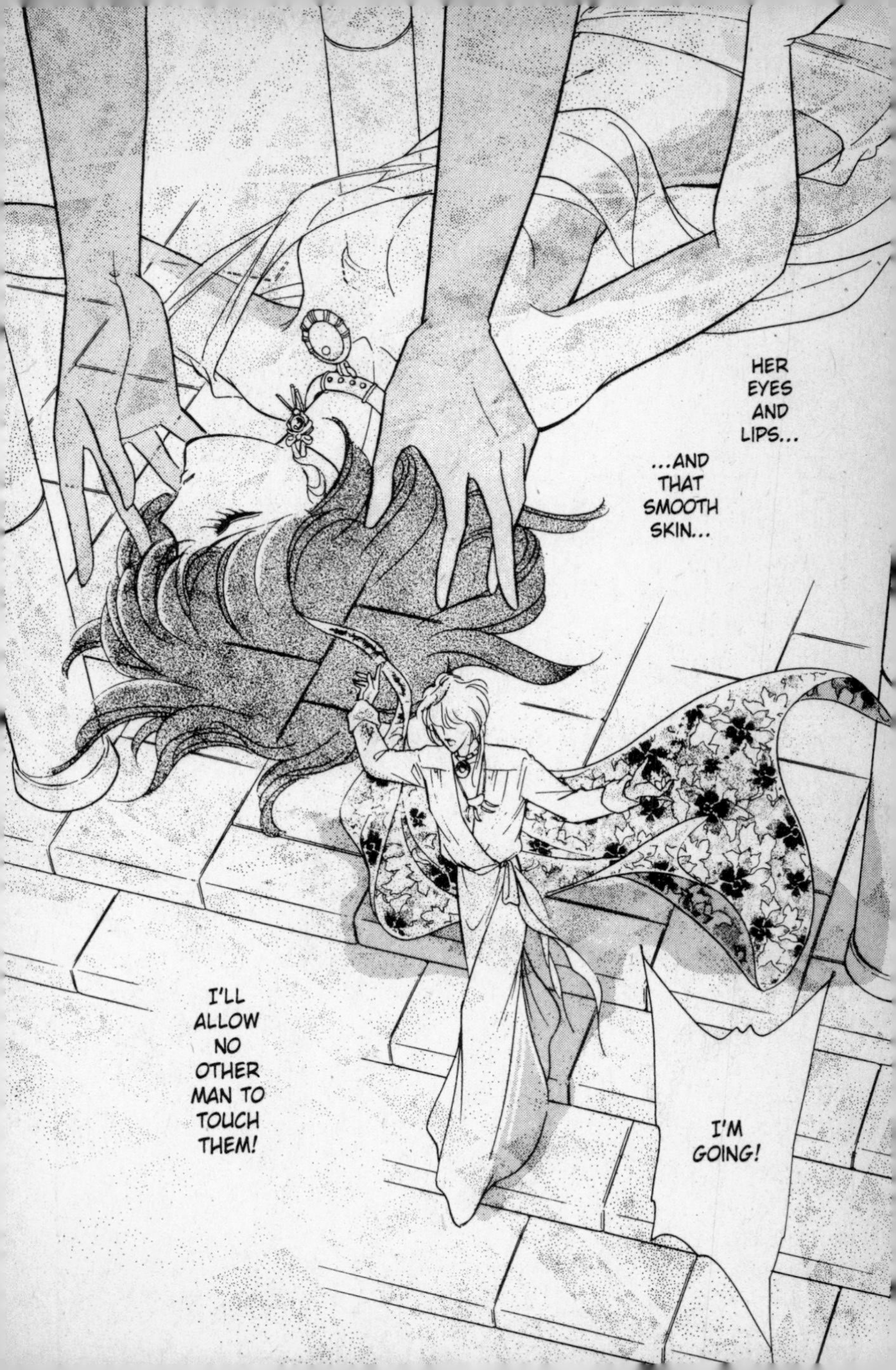
HER EYES AND LIPS...
...AND THAT SMOOTH SKIN...
I'LL ALLOW NO OTHER MAN TO TOUCH THEM!
I'M GOING!

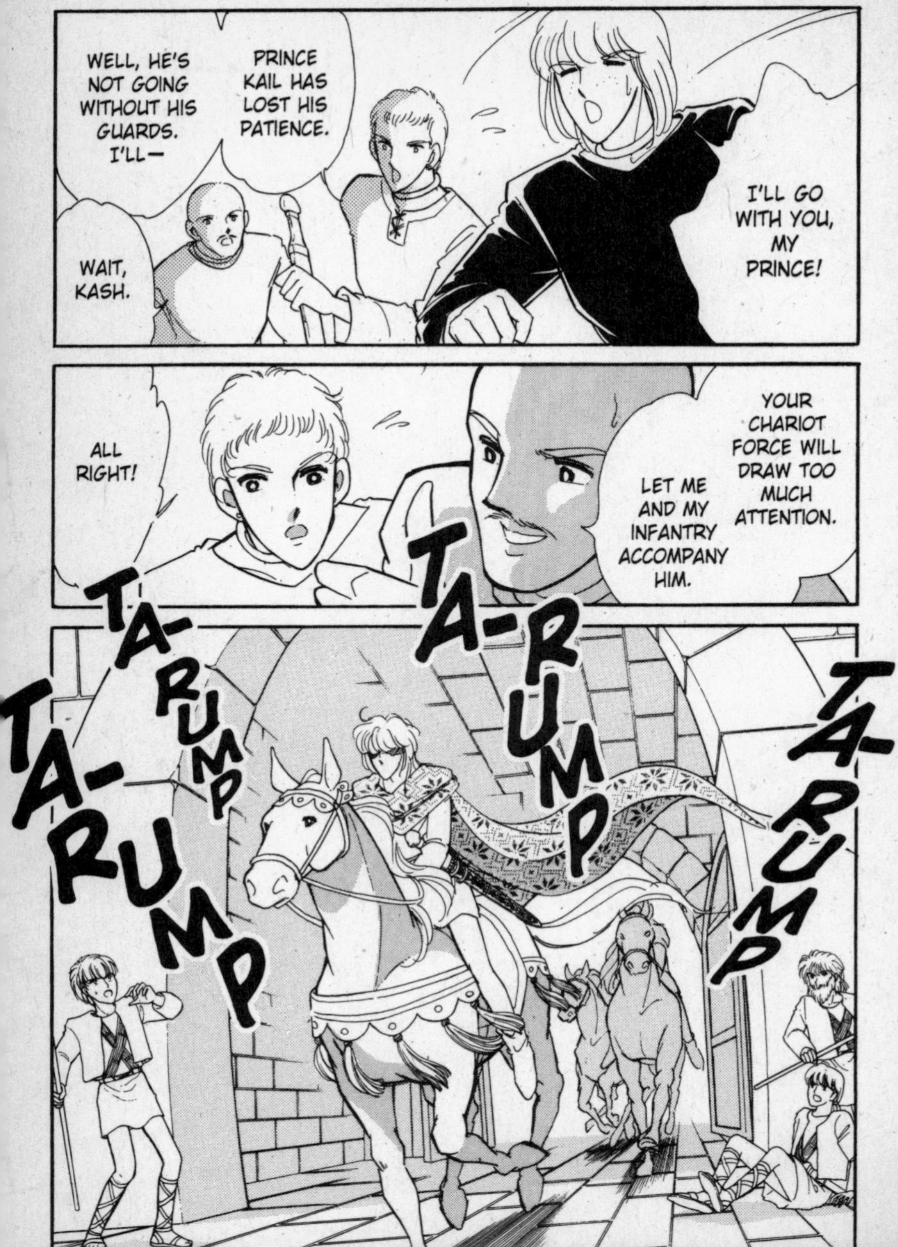
I'LL GO WITH YOU, MY PRINCE!
PRINCE KAIL HAS LOST HIS PATIENCE.
WELL, HE'S NOT GOING WITHOUT HIS GUARDS. I'LL—
WAIT, KASH.
YOUR CHARIOT FORCE WILL DRAW TOO MUCH ATTENTION.
LET ME AND MY INFANTRY ACCOMPANY HIM.
ALL RIGHT!
TA-RUMP
TA-RUMP
TA-RUMP
TA-RUMP

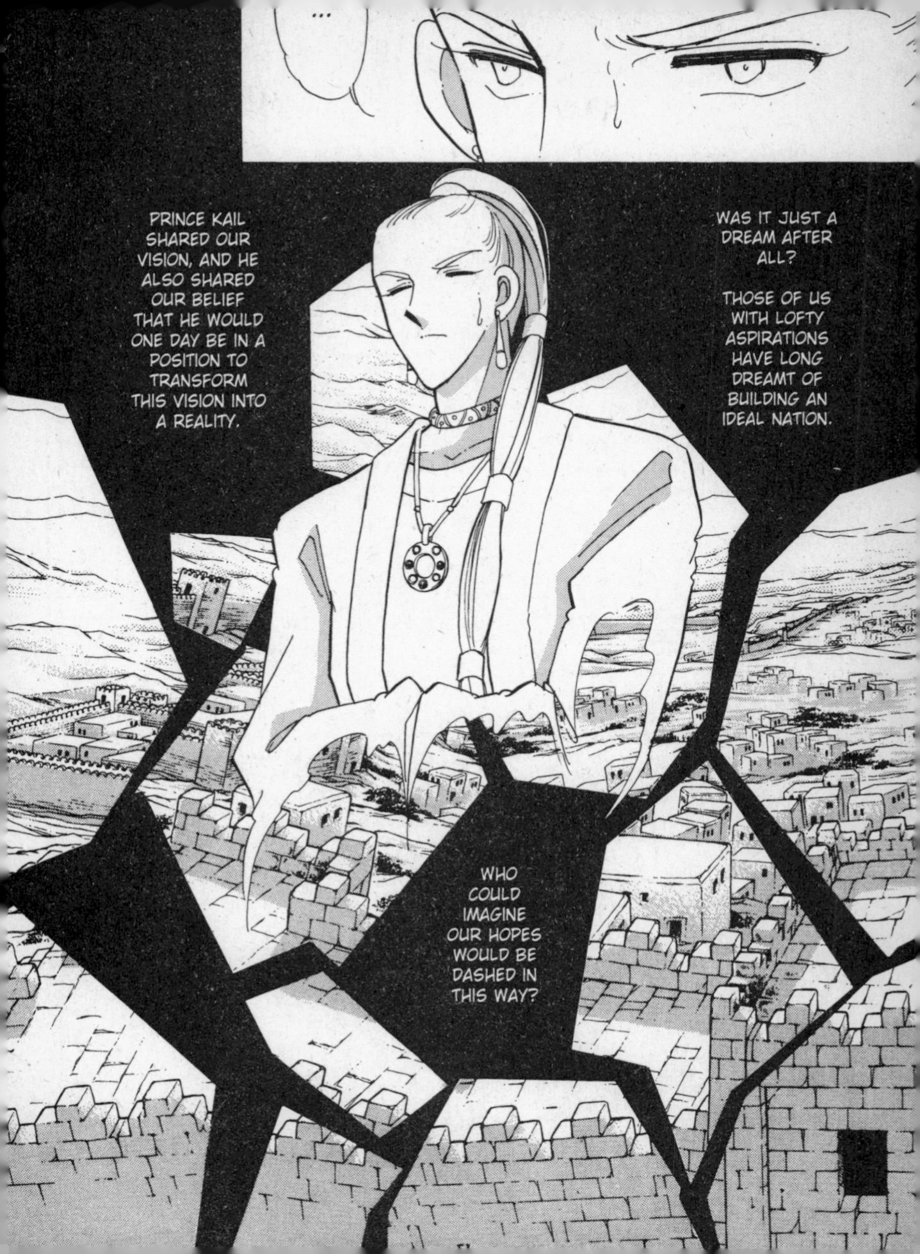
...
WAS IT JUST A DREAM AFTER ALL?
THOSE OF US WITH LOFTY ASPIRATIONS HAVE LONG DREAMT OF BUILDING AN IDEAL NATION.
PRINCE KAIL SHARED OUR VISION, AND HE ALSO SHARED OUR BELIEF THAT HE WOULD ONE DAY BE IN A POSITION TO TRANSFORM THIS VISION INTO A REALITY.
WHO COULD IMAGINE OUR HOPES WOULD BE DASHED IN THIS WAY?

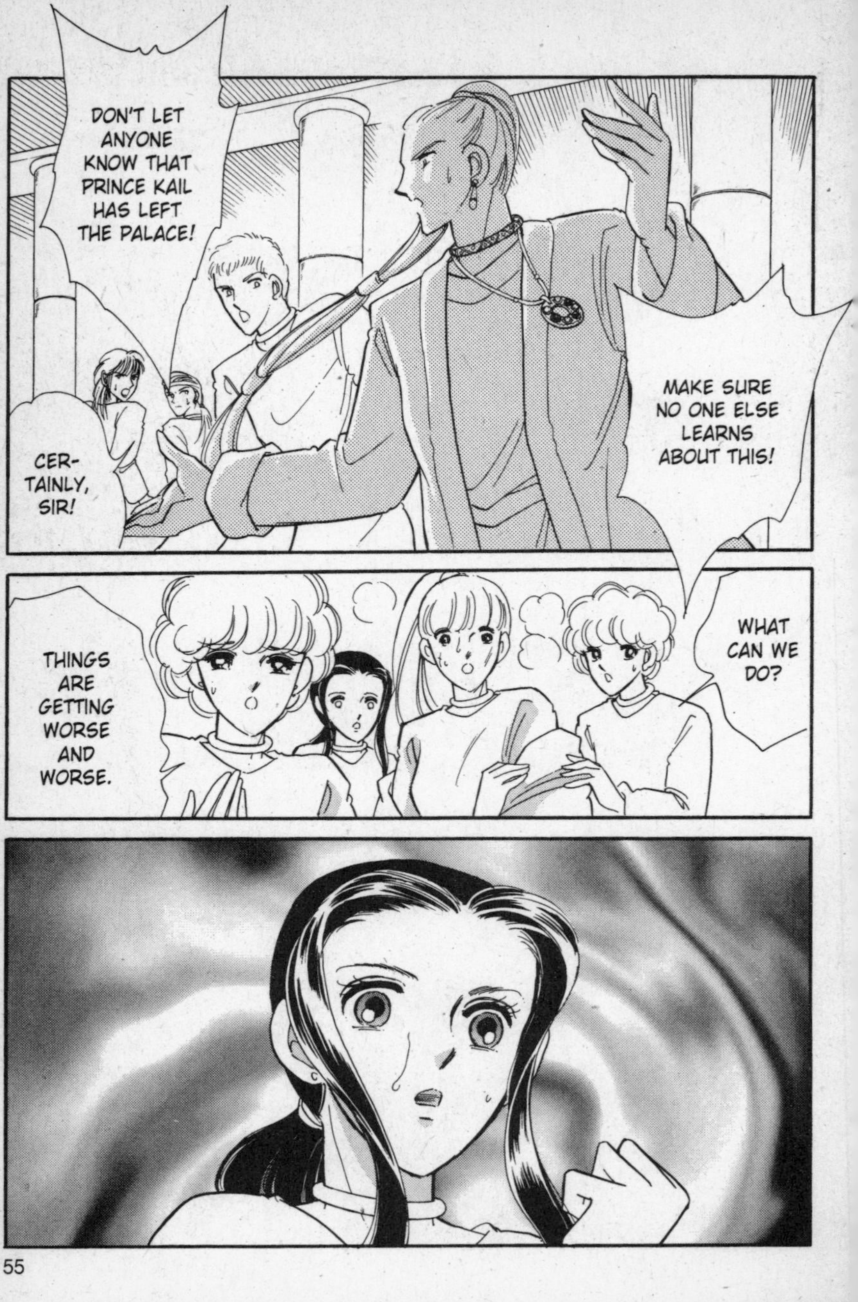
DON'T LET ANYONE KNOW THAT PRINCE KAIL HAS LEFT THE PALACE!
MAKE SURE NO ONE ELSE LEARNS ABOUT THIS!
CER-TAINLY, SIR!
WHAT CAN WE DO?
THINGS ARE GETTING WORSE AND WORSE.

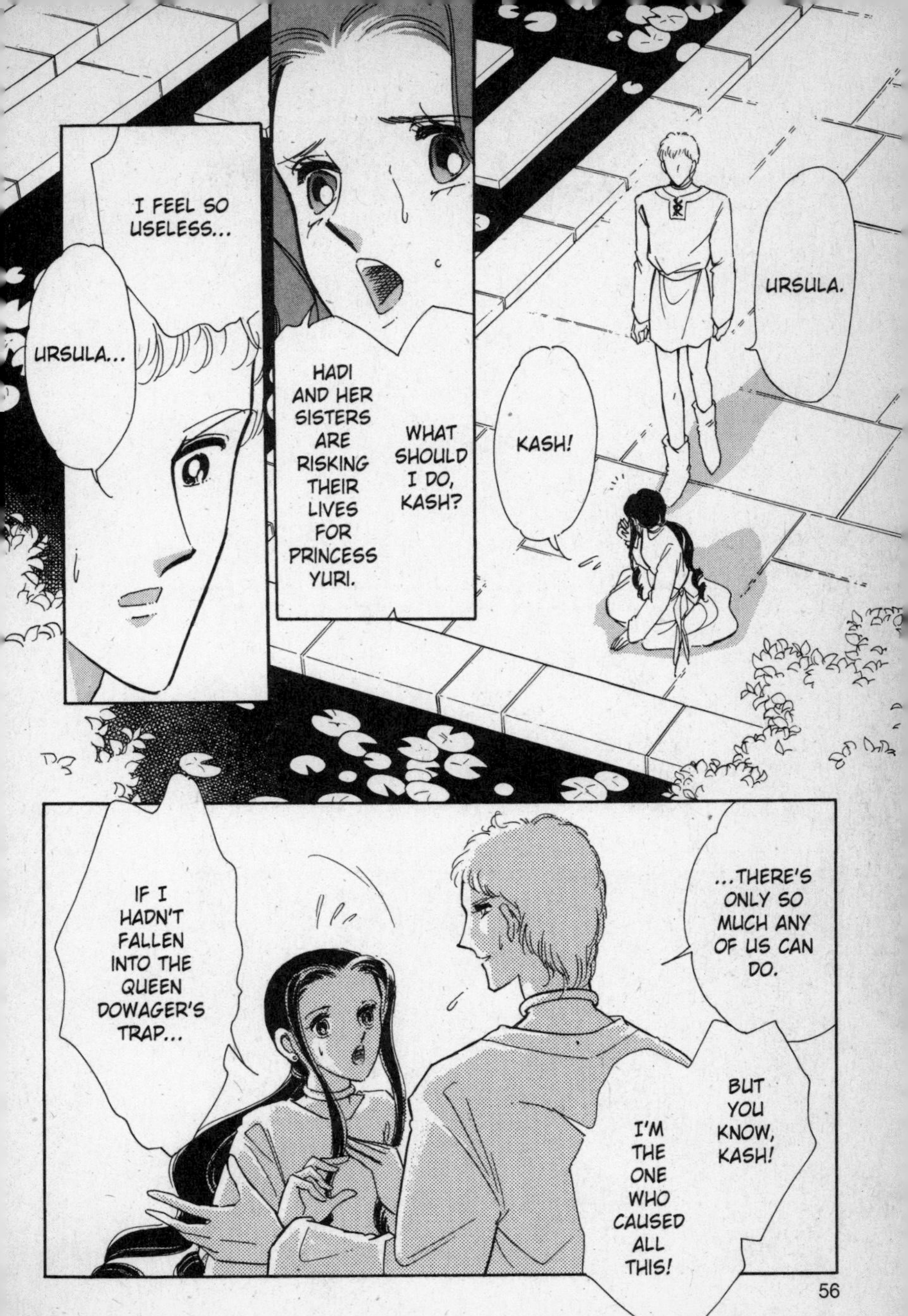
URSULA.
KASH!
WHAT SHOULD I DO, KASH?
HADI AND HER SISTERS ARE RISKING THEIR LIVES FOR PRINCESS YURI.
I FEEL SO USELESS...
URSULA...
...THERE'S ONLY SO MUCH ANY OF US CAN DO.
BUT YOU KNOW, KASH!
I'M THE ONE WHO CAUSED ALL THIS!
IF I HADN'T FALLEN INTO THE QUEEN DOWAGER'S TRAP...

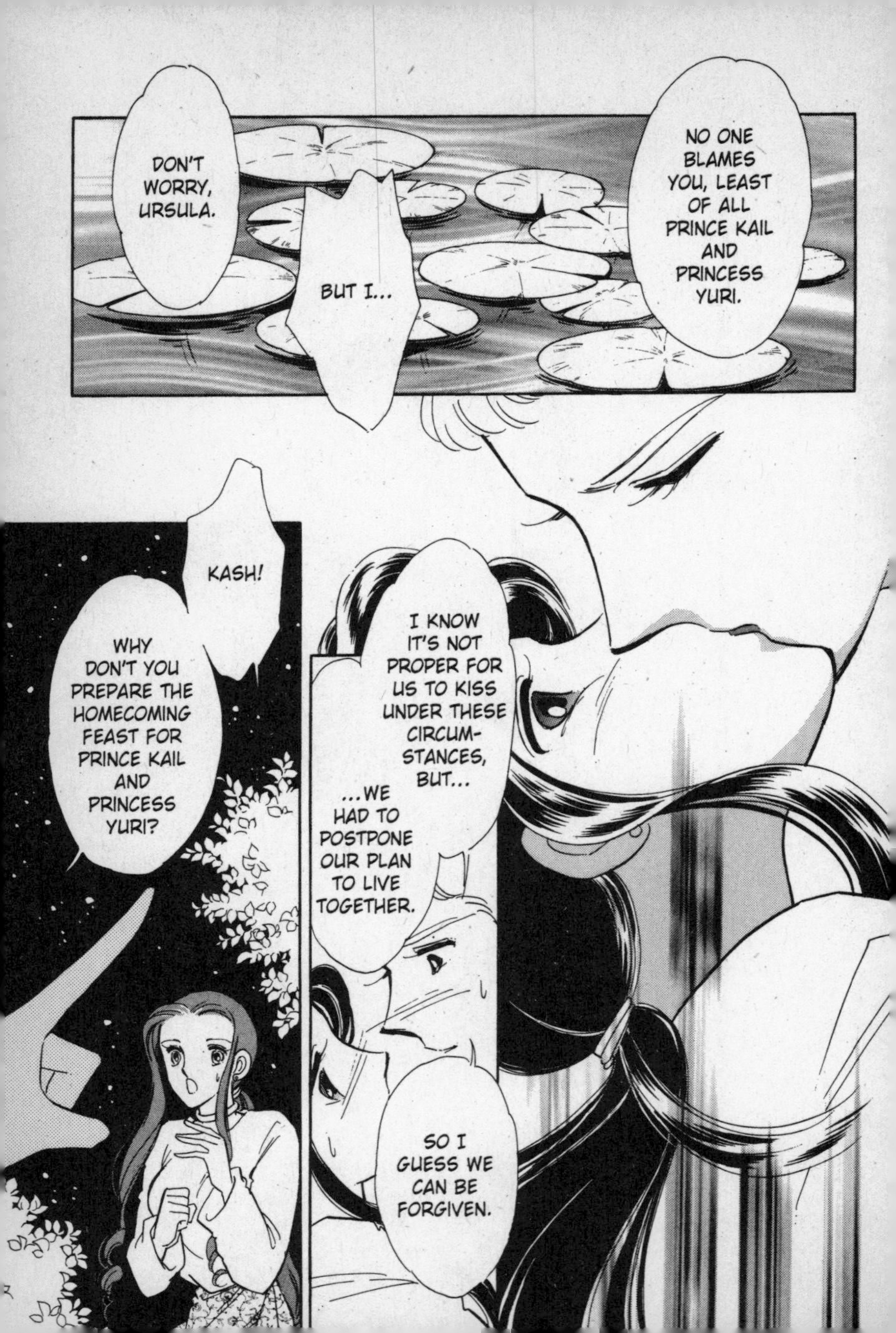
NO ONE BLAMES YOU, LEAST OF ALL PRINCE KAIL AND PRINCESS YURI.
DON'T WORRY, URSULA.
BUT I...
I KNOW IT'S NOT PROPER FOR US TO KISS UNDER THESE CIRCUM-STANCES, BUT...
...WE HAD TO POSTPONE OUR PLAN TO LIVE TOGETHER.
SO I GUESS WE CAN BE FORGIVEN.
KASH!
WHY DON'T YOU PREPARE THE HOMECOMING FEAST FOR PRINCE KAIL AND PRINCESS YURI?

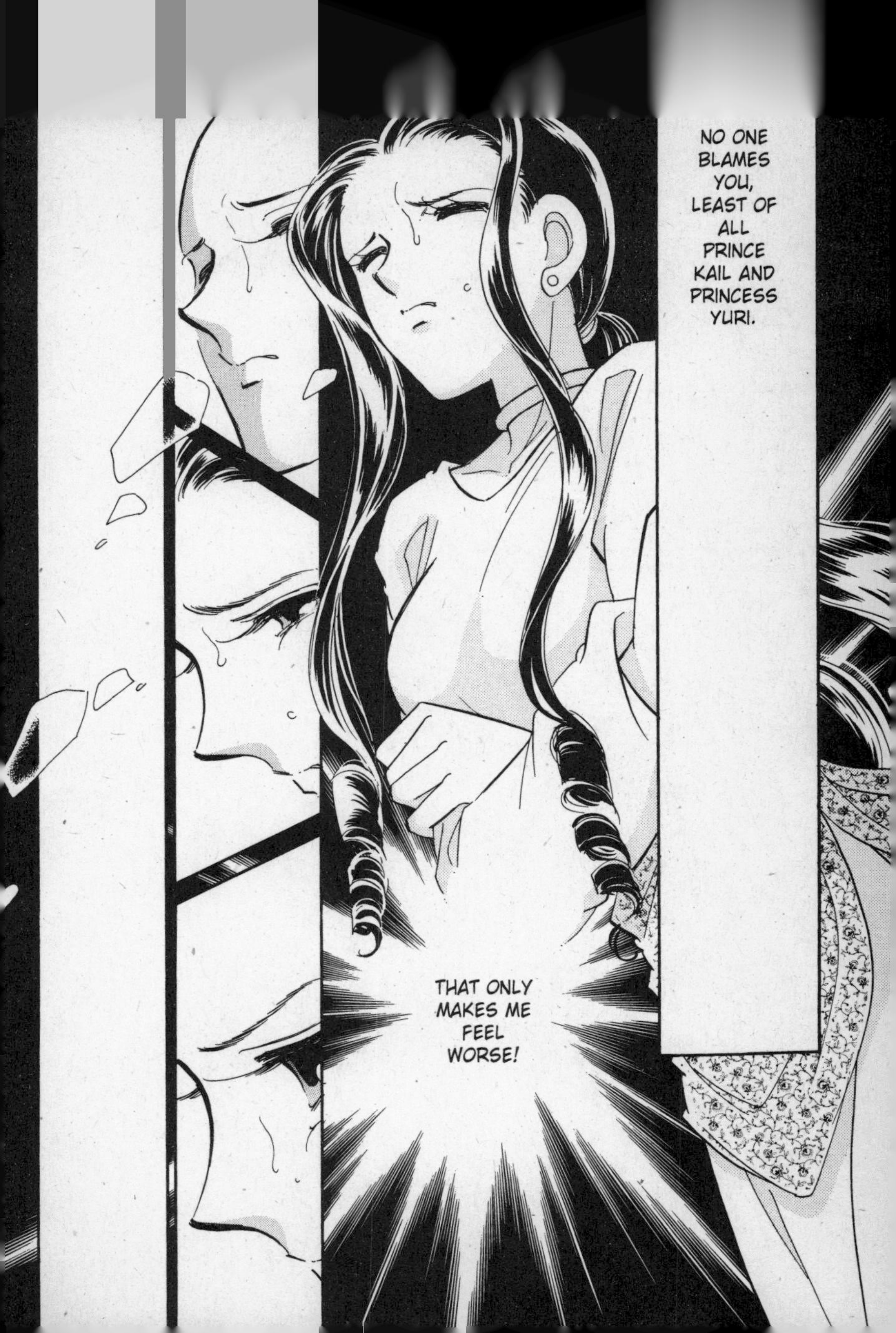
NO ONE BLAMES YOU, LEAST OF ALL PRINCE KAIL AND PRINCESS YURI.
THAT ONLY MAKES ME FEEL WORSE!

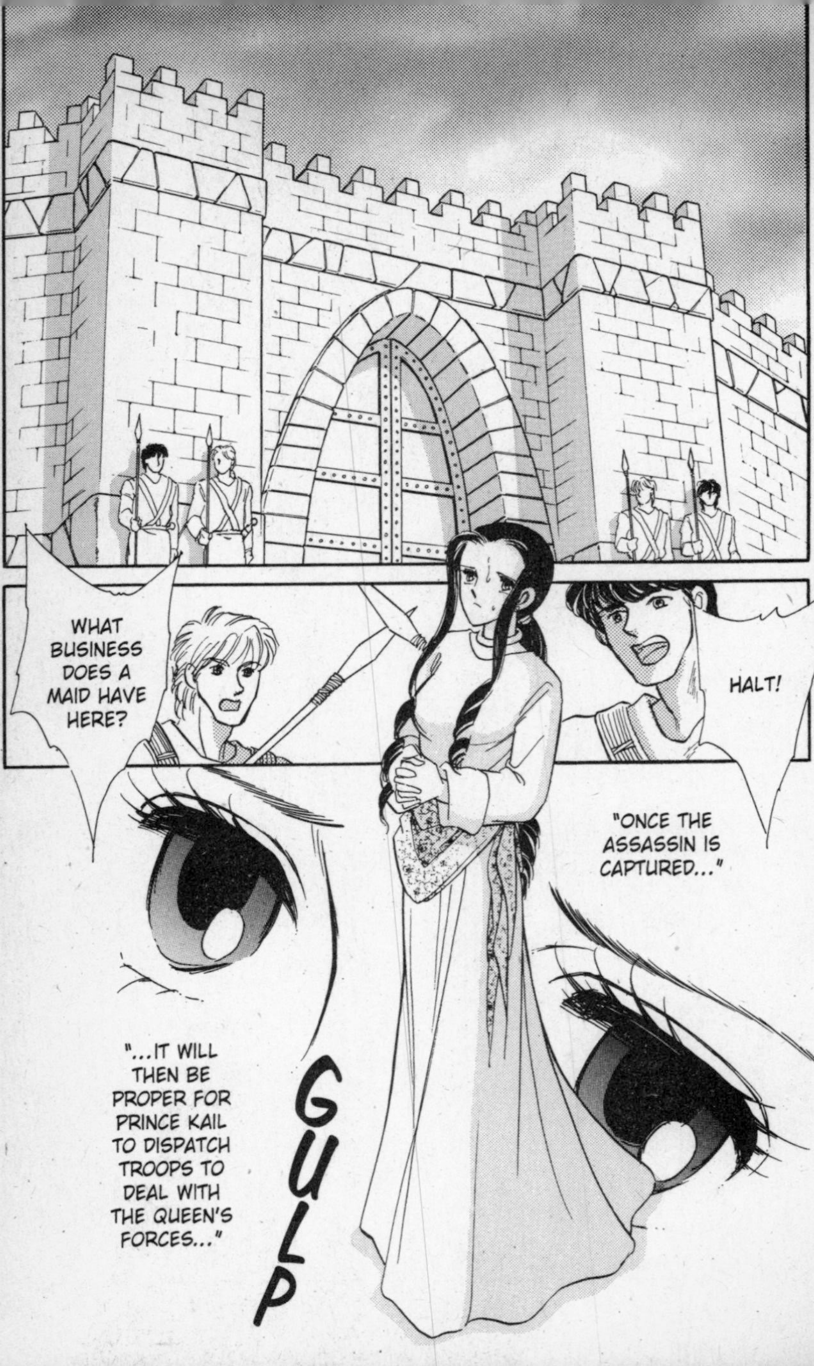
HALT!
WHAT BUSINESS DOES A MAID HAVE HERE?
"ONCE THE ASSASSIN IS CAPTURED..."
"...IT WILL THEN BE PROPER FOR PRINCE KAIL TO DISPATCH TROOPS TO DEAL WITH THE QUEEN'S FORCES..."
GULP

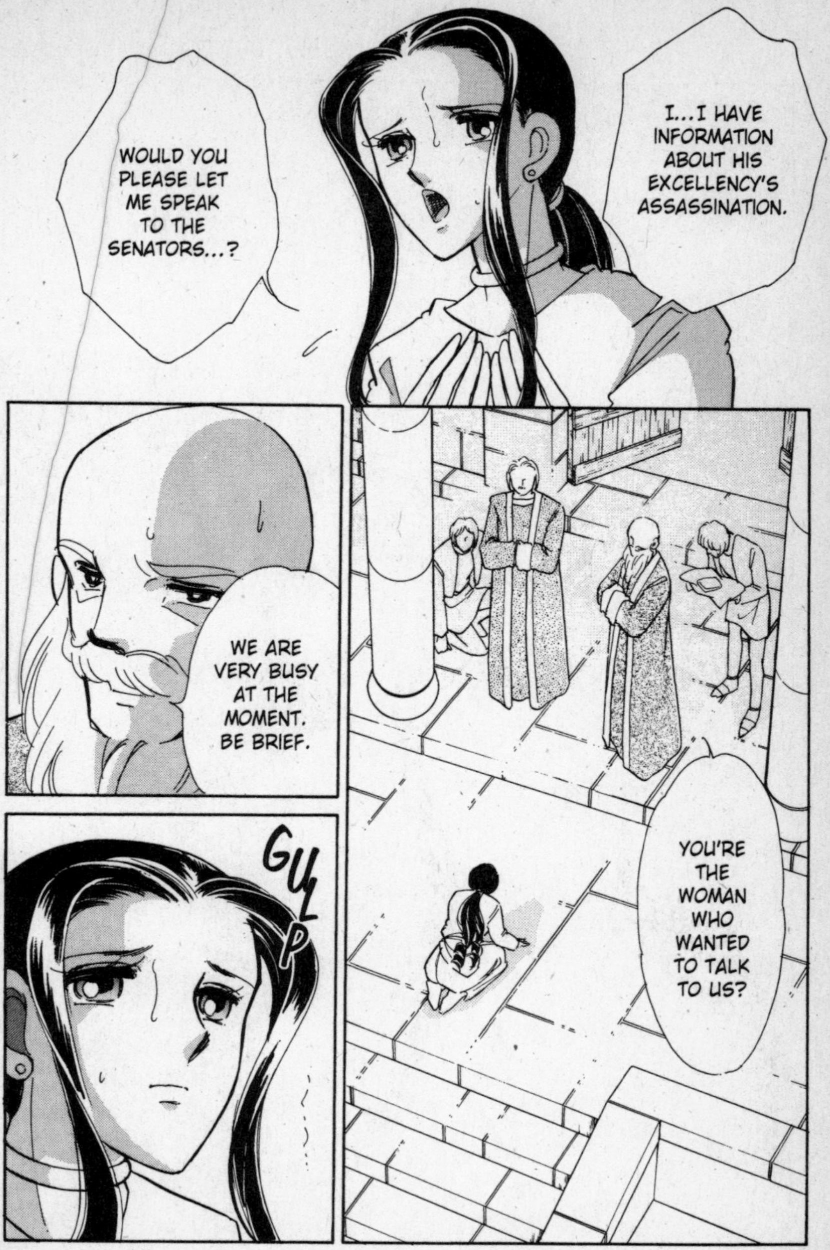
I...I HAVE INFORMATION ABOUT HIS EXCELLENCY'S ASSASSINATION.
WOULD YOU PLEASE LET ME SPEAK TO THE SENATORS...?
YOU'RE THE WOMAN WHO WANTED TO TALK TO US?
WE ARE VERY BUSY AT THE MOMENT. BE BRIEF.
GULP

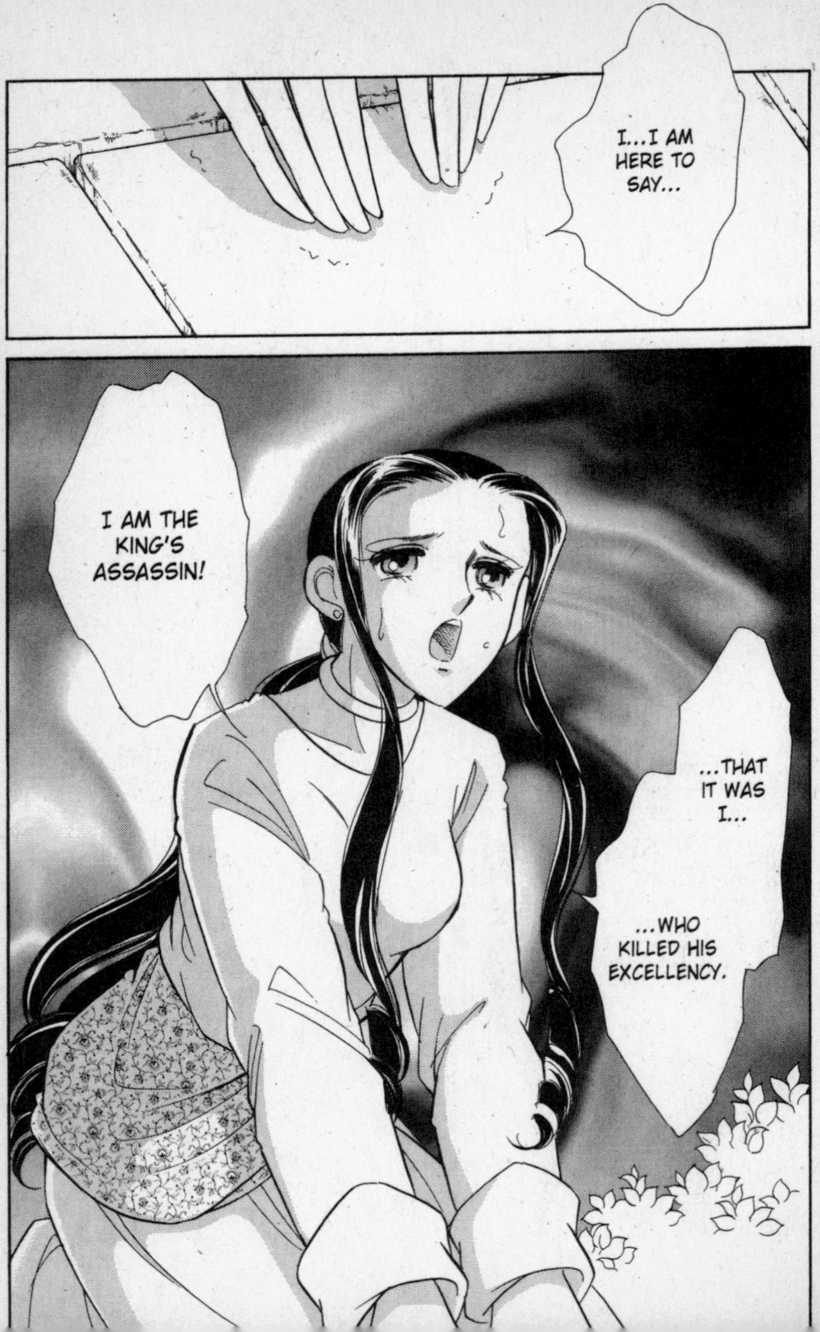
I...I AM HERE TO SAY...
...THAT IT WAS I...
...WHO KILLED HIS EXCELLENCY.
I AM THE KING'S ASSASSIN!

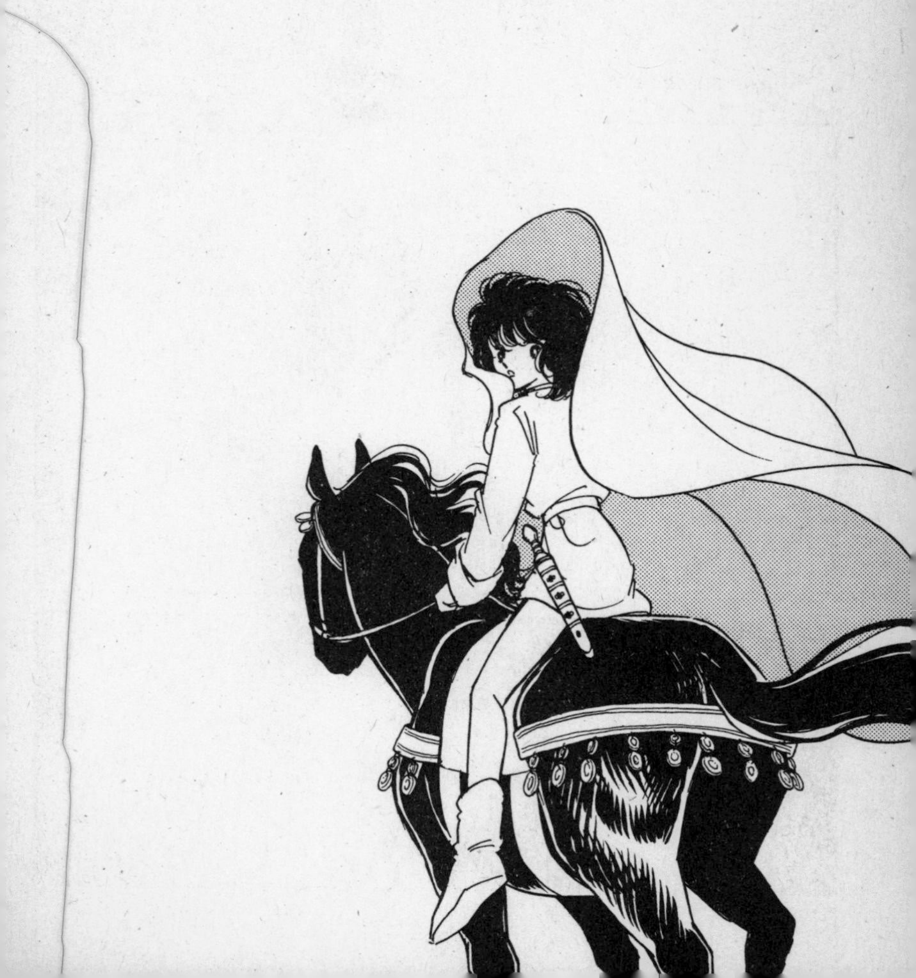

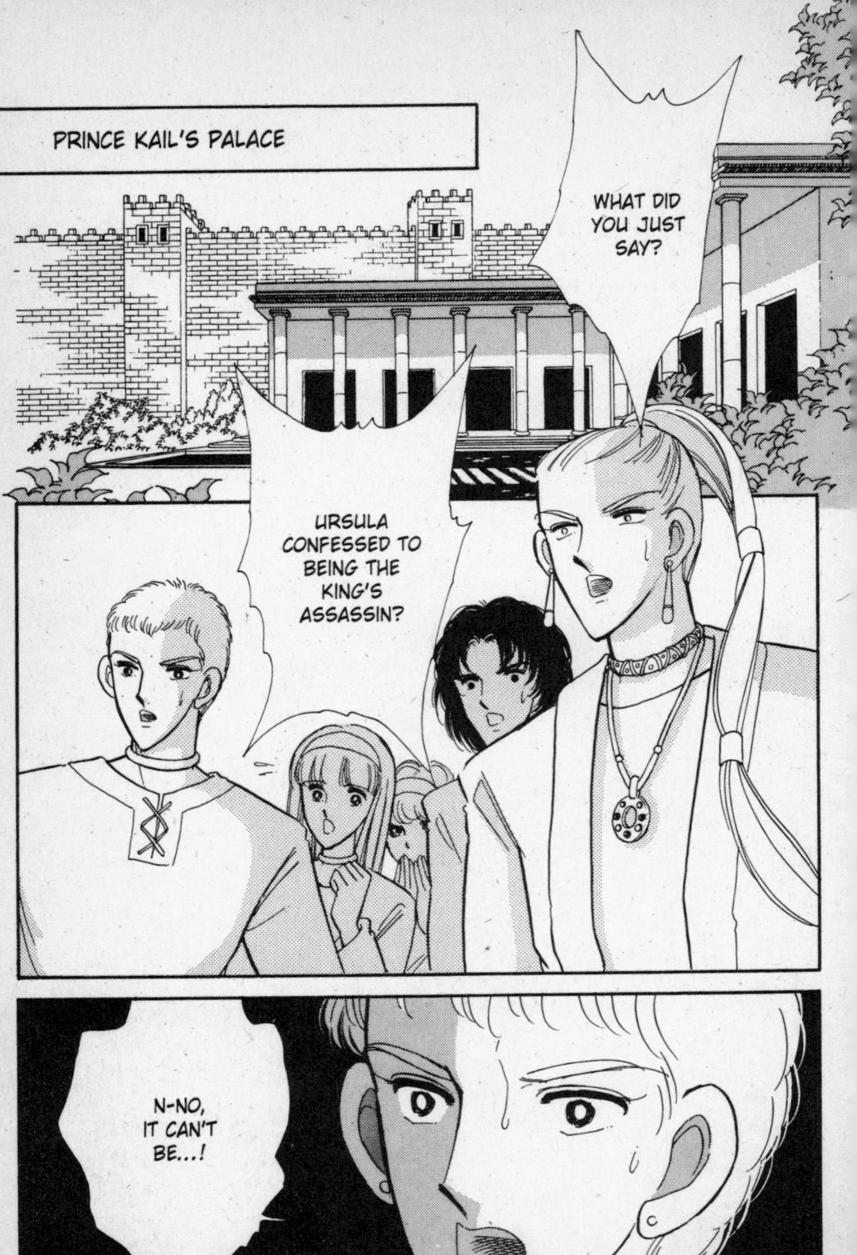
PRINCE KAIL'S PALACE
WHAT DID YOU JUST SAY?
URSULA CONFESSED TO BEING THE KING'S ASSASSIN?
N-NO, IT CAN'T BE...!

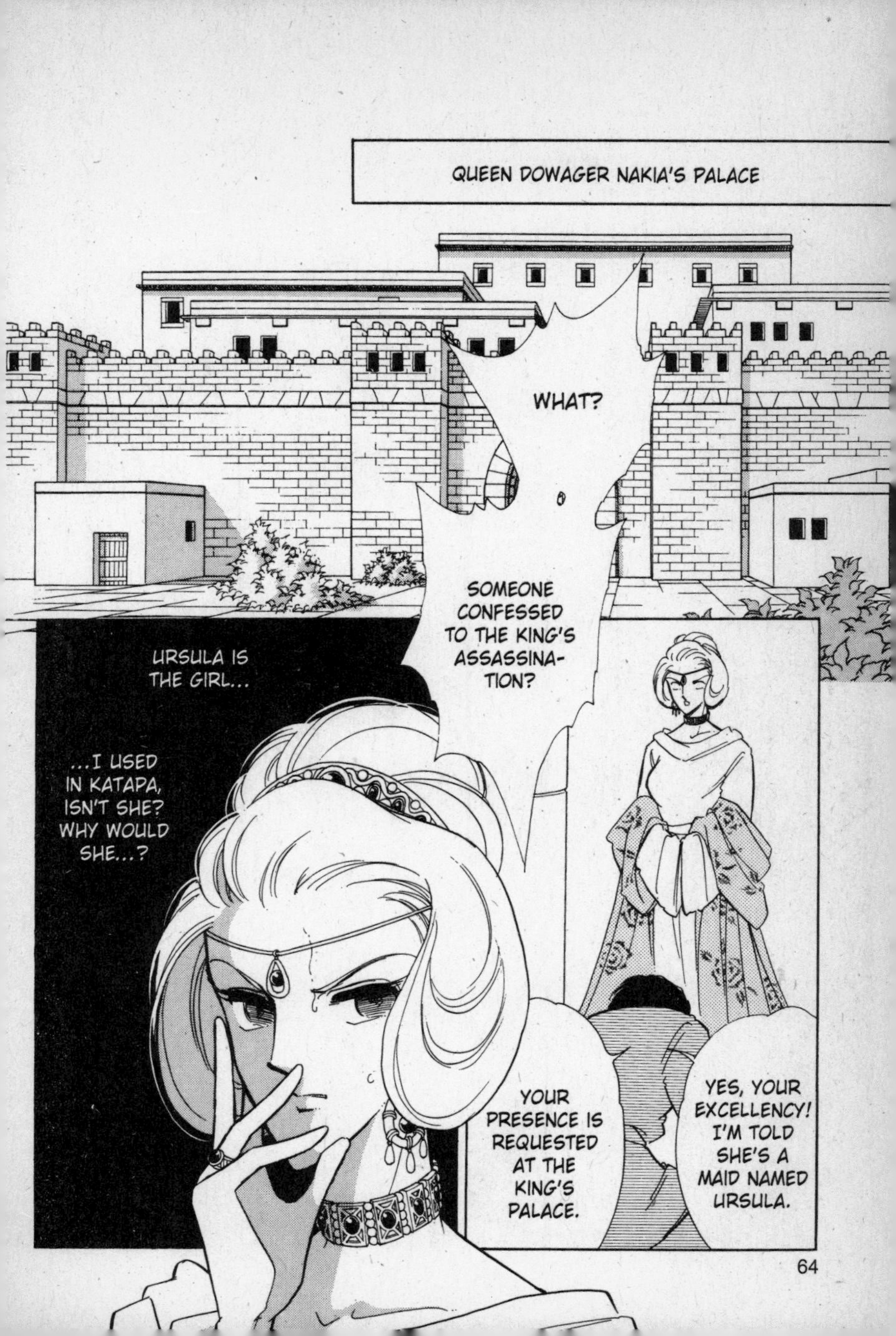
QUEEN DOWAGER NAKIA'S PALACE
WHAT?
SOMEONE CONFESSED TO THE KING'S ASSASSINATION?
YES, YOUR EXCELLENCY! I'M TOLD SHE'S A MAID NAMED URSULA.
YOUR PRESENCE IS REQUESTED AT THE KING'S PALACE.
URSULA IS THE GIRL...
...I USED IN KATAPA, ISN'T SHE? WHY WOULD SHE...?

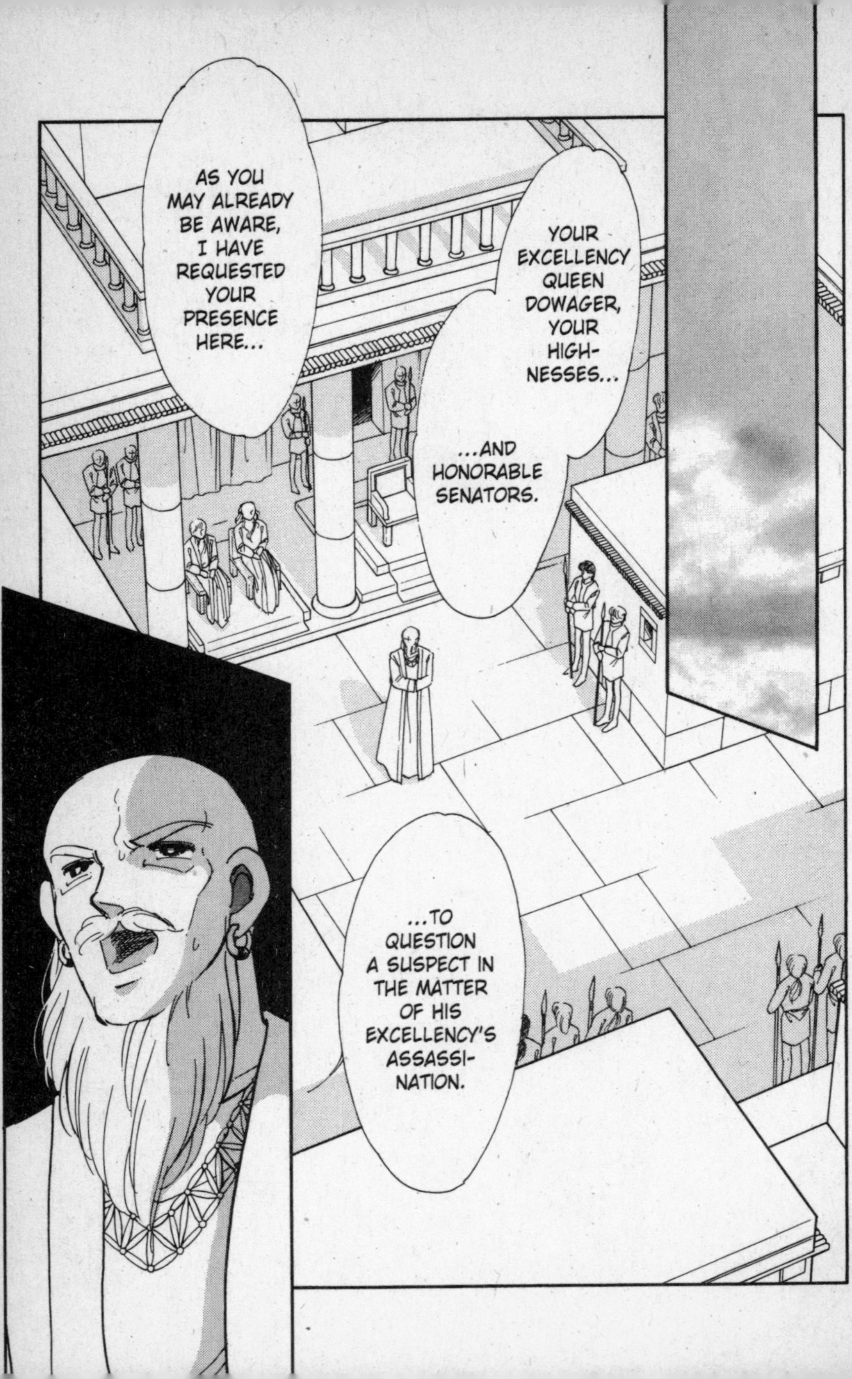
YOUR EXCELLENCY QUEEN DOWAGER, YOUR HIGH-NESSES...
...AND HONORABLE SENATORS.
AS YOU MAY ALREADY BE AWARE, I HAVE REQUESTED YOUR PRESENCE HERE...
...TO QUESTION A SUSPECT IN THE MATTER OF HIS EXCELLENCY'S ASSASSI-NATION.

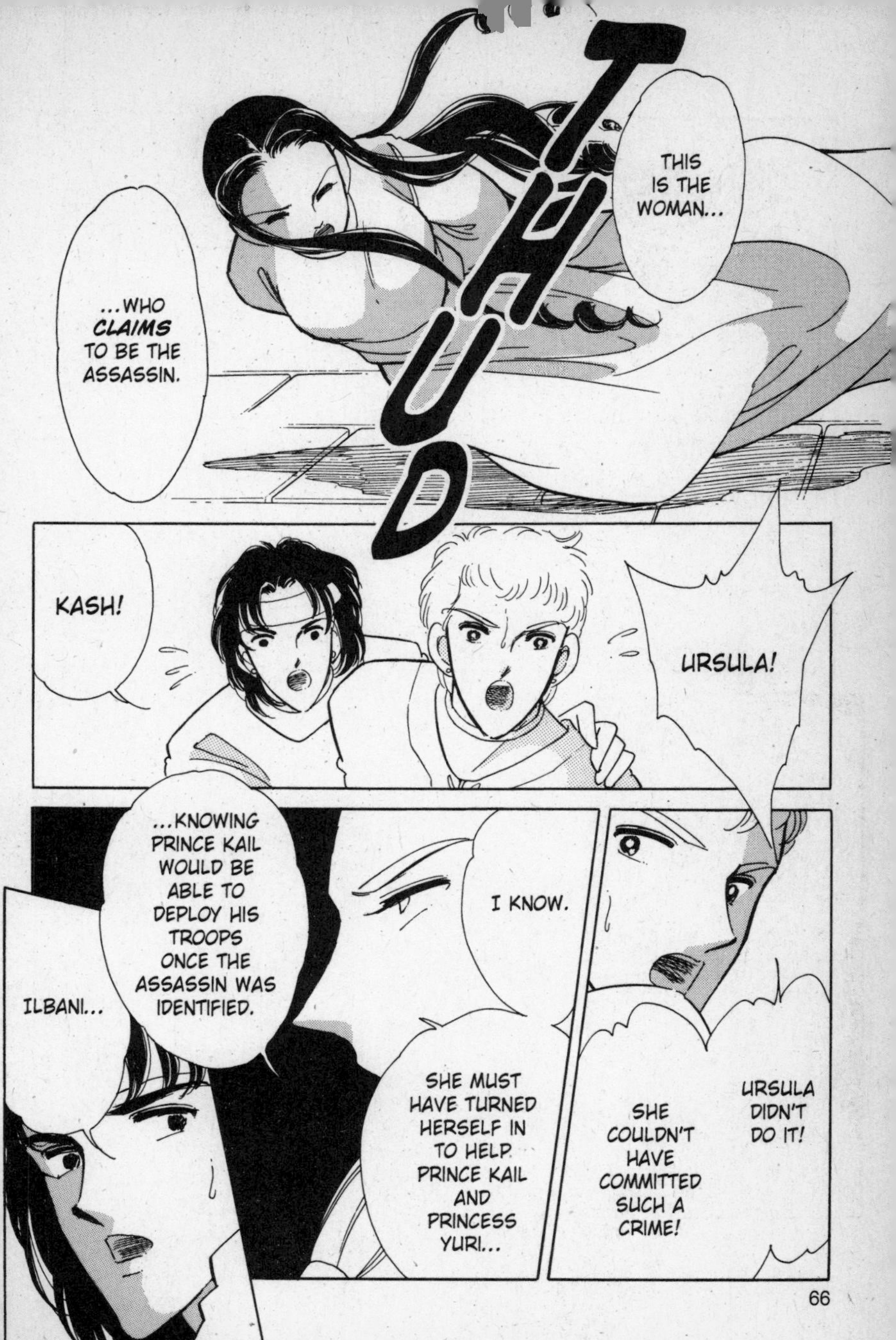

THIS IS THE WOMAN...
THUD
...WHO CLAIMS TO BE THE ASSASSIN.
URSULA!
KASH!
URSULA DIDN'T DO IT!
SHE COULDN'T HAVE COMMITTED SUCH A CRIME!
I KNOW.
SHE MUST HAVE TURNED HERSELF IN TO HELP PRINCE KAIL AND PRINCESS YURI...
...KNOWING PRINCE KAIL WOULD BE ABLE TO DEPLOY HIS TROOPS ONCE THE ASSASSIN WAS IDENTIFIED.
ILBANI...

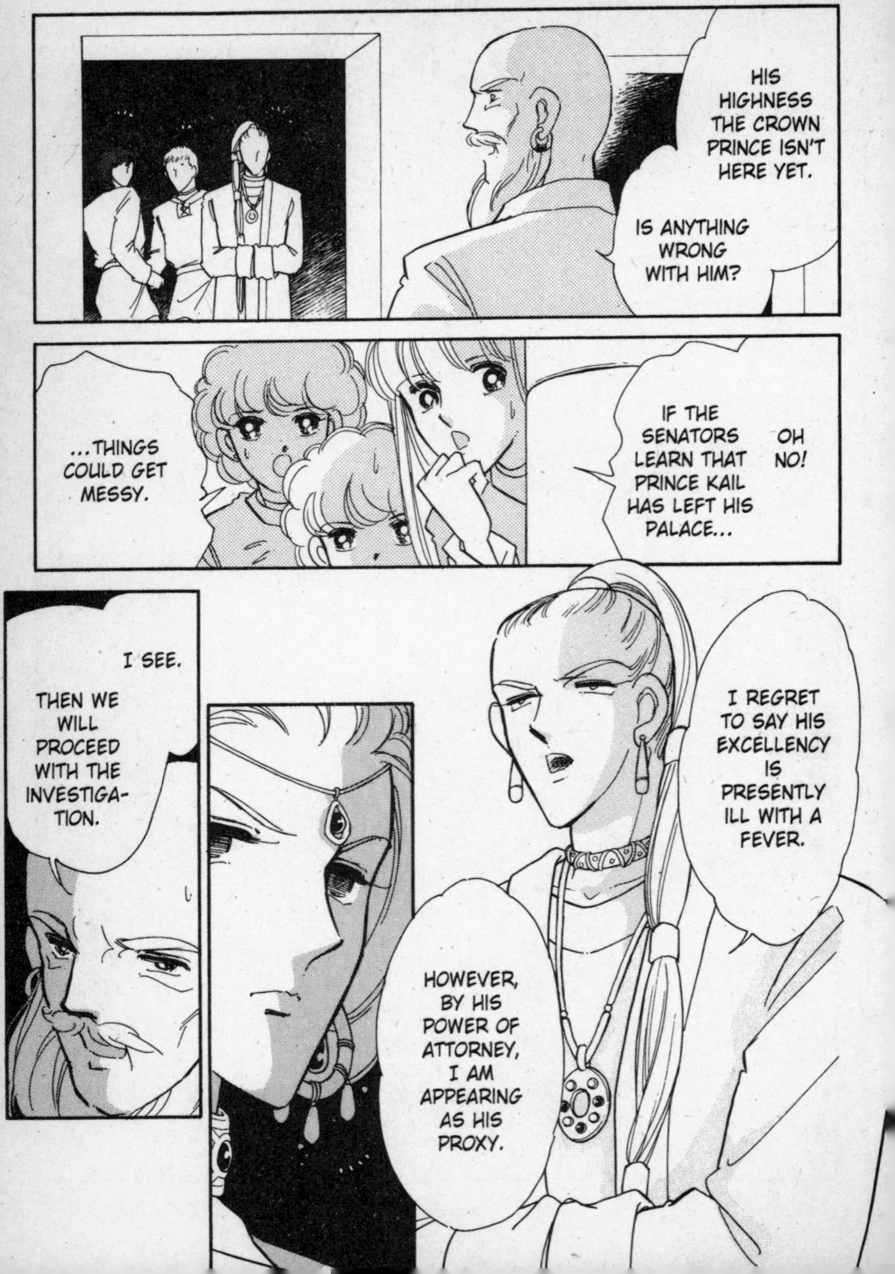
HIS HIGHNESS THE CROWN PRINCE ISN'T HERE YET.
IS ANYTHING WRONG WITH HIM?
OH NO!
IF THE SENATORS LEARN THAT PRINCE KAIL HAS LEFT HIS PALACE...
...THINGS COULD GET MESSY.
I REGRET TO SAY HIS EXCELLENCY IS PRESENTLY ILL WITH A FEVER.
HOWEVER, BY HIS POWER OF ATTORNEY, I AM APPEARING AS HIS PROXY.
I SEE.
THEN WE WILL PROCEED WITH THE INVESTIGATION.

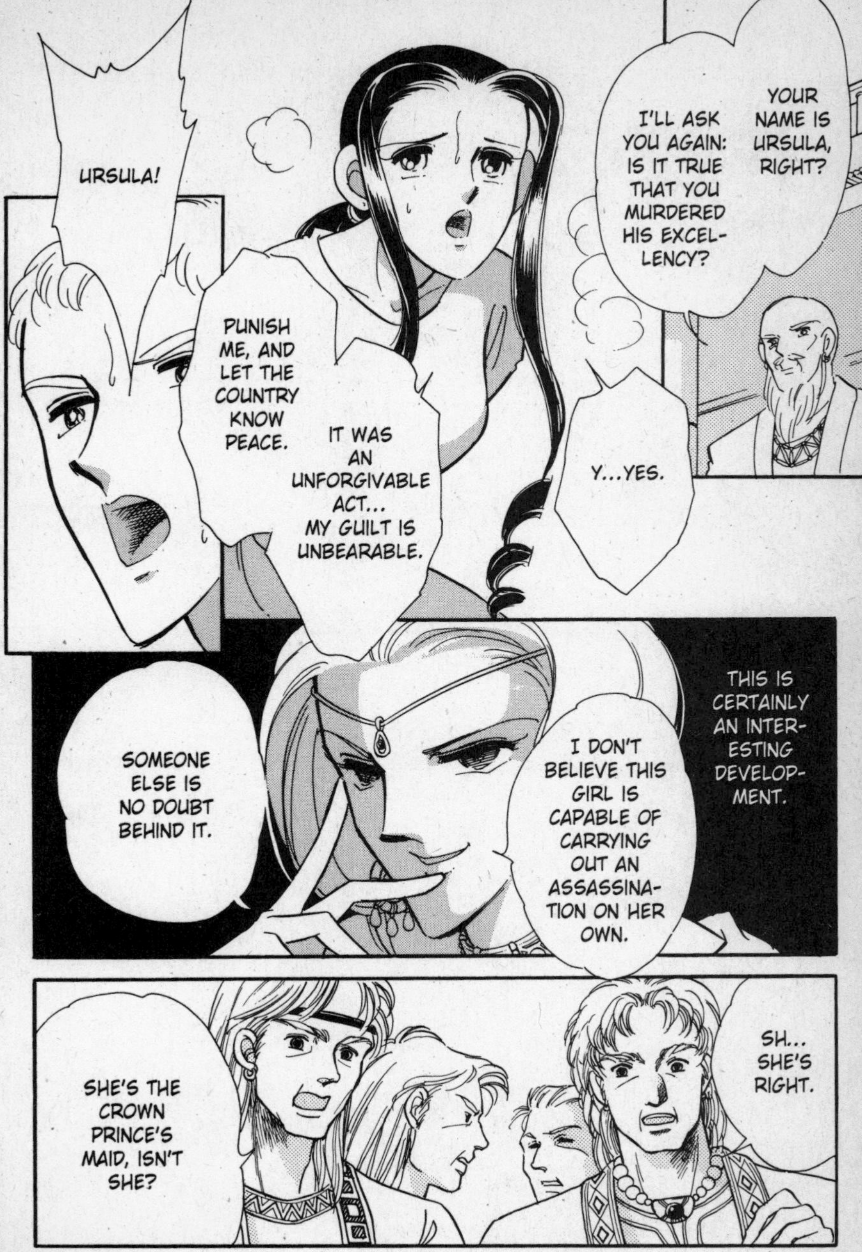
YOUR NAME IS URSULA, RIGHT?
I'LL ASK YOU AGAIN: IS IT TRUE THAT YOU MURDERED HIS EXCELLENCY?
Y...YES.
IT WAS AN UNFORGIVABLE ACT... MY GUILT IS UNBEARABLE.
PUNISH ME, AND LET THE COUNTRY KNOW PEACE.
URSULA!
THIS IS CERTAINLY AN INTERESTING DEVELOPMENT.
I DON'T BELIEVE THIS GIRL IS CAPABLE OF CARRYING OUT AN ASSASSINATION ON HER OWN.
SOMEONE ELSE IS NO DOUBT BEHIND IT.
SH... SHE'S RIGHT.
SHE'S THE CROWN PRINCE'S MAID, ISN'T SHE?

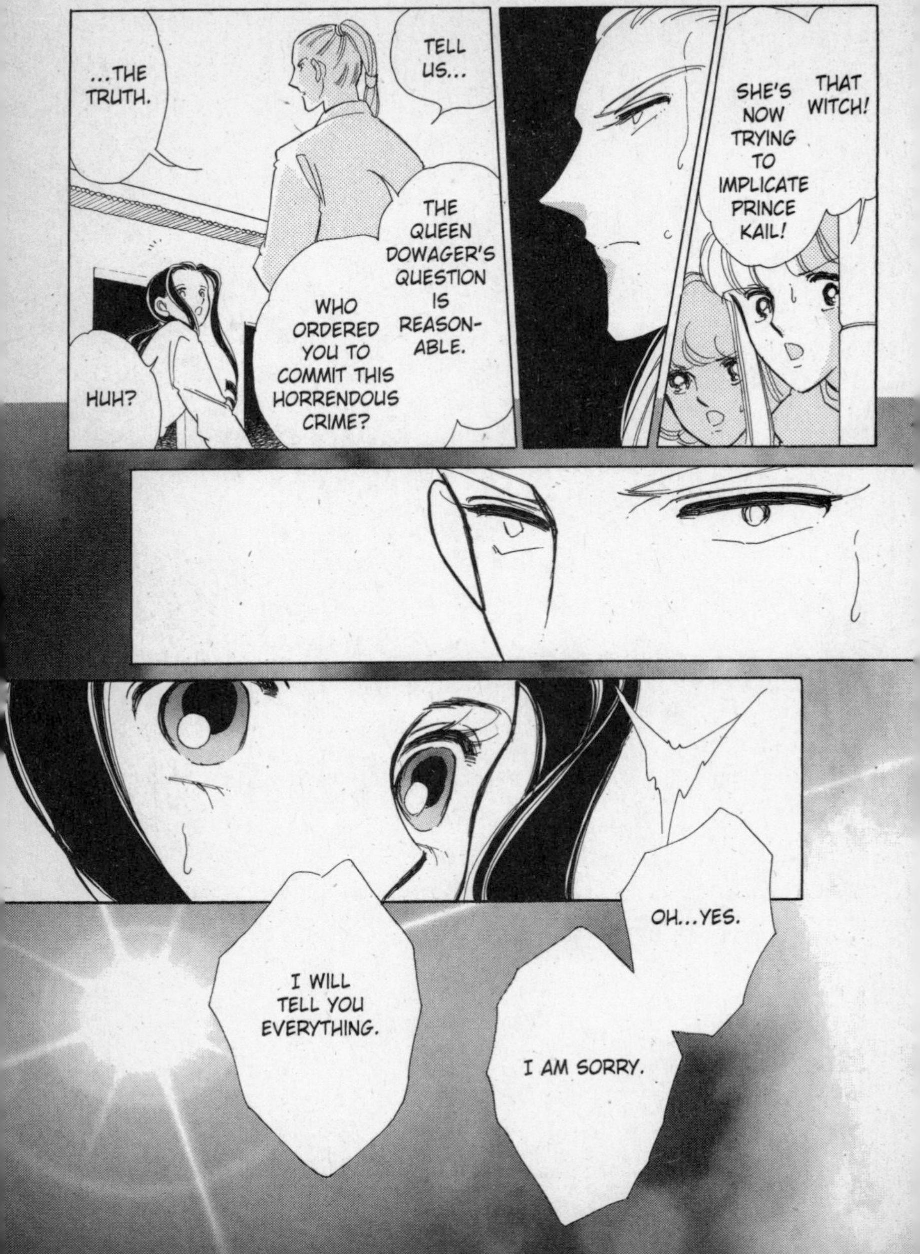
THAT WITCH!
SHE'S NOW TRYING TO IMPLICATE PRINCE KAIL!
TELL US...
...THE TRUTH.
THE QUEEN DOWAGER'S QUESTION IS REASONABLE.
WHO ORDERED YOU TO COMMIT THIS HORRENDOUS CRIME?
HUH?
OH...YES.
I AM SORRY.
I WILL TELL YOU EVERYTHING.

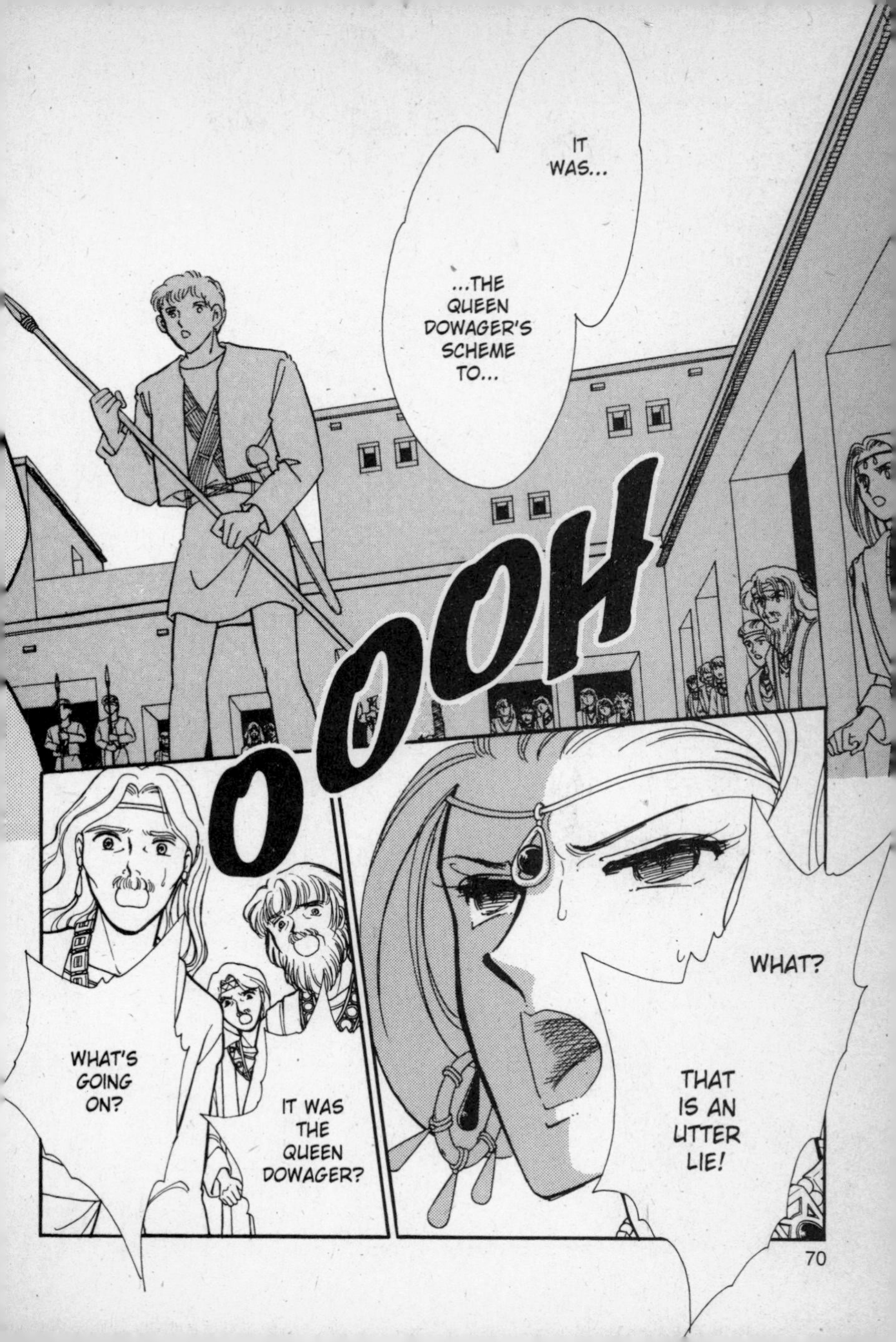
IT WAS...
...THE QUEEN DOWAGER'S SCHEME TO...
OOOH
WHAT?
THAT IS AN UTTER LIE!
IT WAS THE QUEEN DOWAGER?
WHAT'S GOING ON?

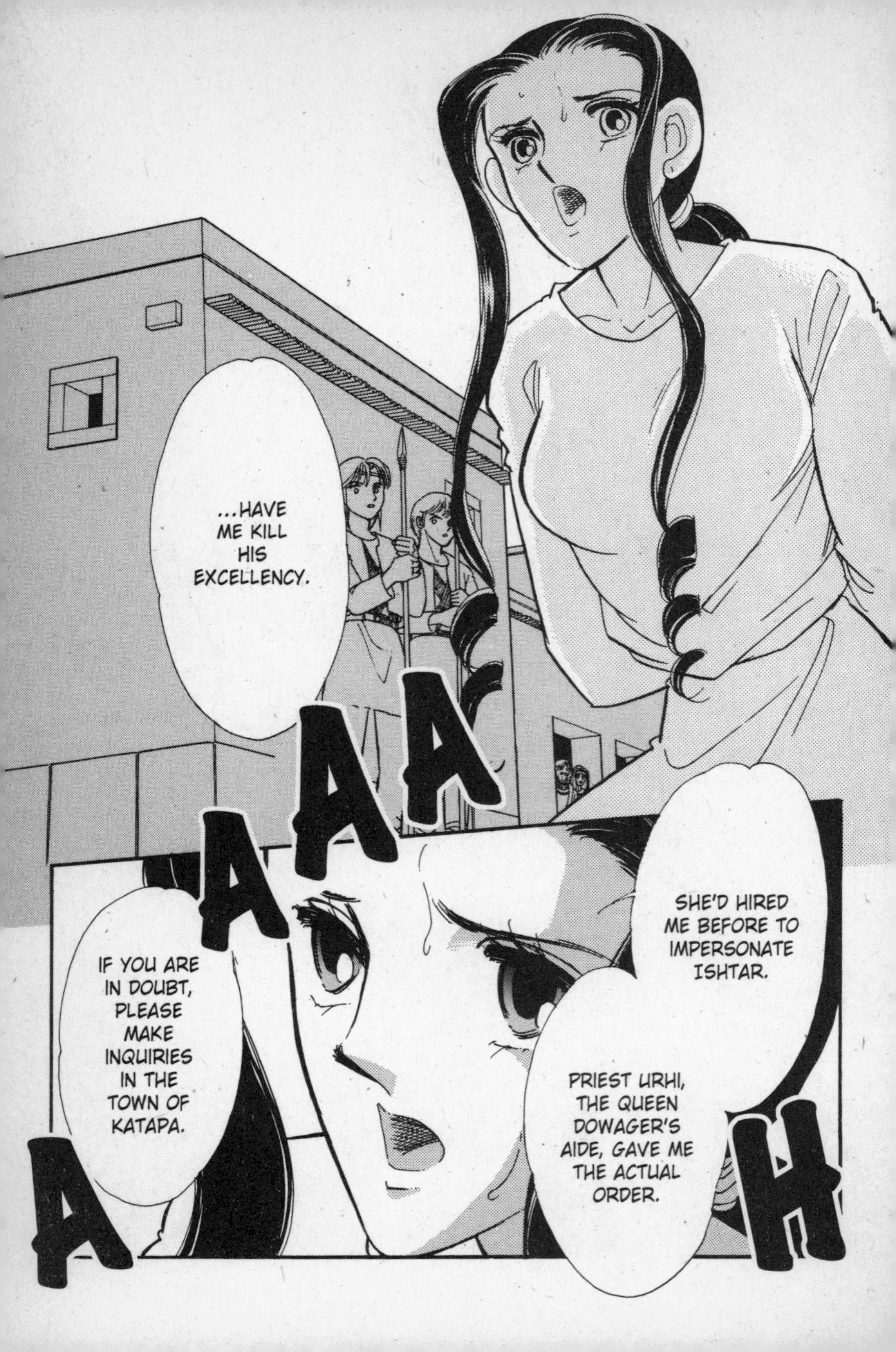
...HAVE ME KILL HIS EXCELLENCY.
AAAAAAH
SHE'D HIRED ME BEFORE TO IMPERSONATE ISHTAR.
PRIEST URHI, THE QUEEN DOWAGER'S AIDE, GAVE ME THE ACTUAL ORDER.
IF YOU ARE IN DOUBT, PLEASE MAKE INQUIRIES IN THE TOWN OF KATAPA.

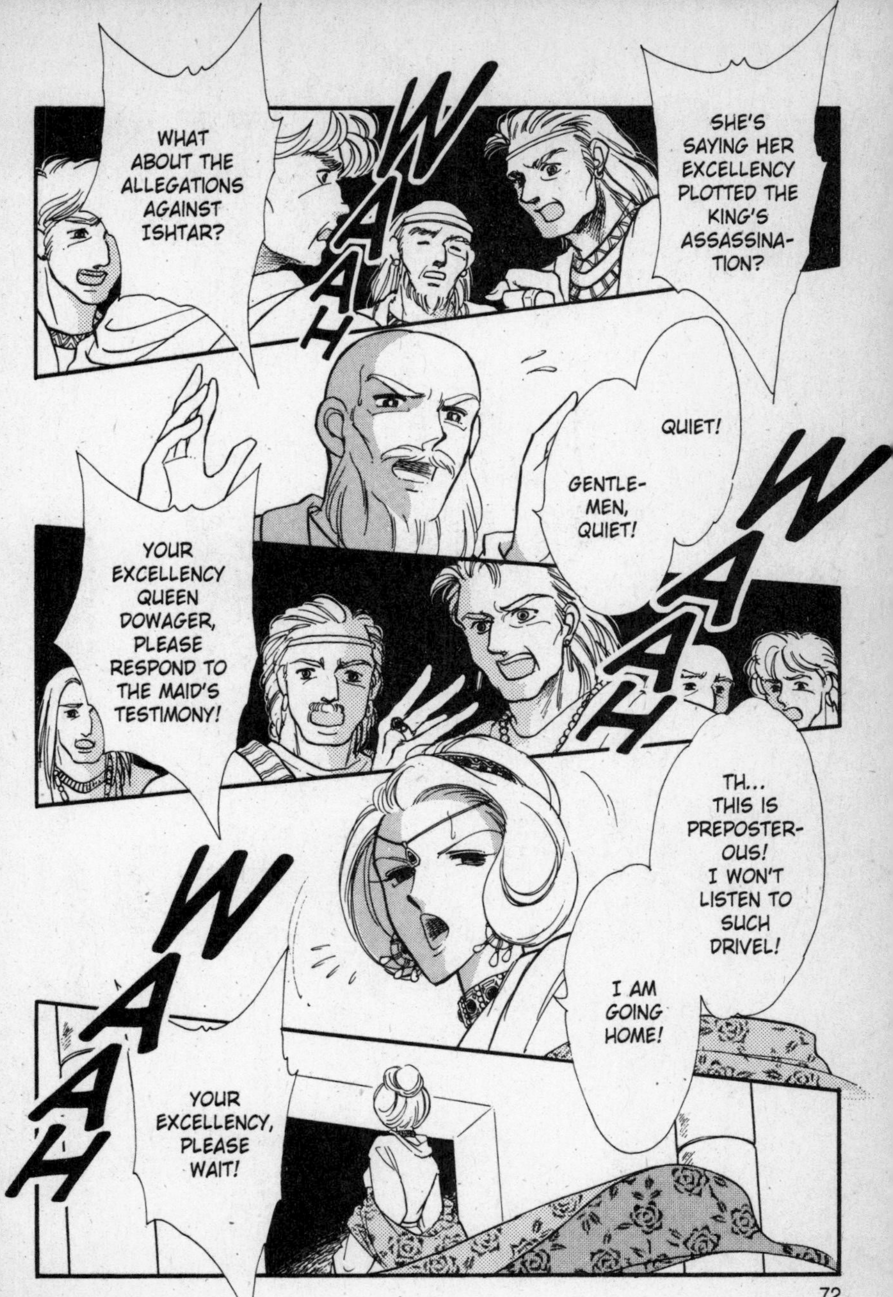
SHE'S SAYING HER EXCELLENCY PLOTTED THE KING'S ASSASSINATION?
WAAH
WHAT ABOUT THE ALLEGATIONS AGAINST ISHTAR?
QUIET!
GENTLEMEN, QUIET!
WAAH
YOUR EXCELLENCY QUEEN DOWAGER, PLEASE RESPOND TO THE MAID'S TESTIMONY!
TH... THIS IS PREPOSTEROUS! I WON'T LISTEN TO SUCH DRIVEL!
I AM GOING HOME!
WAAH
YOUR EXCELLENCY, PLEASE WAIT!

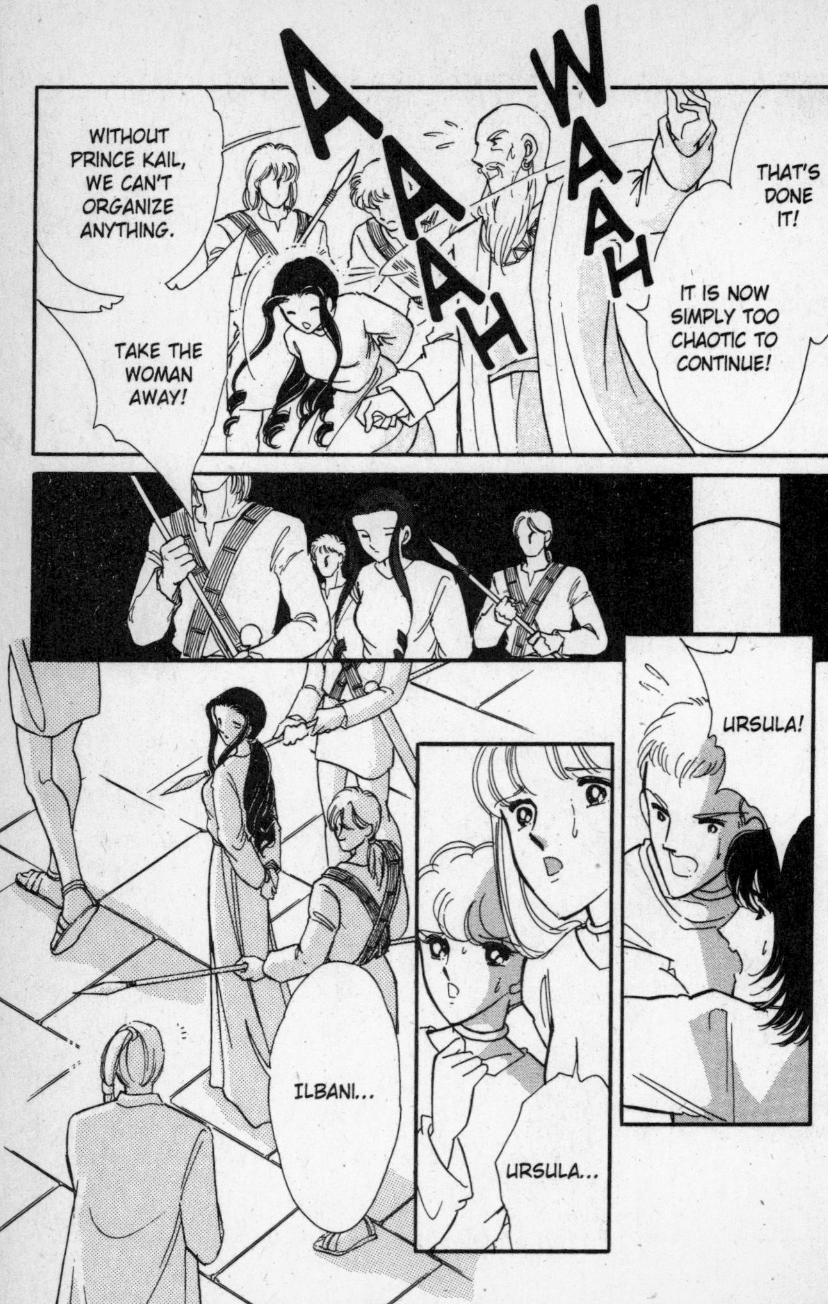
THAT'S DONE IT!
IT IS NOW SIMPLY TOO CHAOTIC TO CONTINUE!
WAAAH
AAAAH
WITHOUT PRINCE KAIL, WE CAN'T ORGANIZE ANYTHING.
TAKE THE WOMAN AWAY!
URSULA!
URSULA...
ILBANI...

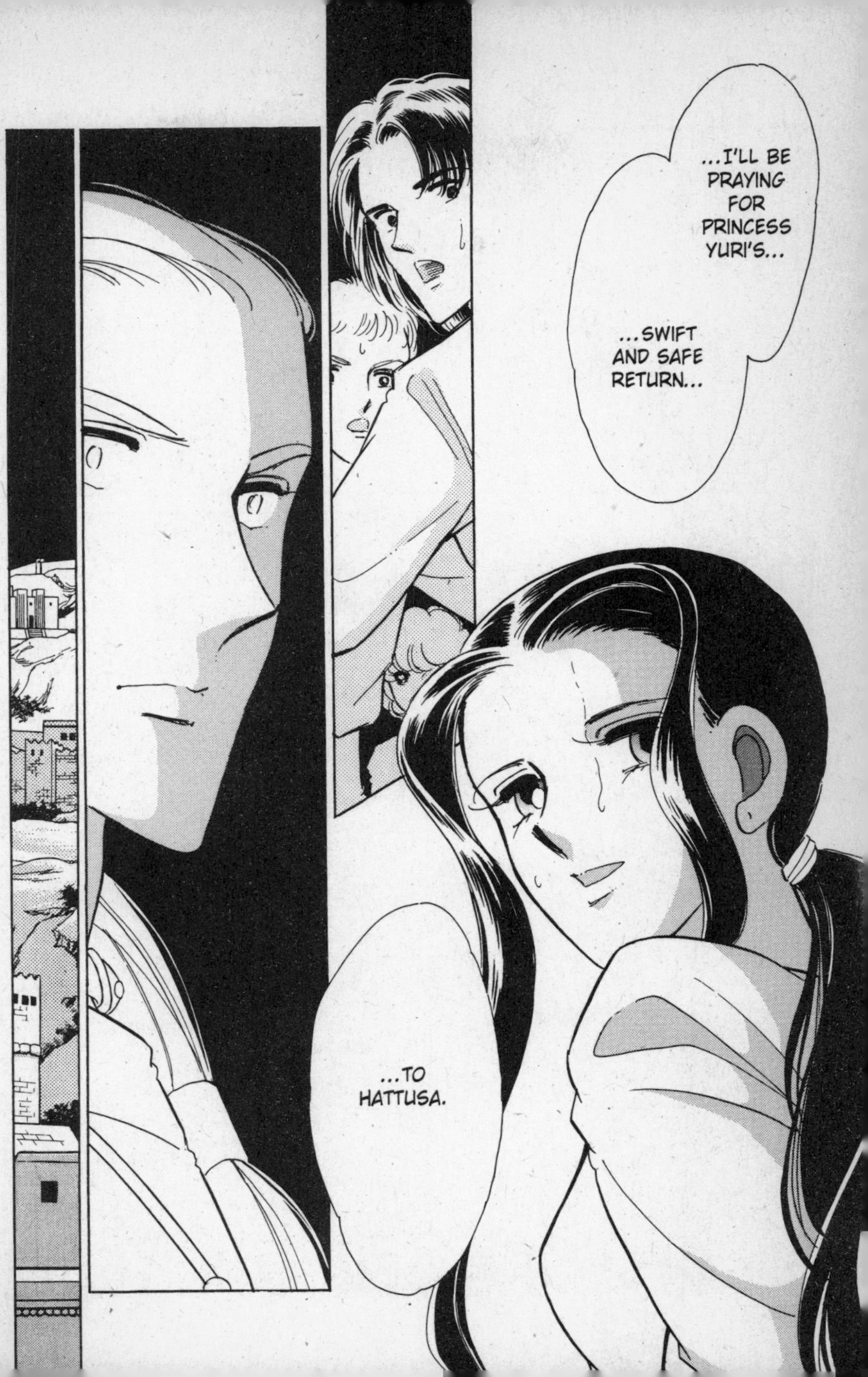
...I'LL BE PRAYING FOR PRINCESS YURI'S...
...SWIFT AND SAFE RETURN...
...TO HATTUSA.

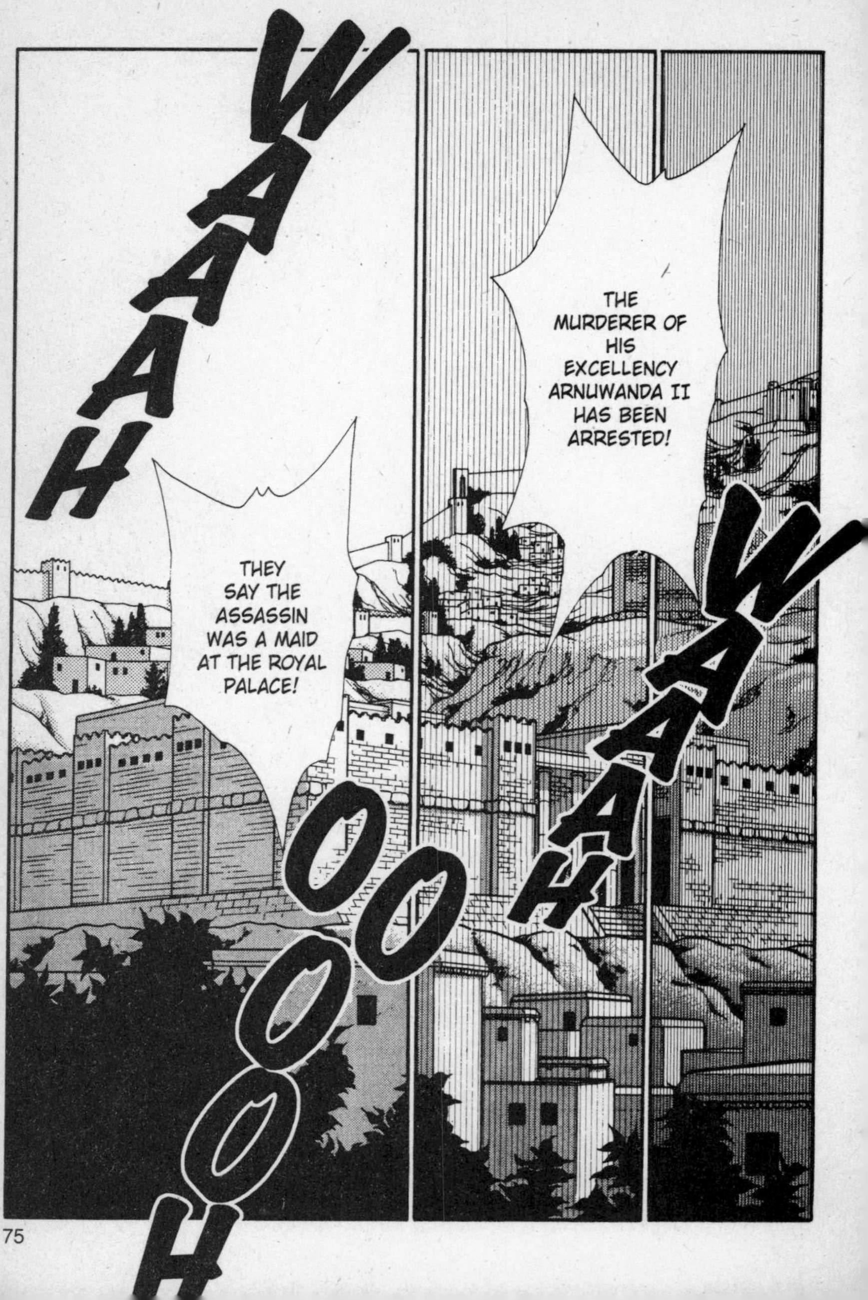
WAAAH
THE MURDERER OF HIS EXCELLENCY ARNUWANDA II HAS BEEN ARRESTED!
OOOOOOH
THEY SAY THE ASSASSIN WAS A MAID AT THE ROYAL PALACE!
WAAAH

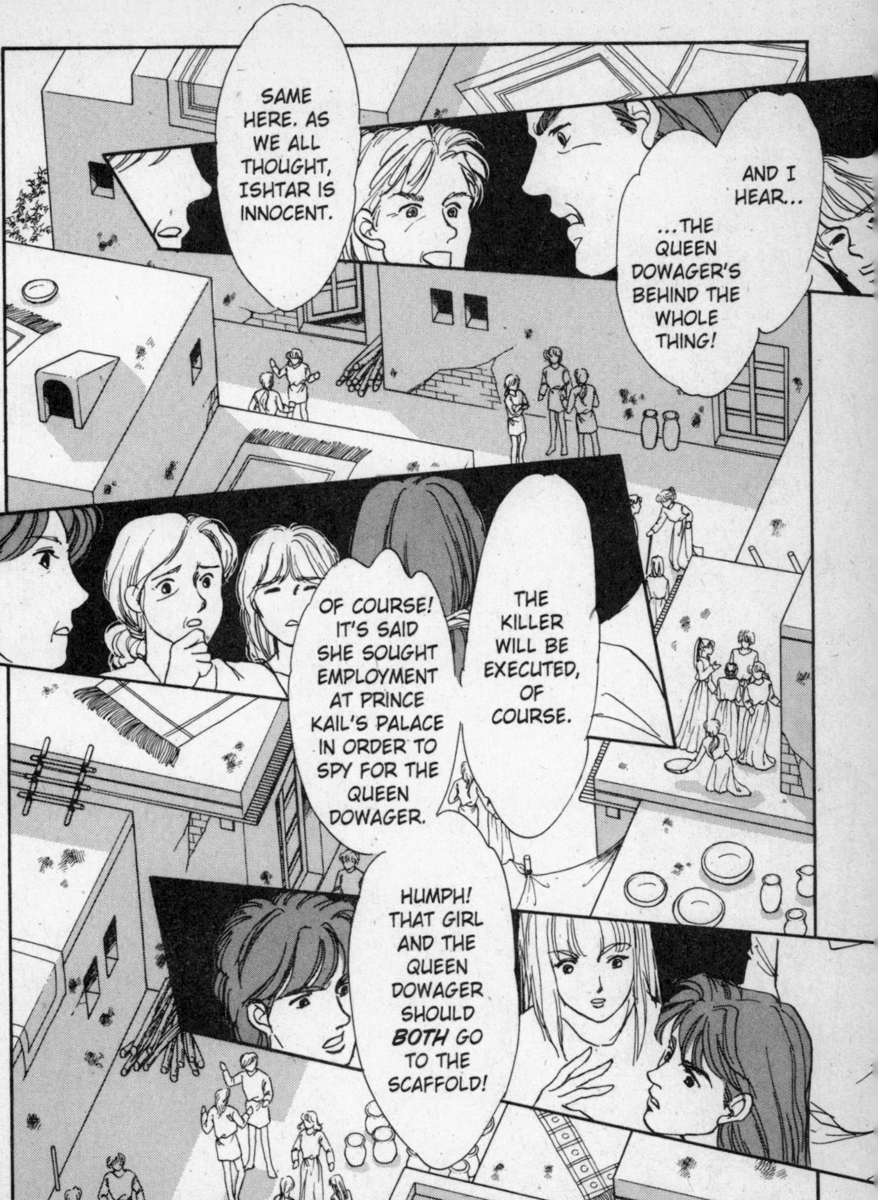
AND I HEAR...
...THE QUEEN DOWAGER'S BEHIND THE WHOLE THING!
SAME HERE. AS WE ALL THOUGHT, ISHTAR IS INNOCENT.
THE KILLER WILL BE EXECUTED, OF COURSE.
OF COURSE! IT'S SAID SHE SOUGHT EMPLOYMENT AT PRINCE KAIL'S PALACE IN ORDER TO SPY FOR THE QUEEN DOWAGER.
HUMPH! THAT GIRL AND THE QUEEN DOWAGER SHOULD ***BOTH*** GO TO THE SCAFFOLD!

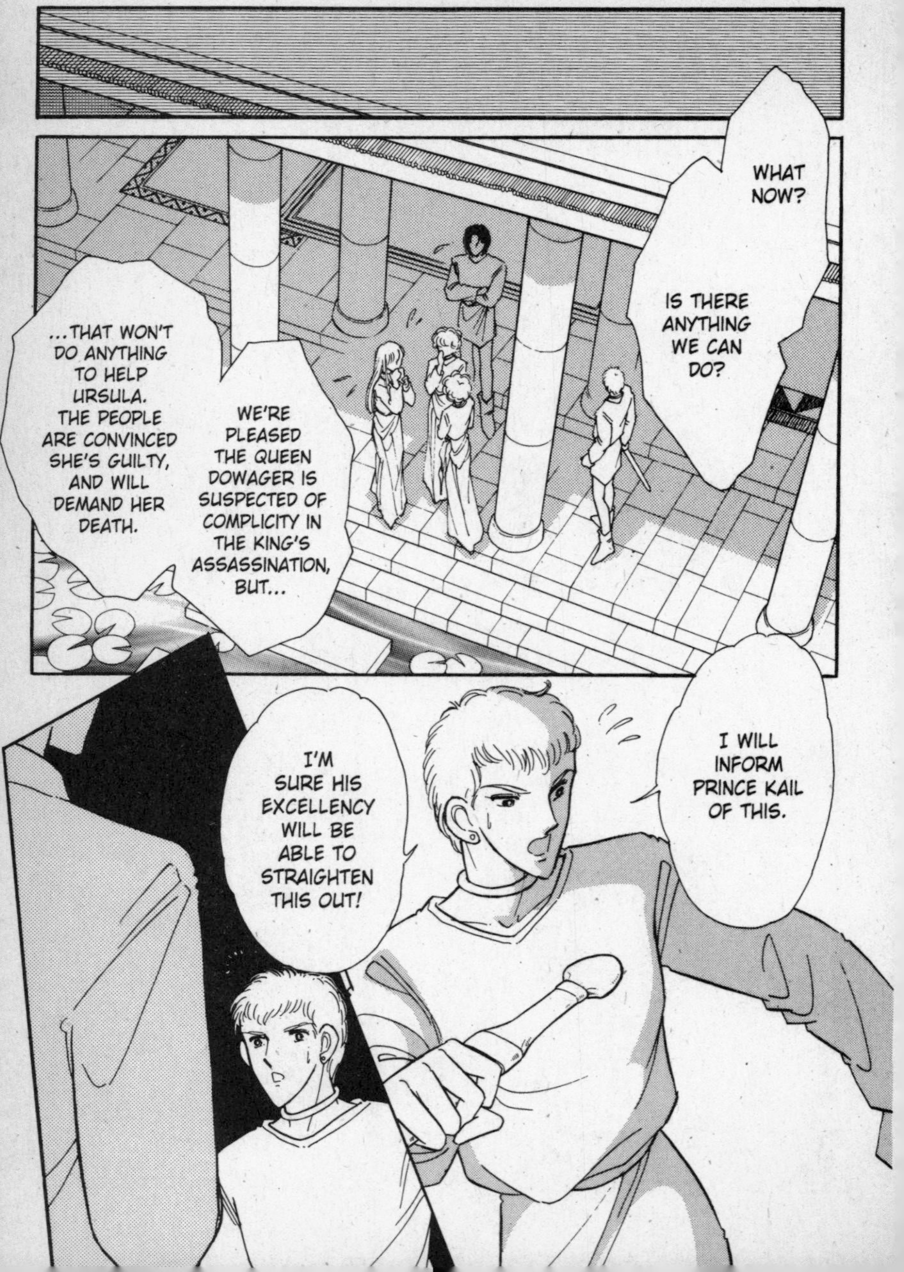
WHAT NOW?
IS THERE ANYTHING WE CAN DO?
WE'RE PLEASED THE QUEEN DOWAGER IS SUSPECTED OF COMPLICITY IN THE KING'S ASSASSINATION, BUT...
...THAT WON'T DO ANYTHING TO HELP URSULA. THE PEOPLE ARE CONVINCED SHE'S GUILTY, AND WILL DEMAND HER DEATH.
I WILL INFORM PRINCE KAIL OF THIS.
I'M SURE HIS EXCELLENCY WILL BE ABLE TO STRAIGHTEN THIS OUT!

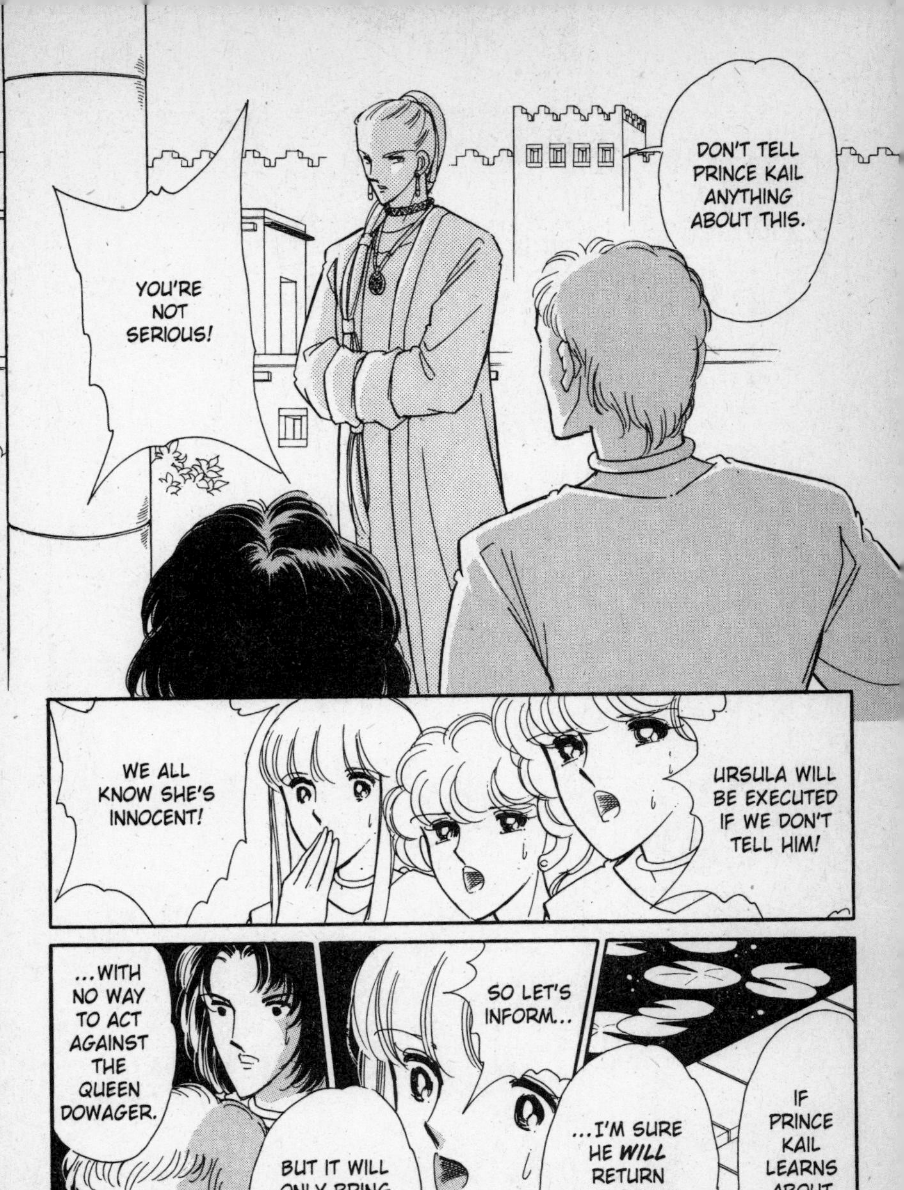
DON'T TELL PRINCE KAIL ANYTHING ABOUT THIS.
YOU'RE NOT SERIOUS!
URSULA WILL BE EXECUTED IF WE DON'T TELL HIM!
WE ALL KNOW SHE'S INNOCENT!
IF PRINCE KAIL LEARNS ABOUT THIS...
...I'M SURE HE ***WILL*** RETURN AND PROVE URSULA'S INNOCENCE.
SO LET'S INFORM...
BUT IT WILL ONLY BRING US BACK TO WHERE WE WERE...
...WITH NO WAY TO ACT AGAINST THE QUEEN DOWAGER.

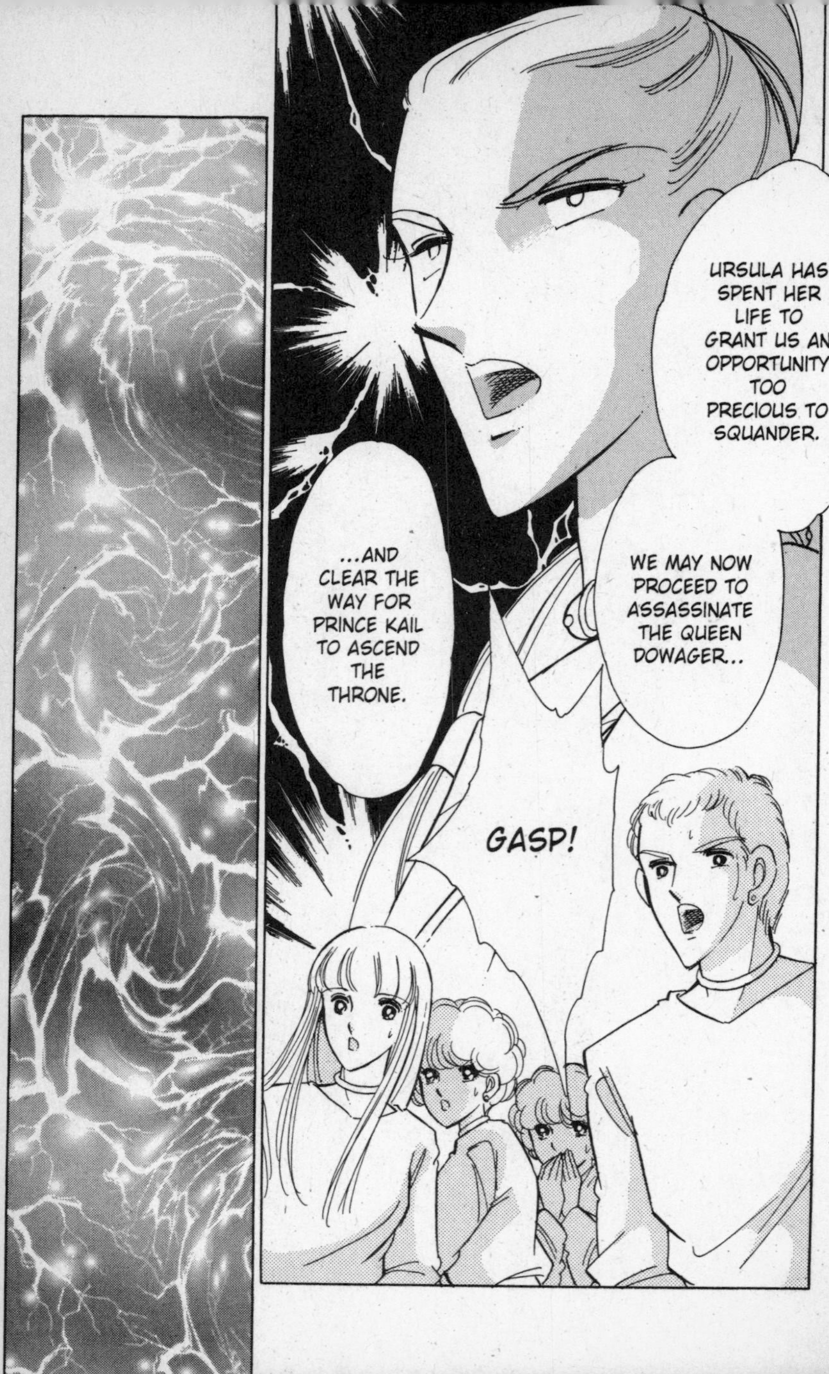
URSULA HAS SPENT HER LIFE TO GRANT US AN OPPORTUNITY TOO PRECIOUS TO SQUANDER.
WE MAY NOW PROCEED TO ASSASSINATE THE QUEEN DOWAGER...
...AND CLEAR THE WAY FOR PRINCE KAIL TO ASCEND THE THRONE.
GASP!

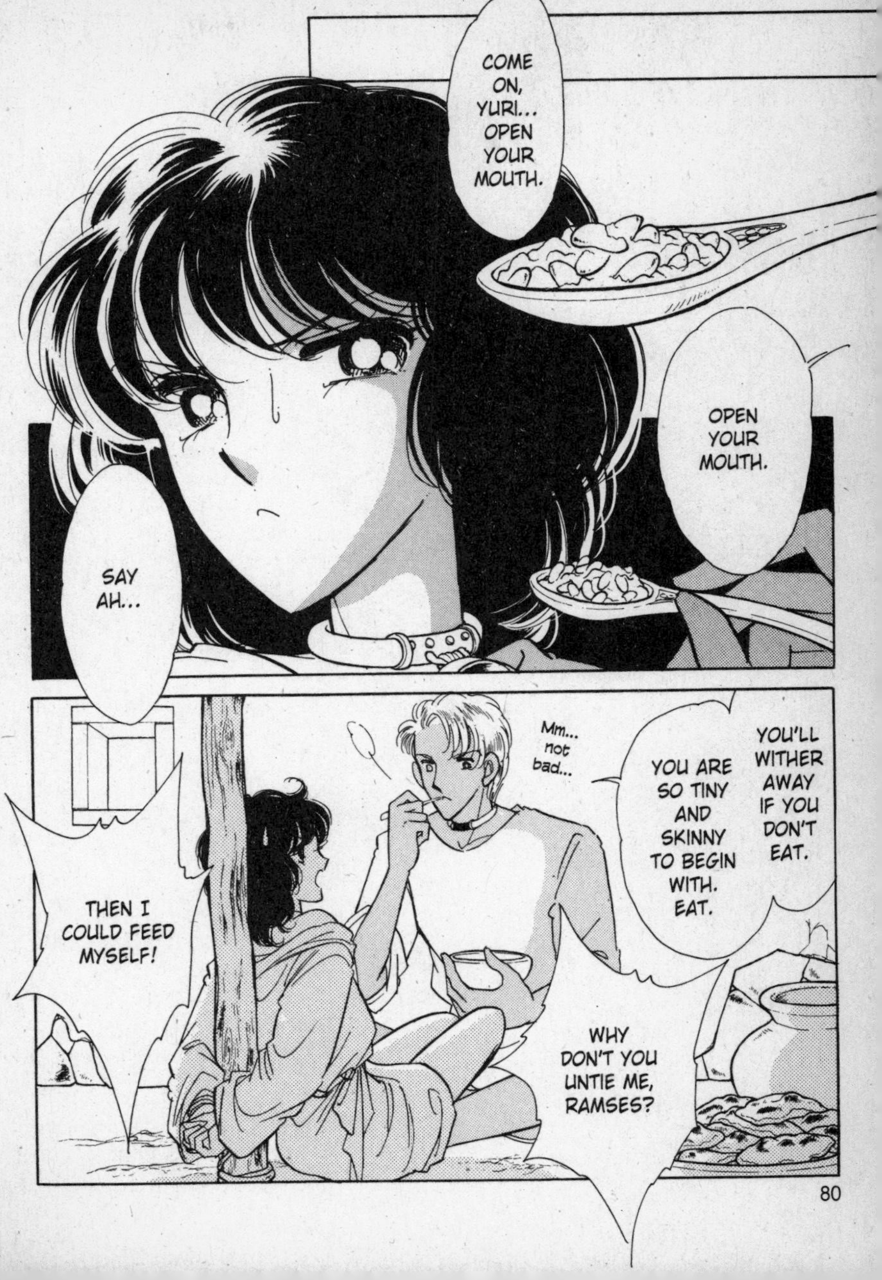
COME ON, YURI... OPEN YOUR MOUTH.
OPEN YOUR MOUTH.
SAY AH...
YOU'LL WITHER AWAY IF YOU DON'T EAT.
YOU ARE SO TINY AND SKINNY TO BEGIN WITH. EAT.
Mm... not bad...
WHY DON'T YOU UNTIE ME, RAMSES?
THEN I COULD FEED MYSELF!

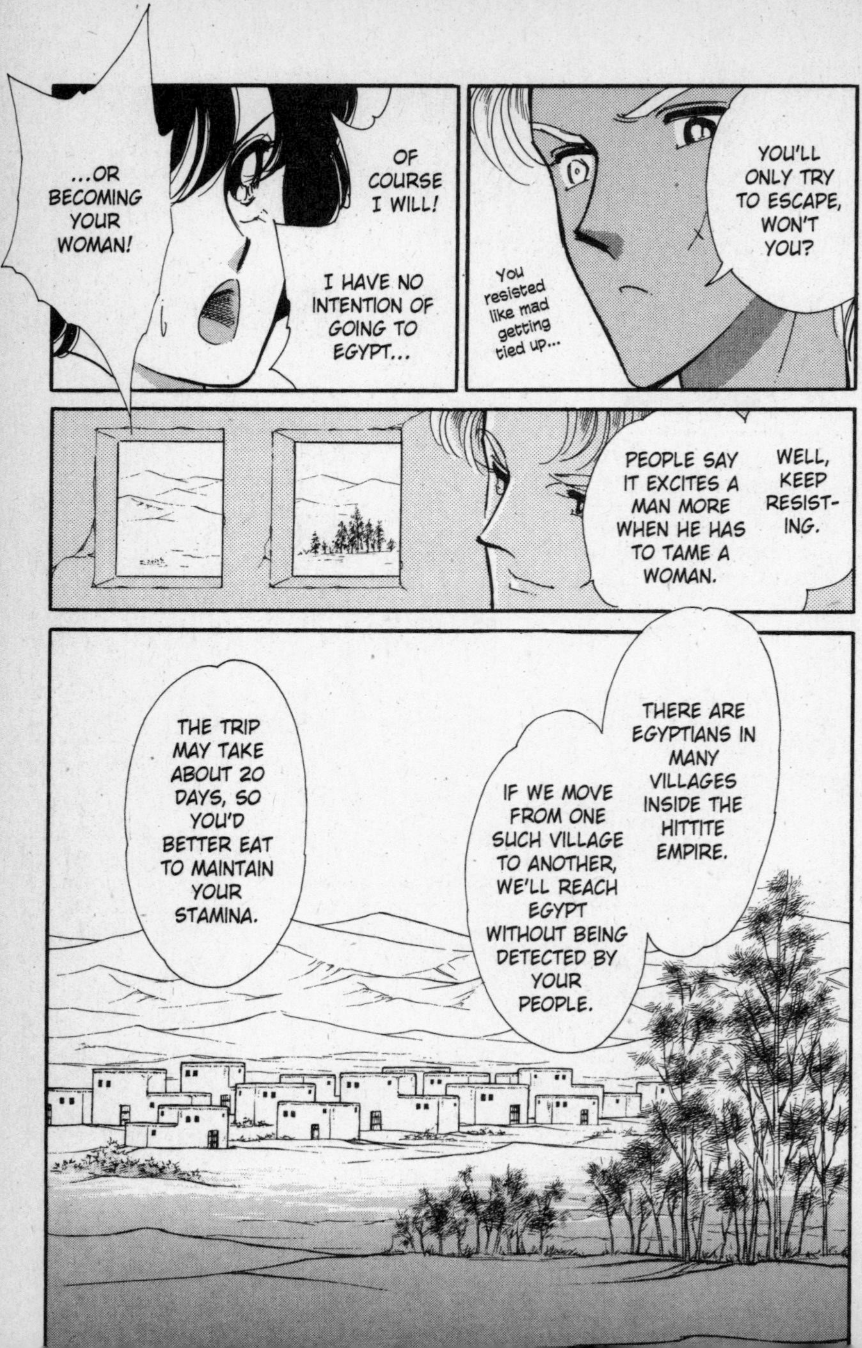
YOU'LL ONLY TRY TO ESCAPE, WON'T YOU?
You resisted like mad getting tied up...
OF COURSE I WILL!
I HAVE NO INTENTION OF GOING TO EGYPT...
...OR BECOMING YOUR WOMAN!
WELL, KEEP RESIST-ING.
PEOPLE SAY IT EXCITES A MAN MORE WHEN HE HAS TO TAME A WOMAN.
THERE ARE EGYPTIANS IN MANY VILLAGES INSIDE THE HITTITE EMPIRE.
IF WE MOVE FROM ONE SUCH VILLAGE TO ANOTHER, WE'LL REACH EGYPT WITHOUT BEING DETECTED BY YOUR PEOPLE.
THE TRIP MAY TAKE ABOUT 20 DAYS, SO YOU'D BETTER EAT TO MAINTAIN YOUR STAMINA.

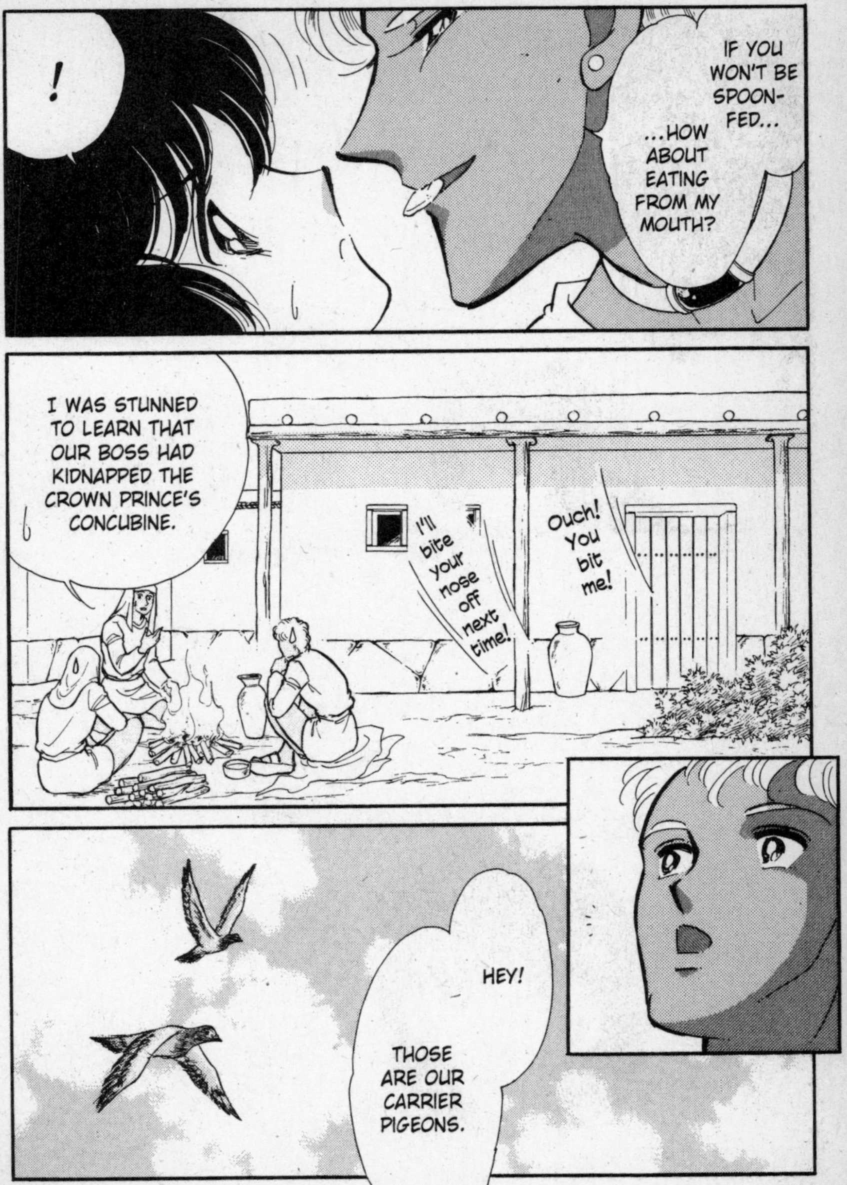
IF YOU WON'T BE SPOON-FED...
...HOW ABOUT EATING FROM MY MOUTH?
!
Ouch! You bit me!
I'll bite your nose off next time!
I WAS STUNNED TO LEARN THAT OUR BOSS HAD KIDNAPPED THE CROWN PRINCE'S CONCUBINE.
HEY!
THOSE ARE OUR CARRIER PIGEONS.

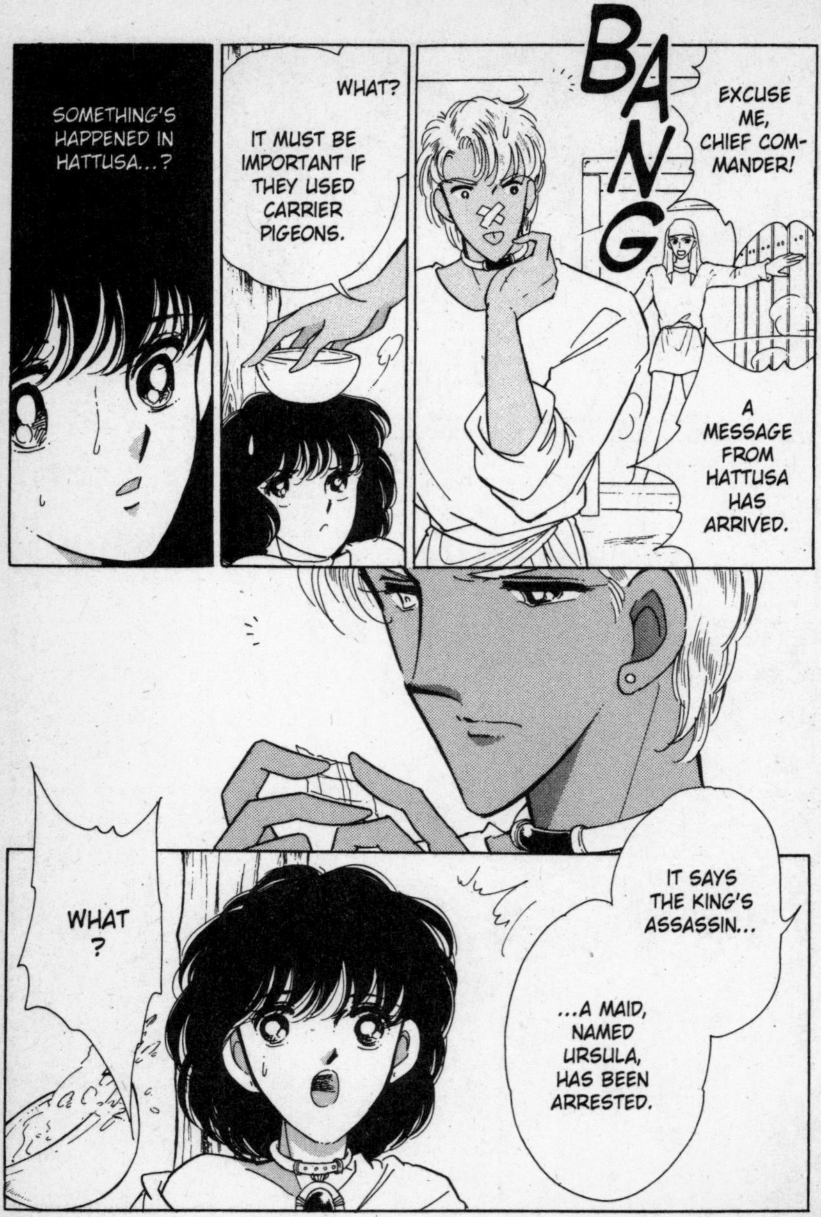
BANG
EXCUSE ME, CHIEF COM-MANDER!
A MESSAGE FROM HATTUSA HAS ARRIVED.
WHAT?
IT MUST BE IMPORTANT IF THEY USED CARRIER PIGEONS.
SOMETHING'S HAPPENED IN HATTUSA...?
IT SAYS THE KING'S ASSASSIN...
...A MAID, NAMED URSULA, HAS BEEN ARRESTED.
WHAT ?

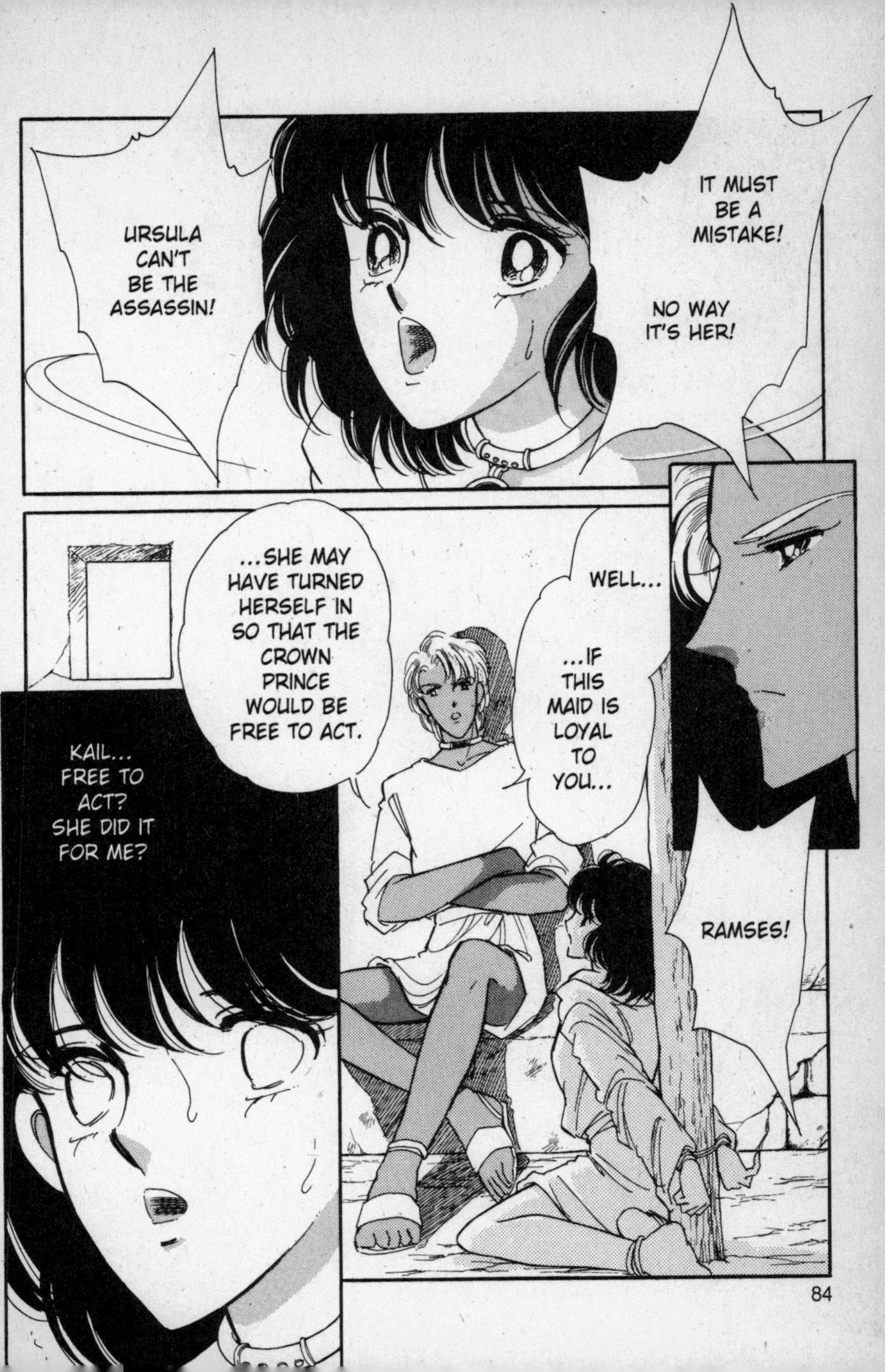
IT MUST BE A MISTAKE!
NO WAY IT'S HER!
URSULA CAN'T BE THE ASSASSIN!
WELL...
...IF THIS MAID IS LOYAL TO YOU...
...SHE MAY HAVE TURNED HERSELF IN SO THAT THE CROWN PRINCE WOULD BE FREE TO ACT.
RAMSES!
KAIL... FREE TO ACT? SHE DID IT FOR ME?

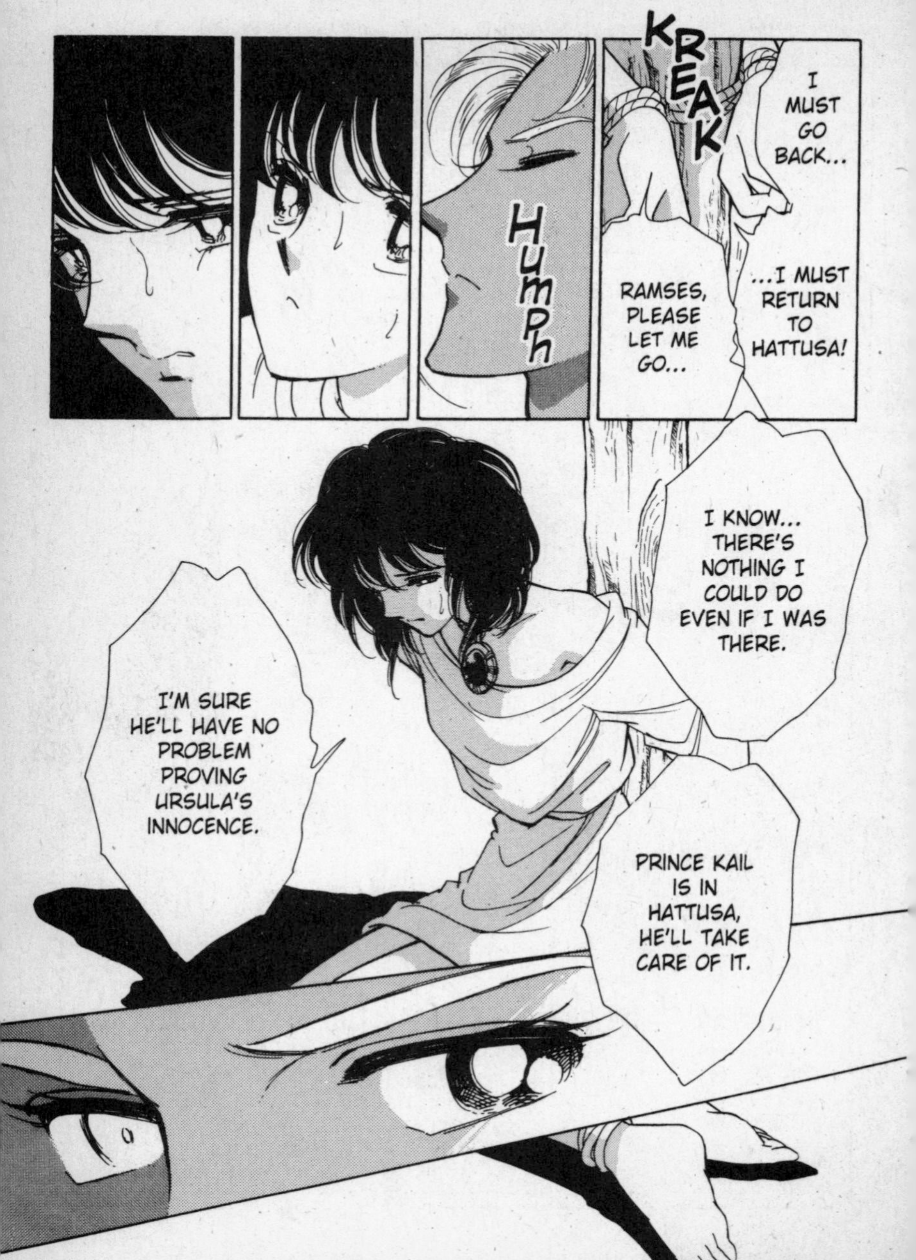
KREAK
I MUST GO BACK...
...I MUST RETURN TO HATTUSA!
RAMSES, PLEASE LET ME GO...
Humph
I KNOW... THERE'S NOTHING I COULD DO EVEN IF I WAS THERE.
PRINCE KAIL IS IN HATTUSA, HE'LL TAKE CARE OF IT.
I'M SURE HE'LL HAVE NO PROBLEM PROVING URSULA'S INNOCENCE.

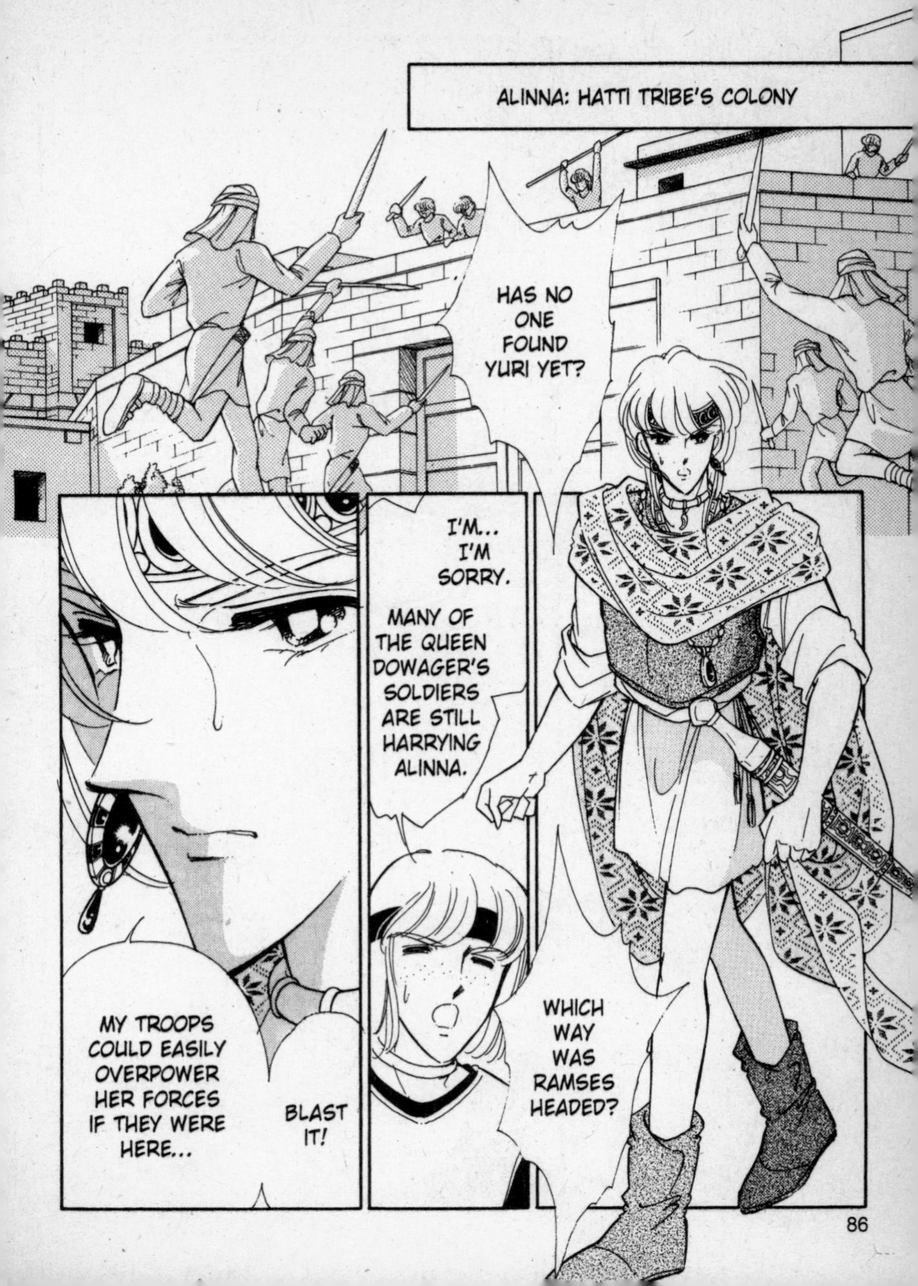
ALINNA: HATTI TRIBE'S COLONY
HAS NO ONE FOUND YURI YET?
WHICH WAY WAS RAMSES HEADED?
I'M... I'M SORRY.
MANY OF THE QUEEN DOWAGER'S SOLDIERS ARE STILL HARRYING ALINNA.
BLAST IT!
MY TROOPS COULD EASILY OVERPOWER HER FORCES IF THEY WERE HERE...

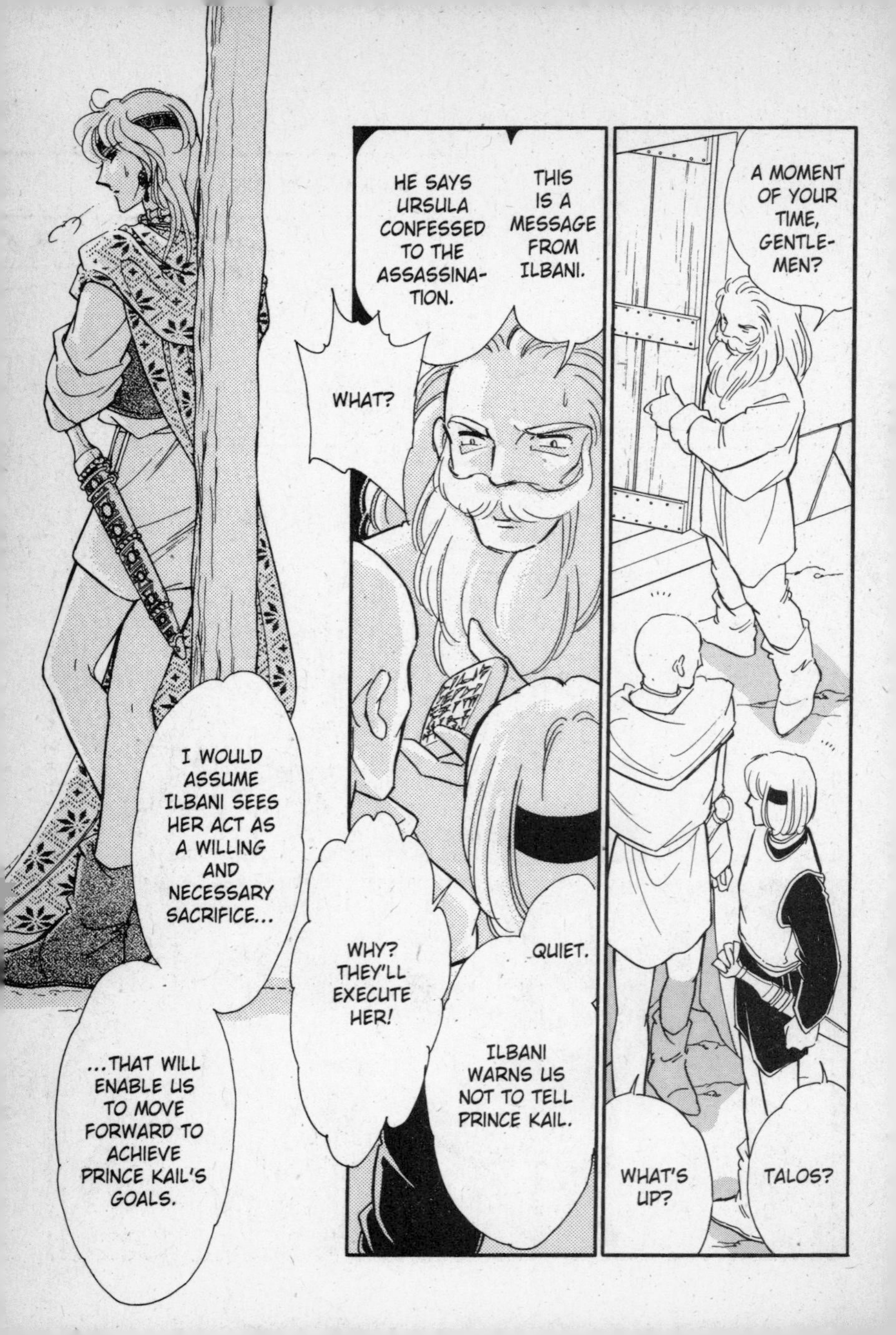
A MOMENT OF YOUR TIME, GENTLE-MEN?
TALOS?
WHAT'S UP?
THIS IS A MESSAGE FROM ILBANI.
HE SAYS URSULA CONFESSED TO THE ASSASSINA-TION.
WHAT?
WHY? THEY'LL EXECUTE HER!
QUIET.
ILBANI WARNS US NOT TO TELL PRINCE KAIL.
I WOULD ASSUME ILBANI SEES HER ACT AS A WILLING AND NECESSARY SACRIFICE...
...THAT WILL ENABLE US TO MOVE FORWARD TO ACHIEVE PRINCE KAIL'S GOALS.

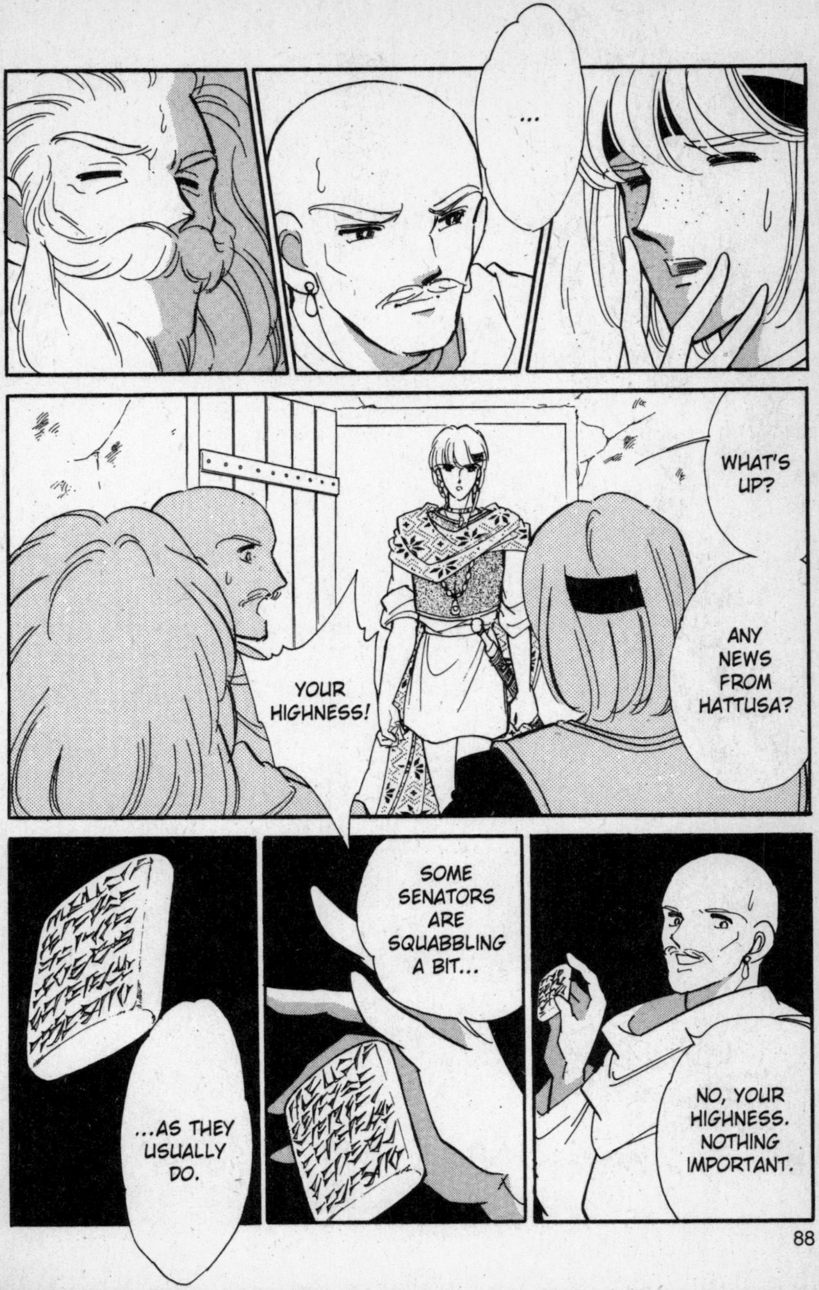
...
WHAT'S UP?
ANY NEWS FROM HATTUSA?
YOUR HIGHNESS!
NO, YOUR HIGHNESS. NOTHING IMPORTANT.
SOME SENATORS ARE SQUABBLING A BIT...
...AS THEY USUALLY DO.

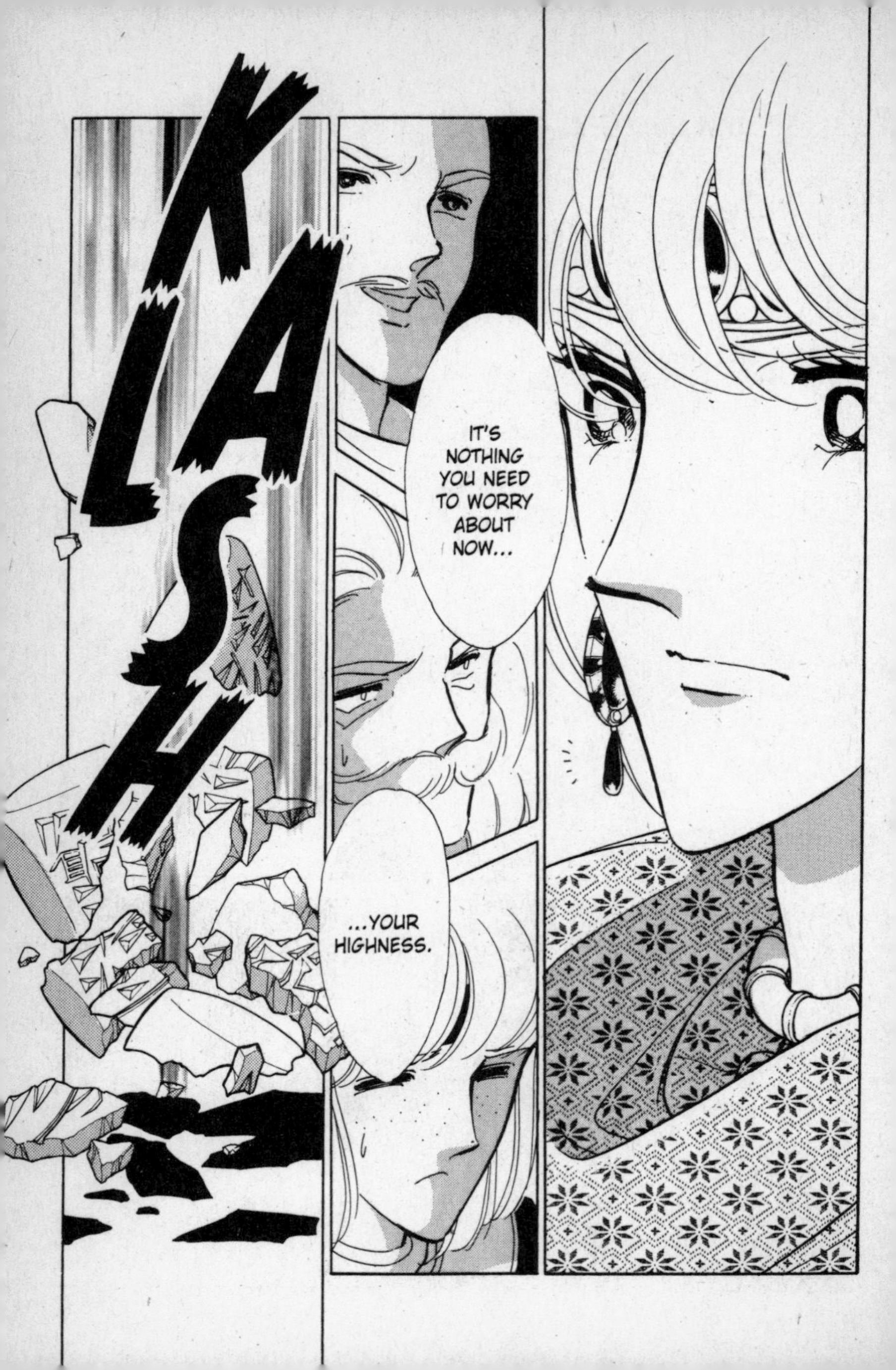
IT'S NOTHING YOU NEED TO WORRY ABOUT NOW...
...YOUR HIGHNESS.
KLASH

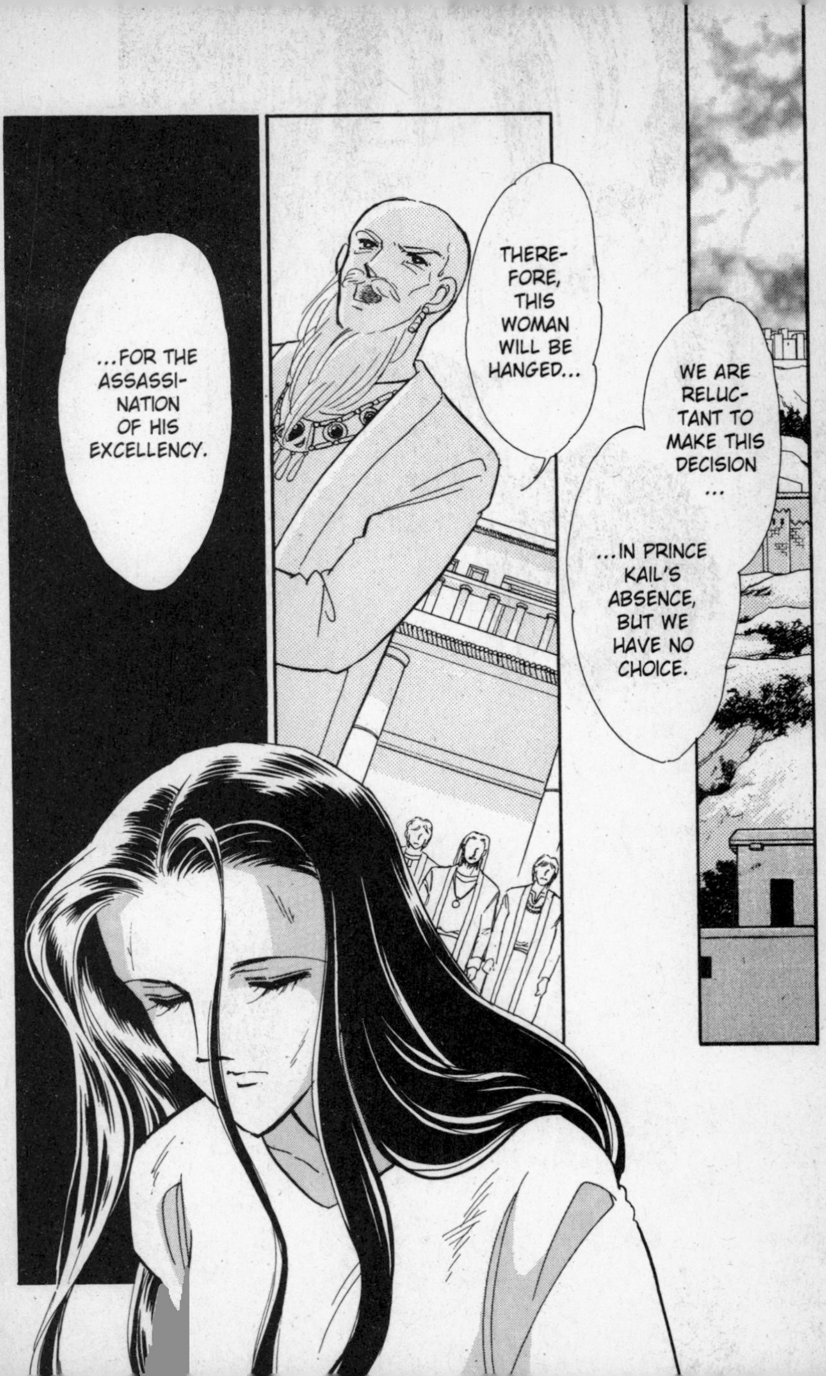
WE ARE RELUCTANT TO MAKE THIS DECISION...
...IN PRINCE KAIL'S ABSENCE, BUT WE HAVE NO CHOICE.
THEREFORE, THIS WOMAN WILL BE HANGED...
...FOR THE ASSASSINATION OF HIS EXCELLENCY.

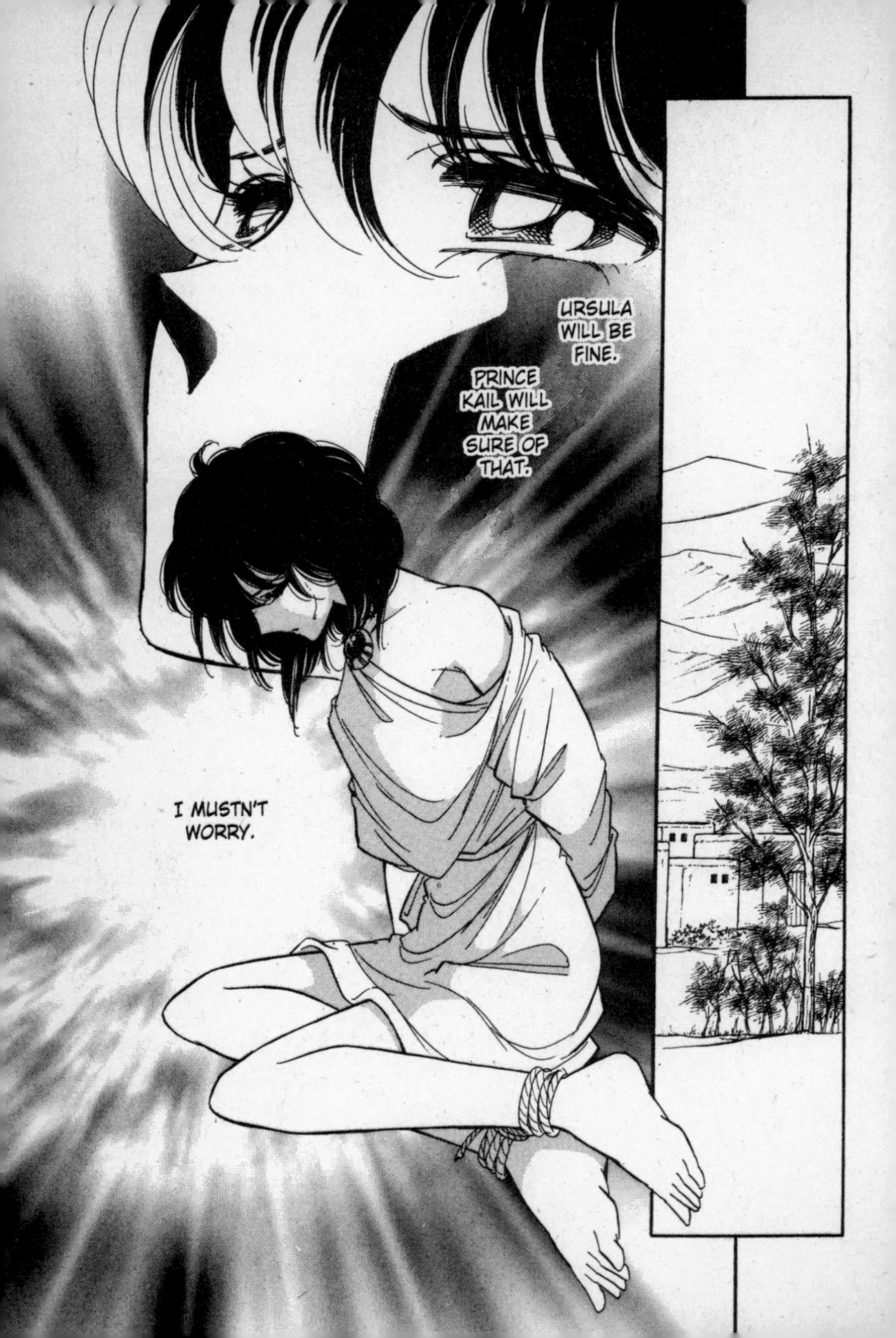
URSULA WILL BE FINE.
PRINCE KAIL WILL MAKE SURE OF THAT.
I MUSTN'T WORRY.

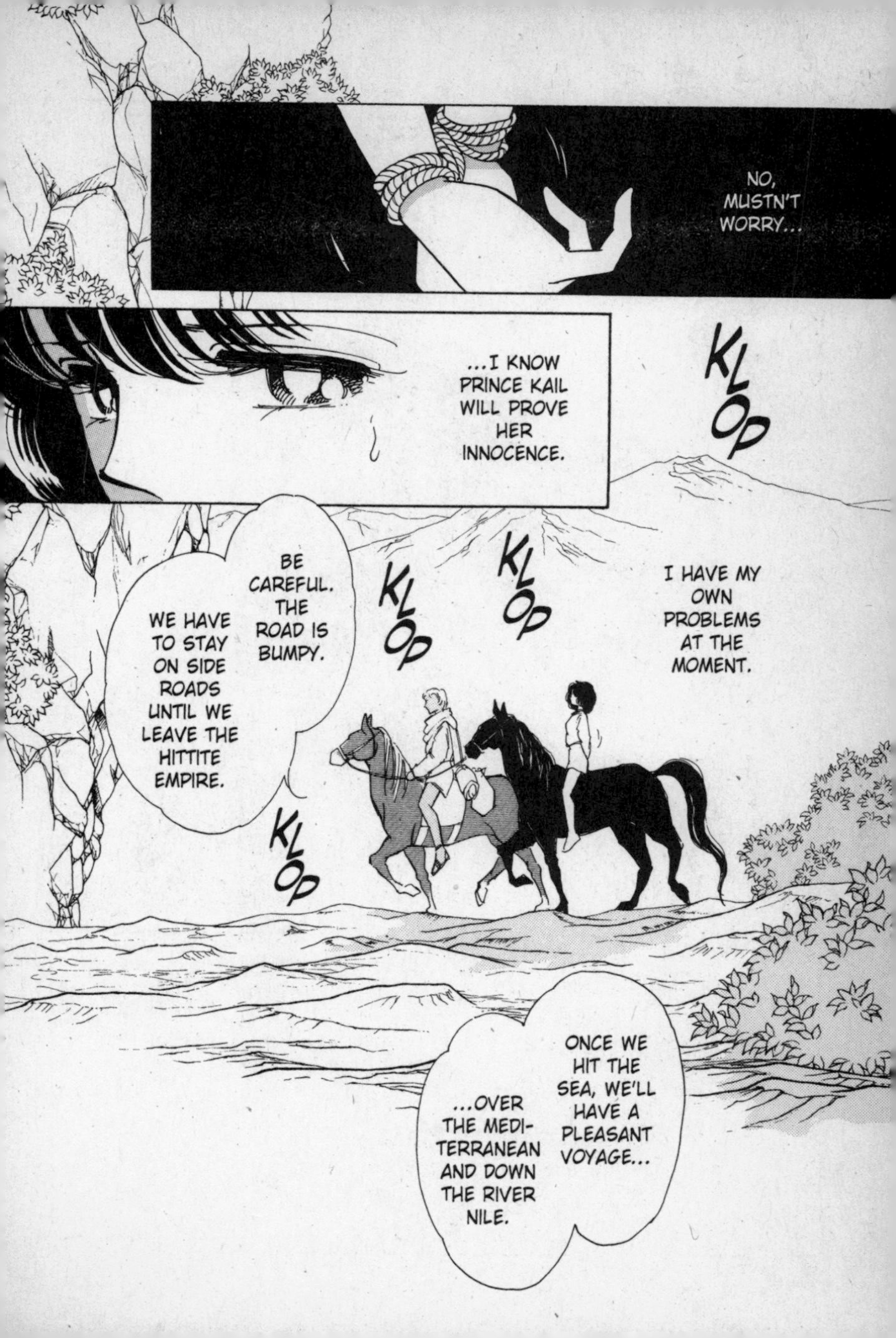
NO, MUSTN'T WORRY...
KLOP
...I KNOW PRINCE KAIL WILL PROVE HER INNOCENCE.
I HAVE MY OWN PROBLEMS AT THE MOMENT.
KLOP
KLOP
BE CAREFUL. THE ROAD IS BUMPY.
WE HAVE TO STAY ON SIDE ROADS UNTIL WE LEAVE THE HITTITE EMPIRE.
KLOP
ONCE WE HIT THE SEA, WE'LL HAVE A PLEASANT VOYAGE...
...OVER THE MEDITERRANEAN AND DOWN THE RIVER NILE.

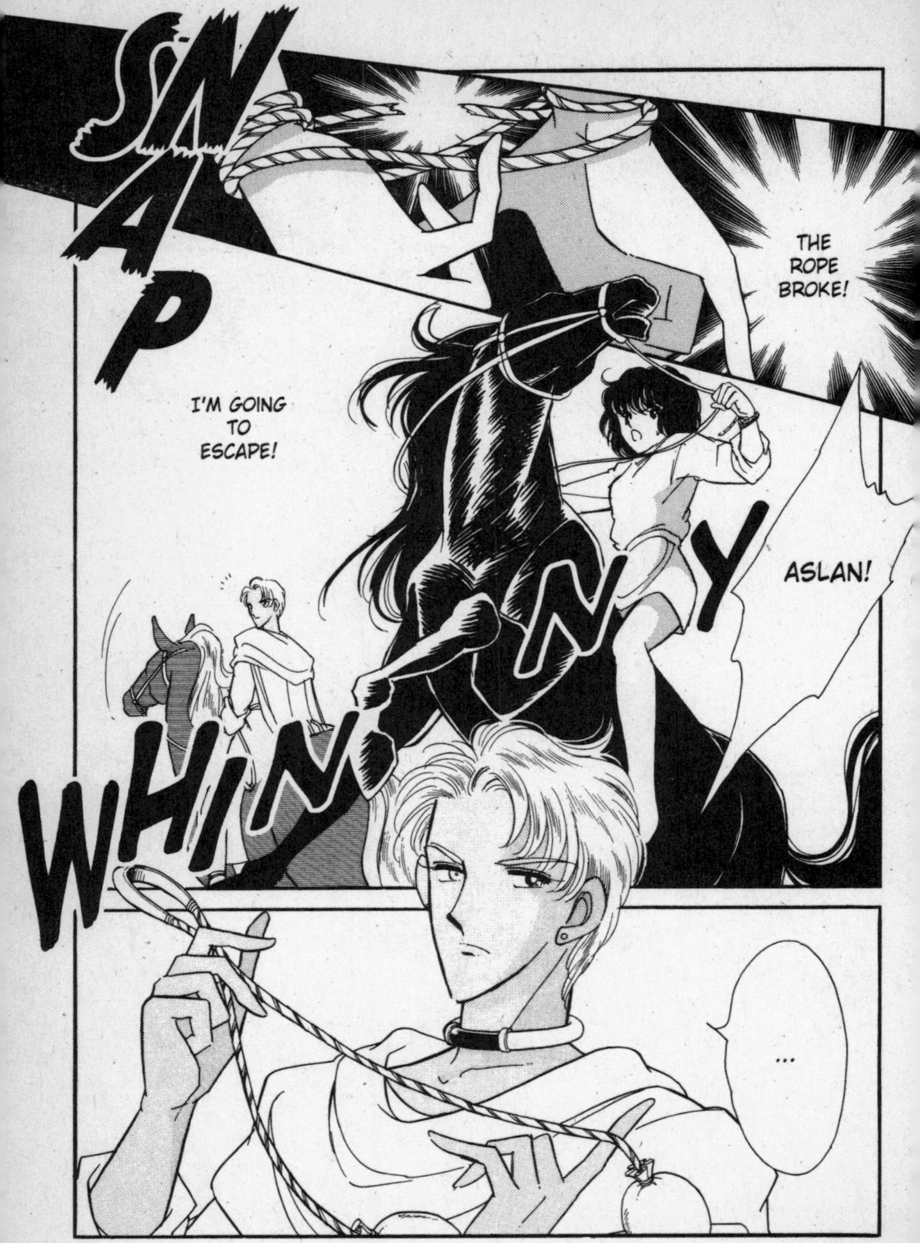
SNAP
THE ROPE BROKE!
I'M GOING TO ESCAPE!
ASLAN!
WHINNY
...

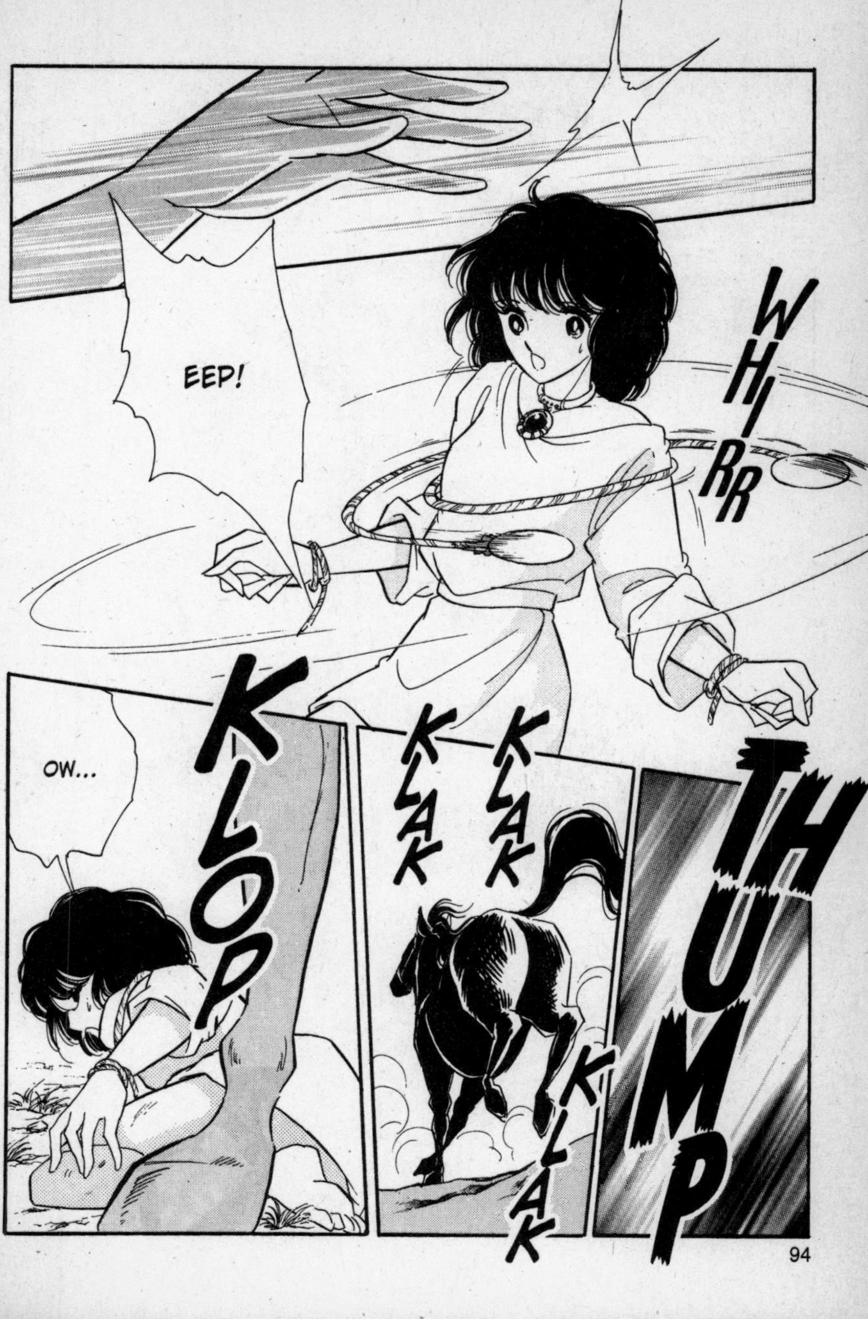
WHIRRR
EEP!
THUMP
KLAK KLAK
KLAK KLAK
KLOP!
OW...

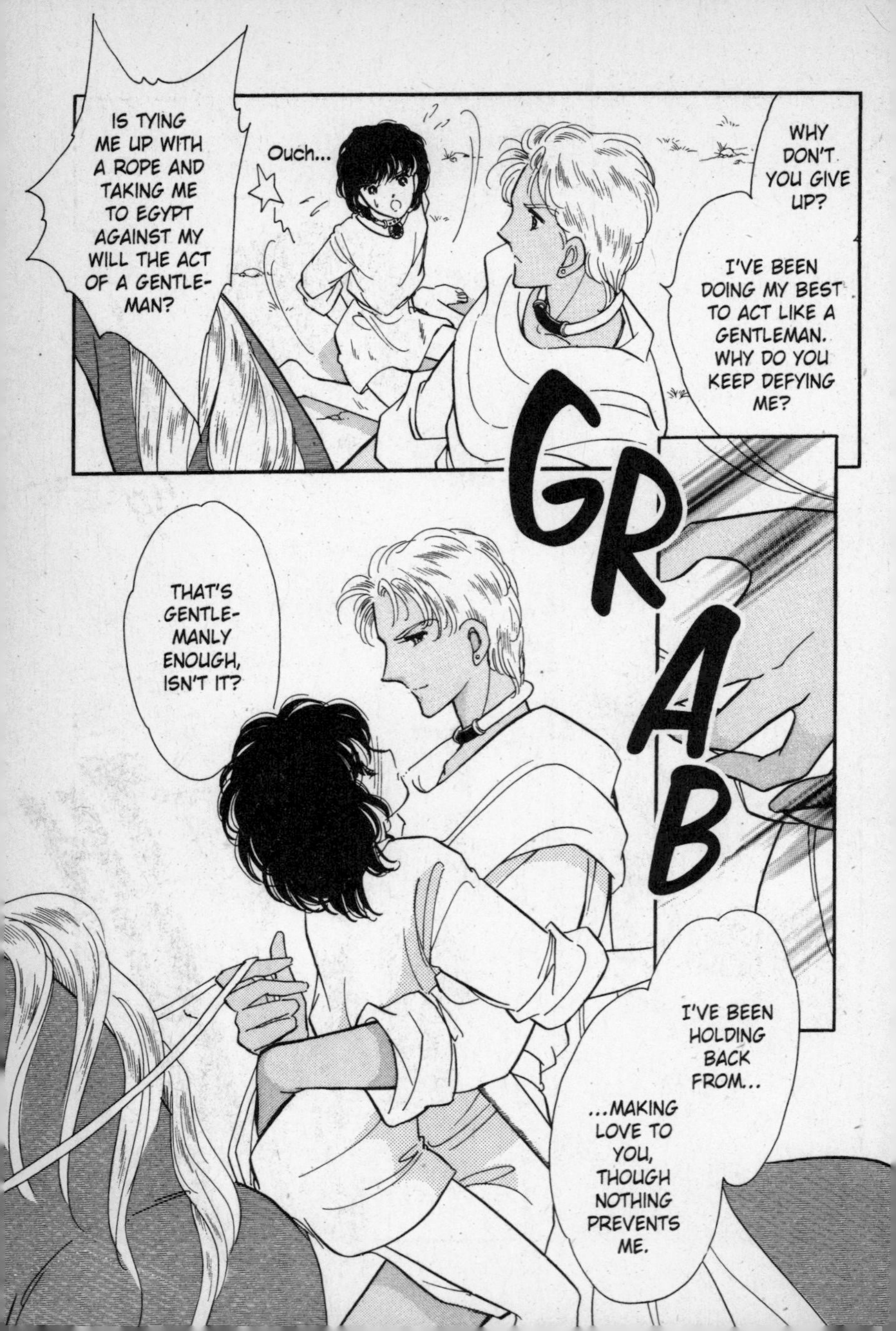
IS TYING ME UP WITH A ROPE AND TAKING ME TO EGYPT AGAINST MY WILL THE ACT OF A GENTLE-MAN?
WHY DON'T YOU GIVE UP?
I'VE BEEN DOING MY BEST TO ACT LIKE A GENTLEMAN. WHY DO YOU KEEP DEFYING ME?
Ouch...
GRAB
THAT'S GENTLE-MANLY ENOUGH, ISN'T IT?
I'VE BEEN HOLDING BACK FROM...
...MAKING LOVE TO YOU, THOUGH NOTHING PREVENTS ME.

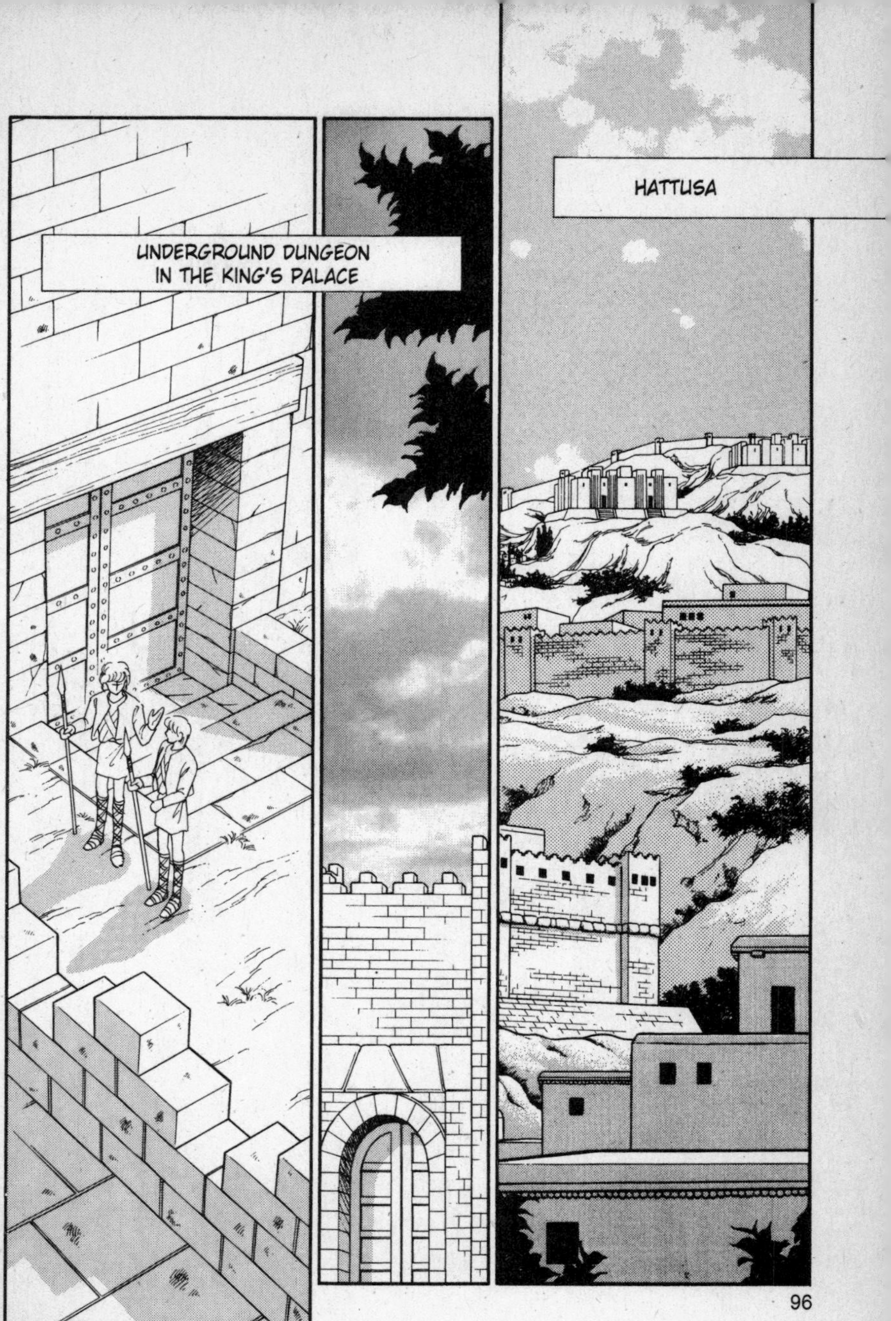
HATTUSA
UNDERGROUND DUNGEON
IN THE KING'S PALACE

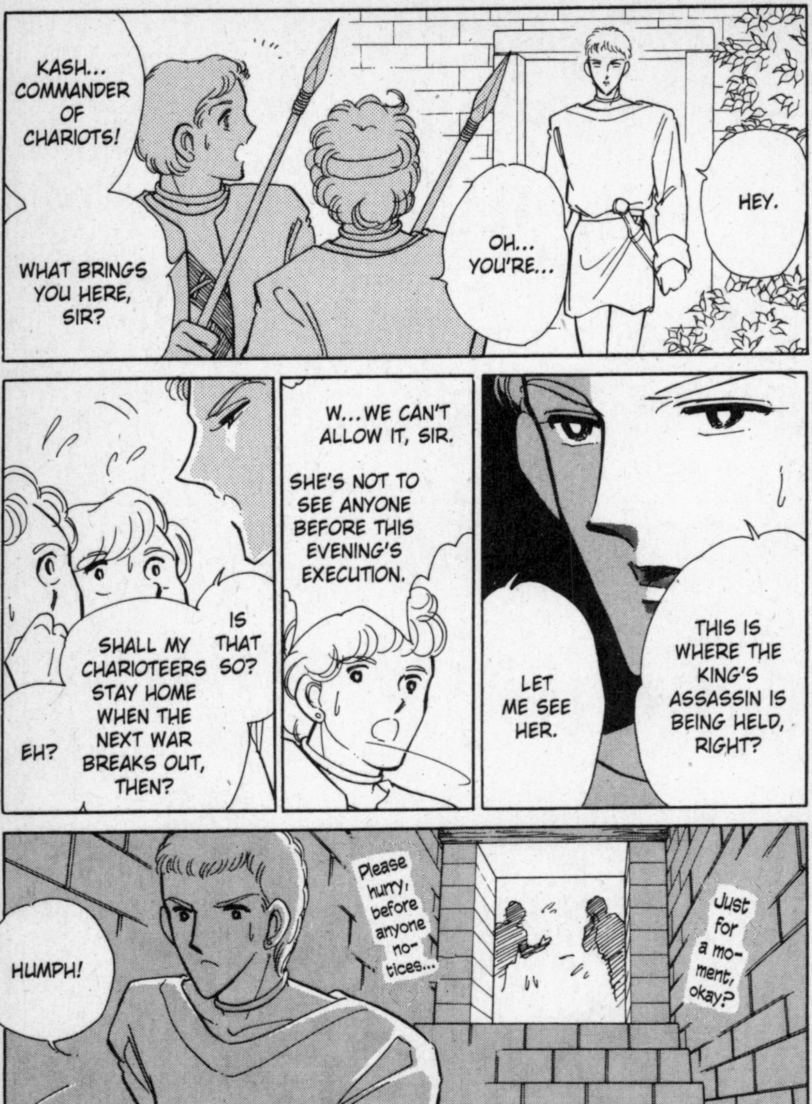
HEY.
OH... YOU'RE...
KASH... COMMANDER OF CHARIOTS!
WHAT BRINGS YOU HERE, SIR?
THIS IS WHERE THE KING'S ASSASSIN IS BEING HELD, RIGHT?
LET ME SEE HER.
W...WE CAN'T ALLOW IT, SIR.
SHE'S NOT TO SEE ANYONE BEFORE THIS EVENING'S EXECUTION.
IS THAT SO?
SHALL MY CHARIOTEERS STAY HOME WHEN THE NEXT WAR BREAKS OUT, THEN?
EH?
Just for a moment, okay?
Please hurry, before anyone notices...
HUMPH!

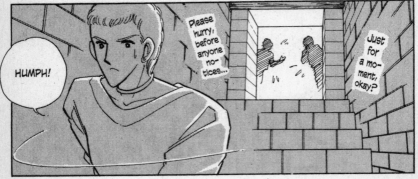

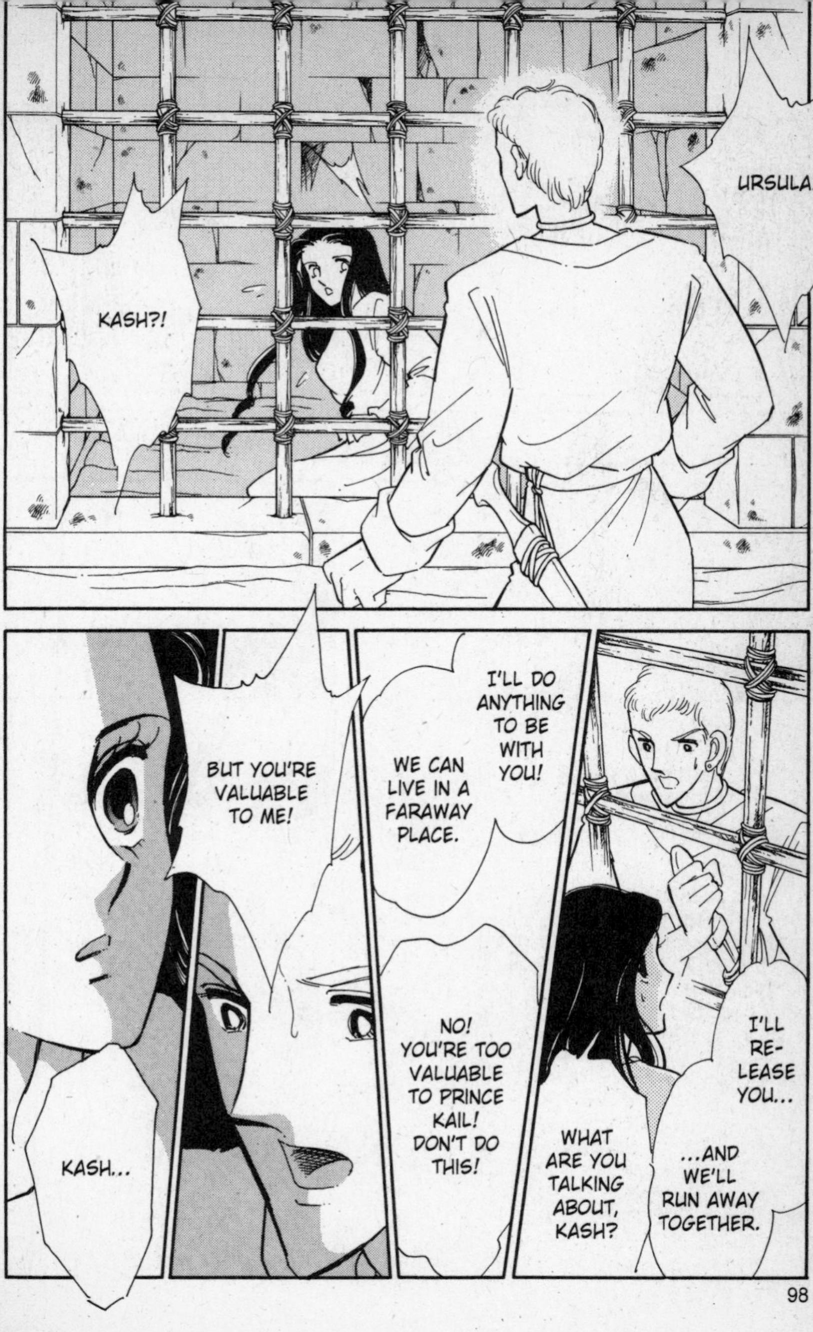

URSULA!
KASH?!
I'LL RE-LEASE YOU...
...AND WE'LL RUN AWAY TOGETHER.
WHAT ARE YOU TALKING ABOUT, KASH?
I'LL DO ANYTHING TO BE WITH YOU!
WE CAN LIVE IN A FARAWAY PLACE.
NO! YOU'RE TOO VALUABLE TO PRINCE KAIL! DON'T DO THIS!
BUT YOU'RE VALUABLE TO ME!
KASH...

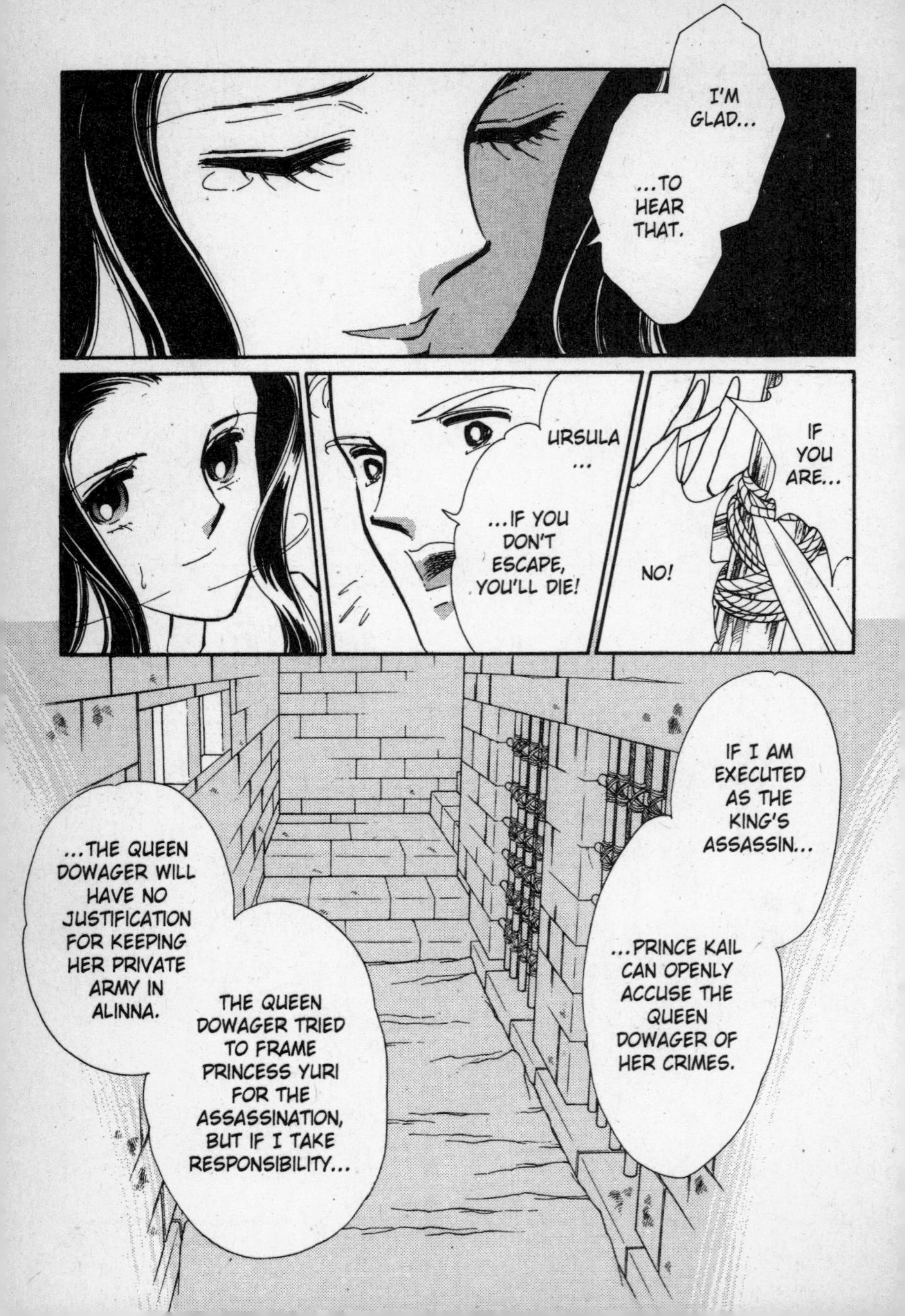
I'M GLAD...
...TO HEAR THAT.
IF YOU ARE...
NO!
URSULA...
...IF YOU DON'T ESCAPE, YOU'LL DIE!
IF I AM EXECUTED AS THE KING'S ASSASSIN...
...PRINCE KAIL CAN OPENLY ACCUSE THE QUEEN DOWAGER OF HER CRIMES.
THE QUEEN DOWAGER TRIED TO FRAME PRINCESS YURI FOR THE ASSASSINATION, BUT IF I TAKE RESPONSIBILITY...
...THE QUEEN DOWAGER WILL HAVE NO JUSTIFICATION FOR KEEPING HER PRIVATE ARMY IN ALINNA.

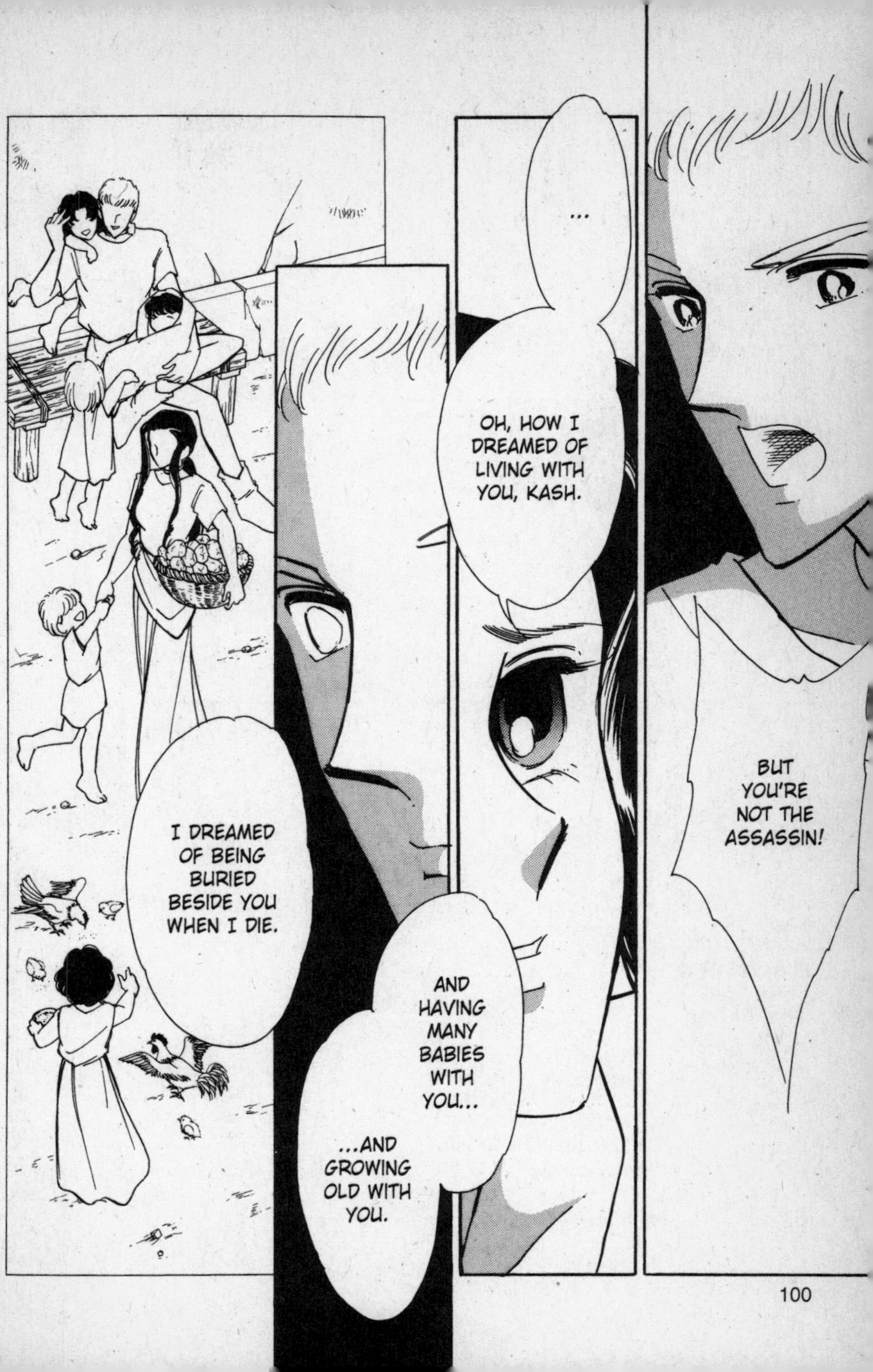

BUT YOU'RE NOT THE ASSASSIN!
...
OH, HOW I DREAMED OF LIVING WITH YOU, KASH.
AND HAVING MANY BABIES WITH YOU...
...AND GROWING OLD WITH YOU.
I DREAMED OF BEING BURIED BESIDE YOU WHEN I DIE.

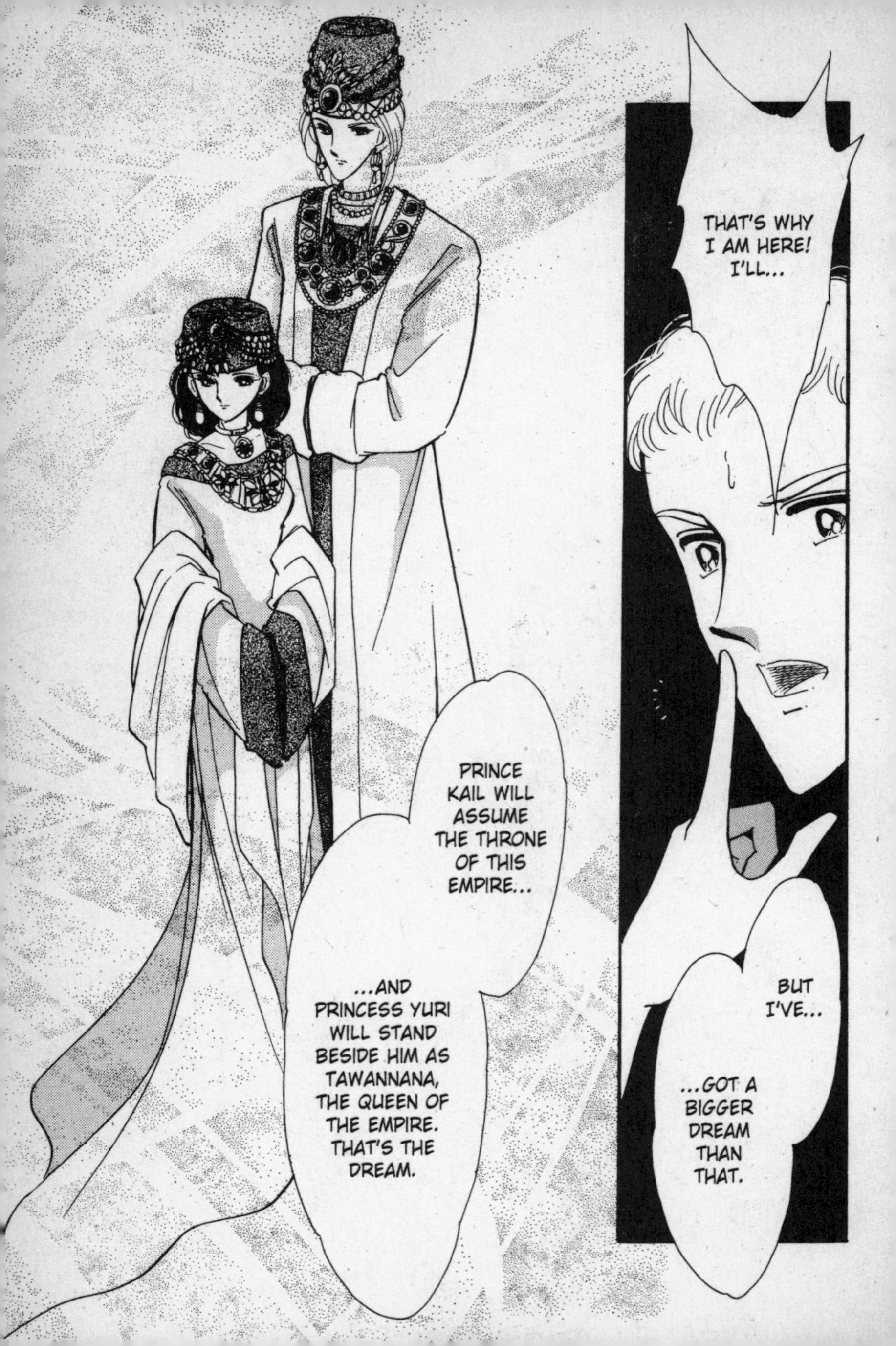
THAT'S WHY I AM HERE! I'LL...
BUT I'VE...
...GOT A BIGGER DREAM THAN THAT.
PRINCE KAIL WILL ASSUME THE THRONE OF THIS EMPIRE...
...AND PRINCESS YURI WILL STAND BESIDE HIM AS TAWANNANA, THE QUEEN OF THE EMPIRE. THAT'S THE DREAM.

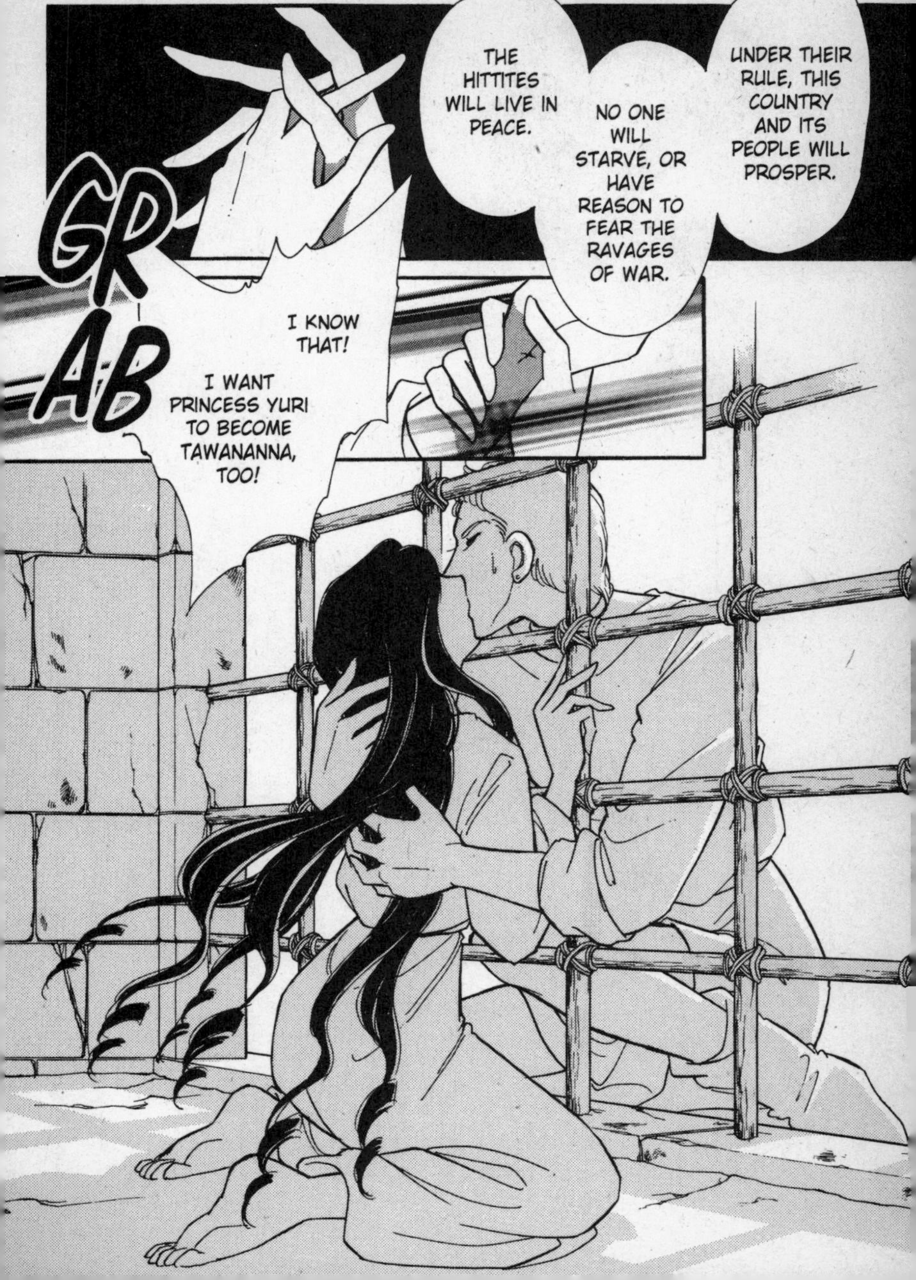
UNDER THEIR RULE, THIS COUNTRY AND ITS PEOPLE WILL PROSPER.
NO ONE WILL STARVE, OR HAVE REASON TO FEAR THE RAVAGES OF WAR.
THE HITTITES WILL LIVE IN PEACE.
GR-AB
I KNOW THAT!
I WANT PRINCESS YURI TO BECOME TAWANANNA, TOO!

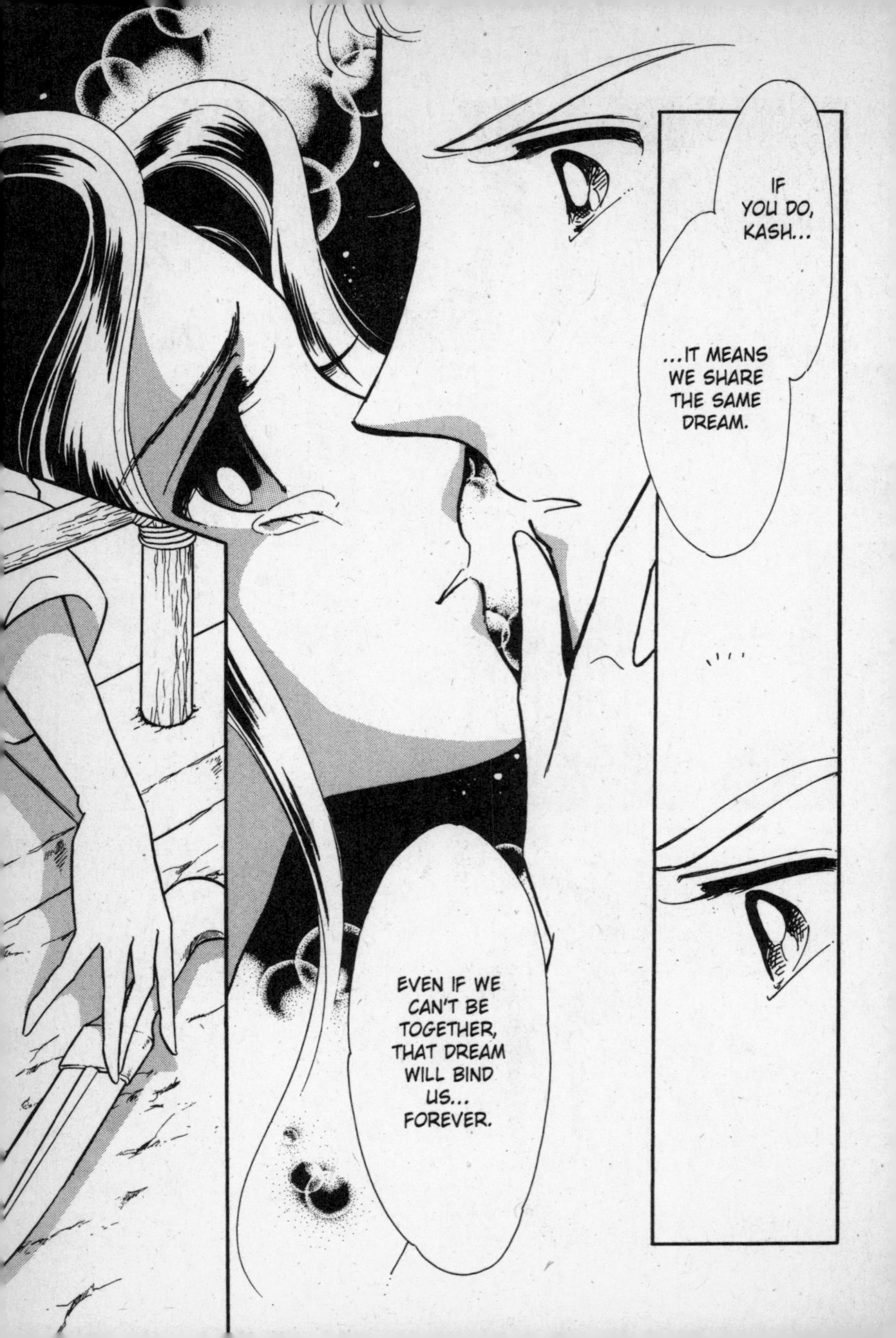
IF YOU DO, KASH...
...IT MEANS WE SHARE THE SAME DREAM.
EVEN IF WE CAN'T BE TOGETHER, THAT DREAM WILL BIND US... FOREVER.

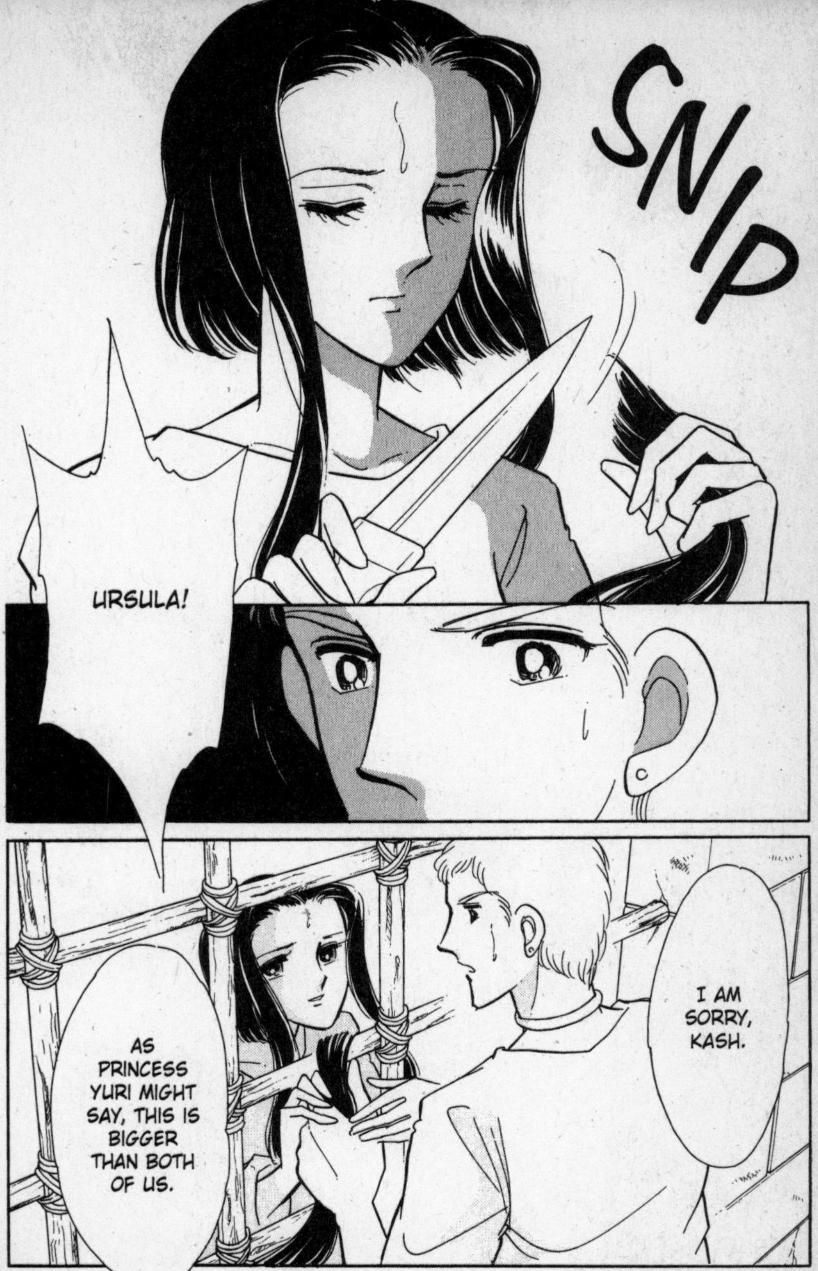
SNIP
URSULA!
I AM SORRY, KASH.
AS PRINCESS YURI MIGHT SAY, THIS IS BIGGER THAN BOTH OF US.

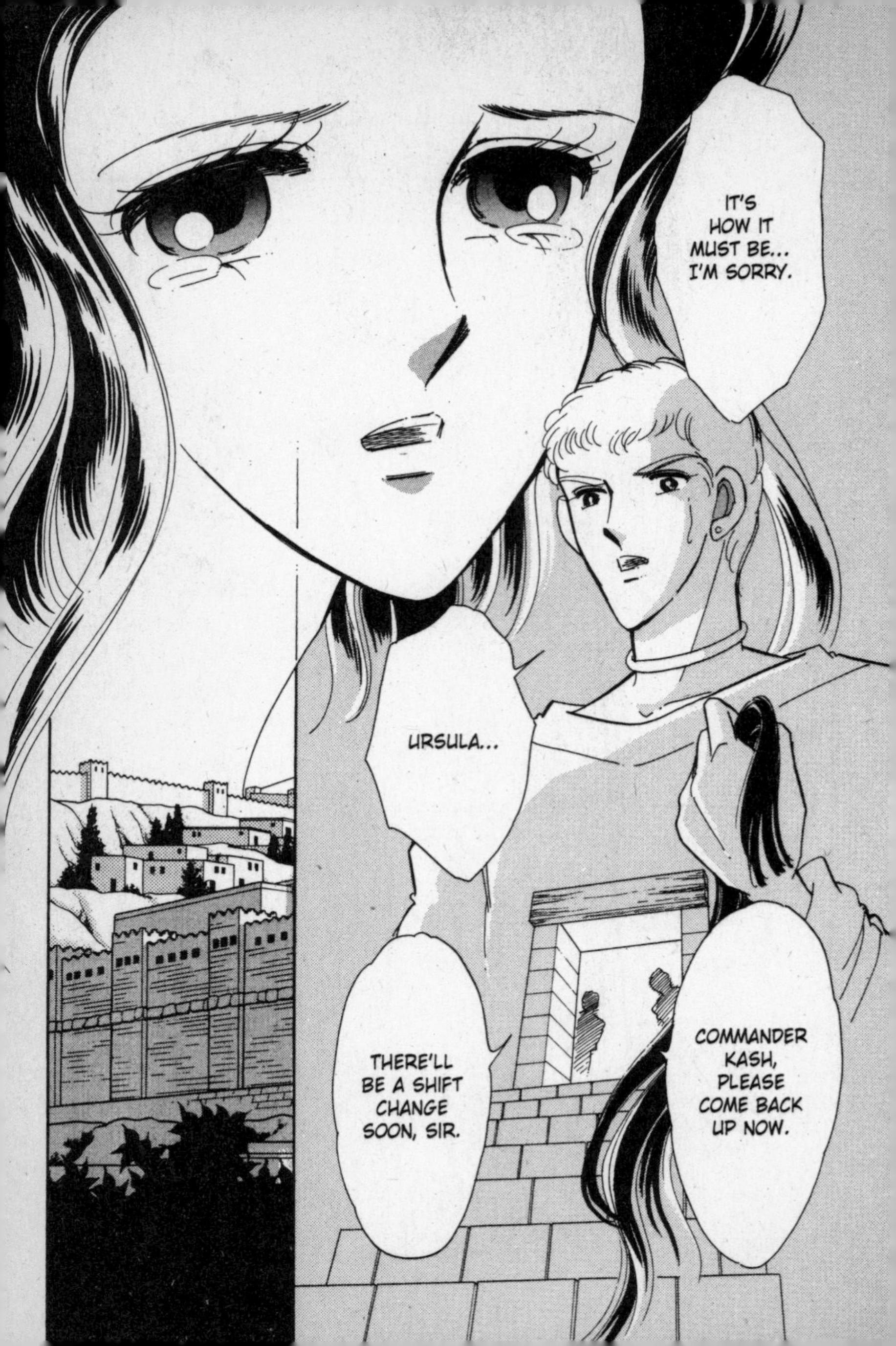
IT'S HOW IT MUST BE... I'M SORRY.
URSULA...
COMMANDER KASH, PLEASE COME BACK UP NOW.
THERE'LL BE A SHIFT CHANGE SOON, SIR.

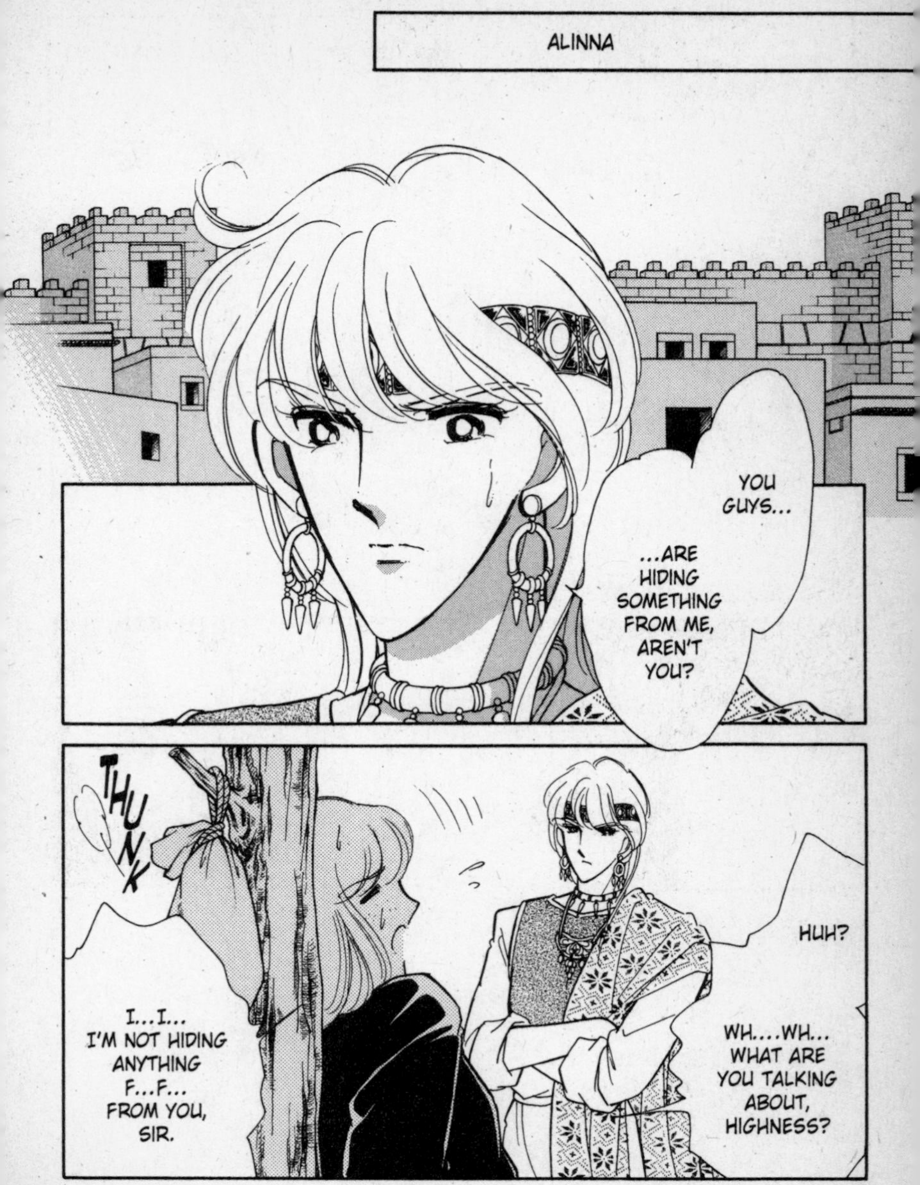
ALINNA
YOU GUYS...
...ARE HIDING SOMETHING FROM ME, AREN'T YOU?
HUH?
THUNK
WH....WH... WHAT ARE YOU TALKING ABOUT, HIGHNESS?
I...I... I'M NOT HIDING ANYTHING F...F... FROM YOU, SIR.

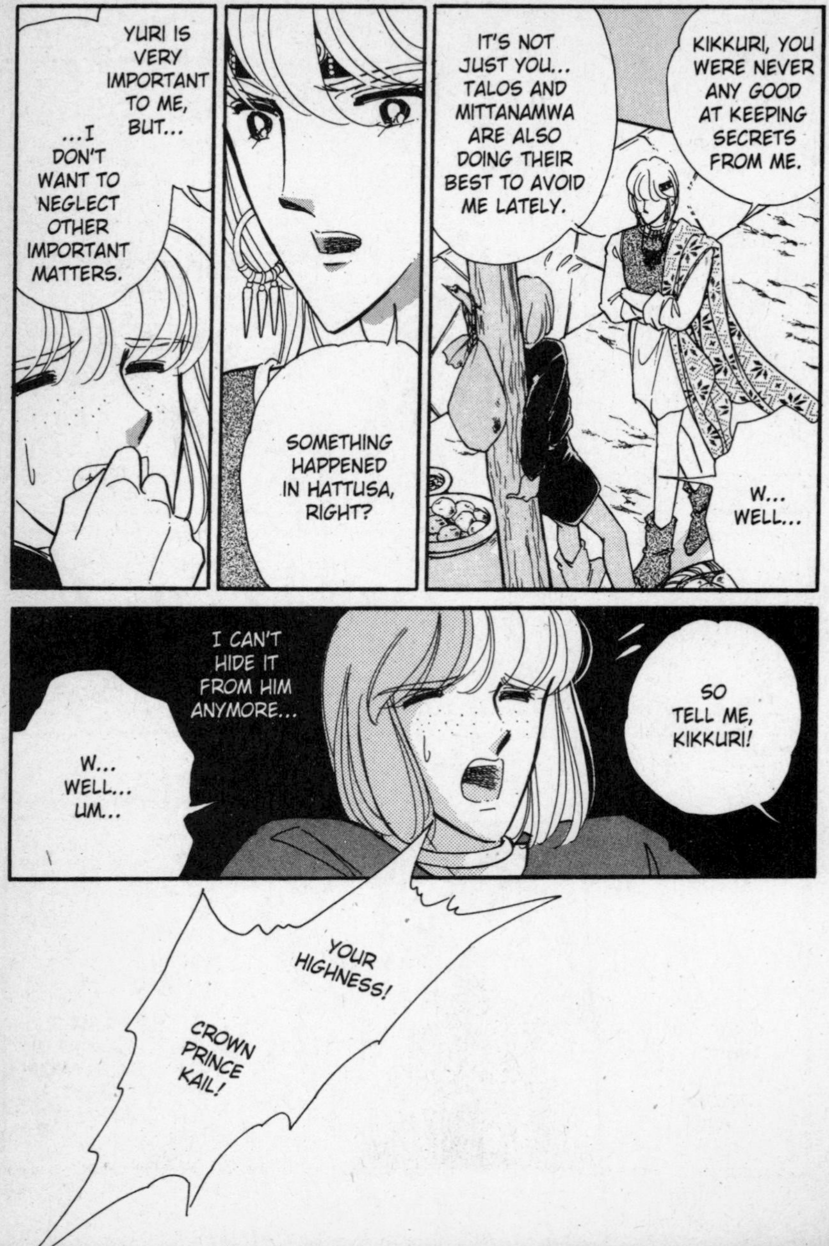
KIKKURI, YOU WERE NEVER ANY GOOD AT KEEPING SECRETS FROM ME.
IT'S NOT JUST YOU... TALOS AND MITTANAMWA ARE ALSO DOING THEIR BEST TO AVOID ME LATELY.
W... WELL...
SOMETHING HAPPENED IN HATTUSA, RIGHT?
YURI IS VERY IMPORTANT TO ME, BUT...
...I DON'T WANT TO NEGLECT OTHER IMPORTANT MATTERS.
SO TELL ME, KIKKURI!
I CAN'T HIDE IT FROM HIM ANYMORE...
W... WELL... UM...
YOUR HIGHNESS!
CROWN PRINCE KAIL!

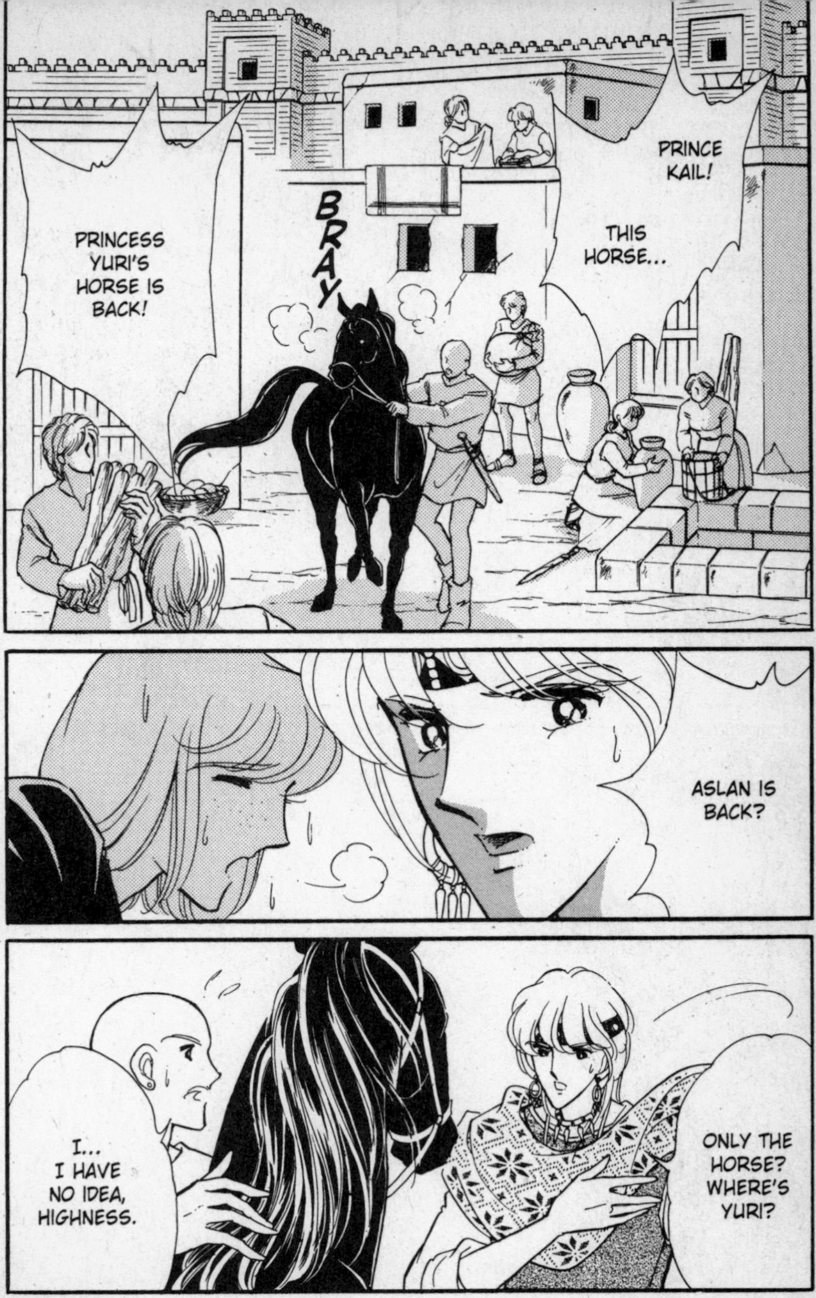
PRINCE KAIL!
THIS HORSE...
BRAY
PRINCESS YURI'S HORSE IS BACK!
ASLAN IS BACK?
ONLY THE HORSE? WHERE'S YURI?
I... I HAVE NO IDEA, HIGHNESS.

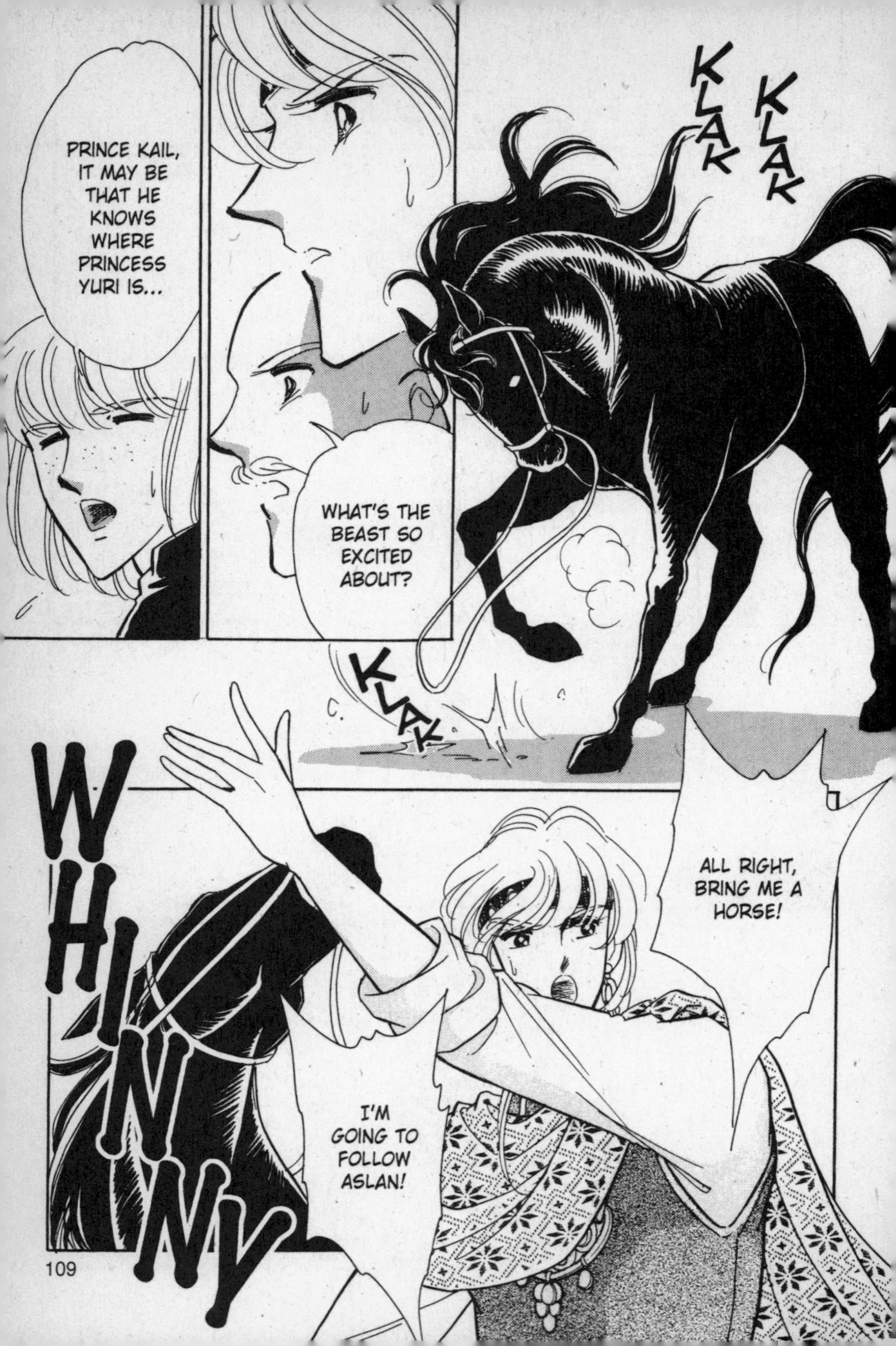
KLAK KLAK
KLAK
WHAT'S THE BEAST SO EXCITED ABOUT?
PRINCE KAIL, IT MAY BE THAT HE KNOWS WHERE PRINCESS YURI IS...
ALL RIGHT, BRING ME A HORSE!
I'M GOING TO FOLLOW ASLAN!
WHINNY

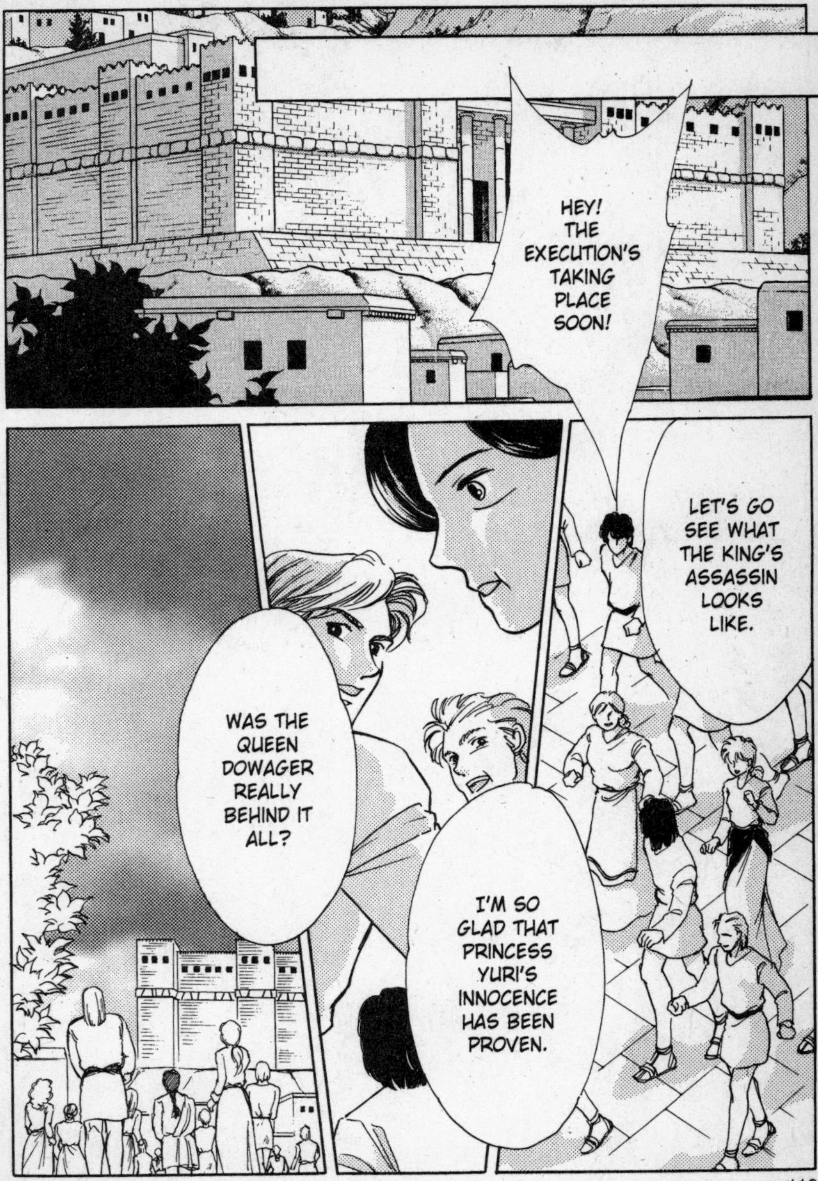
HEY! THE EXECUTION'S TAKING PLACE SOON!
LET'S GO SEE WHAT THE KING'S ASSASSIN LOOKS LIKE.
I'M SO GLAD THAT PRINCESS YURI'S INNOCENCE HAS BEEN PROVEN.
WAS THE QUEEN DOWAGER REALLY BEHIND IT ALL?

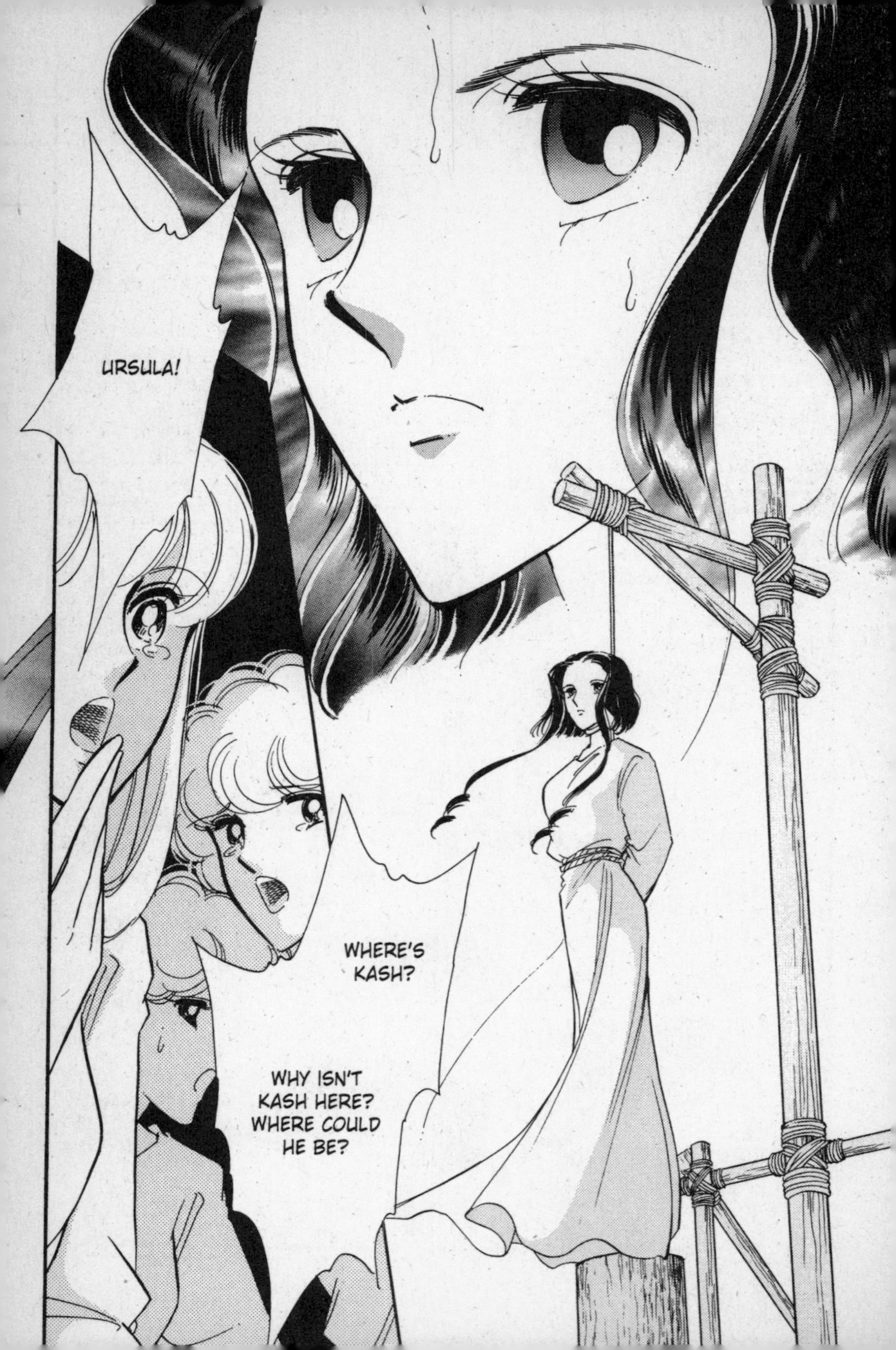
URSULA!
WHERE'S KASH?
WHY ISN'T KASH HERE? WHERE COULD HE BE?

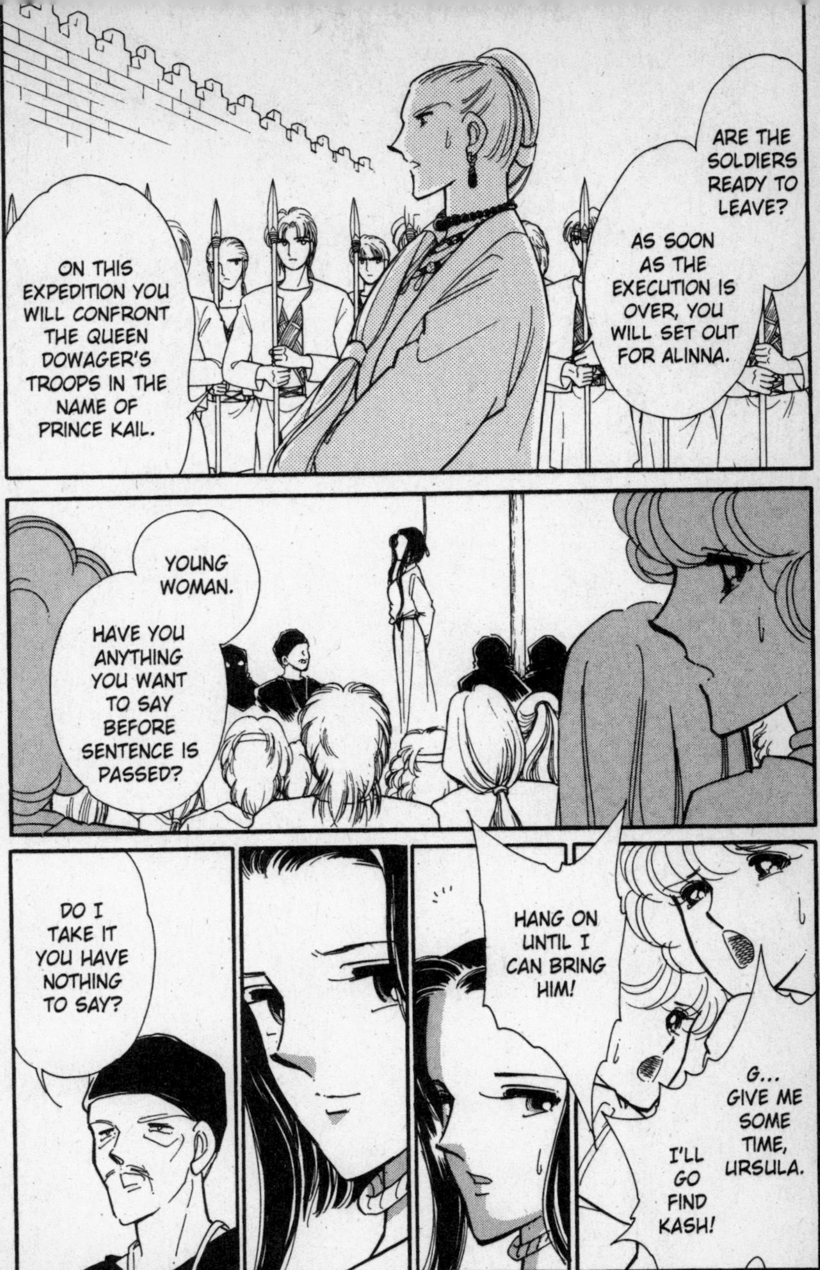
ARE THE SOLDIERS READY TO LEAVE?
AS SOON AS THE EXECUTION IS OVER, YOU WILL SET OUT FOR ALINNA.
ON THIS EXPEDITION YOU WILL CONFRONT THE QUEEN DOWAGER'S TROOPS IN THE NAME OF PRINCE KAIL.
YOUNG WOMAN.
HAVE YOU ANYTHING YOU WANT TO SAY BEFORE SENTENCE IS PASSED?
G... GIVE ME SOME TIME, URSULA.
I'LL GO FIND KASH!
HANG ON UNTIL I CAN BRING HIM!
DO I TAKE IT YOU HAVE NOTHING TO SAY?

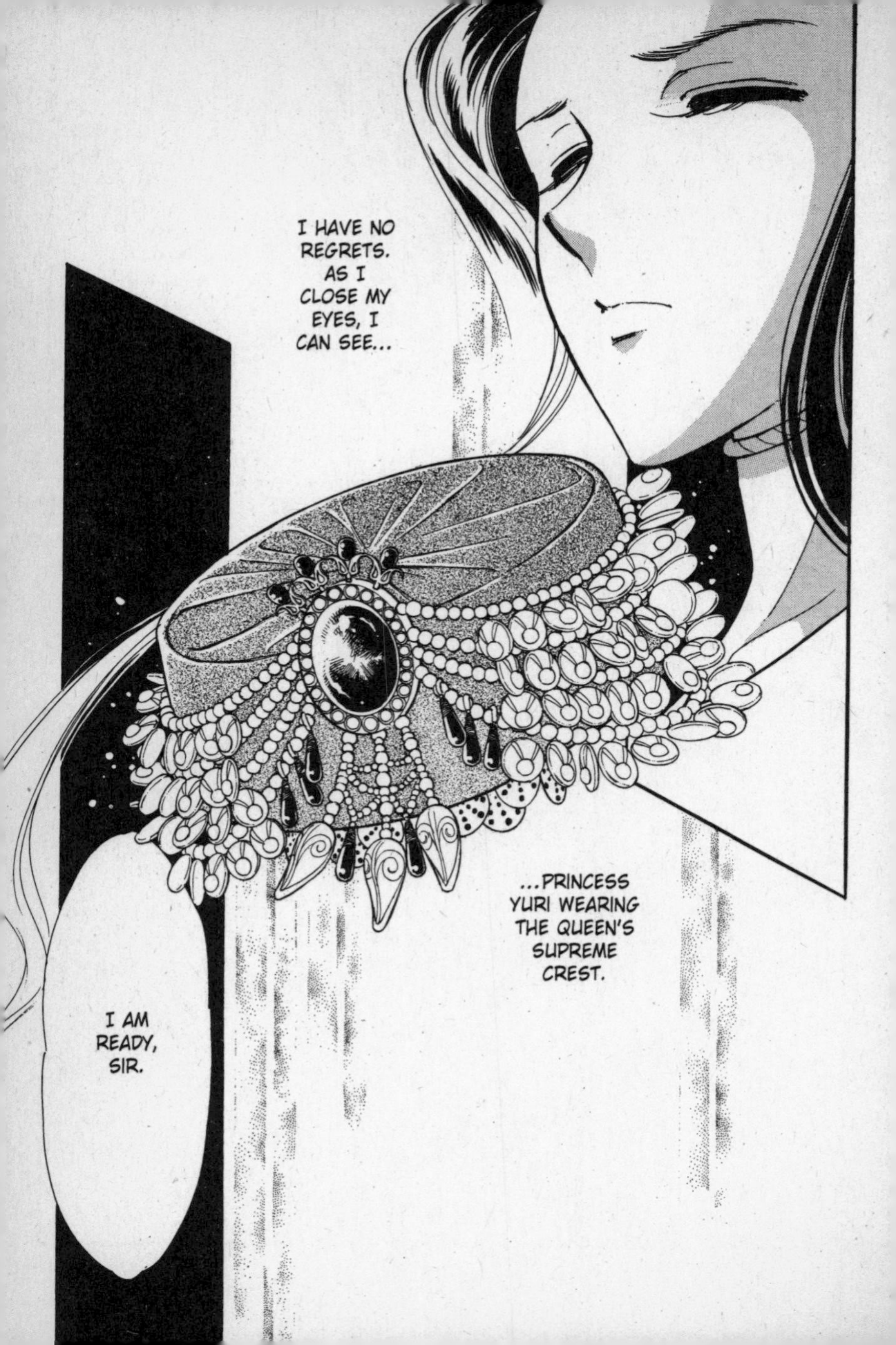
I HAVE NO REGRETS. AS I CLOSE MY EYES, I CAN SEE...
...PRINCESS YURI WEARING THE QUEEN'S SUPREME CREST.
I AM READY, SIR.

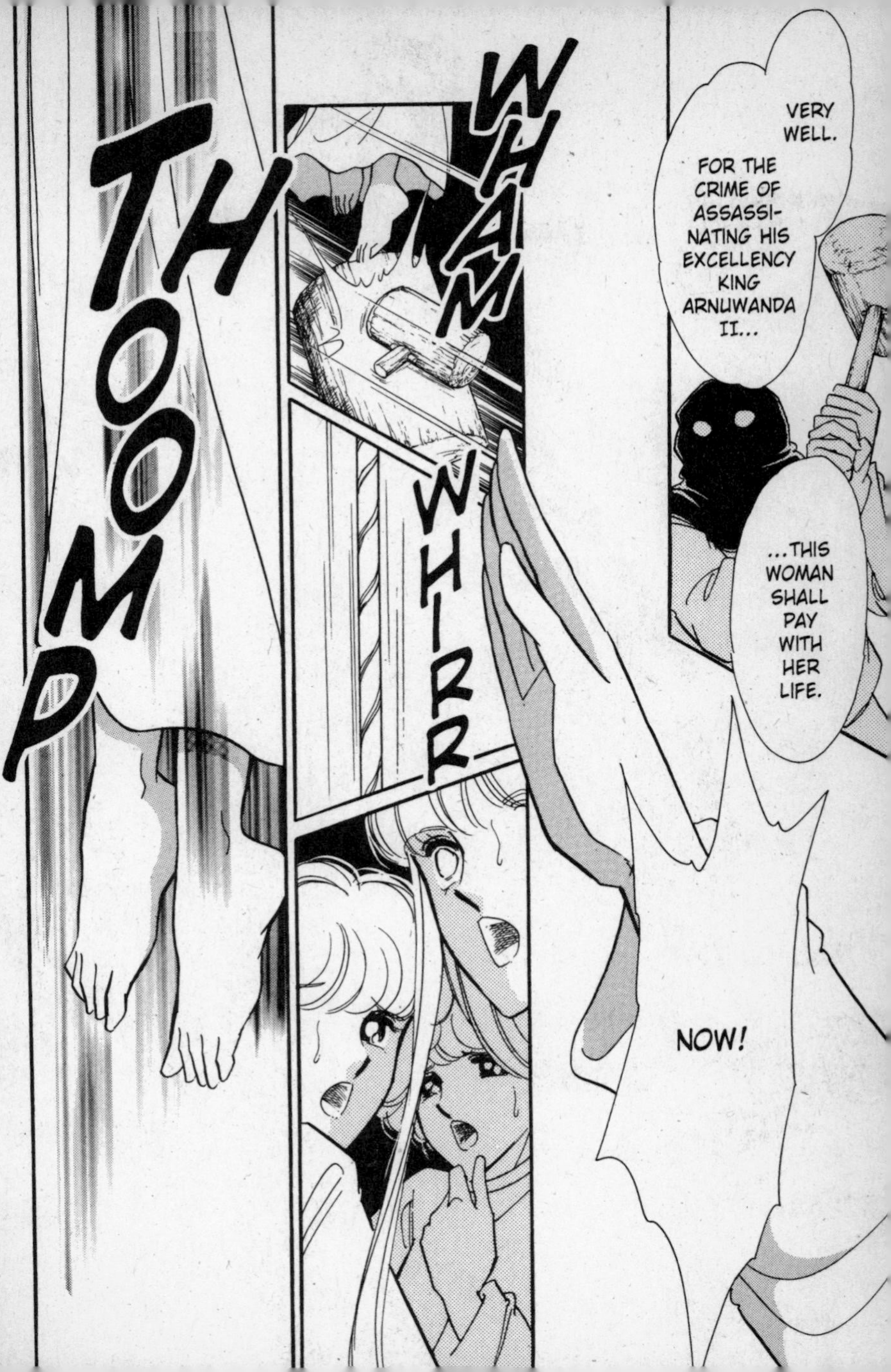
VERY WELL.
FOR THE CRIME OF ASSASSI-NATING HIS EXCELLENCY KING ARNUWANDA II...
...THIS WOMAN SHALL PAY WITH HER LIFE.
NOW!
WHAM
WHIRR
THOOMP

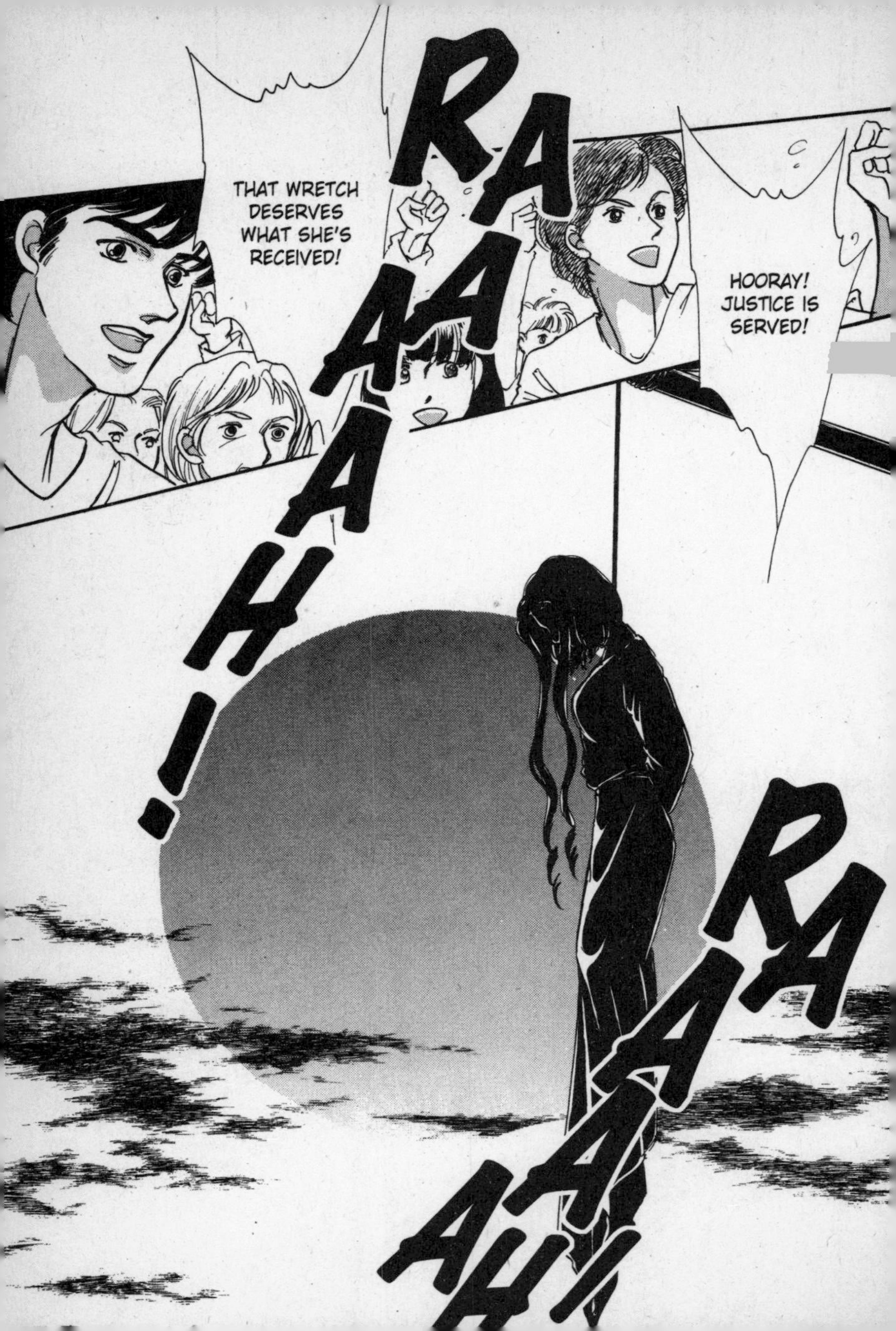
HOORAY! JUSTICE IS SERVED!
THAT WRETCH DESERVES WHAT SHE'S RECEIVED!
RAAAAH!!
RAAAAAH!!

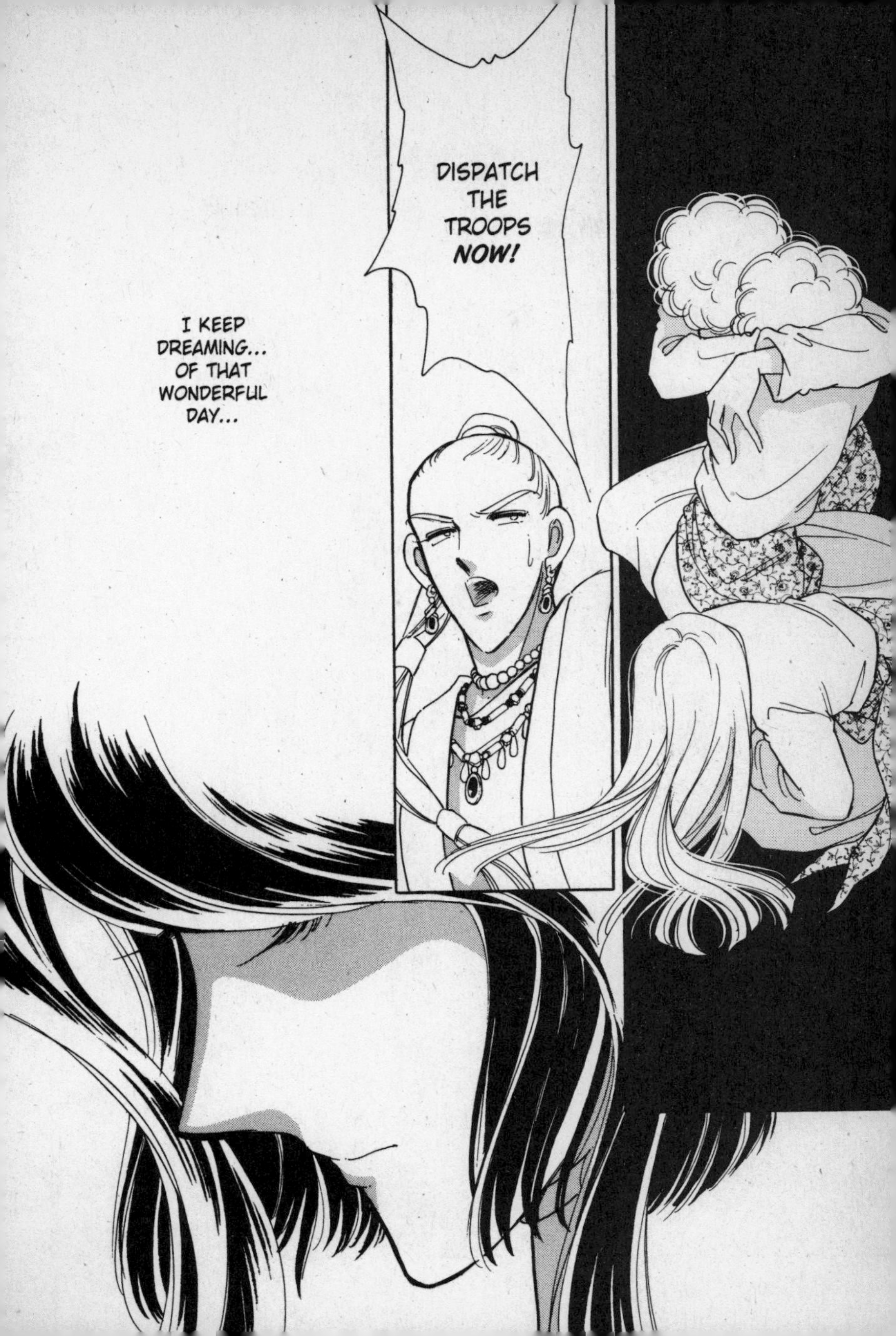
DISPATCH THE TROOPS NOW!
I KEEP DREAMING... OF THAT WONDERFUL DAY...

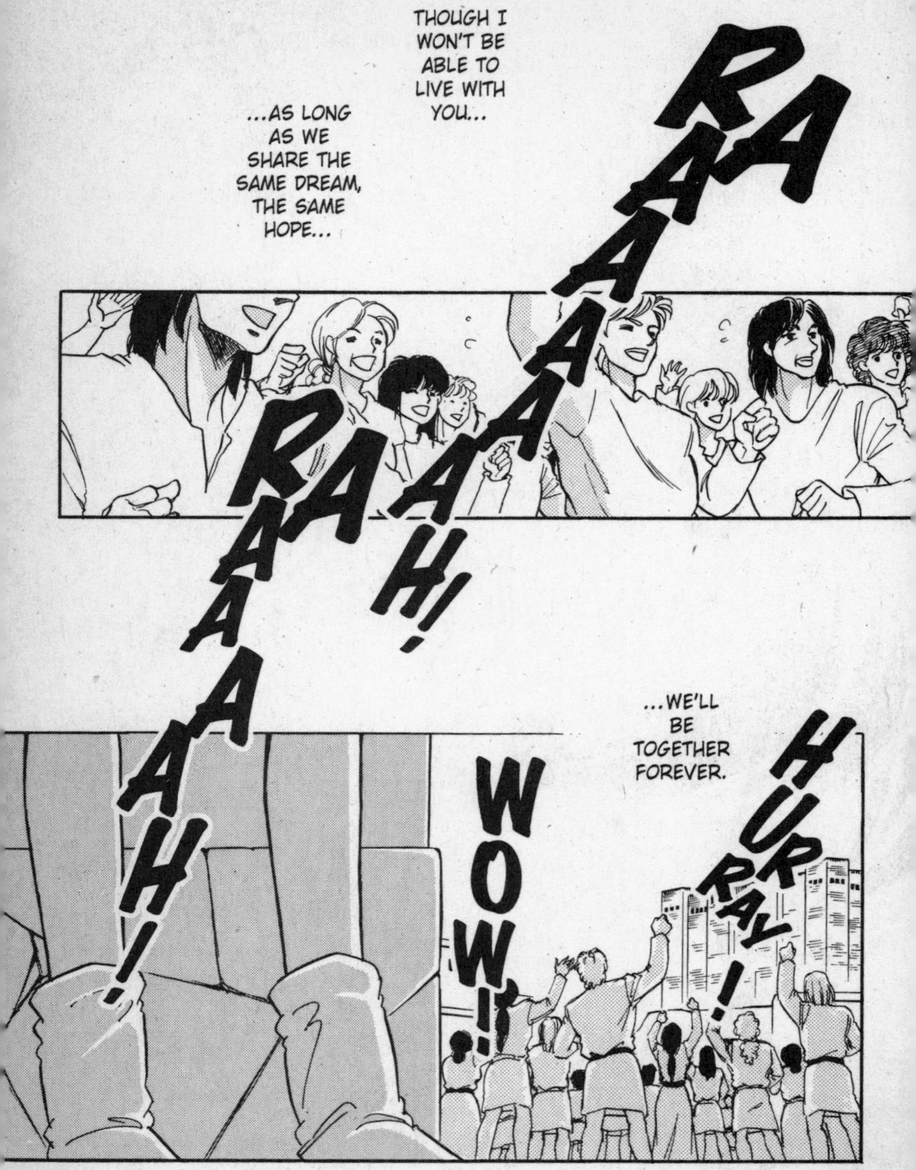
THOUGH I WON'T BE ABLE TO LIVE WITH YOU...
...AS LONG AS WE SHARE THE SAME DREAM, THE SAME HOPE...
RAAAAAAH!
RAAAAAAAH!
...WE'LL BE TOGETHER FOREVER.
HURRAY!!
WOW!!

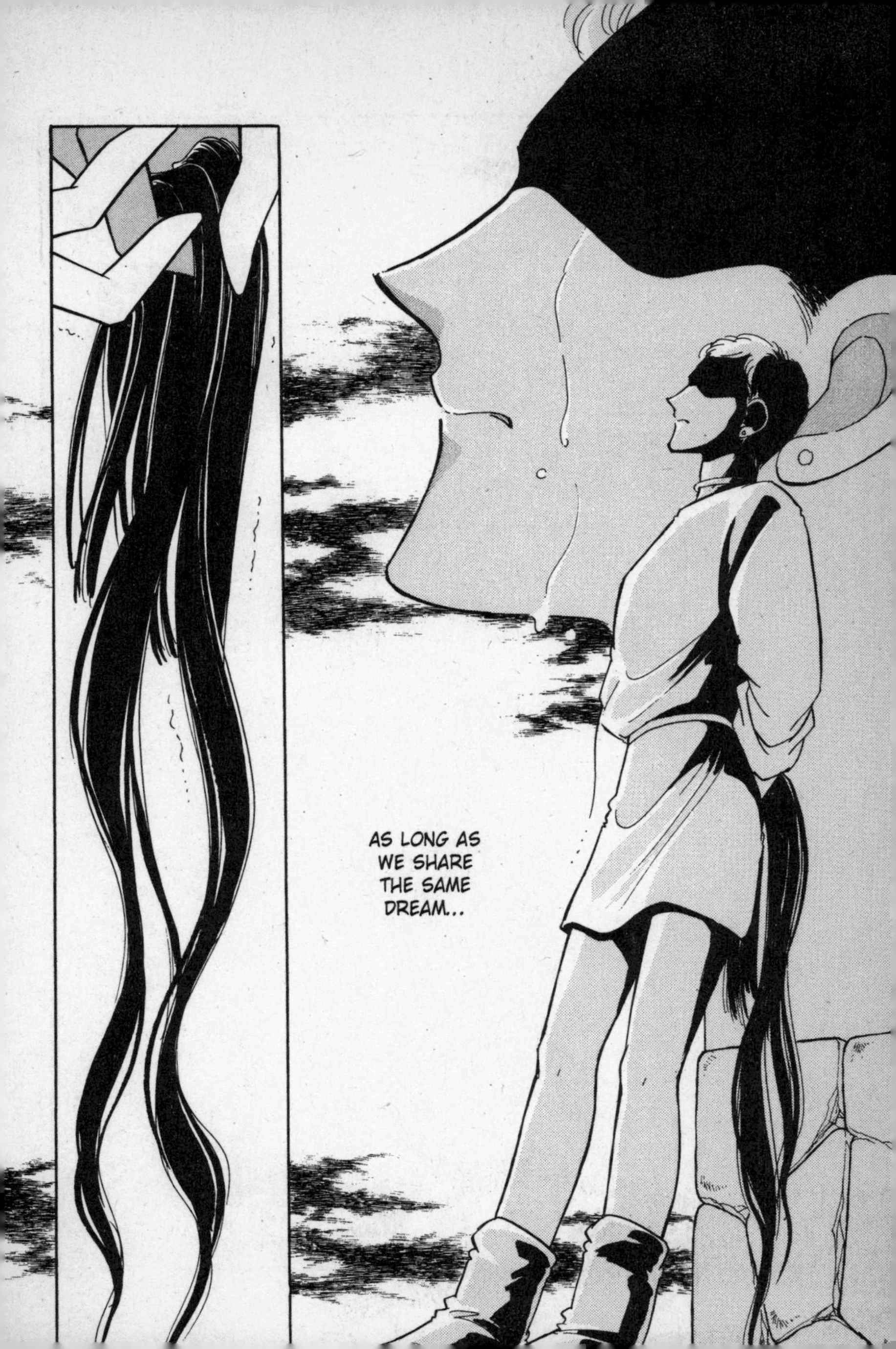
AS LONG AS WE SHARE THE SAME DREAM...

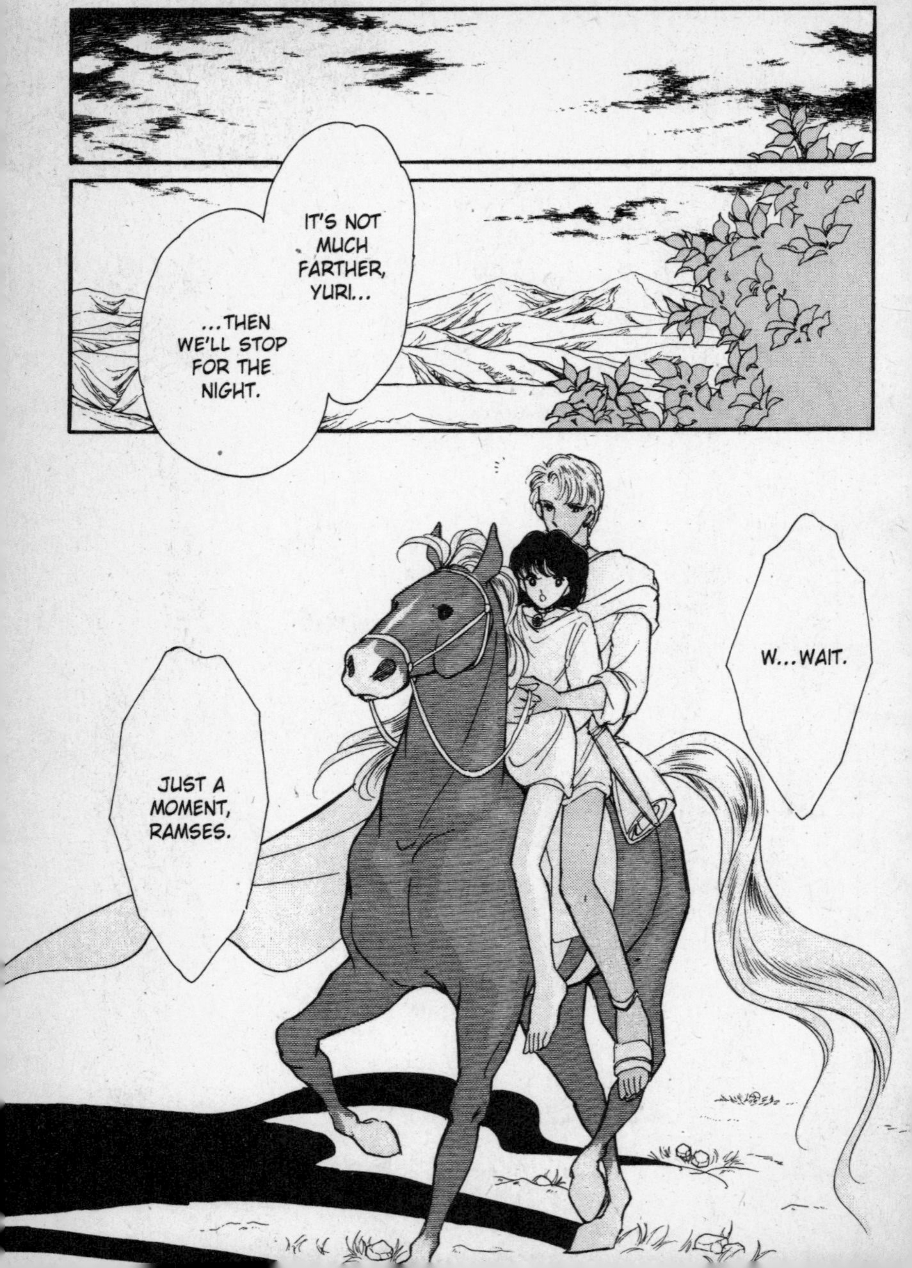
IT'S NOT MUCH FARTHER, YURI...
...THEN WE'LL STOP FOR THE NIGHT.
W...WAIT.
JUST A MOMENT, RAMSES.

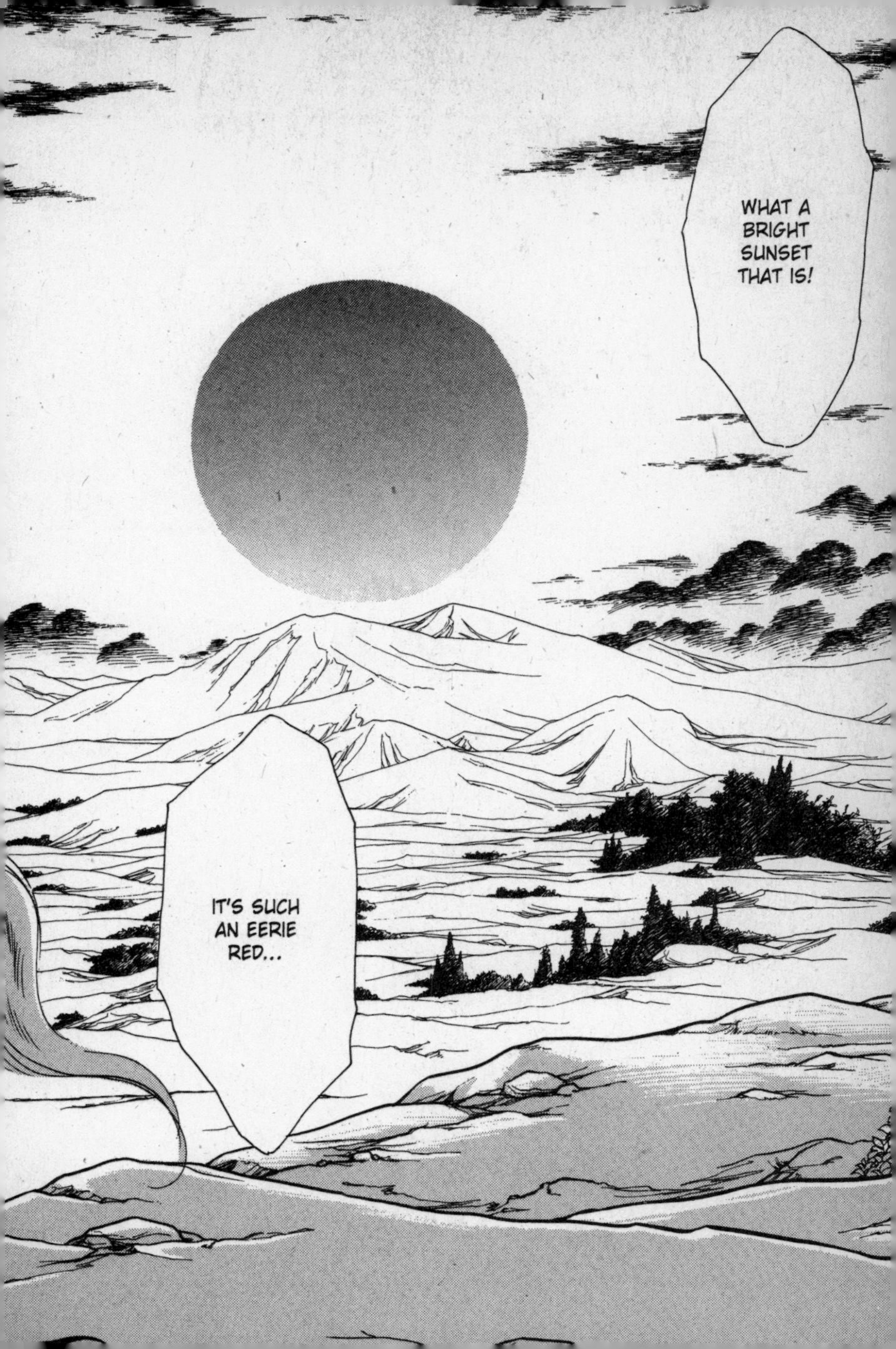
WHAT A BRIGHT SUNSET THAT IS!
IT'S SUCH AN EERIE RED...

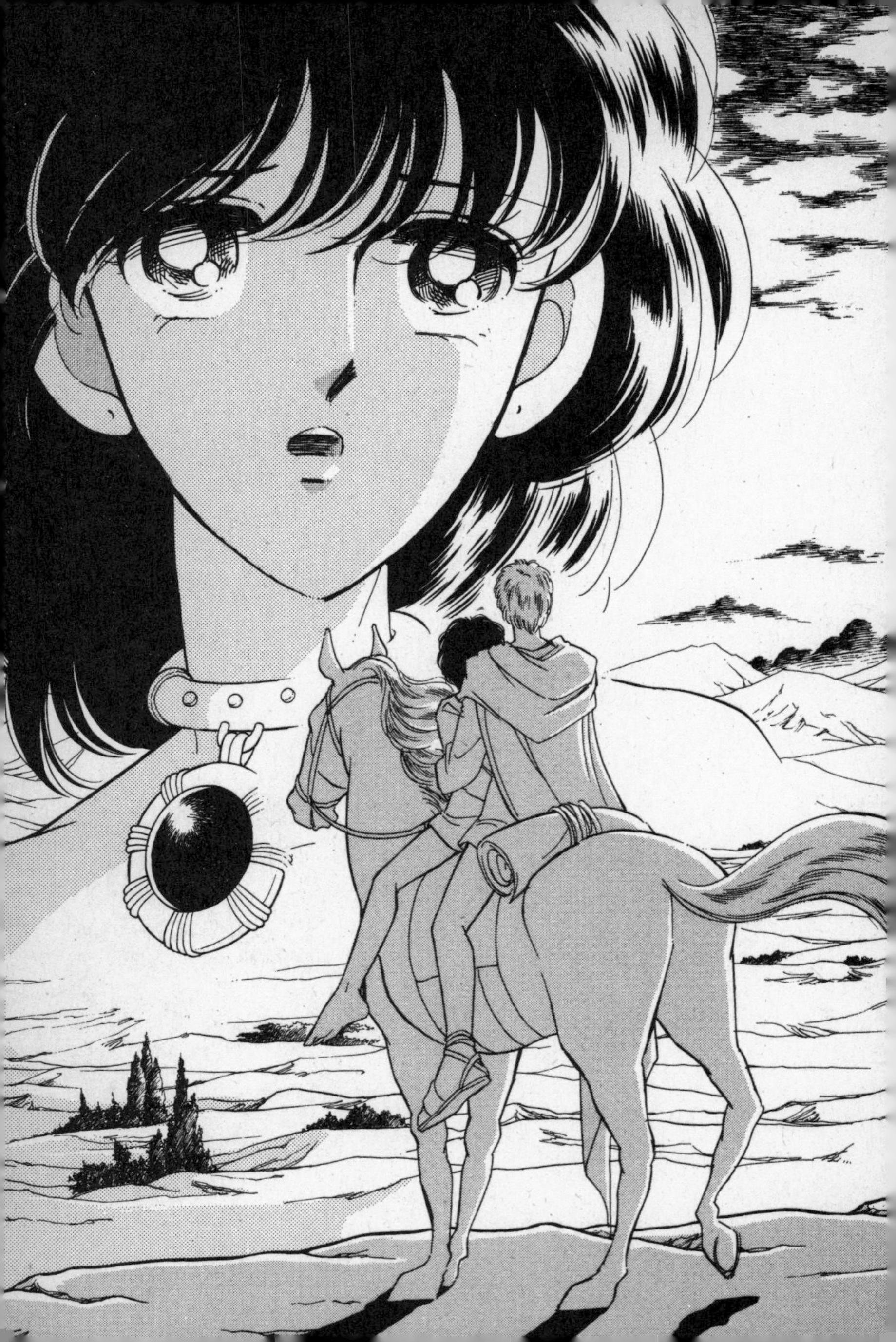

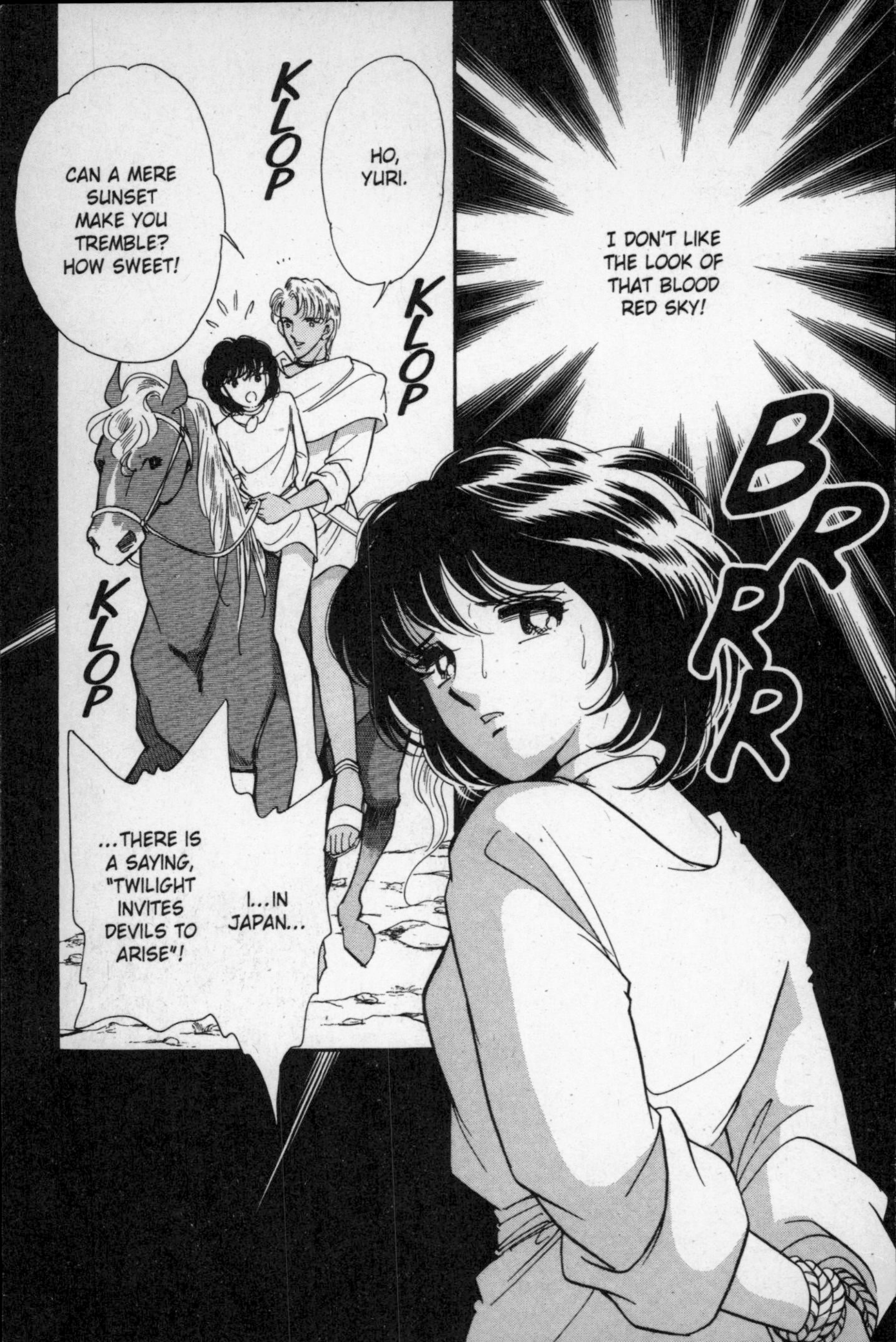
I DON'T LIKE THE LOOK OF THAT BLOOD RED SKY!
BRRR
KLOP KLOP
HO, YURI.
KLOP KLOP
CAN A MERE SUNSET MAKE YOU TREMBLE? HOW SWEET!
...
KLOP KLOP
I...IN JAPAN...
...THERE IS A SAYING, "TWILIGHT INVITES DEVILS TO ARISE"!

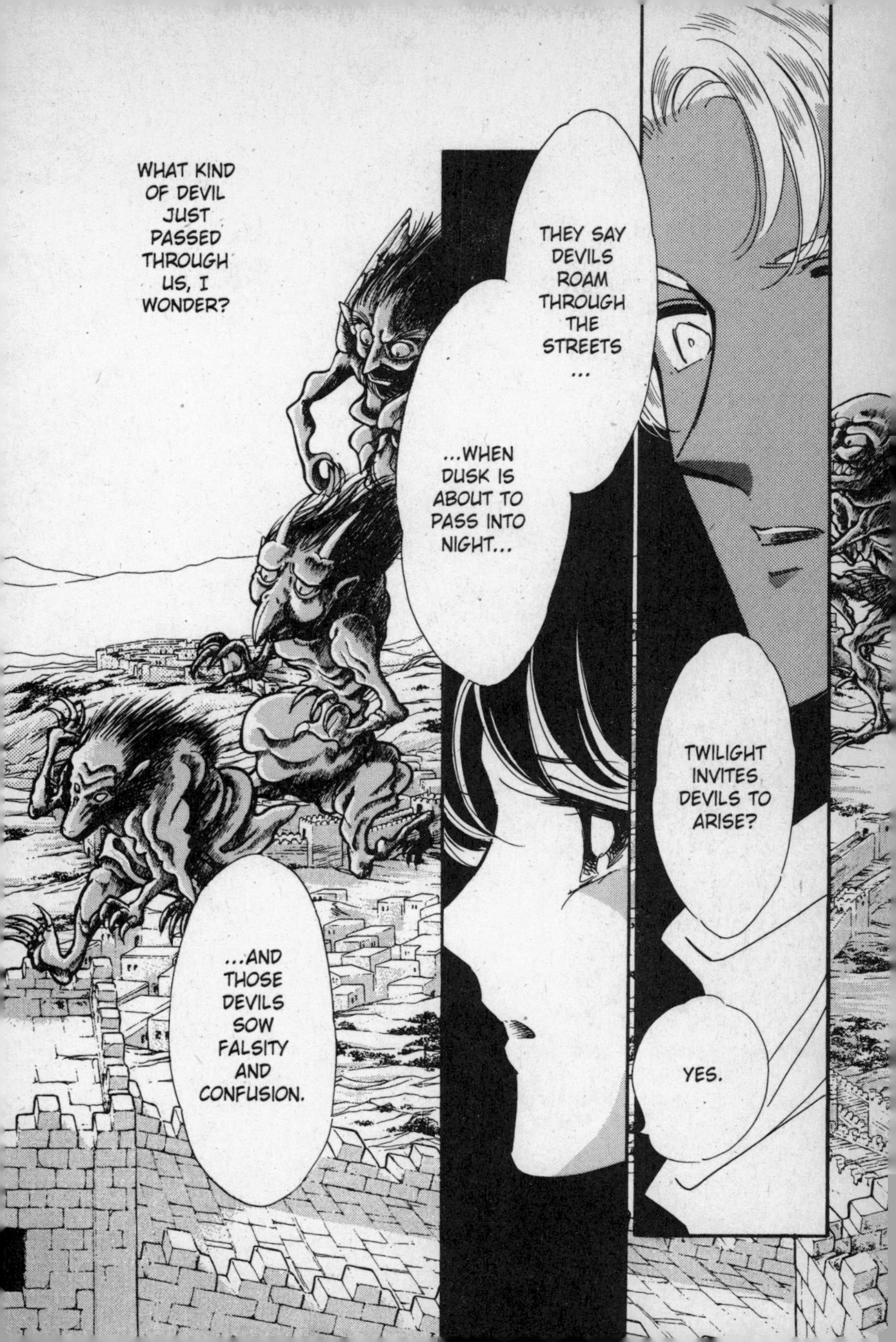
THEY SAY DEVILS ROAM THROUGH THE STREETS...
...WHEN DUSK IS ABOUT TO PASS INTO NIGHT...
TWILIGHT INVITES DEVILS TO ARISE?
YES.
...AND THOSE DEVILS SOW FALSITY AND CONFUSION.
WHAT KIND OF DEVIL JUST PASSED THROUGH US, I WONDER?

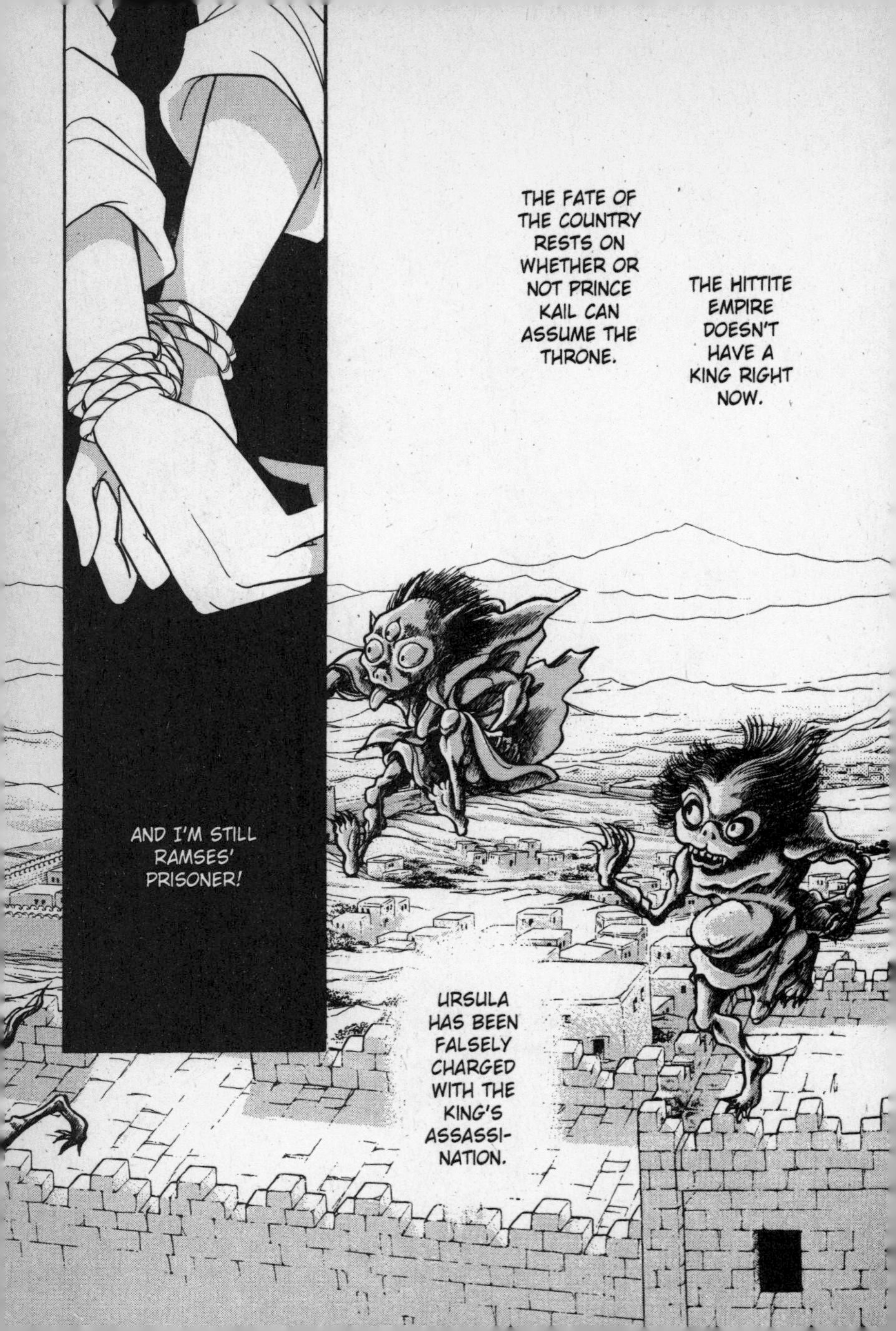
THE HITTITE EMPIRE DOESN'T HAVE A KING RIGHT NOW.
THE FATE OF THE COUNTRY RESTS ON WHETHER OR NOT PRINCE KAIL CAN ASSUME THE THRONE.
URSULA HAS BEEN FALSELY CHARGED WITH THE KING'S ASSASSI-NATION.
AND I'M STILL RAMSES' PRISONER!

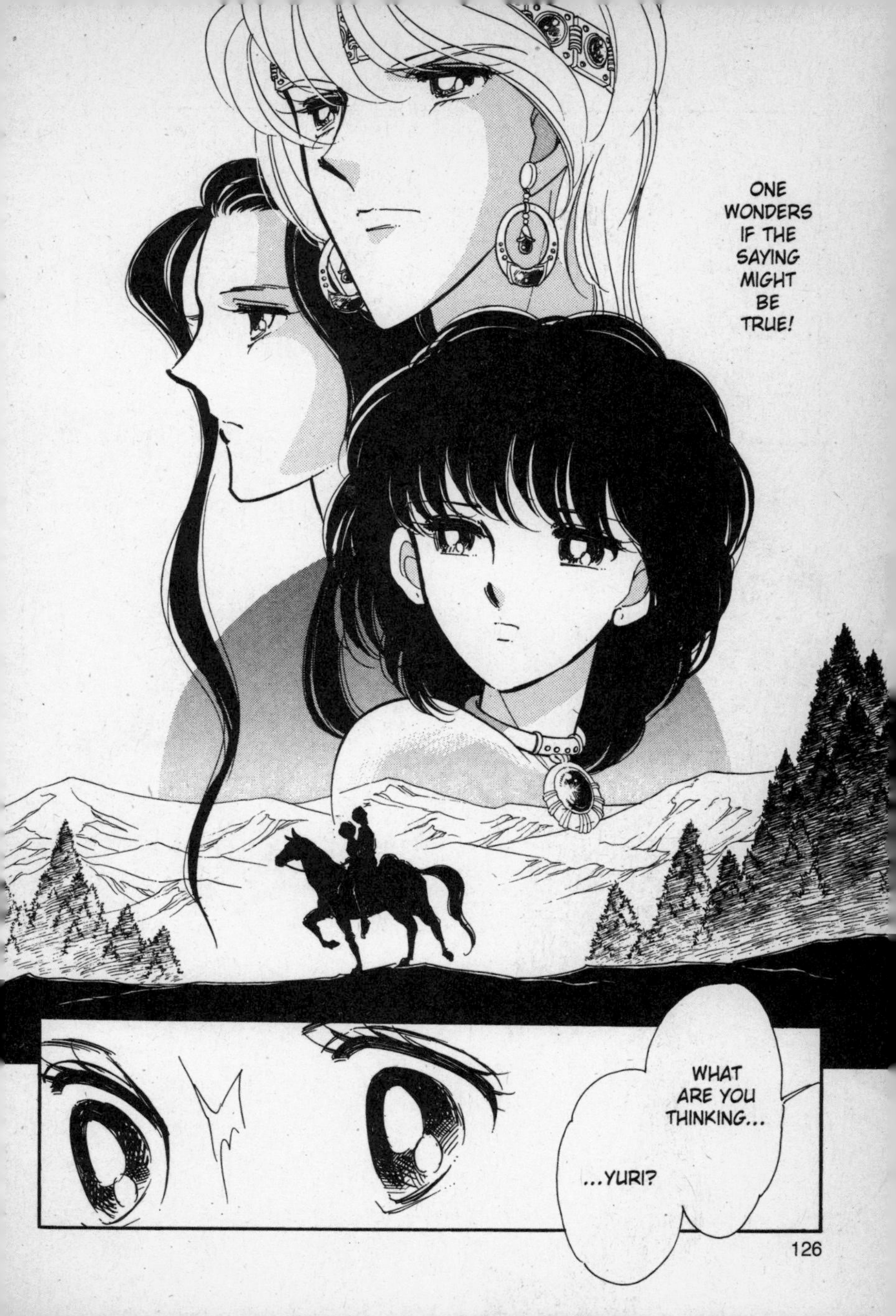
ONE WONDERS IF THE SAYING MIGHT BE TRUE!
WHAT ARE YOU THINKING...
...YURI?

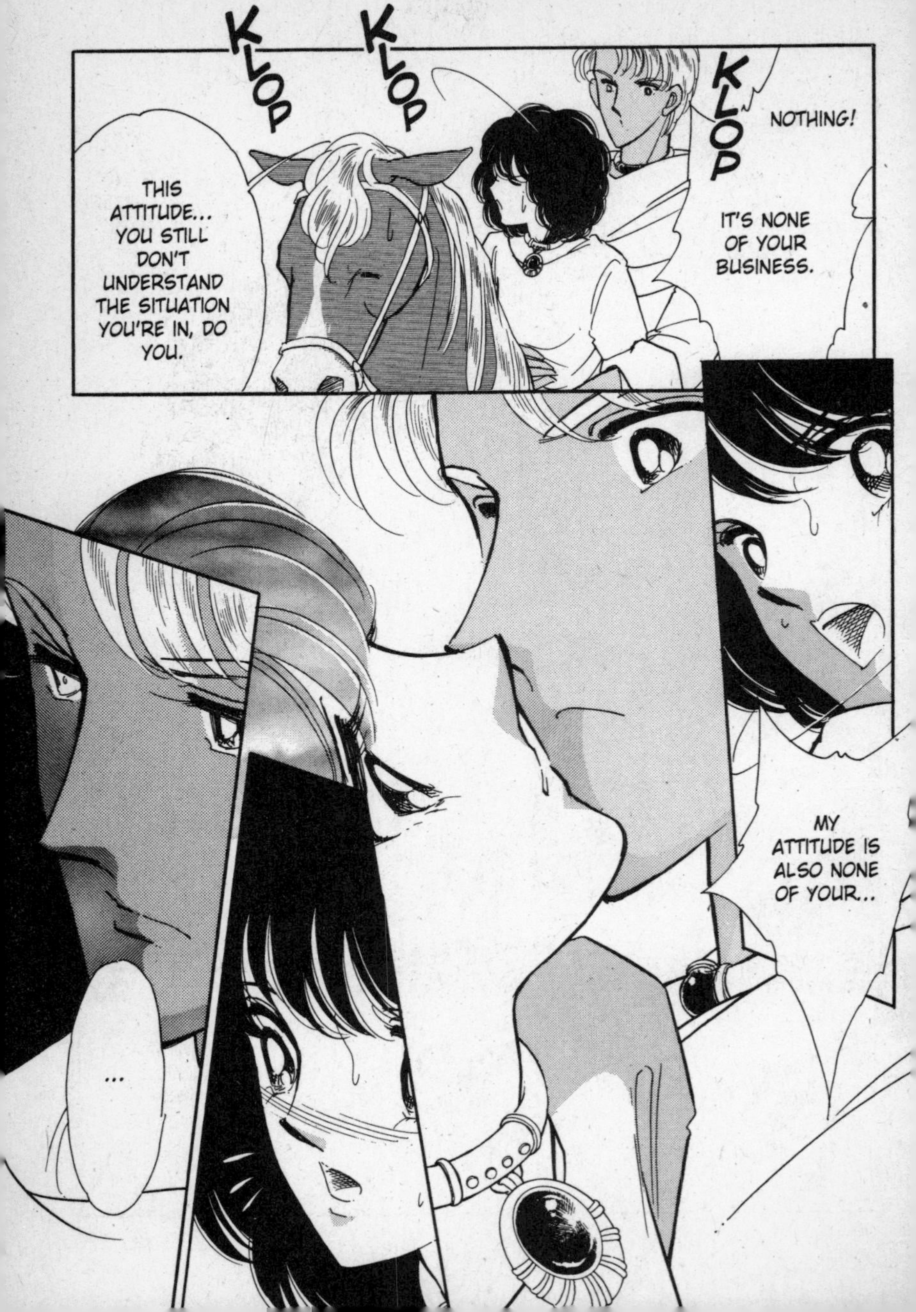
KLOP
NOTHING!
IT'S NONE OF YOUR BUSINESS.
KLOP
KLOP
THIS ATTITUDE... YOU STILL DON'T UNDERSTAND THE SITUATION YOU'RE IN, DO YOU.
MY ATTITUDE IS ALSO NONE OF YOUR...
...

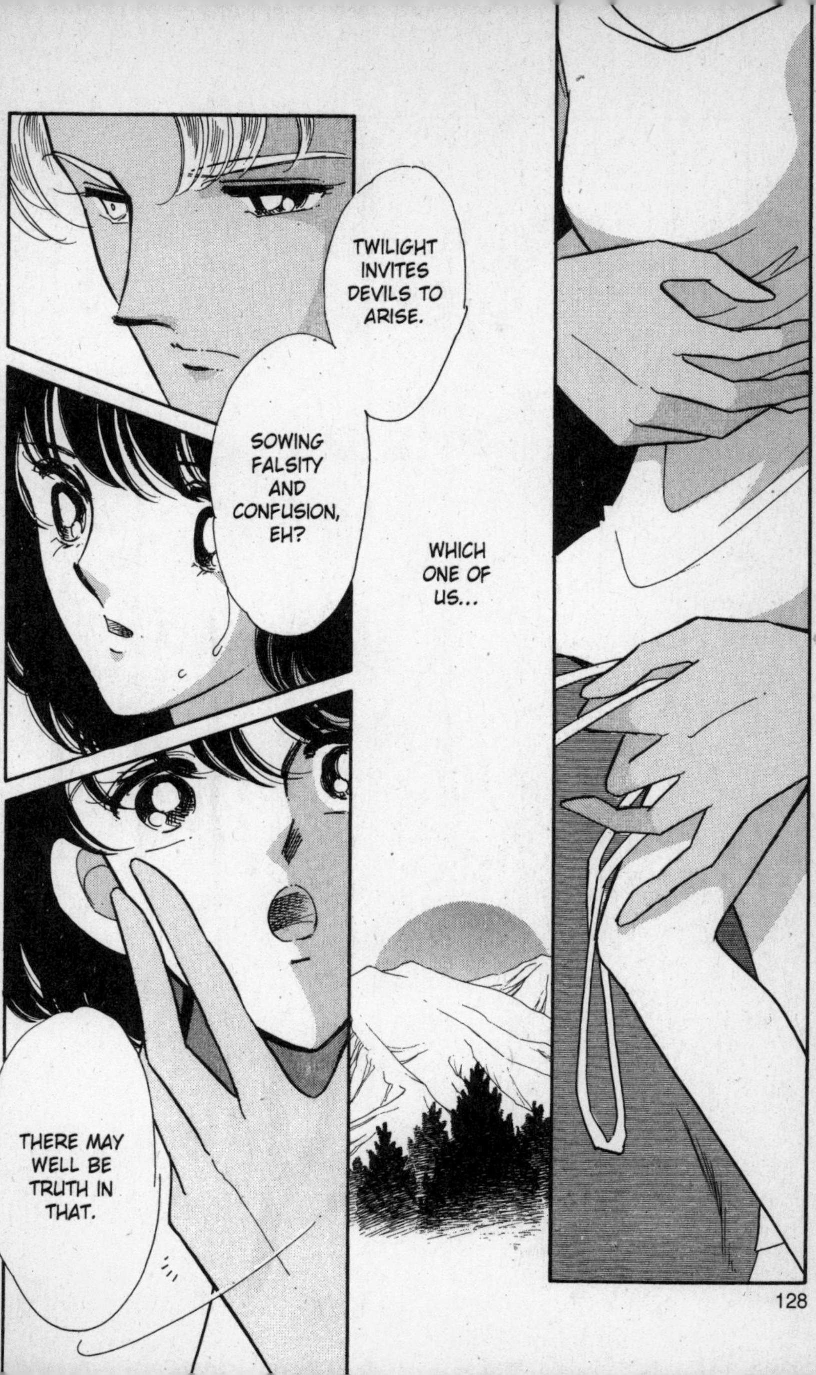
TWILIGHT INVITES DEVILS TO ARISE.
SOWING FALSITY AND CONFUSION, EH?
WHICH ONE OF US...
THERE MAY WELL BE TRUTH IN THAT.

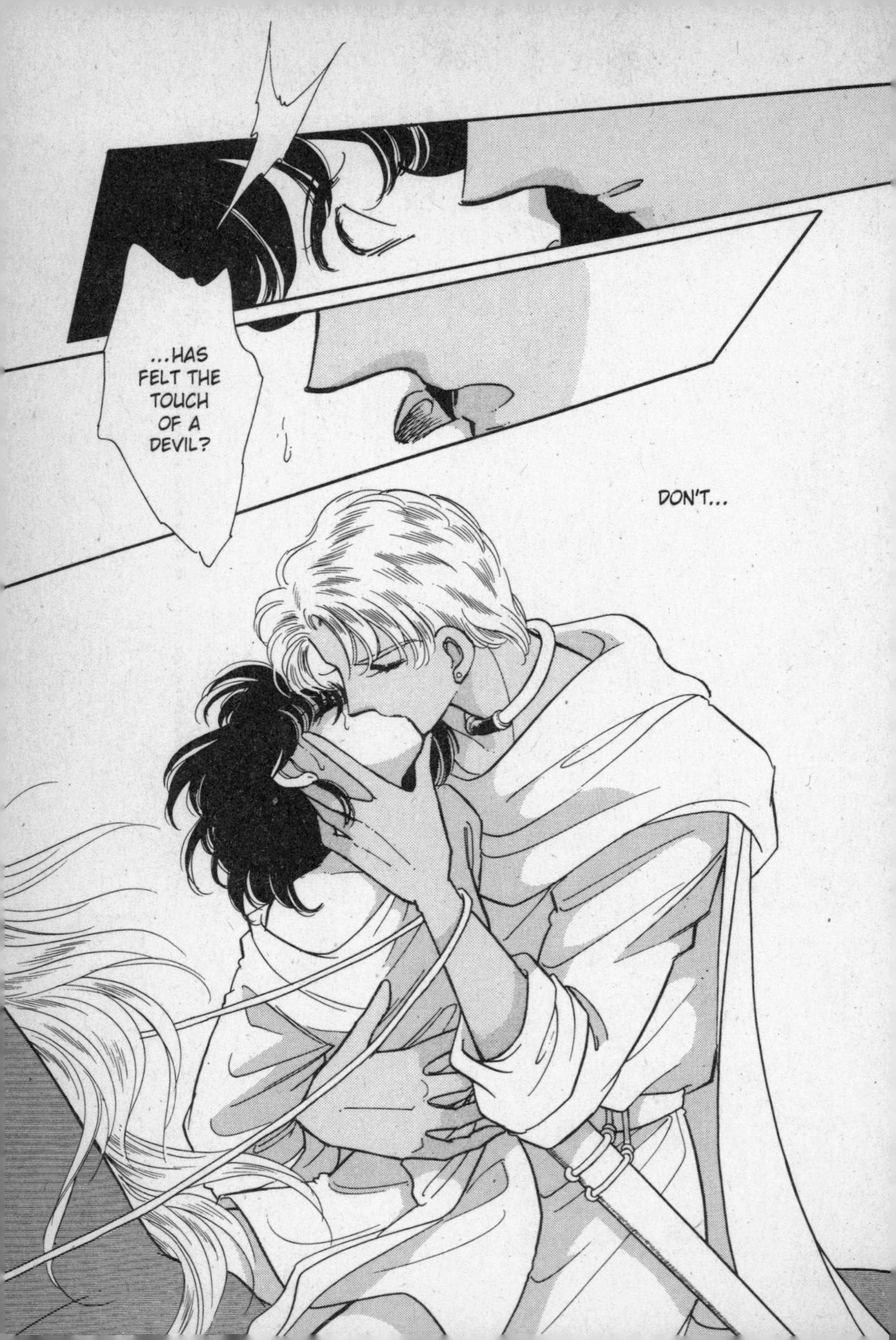
...HAS FELT THE TOUCH OF A DEVIL?
DON'T...

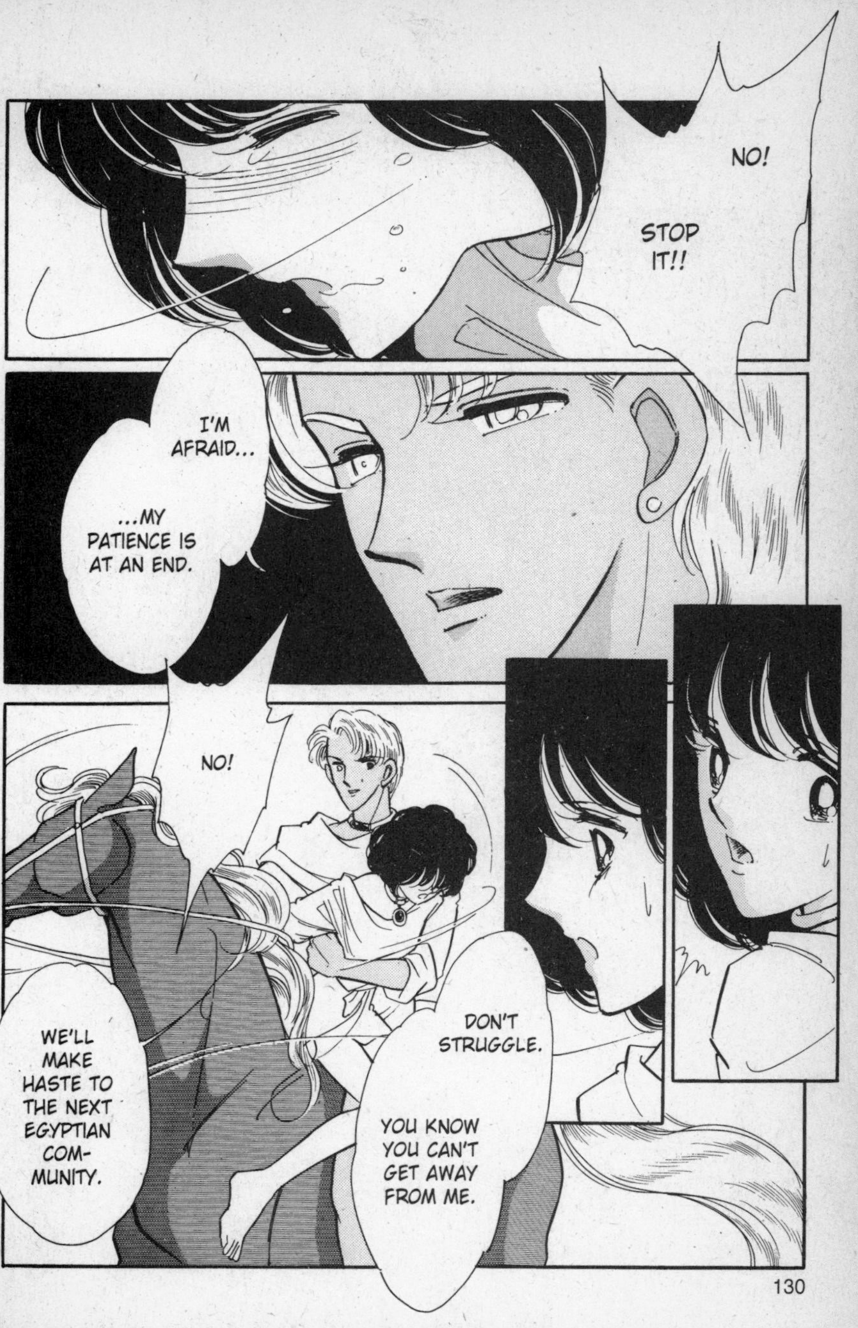
NO!
STOP IT!!
I'M AFRAID...
...MY PATIENCE IS AT AN END.
NO!
DON'T STRUGGLE.
YOU KNOW YOU CAN'T GET AWAY FROM ME.
WE'LL MAKE HASTE TO THE NEXT EGYPTIAN COM-MUNITY.

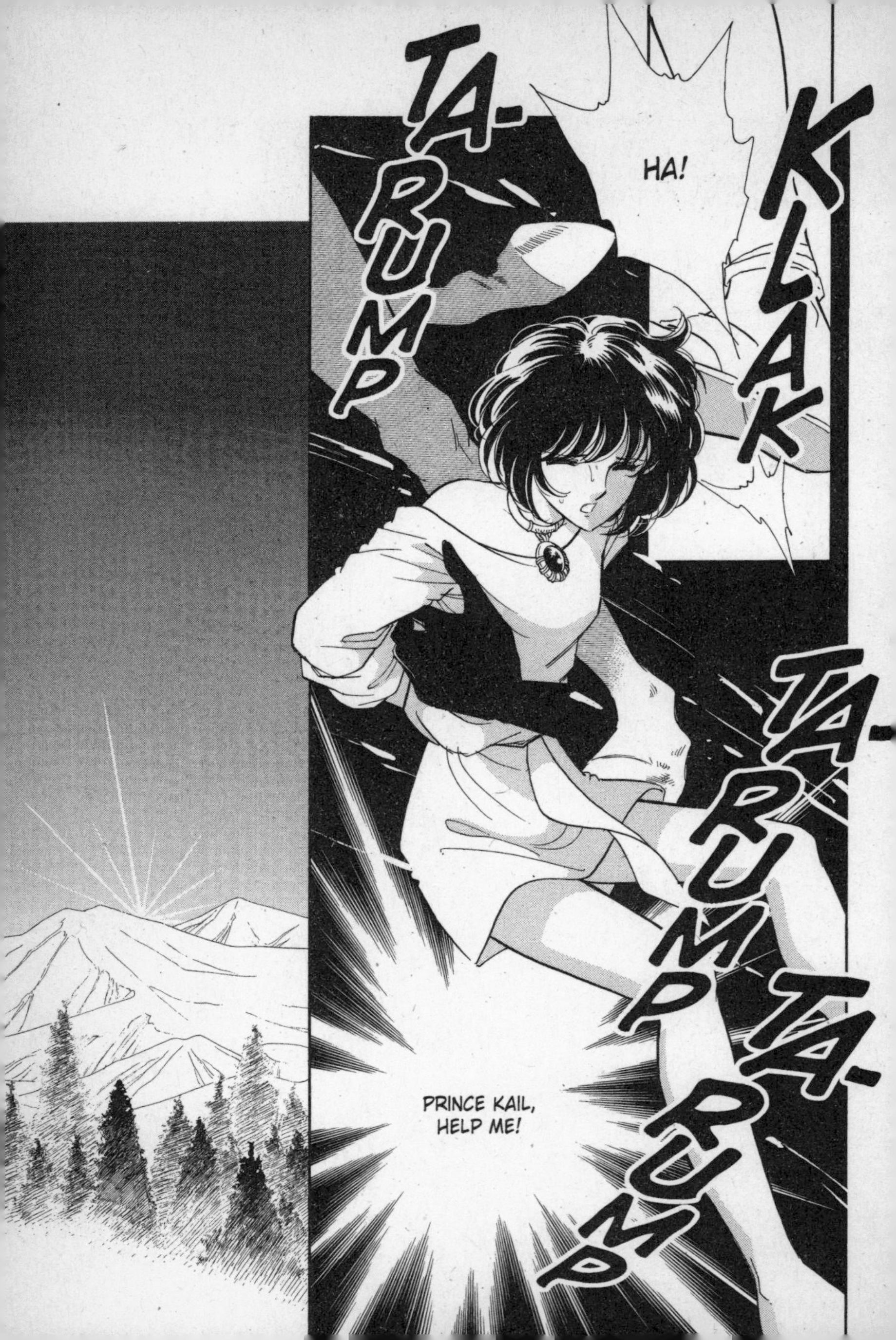
KLAK
HA!
TA-RUMP
TA-RUMP TA-RUMP
PRINCE KAIL,
HELP ME!

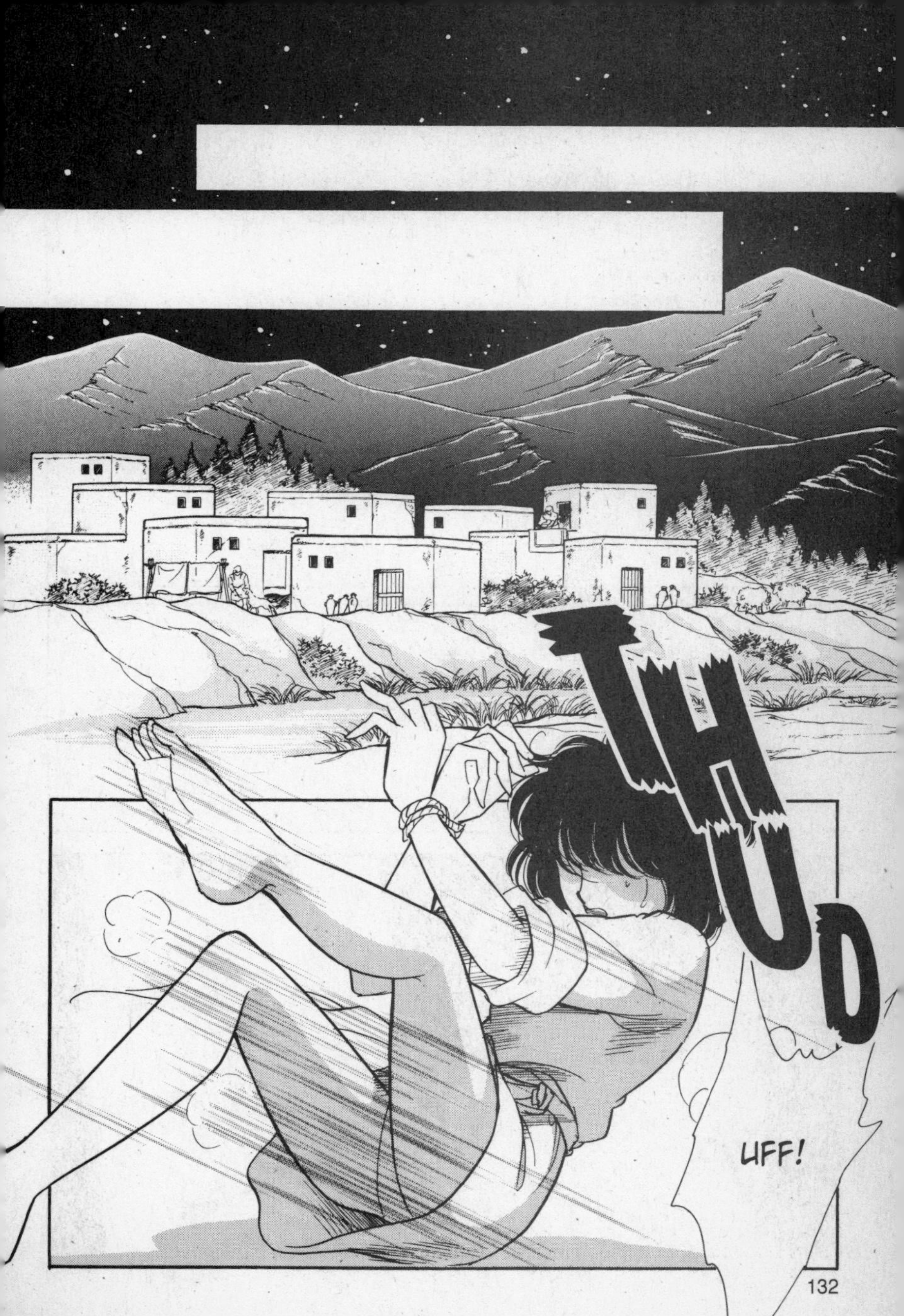
THUD
UFF!

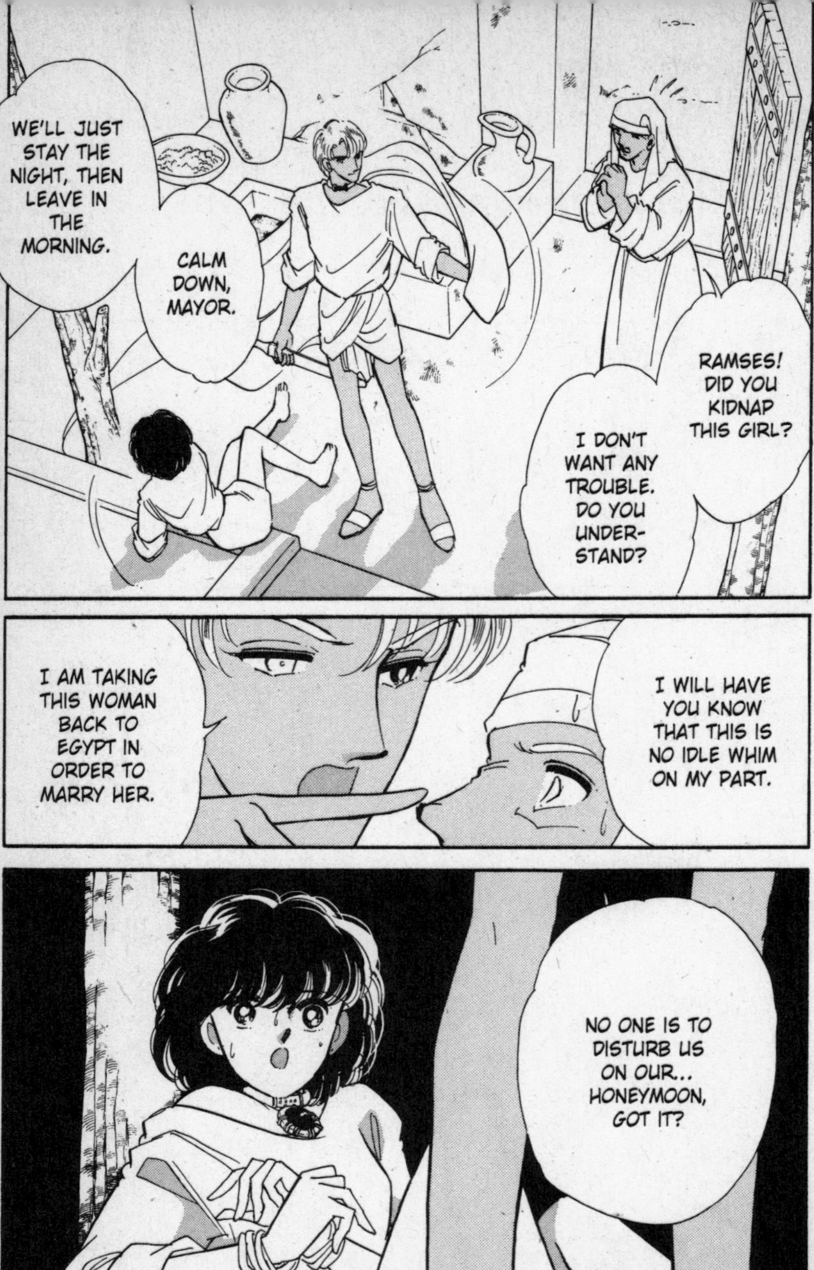
RAMSES! DID YOU KIDNAP THIS GIRL?
I DON'T WANT ANY TROUBLE. DO YOU UNDER-STAND?
CALM DOWN, MAYOR.
WE'LL JUST STAY THE NIGHT, THEN LEAVE IN THE MORNING.
I WILL HAVE YOU KNOW THAT THIS IS NO IDLE WHIM ON MY PART.
I AM TAKING THIS WOMAN BACK TO EGYPT IN ORDER TO MARRY HER.
NO ONE IS TO DISTURB US ON OUR... HONEYMOON, GOT IT?

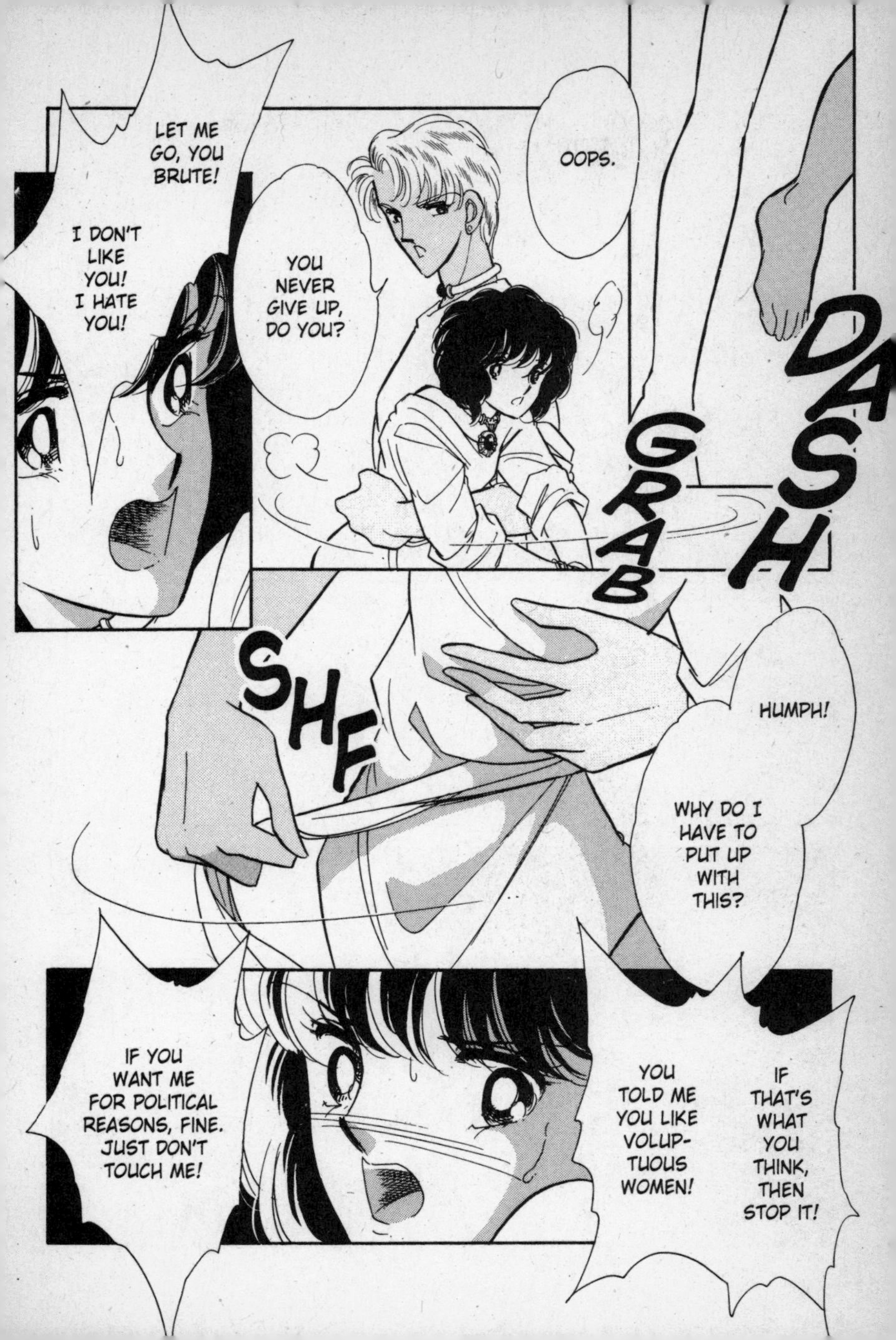
DASH
OOPS.
YOU NEVER GIVE UP, DO YOU?
GRAB
LET ME GO, YOU BRUTE!
I DON'T LIKE YOU! I HATE YOU!
HUMPH!
WHY DO I HAVE TO PUT UP WITH THIS?
SHF
IF THAT'S WHAT YOU THINK, THEN STOP IT!
YOU TOLD ME YOU LIKE VOLUP-TUOUS WOMEN!
IF YOU WANT ME FOR POLITICAL REASONS, FINE. JUST DON'T TOUCH ME!

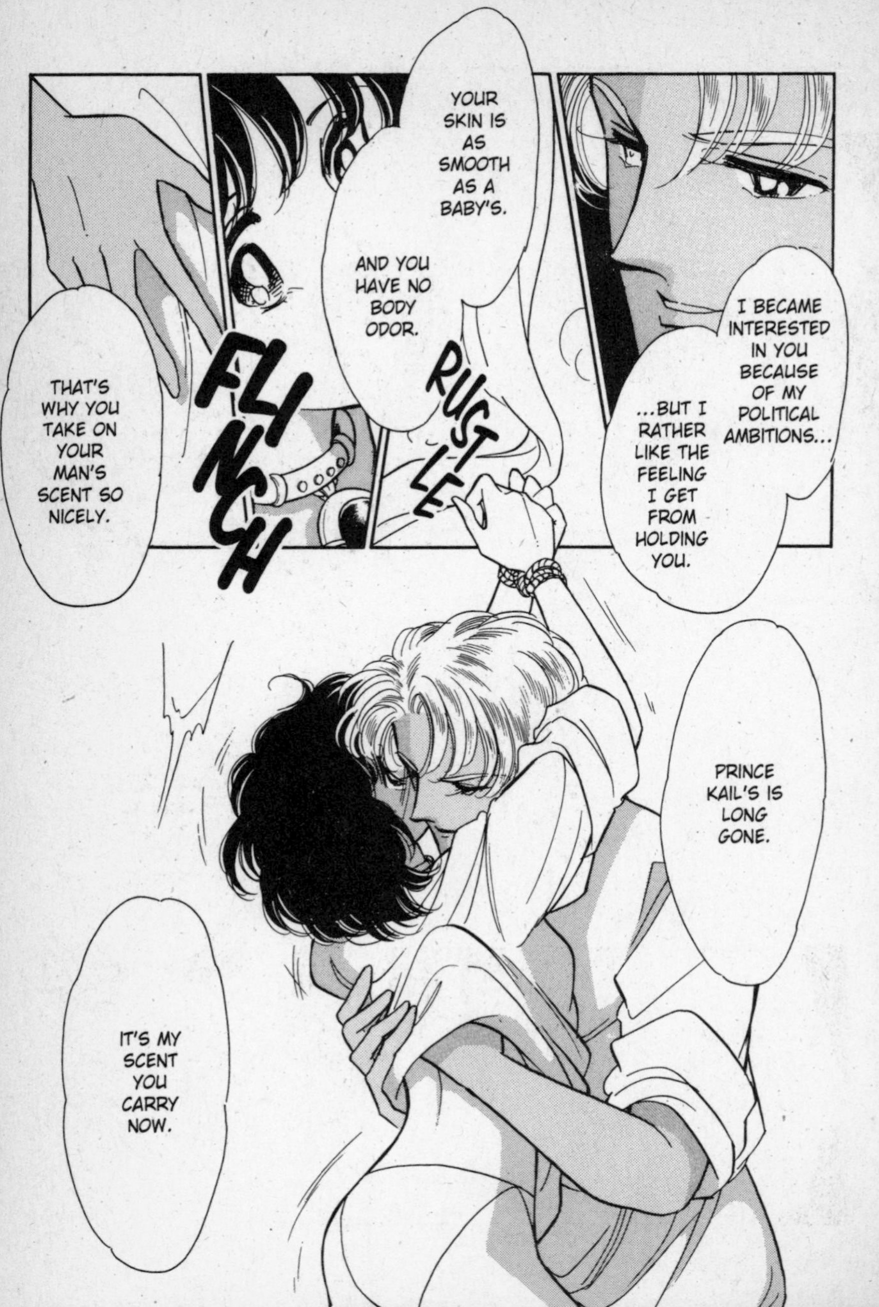
I BECAME INTERESTED IN YOU BECAUSE OF MY POLITICAL AMBITIONS...
...BUT I RATHER LIKE THE FEELING I GET FROM HOLDING YOU.
RUSTLE
YOUR SKIN IS AS SMOOTH AS A BABY'S.
AND YOU HAVE NO BODY ODOR.
FLINCH
THAT'S WHY YOU TAKE ON YOUR MAN'S SCENT SO NICELY.
PRINCE KAIL'S IS LONG GONE.
IT'S MY SCENT YOU CARRY NOW.

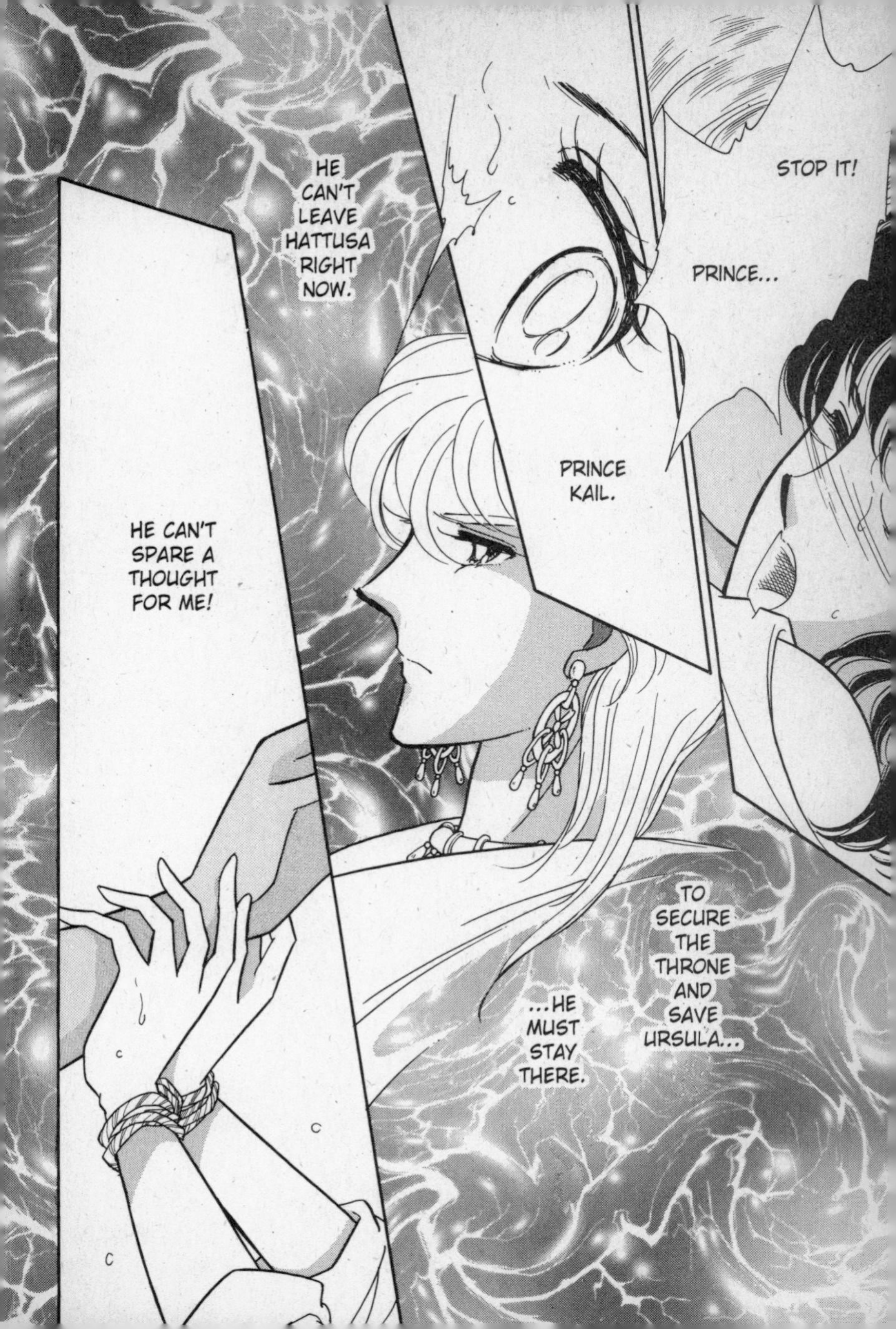
STOP IT!
PRINCE...
PRINCE KAIL.
HE CAN'T LEAVE HATTUSA RIGHT NOW.
TO SECURE THE THRONE AND SAVE URSULA...
...HE MUST STAY THERE.
HE CAN'T SPARE A THOUGHT FOR ME!

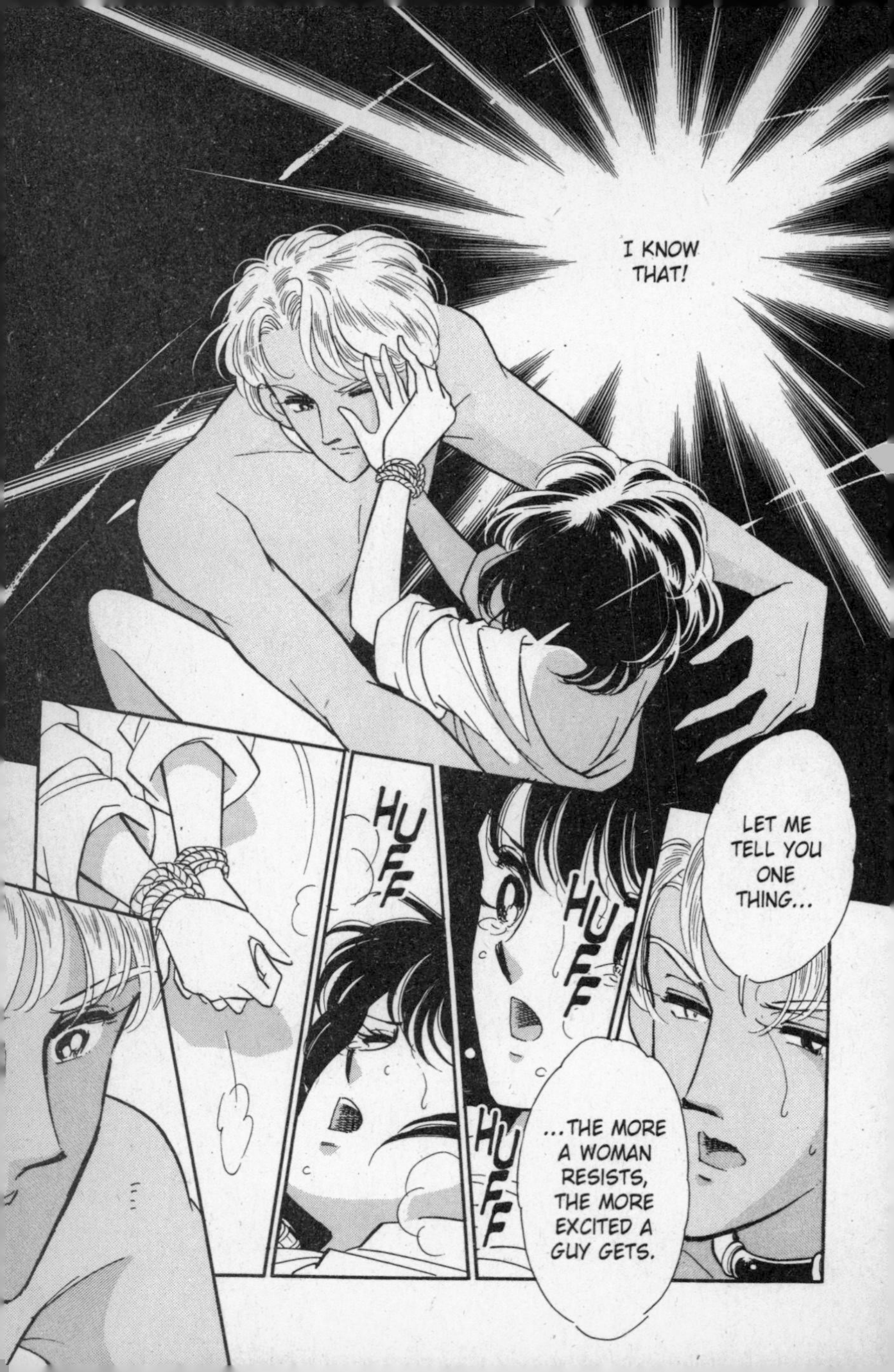

I KNOW THAT!
LET ME TELL YOU ONE THING...
...THE MORE A WOMAN RESISTS, THE MORE EXCITED A GUY GETS.
HUFF
HUFF
HUFF

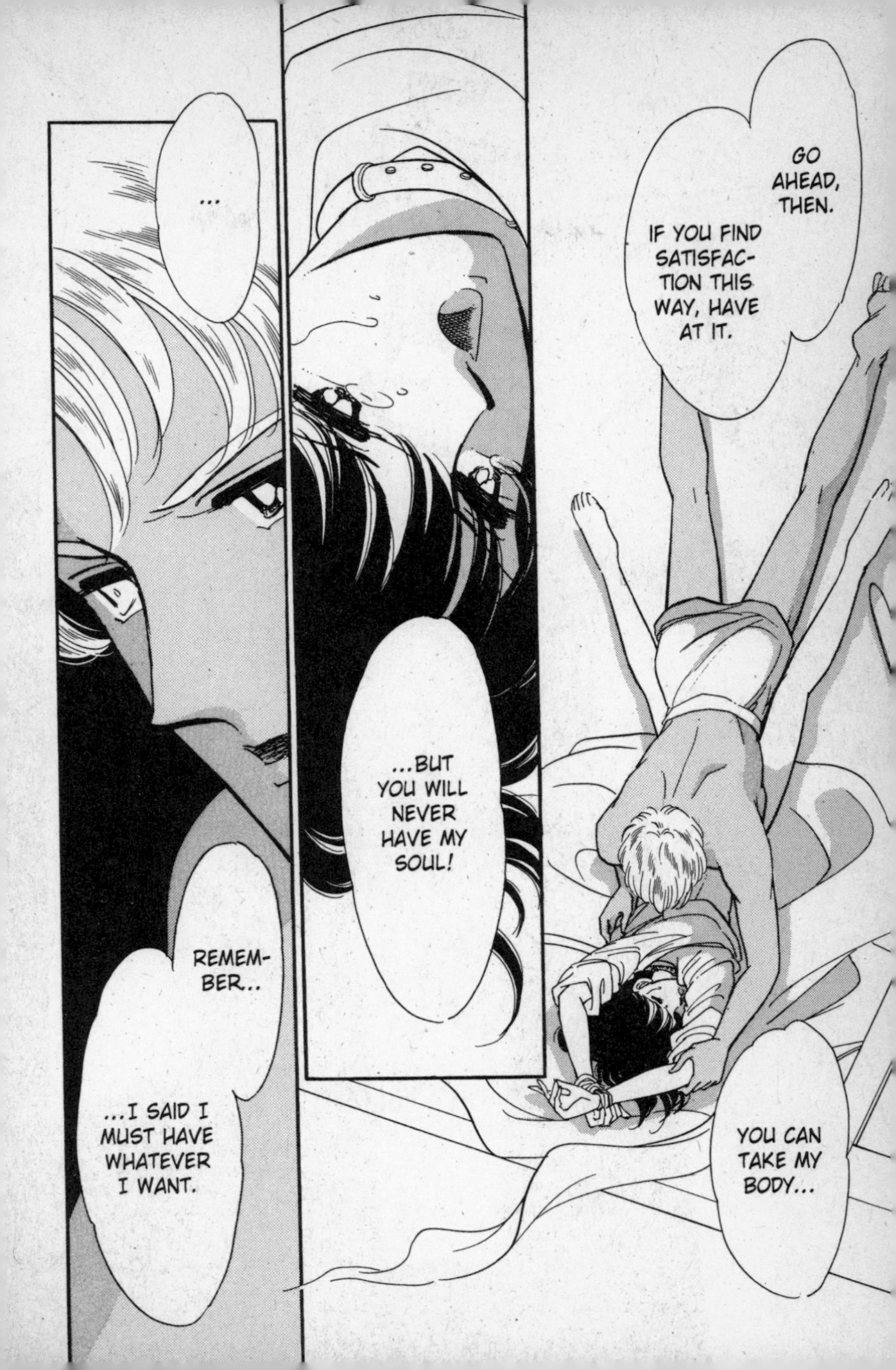
GO AHEAD, THEN.
IF YOU FIND SATISFACTION THIS WAY, HAVE AT IT.
YOU CAN TAKE MY BODY...
...BUT YOU WILL NEVER HAVE MY SOUL!
...
REMEMBER...
...I SAID I MUST HAVE WHATEVER I WANT.

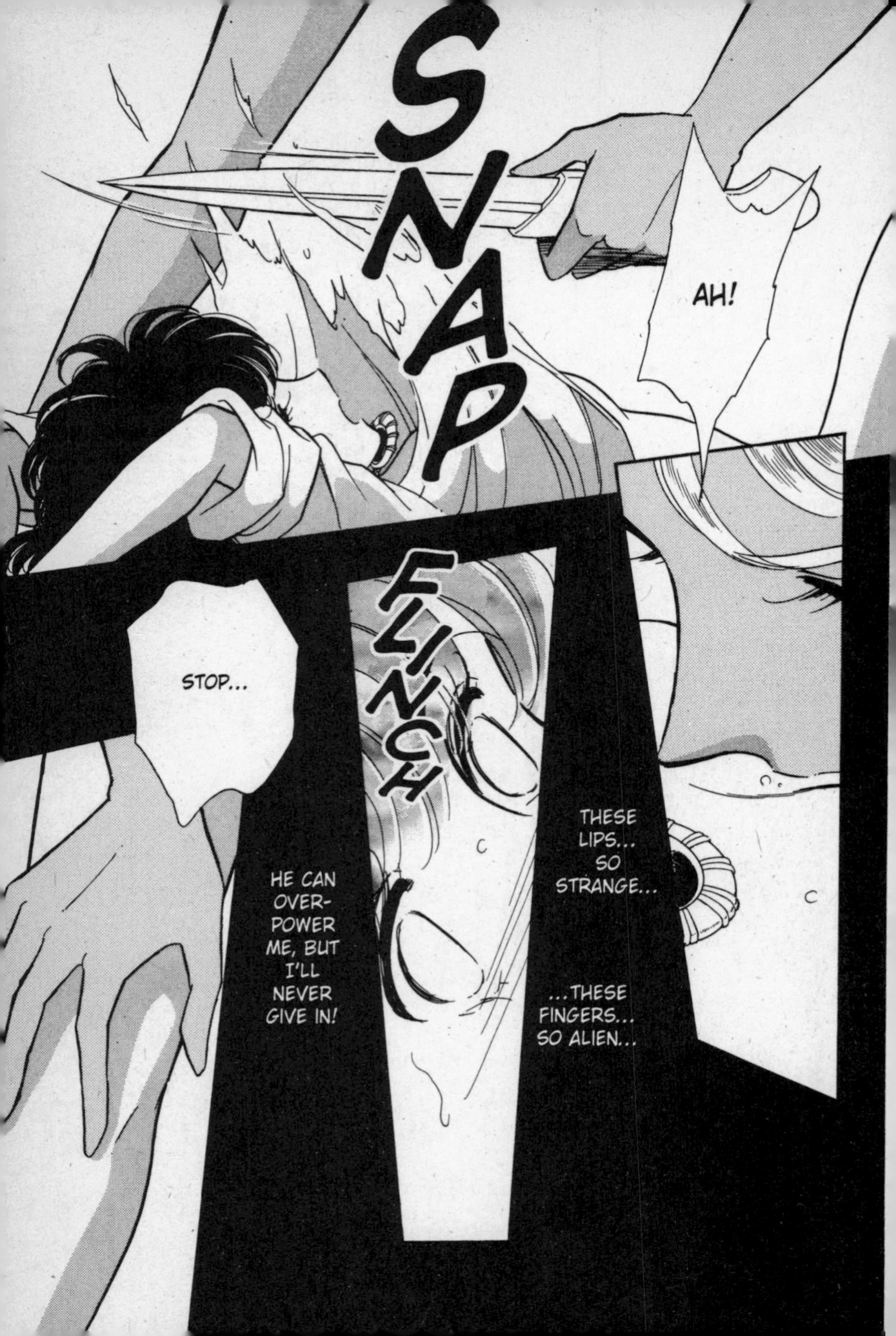
SNAP
AH!
THESE LIPS... SO STRANGE...
...THESE FINGERS... SO ALIEN...
FLINCH
HE CAN OVER-POWER ME, BUT I'LL NEVER GIVE IN!
STOP...

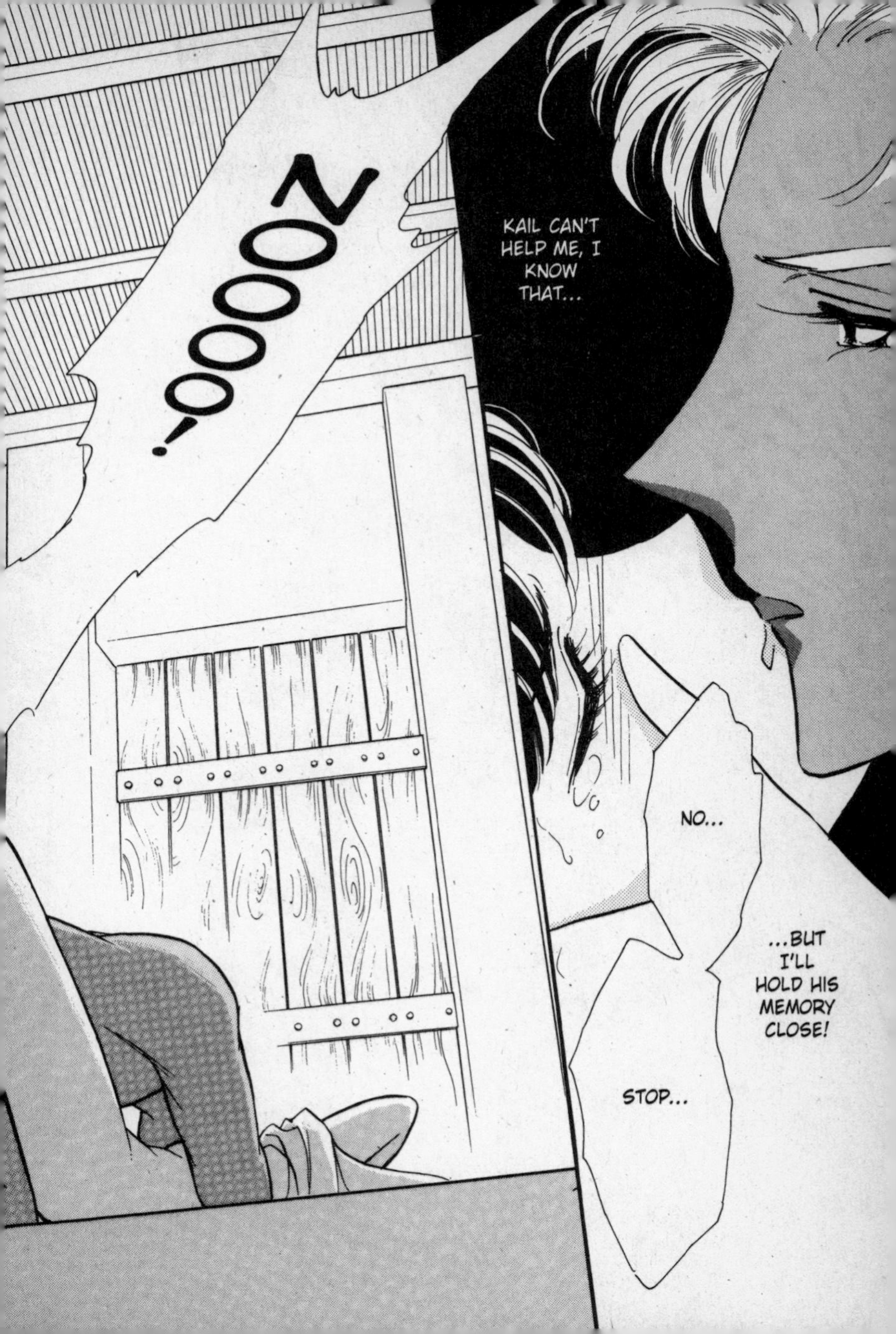
KAIL CAN'T HELP ME, I KNOW THAT...
...BUT I'LL HOLD HIS MEMORY CLOSE!
NO...
STOP...
NOOOO!

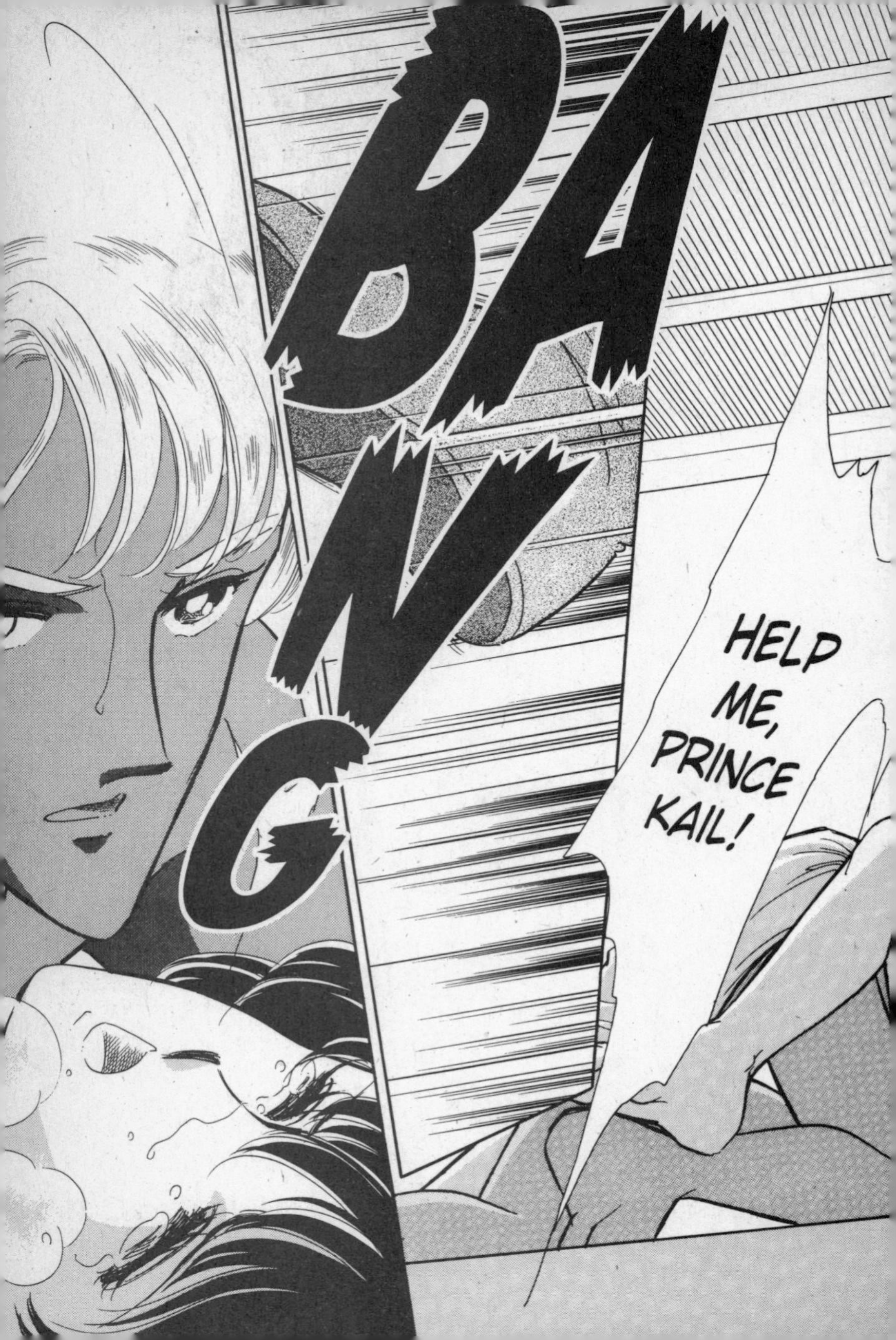
BANG
HELP ME, PRINCE KAIL!

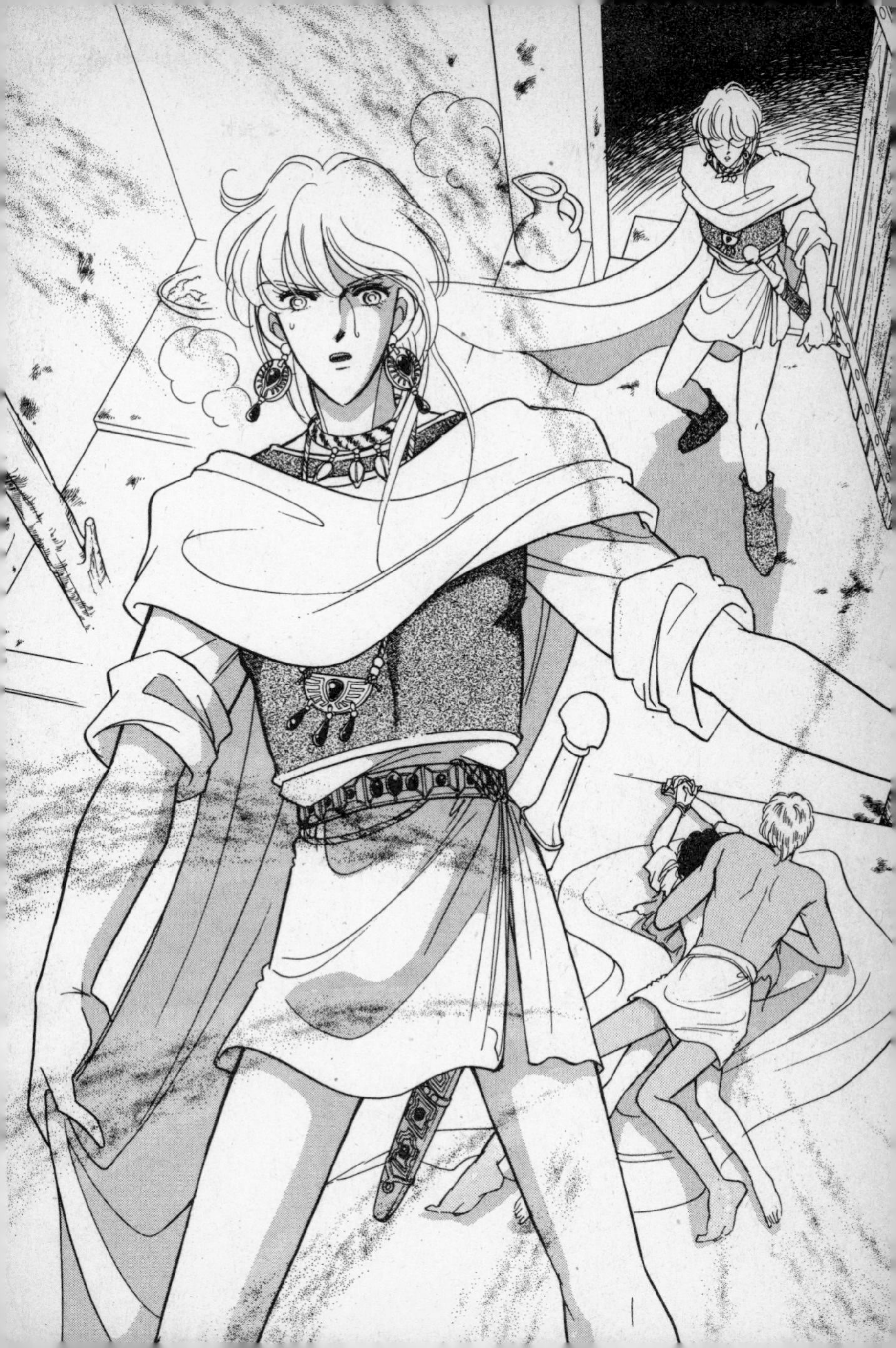

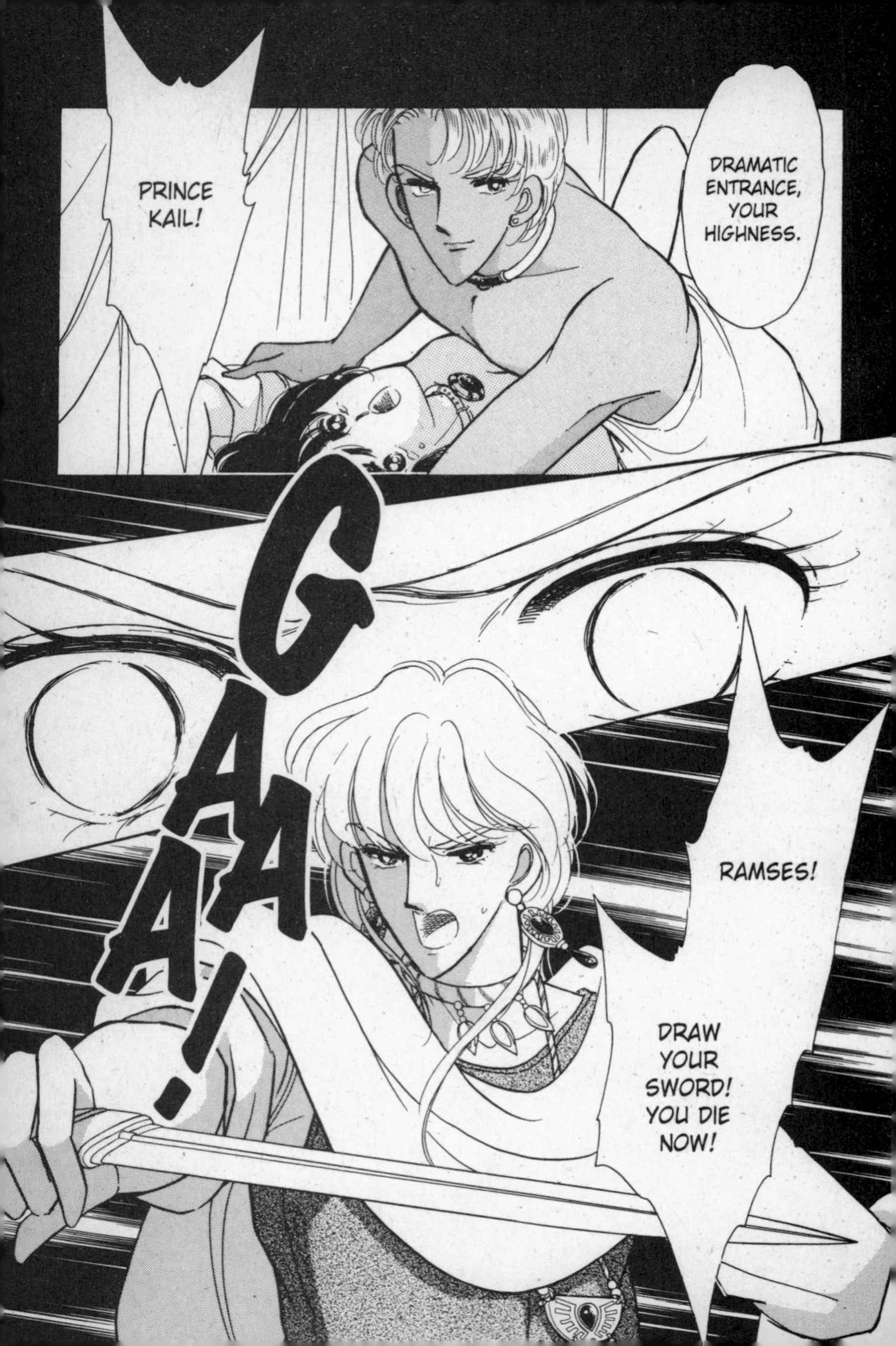
DRAMATIC ENTRANCE, YOUR HIGHNESS.
PRINCE KAIL!
RAMSES!
DRAW YOUR SWORD! YOU DIE NOW!
GAAA!

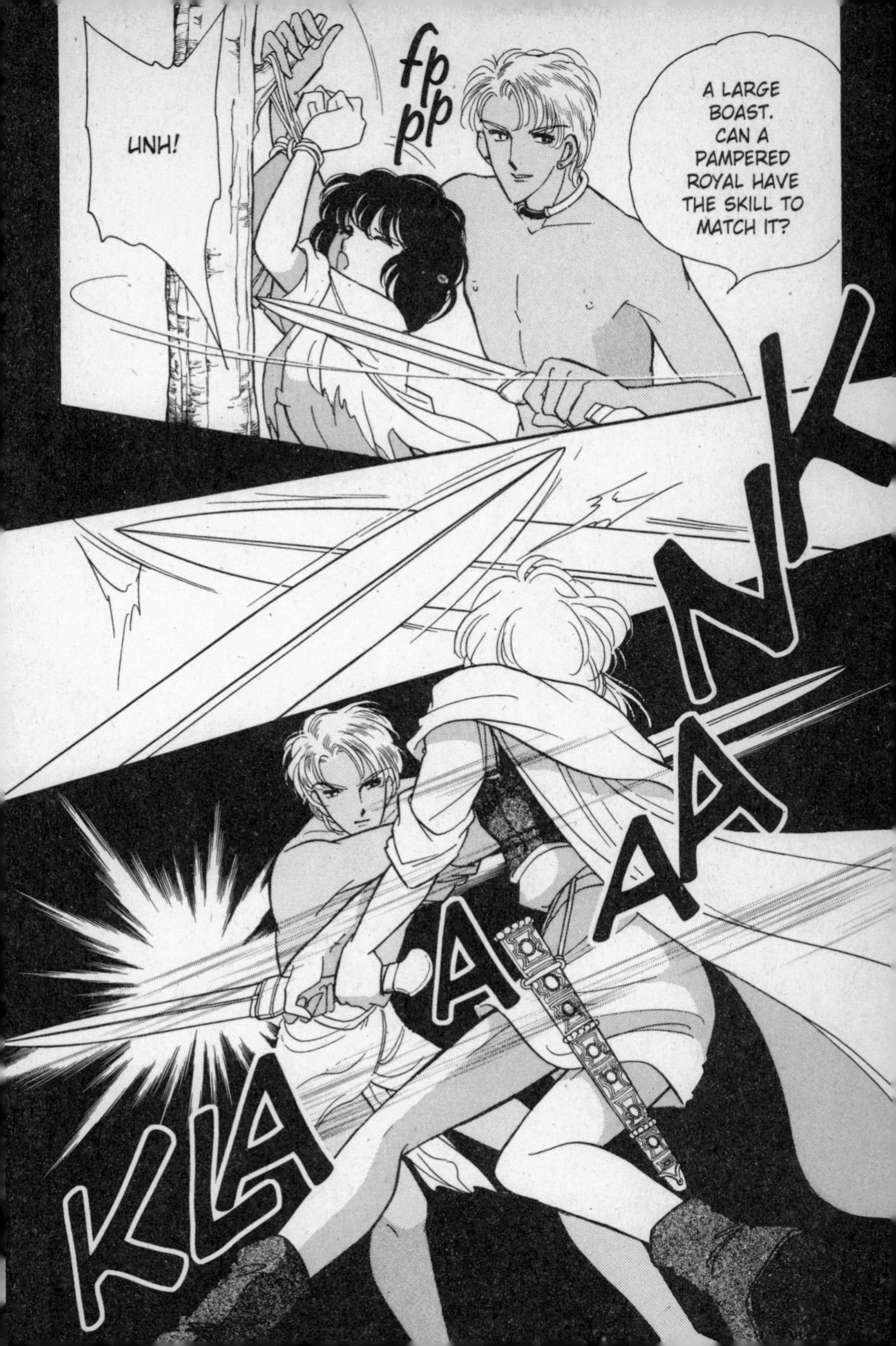
A LARGE BOAST. CAN A PAMPERED ROYAL HAVE THE SKILL TO MATCH IT?
fppp
UNH!
KLAAAANK

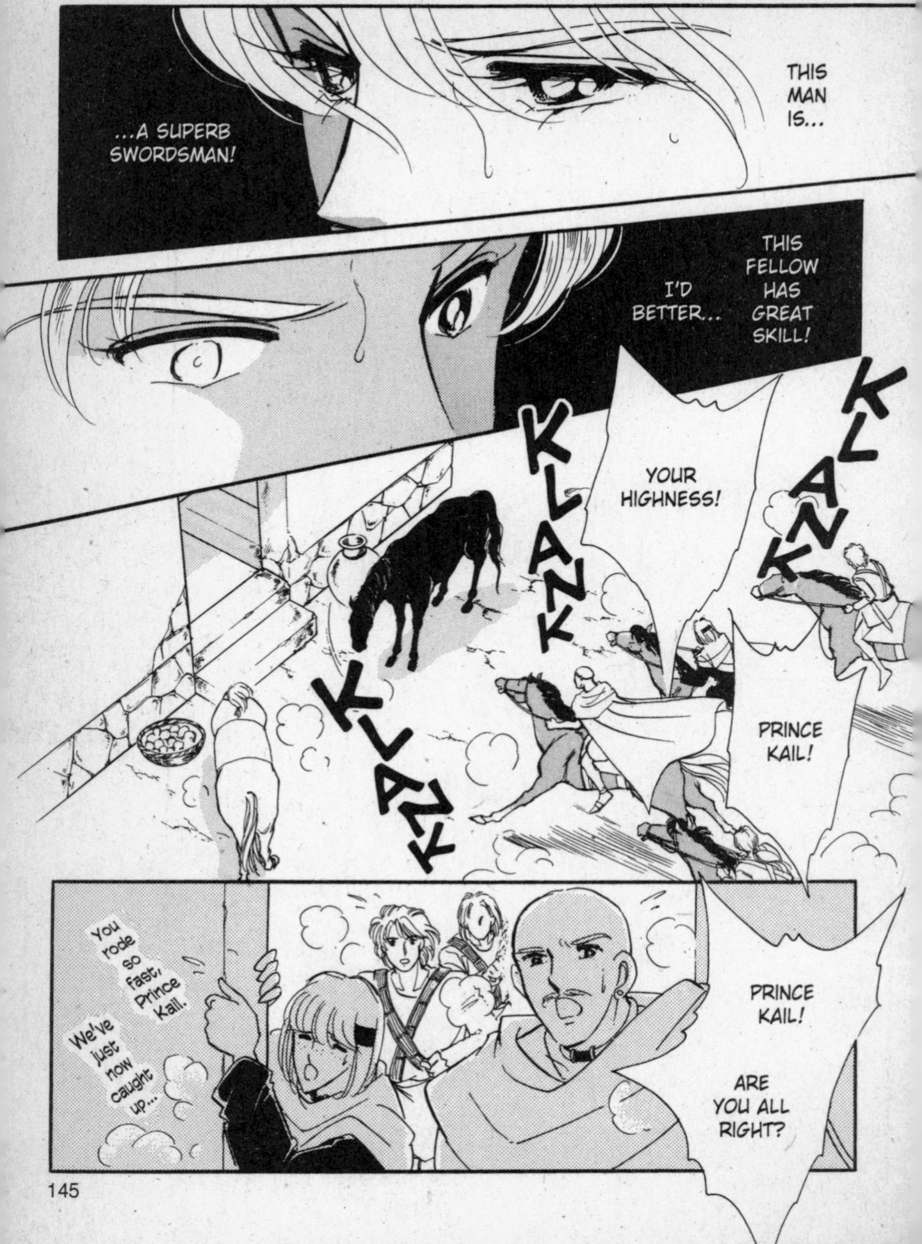
THIS MAN IS...
...A SUPERB SWORDSMAN!
THIS FELLOW HAS GREAT SKILL!
I'D BETTER...
KLANK
YOUR HIGHNESS!
PRINCE KAIL!
KLANK
KLANK
PRINCE KAIL!
ARE YOU ALL RIGHT?
You rode so fast, Prince Kail.
We've just now caught up...

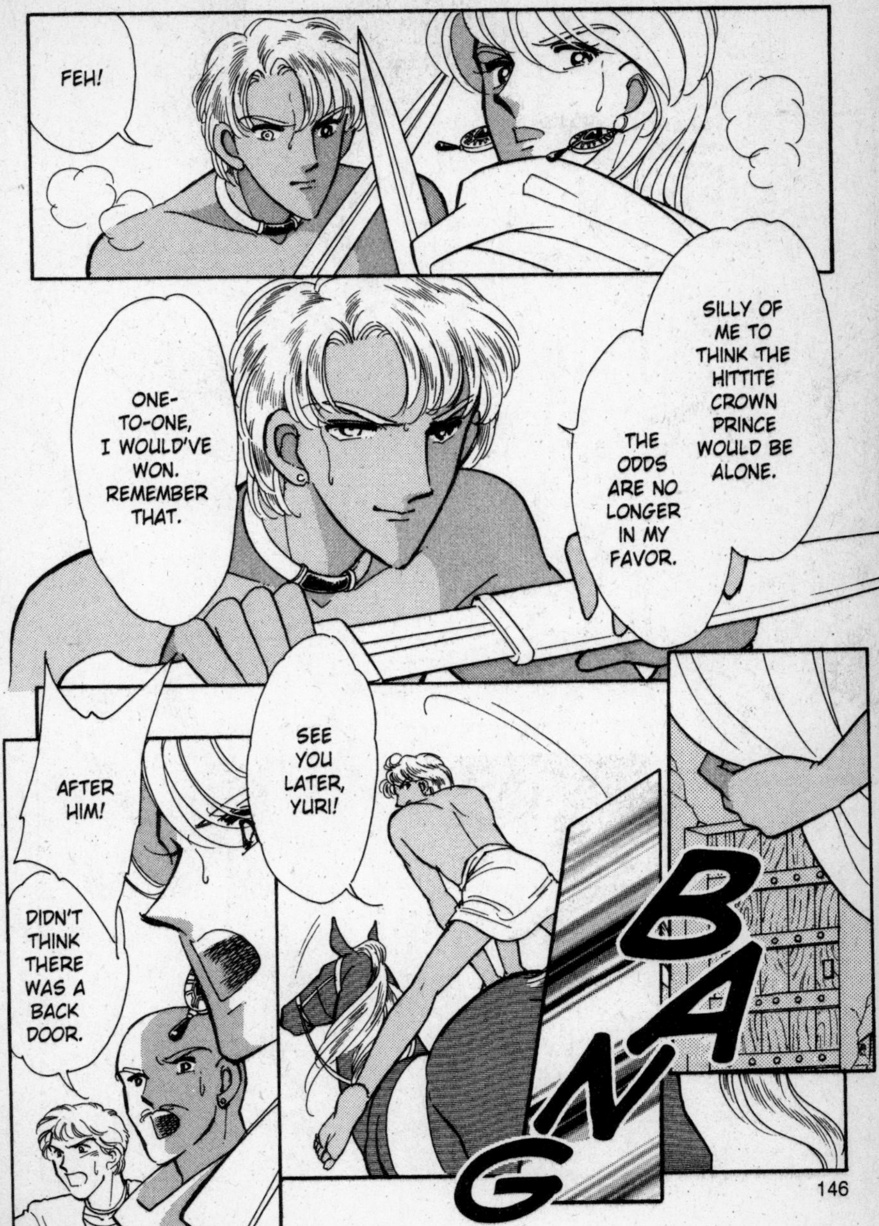
FEH!
SILLY OF ME TO THINK THE HITTITE CROWN PRINCE WOULD BE ALONE.
THE ODDS ARE NO LONGER IN MY FAVOR.
ONE-TO-ONE, I WOULD'VE WON. REMEMBER THAT.
BANG
SEE YOU LATER, YURI!
AFTER HIM!
DIDN'T THINK THERE WAS A BACK DOOR.

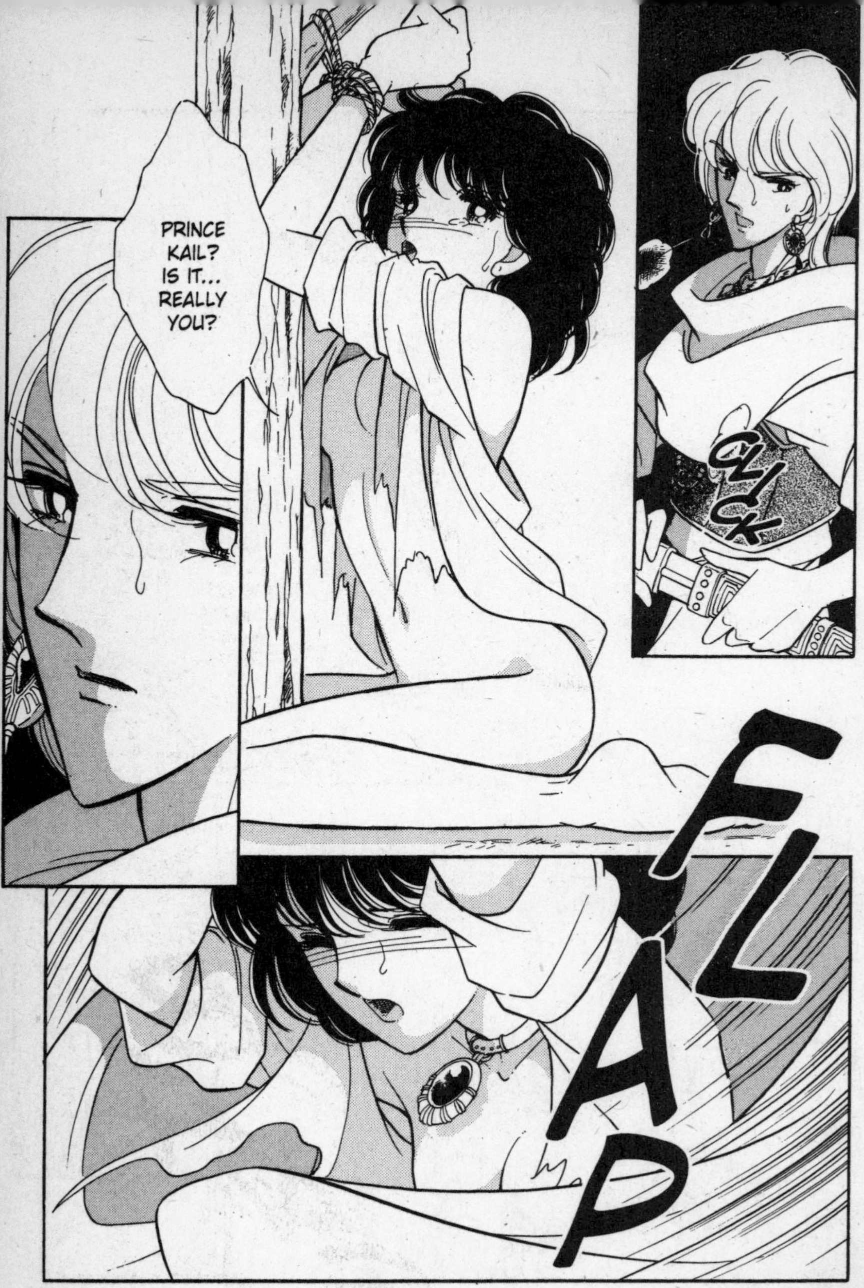
CLICK
PRINCE KAIL? IS IT... REALLY YOU?
FLAP

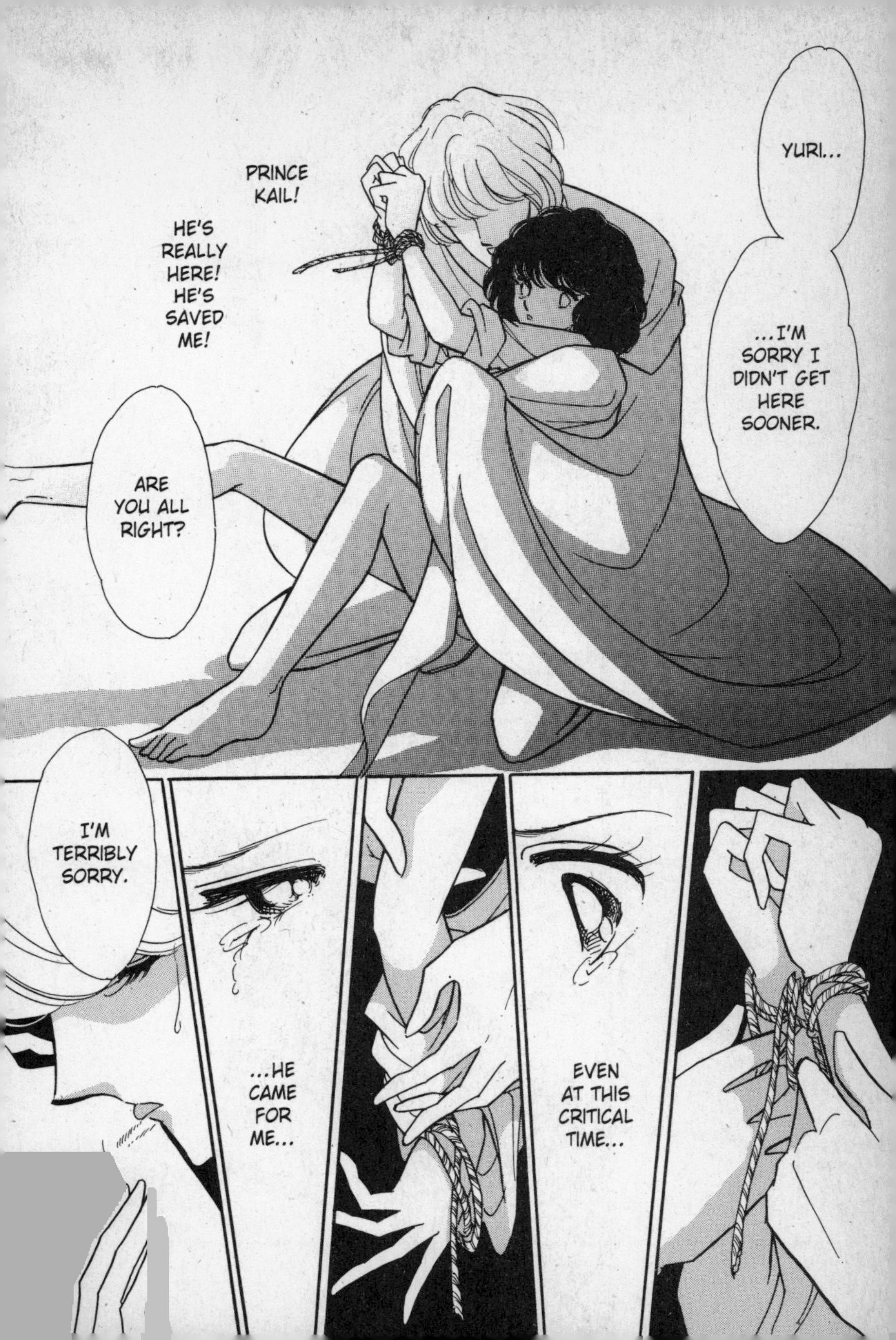
YURI...
...I'M SORRY I DIDN'T GET HERE SOONER.
PRINCE KAIL!
HE'S REALLY HERE! HE'S SAVED ME!
ARE YOU ALL RIGHT?
EVEN AT THIS CRITICAL TIME...
...HE CAME FOR ME...
I'M TERRIBLY SORRY.

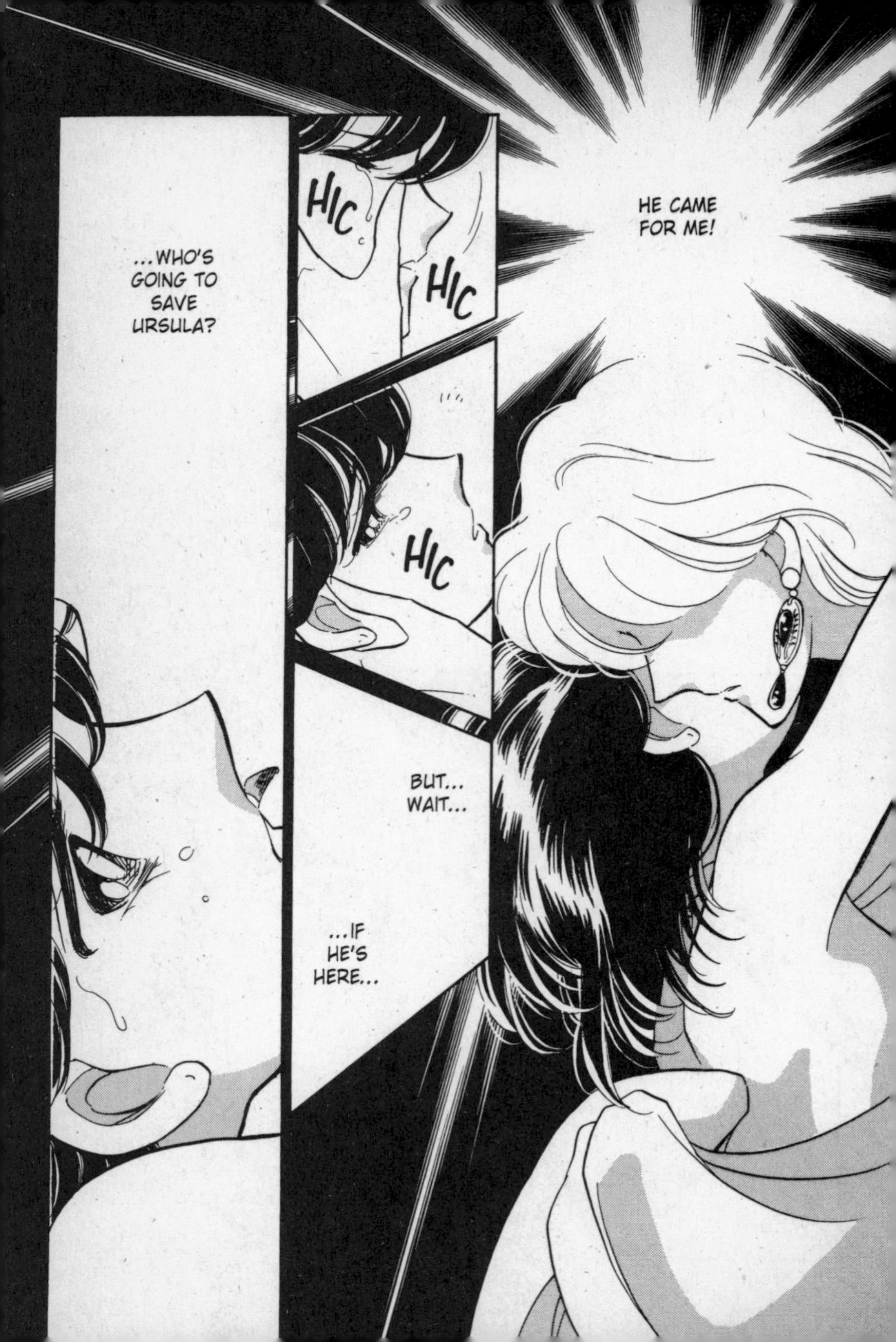
HE CAME FOR ME!
HIC
HIC
HIC
BUT... WAIT...
...IF HE'S HERE...
...WHO'S GOING TO SAVE URSULA?

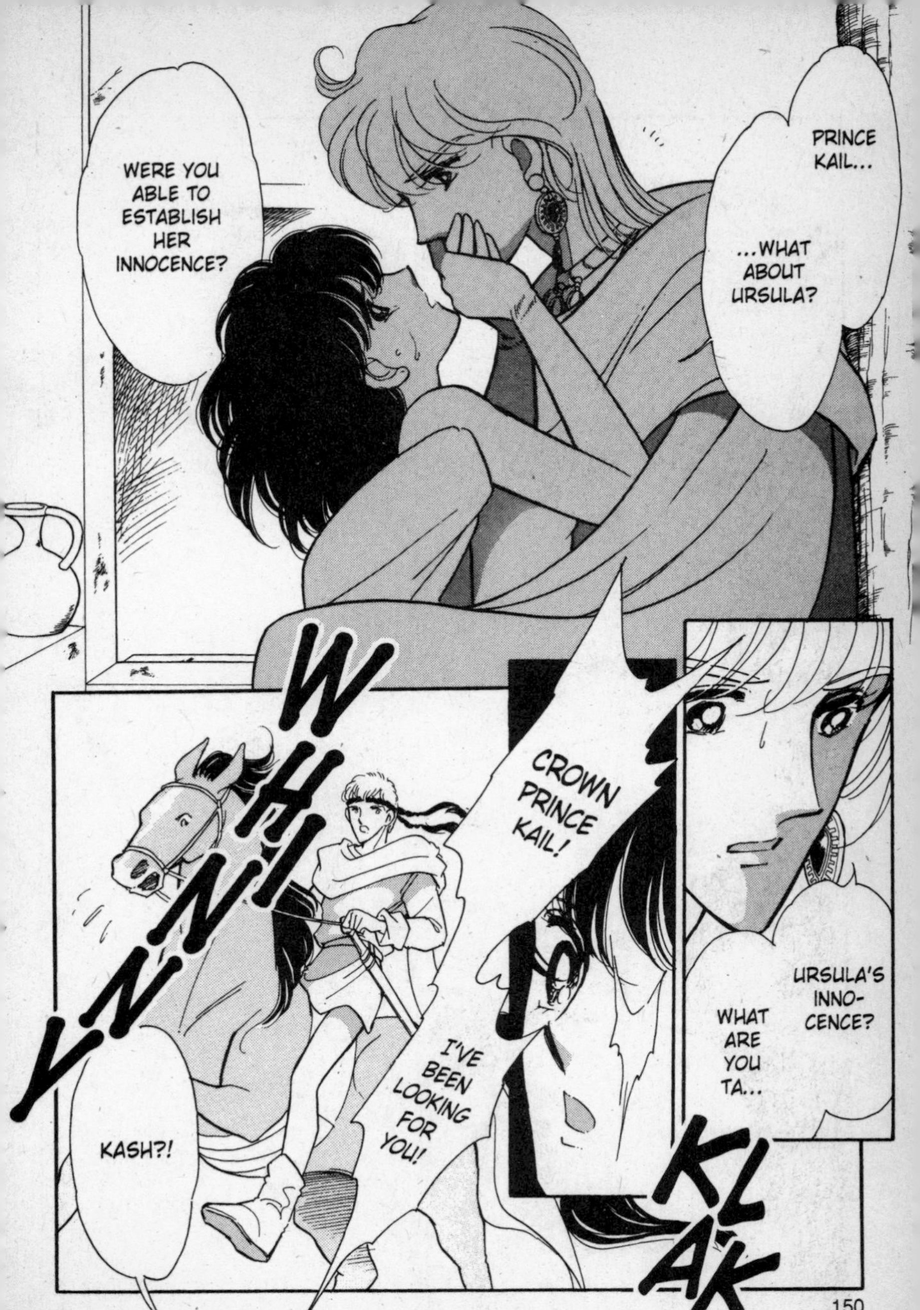
PRINCE KAIL...
...WHAT ABOUT URSULA?
WERE YOU ABLE TO ESTABLISH HER INNOCENCE?
URSULA'S INNO-CENCE?
WHAT ARE YOU TA...
KLAK
CROWN PRINCE KAIL!
I'VE BEEN LOOKING FOR YOU!
WHINNY
KASH?!

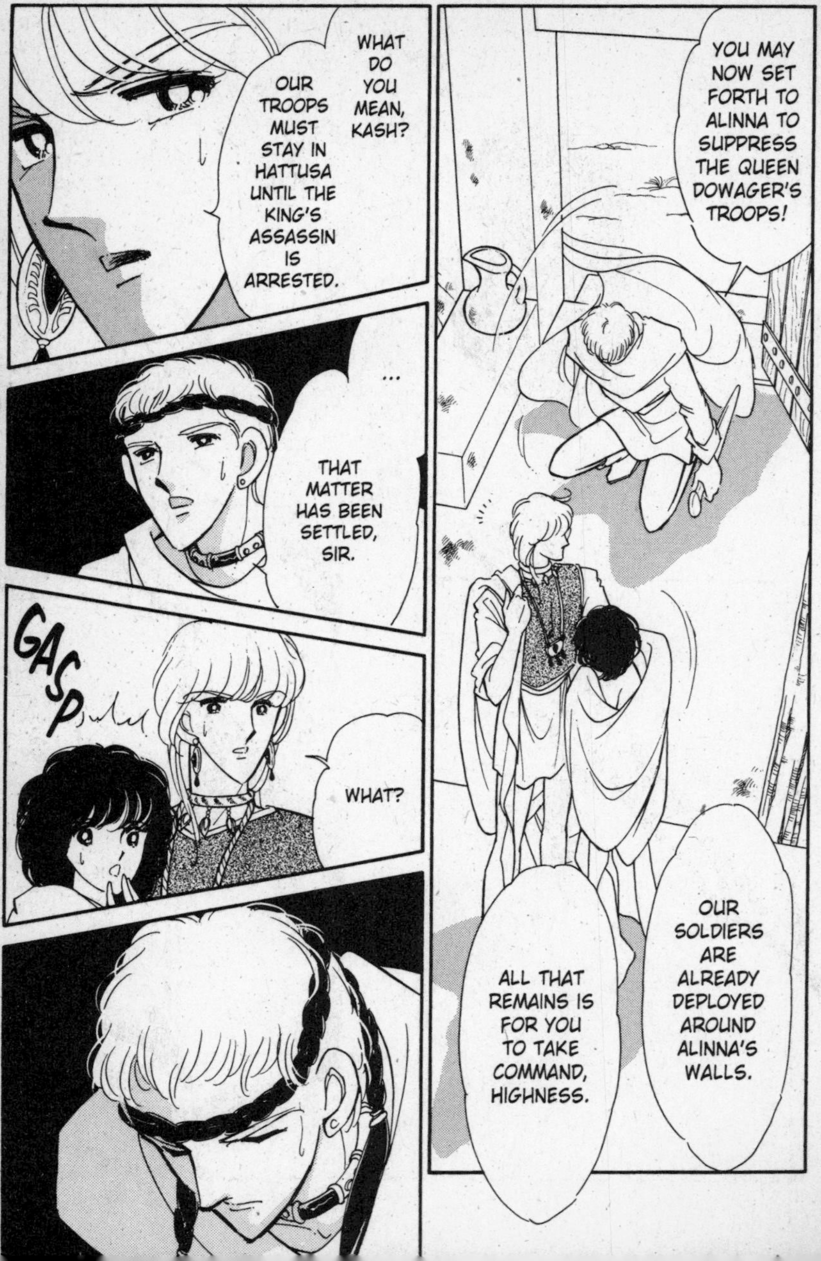
YOU MAY NOW SET FORTH TO ALINNA TO SUPPRESS THE QUEEN DOWAGER'S TROOPS!
OUR SOLDIERS ARE ALREADY DEPLOYED AROUND ALINNA'S WALLS.
ALL THAT REMAINS IS FOR YOU TO TAKE COMMAND, HIGHNESS.
WHAT DO YOU MEAN, KASH?
OUR TROOPS MUST STAY IN HATTUSA UNTIL THE KING'S ASSASSIN IS ARRESTED.
...
THAT MATTER HAS BEEN SETTLED, SIR.
WHAT?
GASP

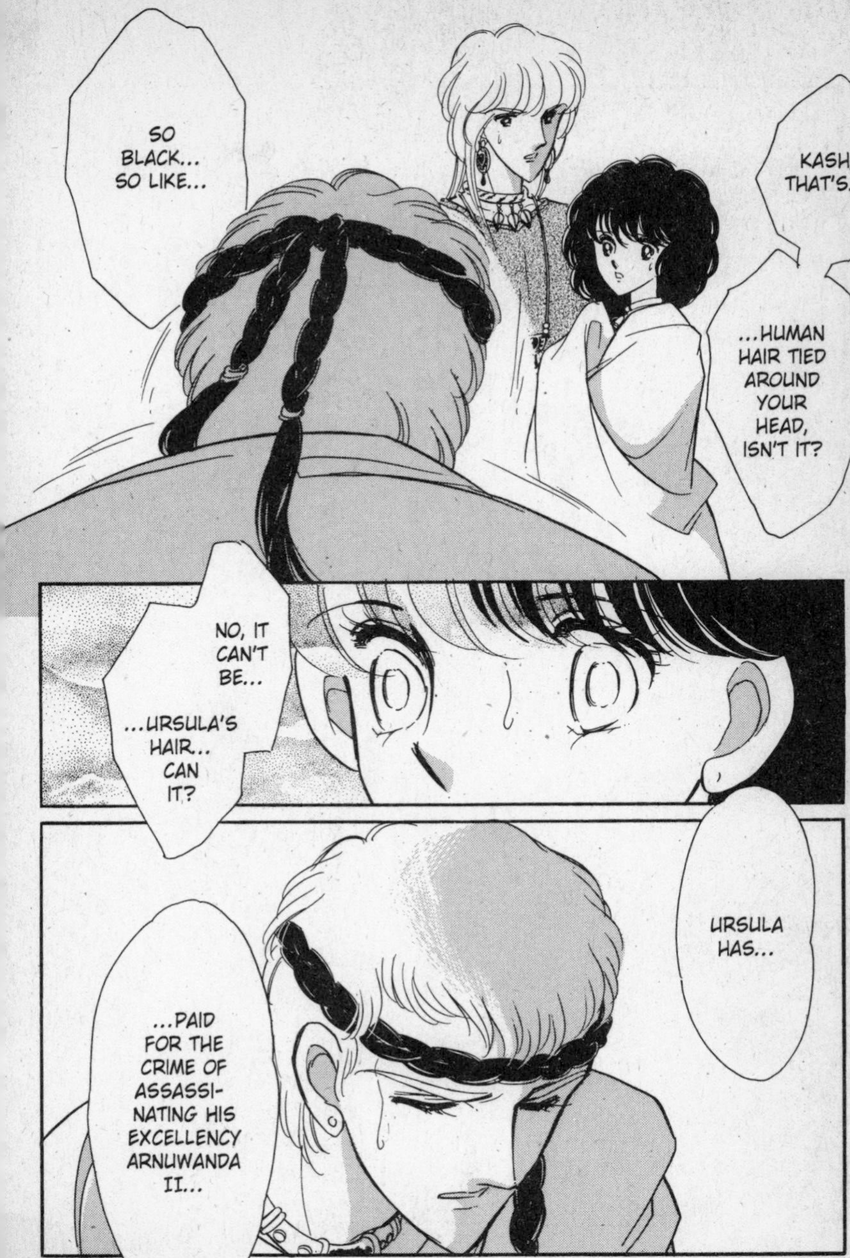
KASH, THAT'S...
...HUMAN HAIR TIED AROUND YOUR HEAD, ISN'T IT?
SO BLACK... SO LIKE...
NO, IT CAN'T BE...
...URSULA'S HAIR... CAN IT?
URSULA HAS...
...PAID FOR THE CRIME OF ASSASSI-NATING HIS EXCELLENCY ARNUWANDA II...

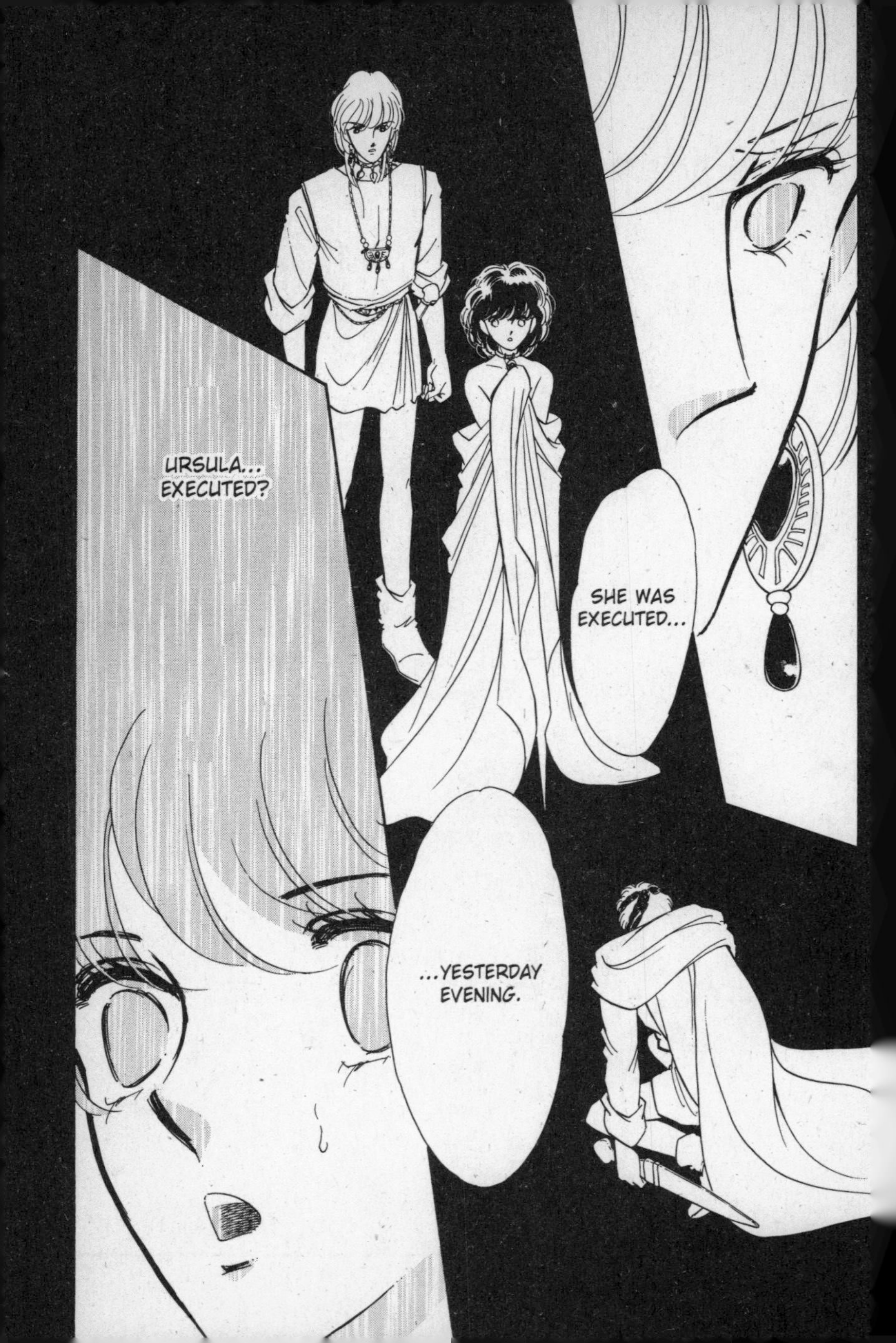
SHE WAS EXECUTED...
...YESTERDAY EVENING.
URSULA... EXECUTED?

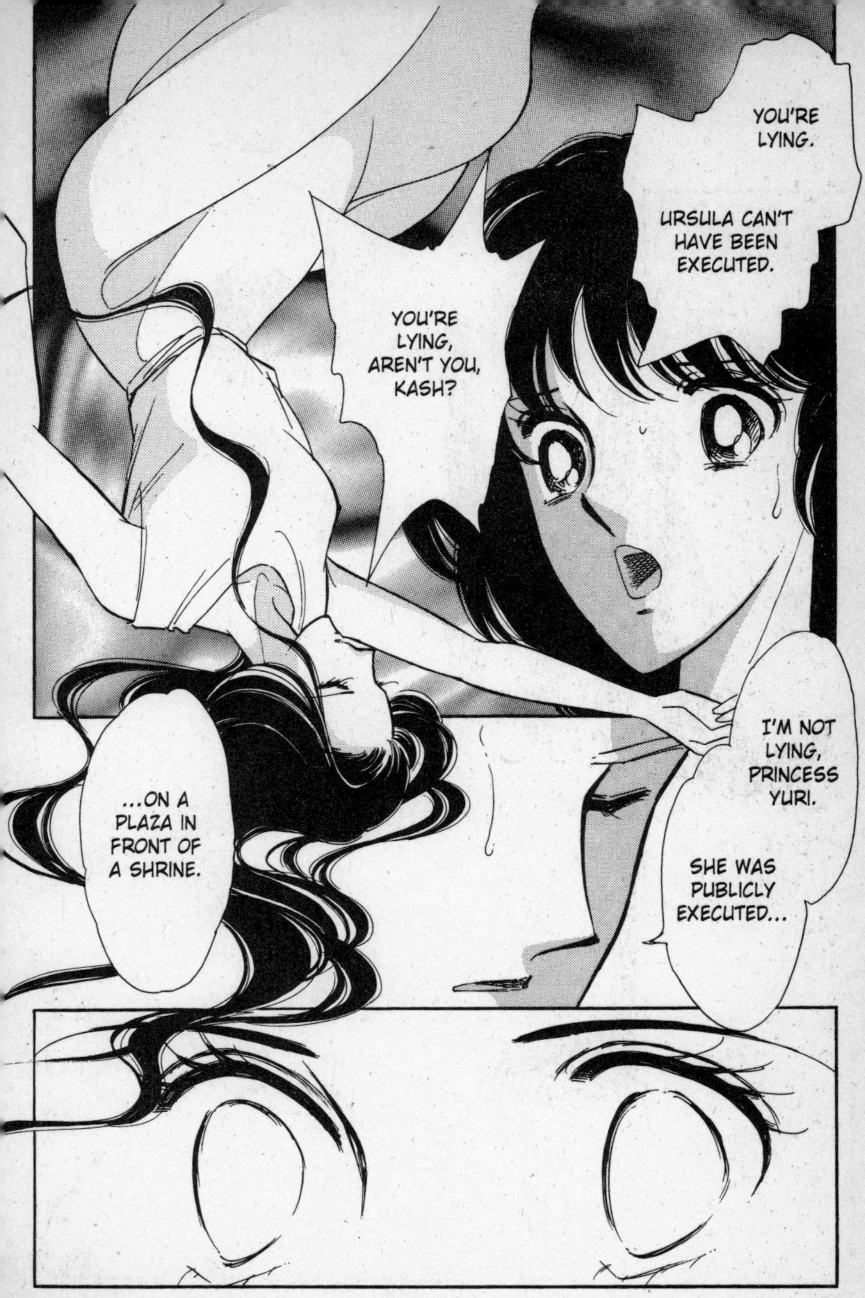
YOU'RE LYING.
URSULA CAN'T HAVE BEEN EXECUTED.
YOU'RE LYING, AREN'T YOU, KASH?
I'M NOT LYING, PRINCESS YURI.
SHE WAS PUBLICLY EXECUTED...
...ON A PLAZA IN FRONT OF A SHRINE.

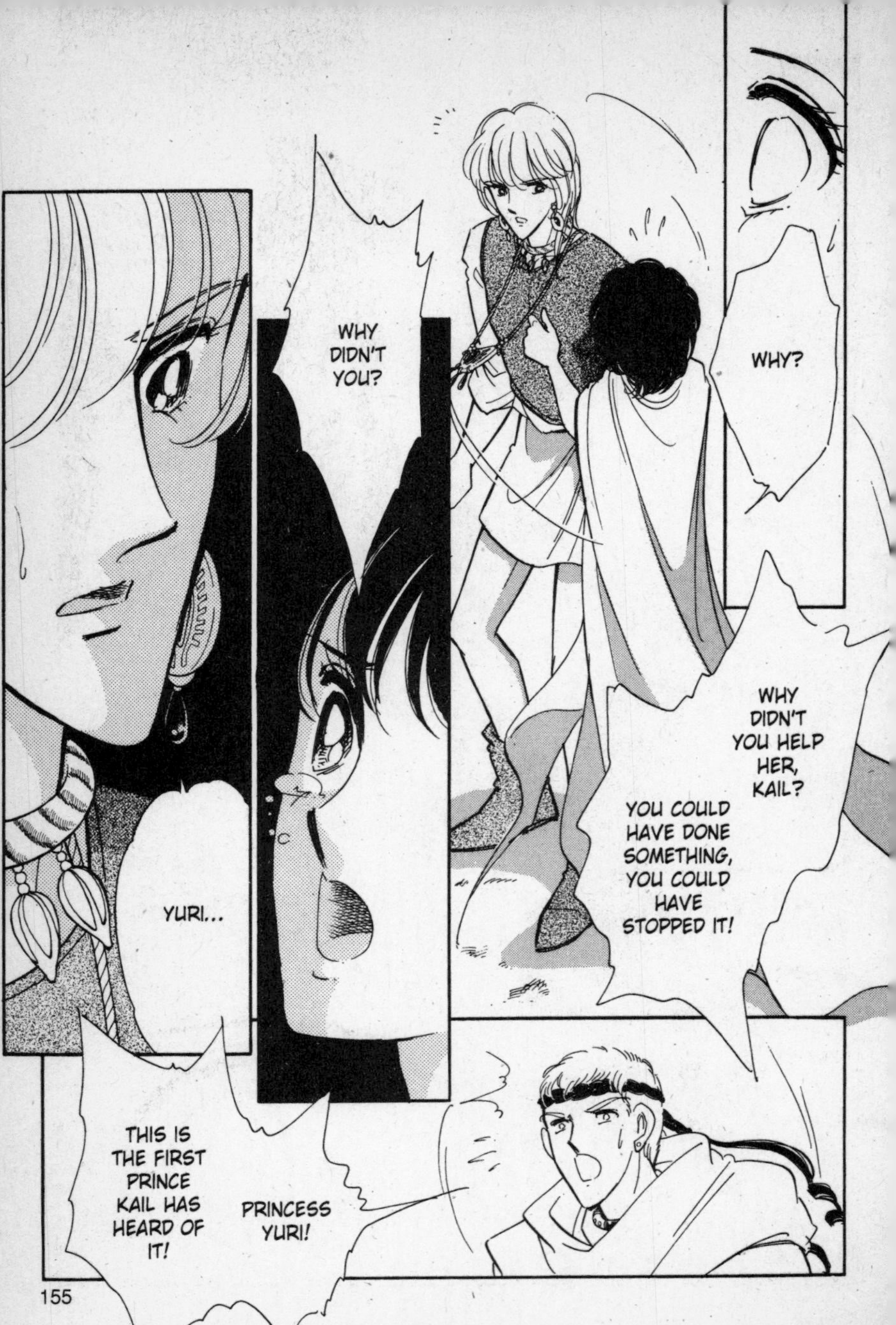
WHY?
WHY DIDN'T YOU HELP HER, KAIL?
YOU COULD HAVE DONE SOMETHING, YOU COULD HAVE STOPPED IT!
WHY DIDN'T YOU?
YURI...
PRINCESS YURI!
THIS IS THE FIRST PRINCE KAIL HAS HEARD OF IT!

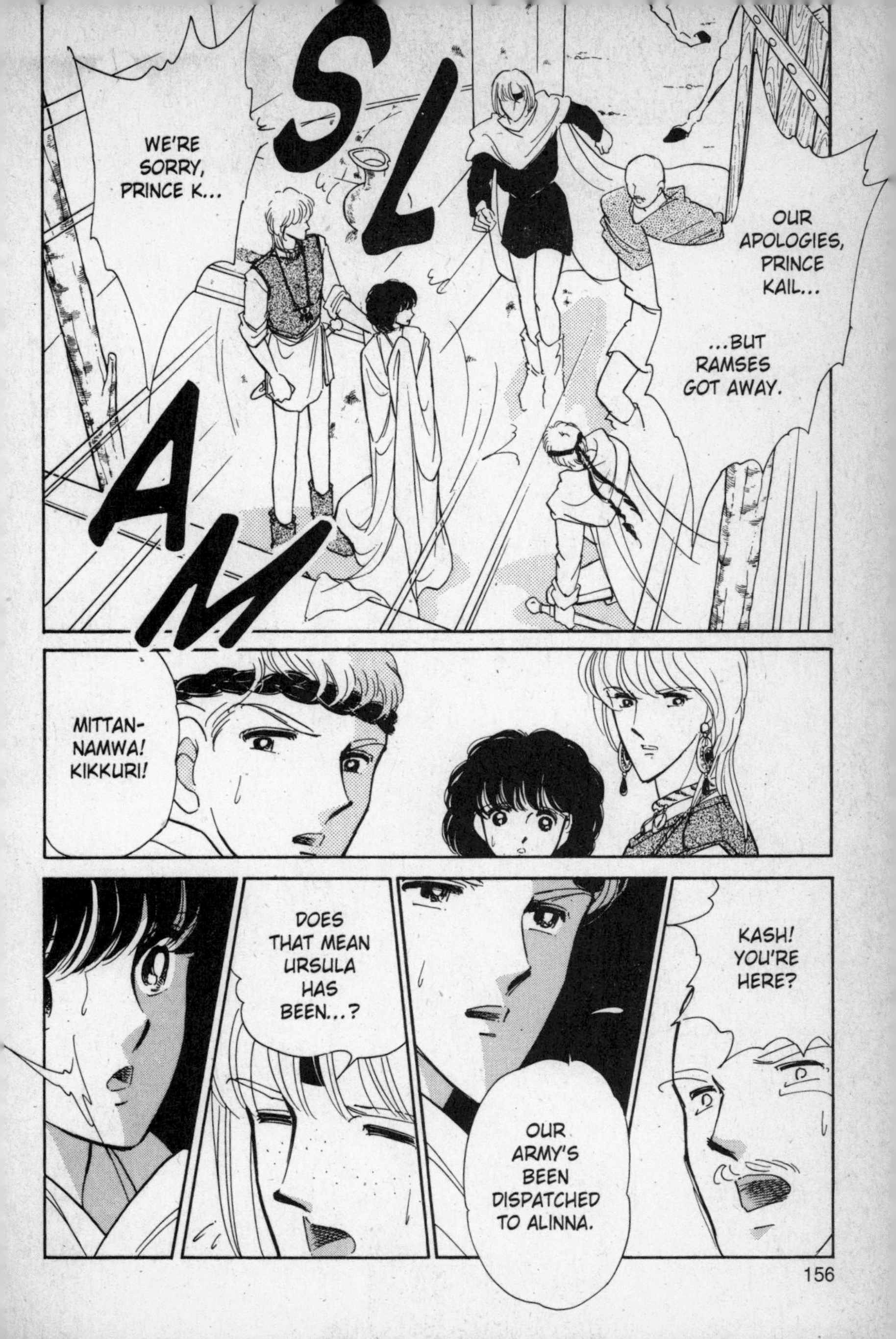
SLAM
OUR APOLOGIES, PRINCE KAIL...
...BUT RAMSES GOT AWAY.
WE'RE SORRY, PRINCE K...
MITTANNAMWA! KIKKURI!
KASH! YOU'RE HERE?
OUR ARMY'S BEEN DISPATCHED TO ALINNA.
DOES THAT MEAN URSULA HAS BEEN...?

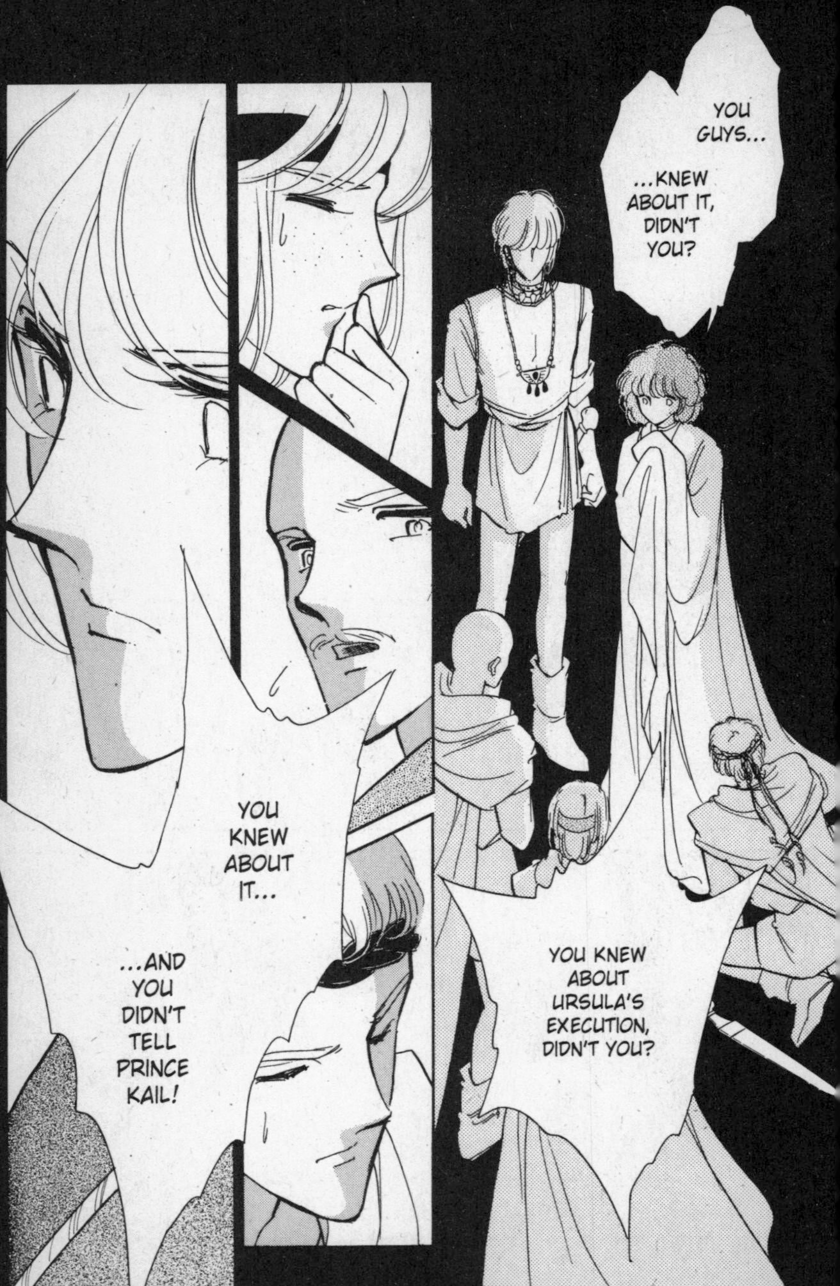
YOU GUYS...
...KNEW ABOUT IT, DIDN'T YOU?
YOU KNEW ABOUT URSULA'S EXECUTION, DIDN'T YOU?
YOU KNEW ABOUT IT...
...AND YOU DIDN'T TELL PRINCE KAIL!

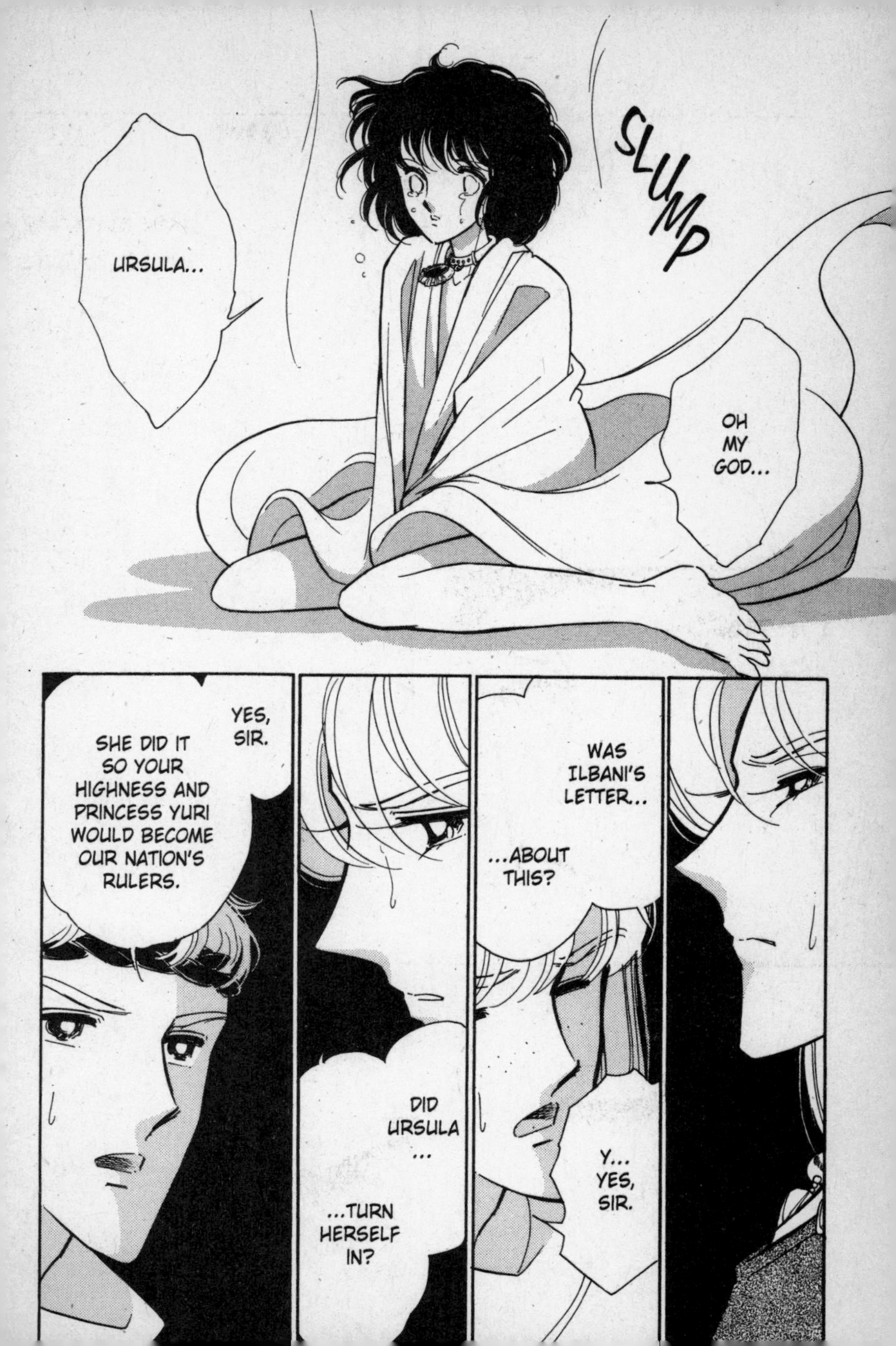
SLUMP
OH MY GOD...
URSULA...
WAS ILBANI'S LETTER...
...ABOUT THIS?
Y... YES, SIR.
DID URSULA ...
...TURN HERSELF IN?
YES, SIR.
SHE DID IT SO YOUR HIGHNESS AND PRINCESS YURI WOULD BECOME OUR NATION'S RULERS.

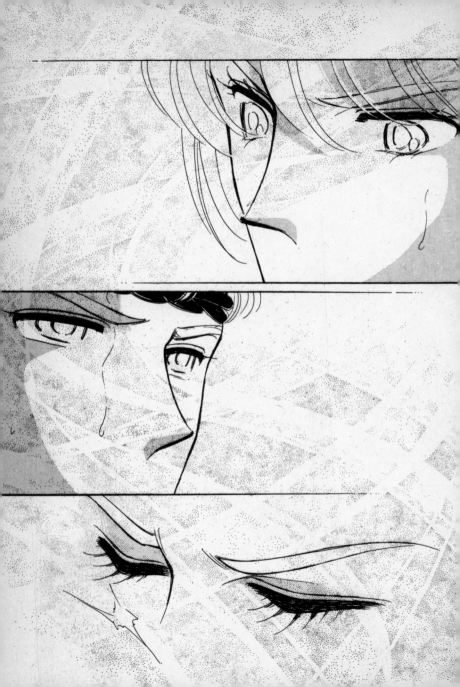

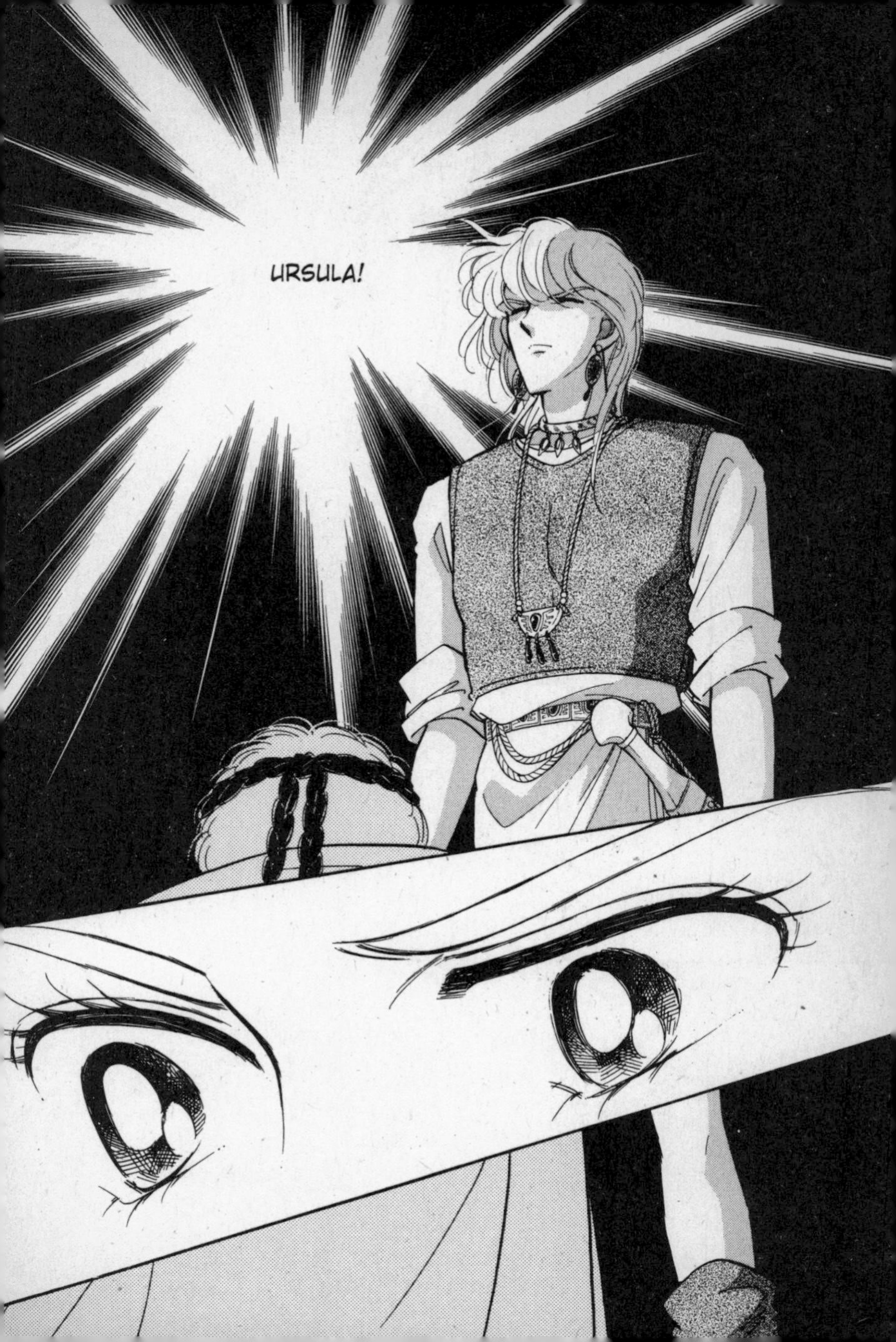
URSULA!

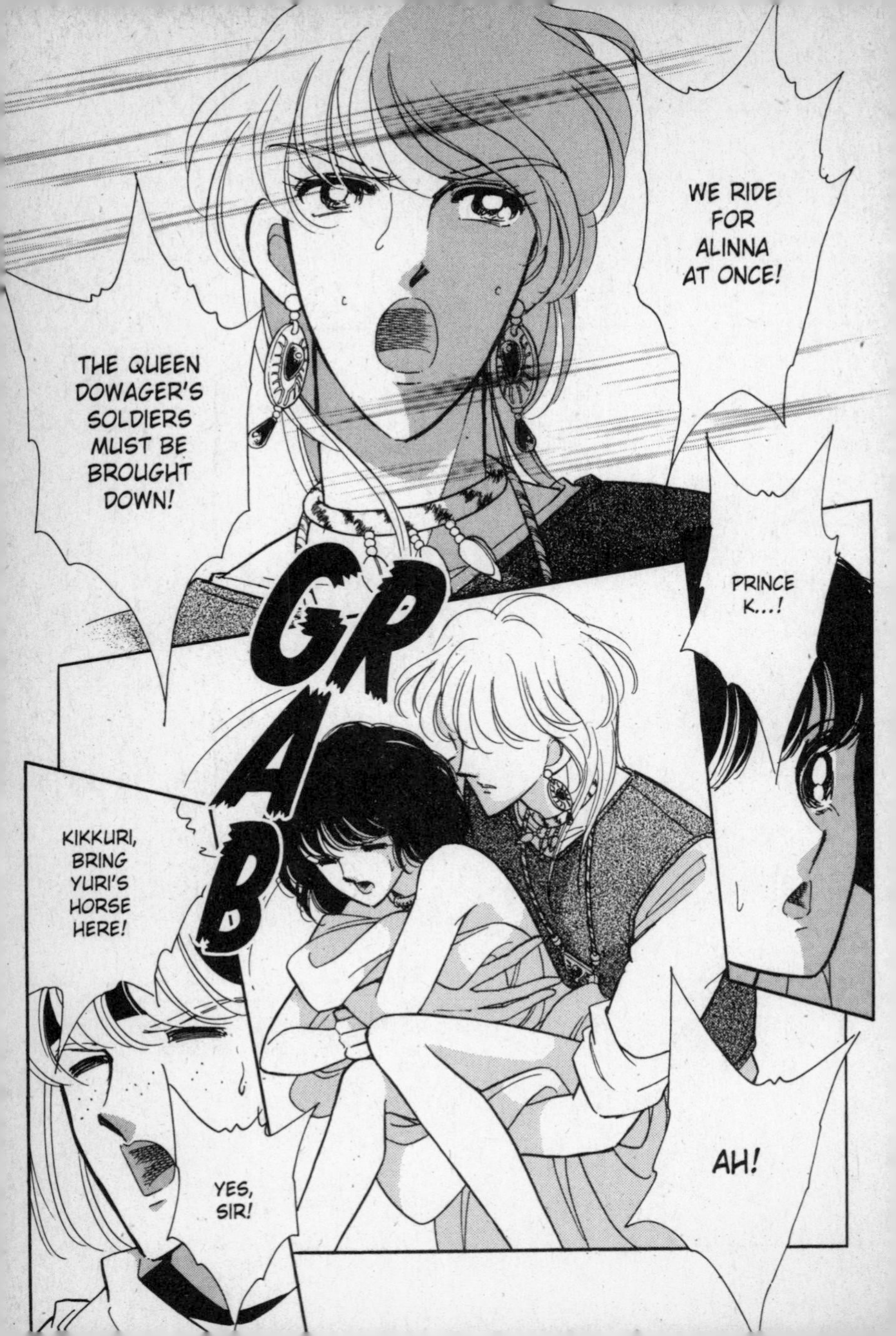
WE RIDE FOR ALINNA AT ONCE!
THE QUEEN DOWAGER'S SOLDIERS MUST BE BROUGHT DOWN!
PRINCE K...!
GRAB
AH!
KIKKURI, BRING YURI'S HORSE HERE!
YES, SIR!

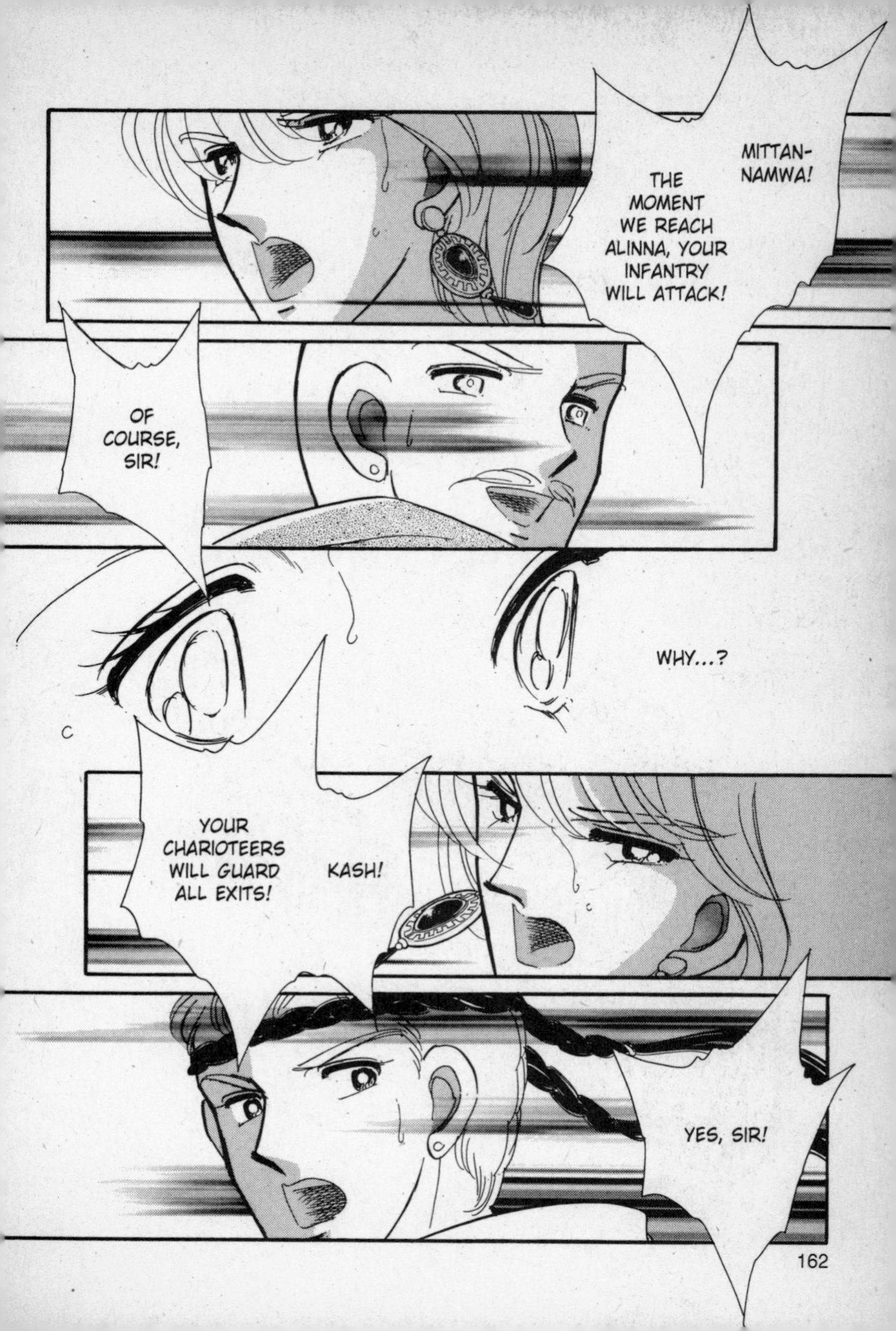
MITTAN-NAMWA!
THE MOMENT WE REACH ALINNA, YOUR INFANTRY WILL ATTACK!
OF COURSE, SIR!
WHY...?
KASH!
YOUR CHARIOTEERS WILL GUARD ALL EXITS!
YES, SIR!

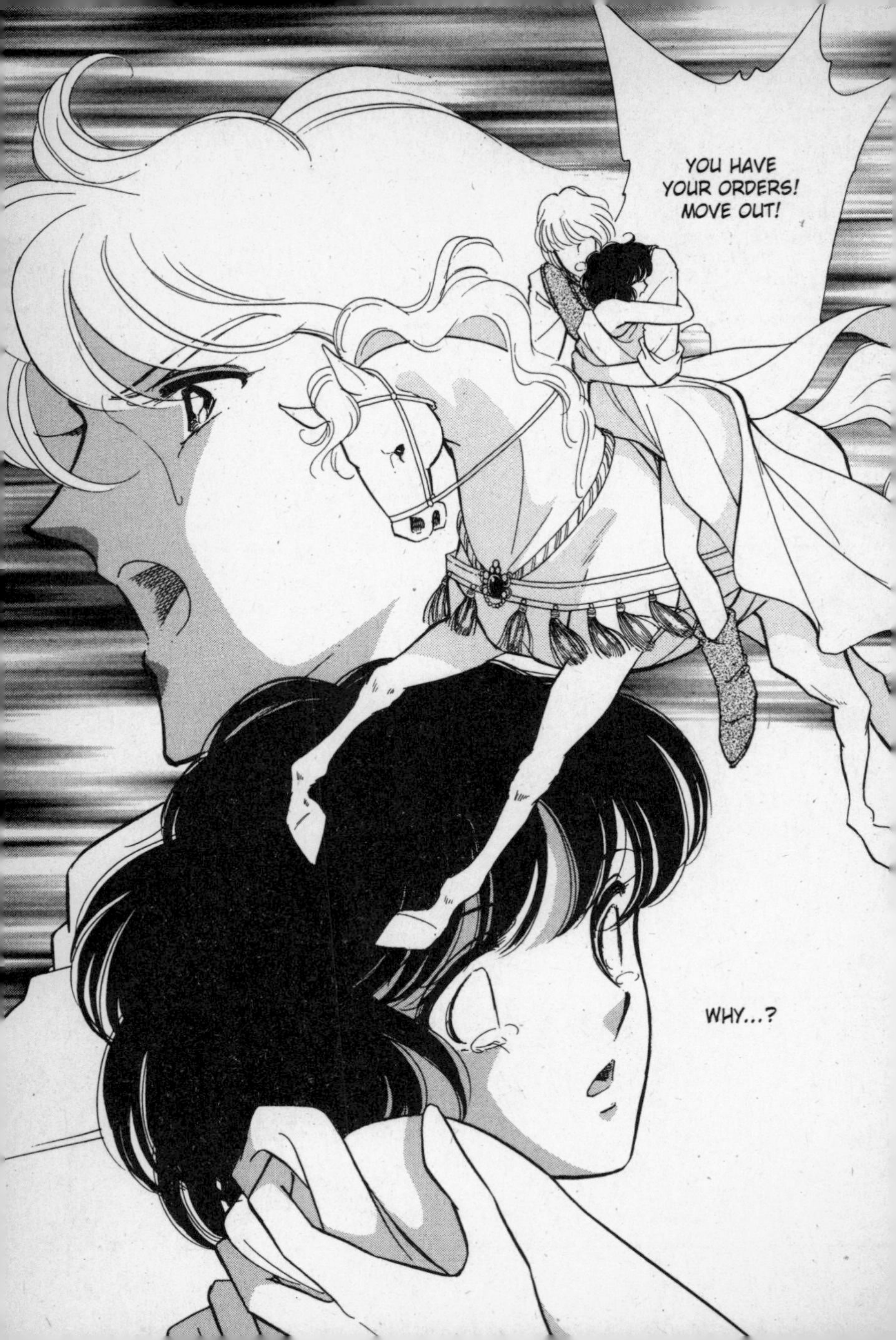
YOU HAVE YOUR ORDERS! MOVE OUT!
WHY...?

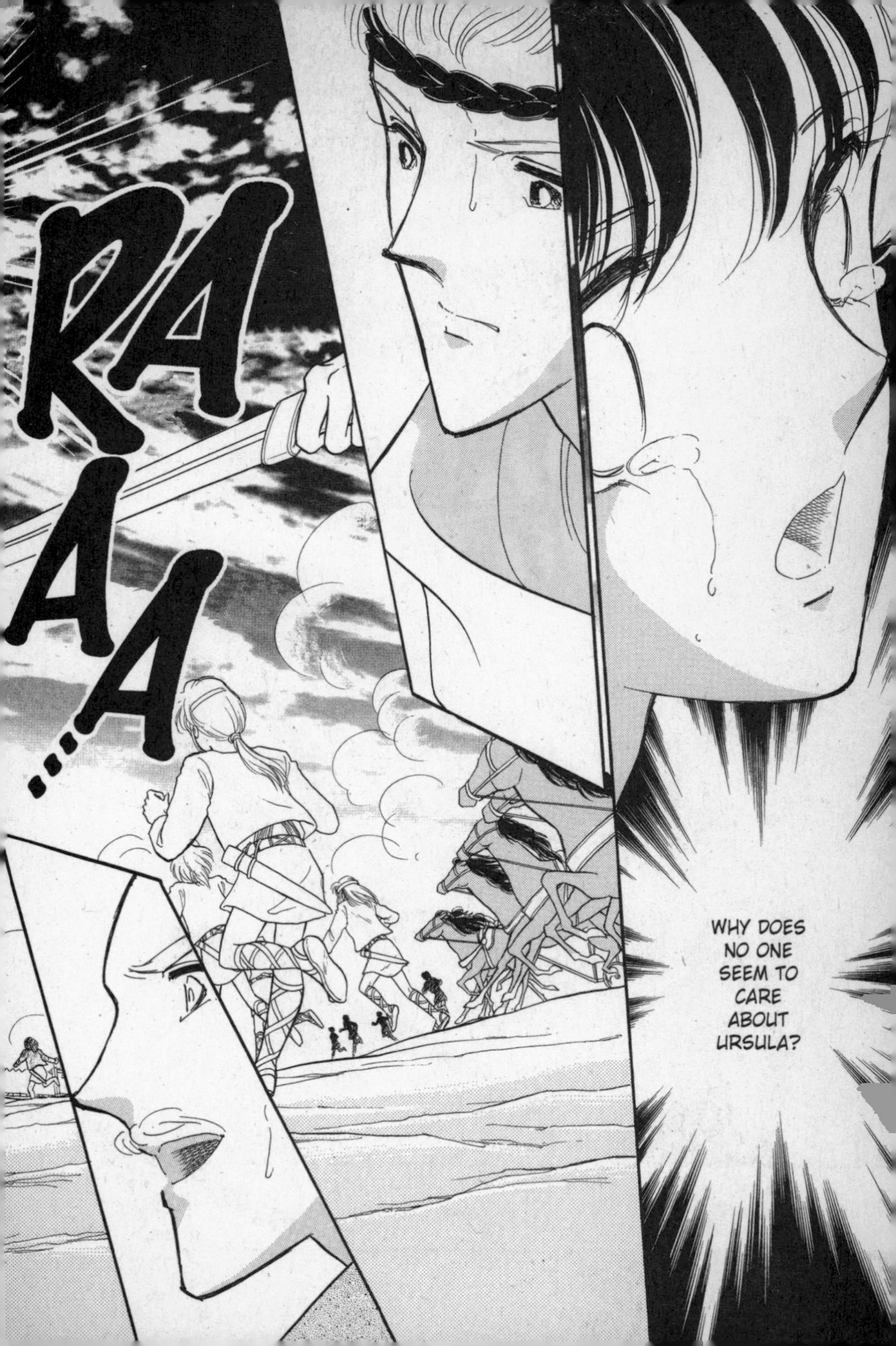
WHY DOES NO ONE SEEM TO CARE ABOUT URSULA?
RAAA...

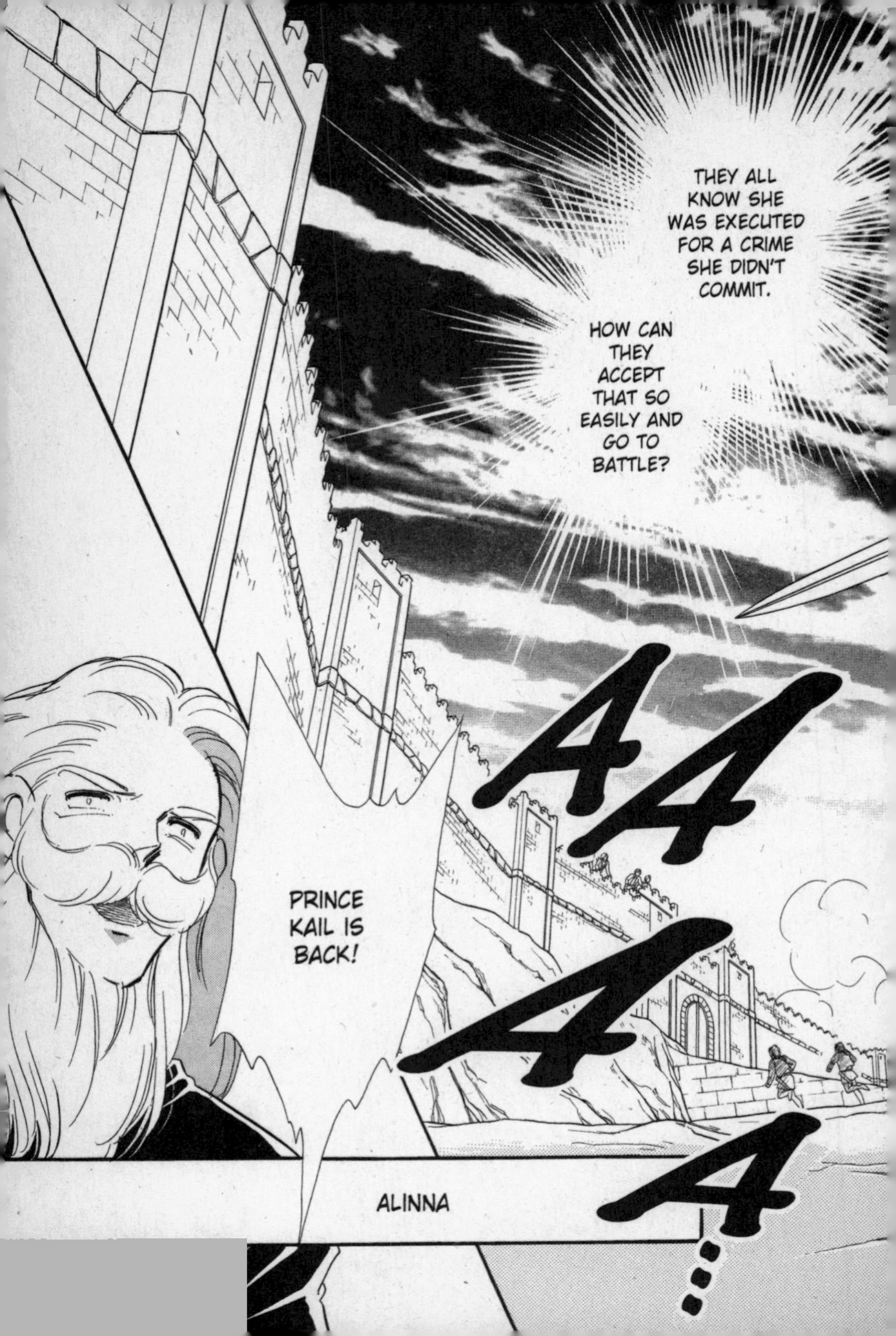
THEY ALL KNOW SHE WAS EXECUTED FOR A CRIME SHE DIDN'T COMMIT.
HOW CAN THEY ACCEPT THAT SO EASILY AND GO TO BATTLE?
AAAA...
PRINCE KAIL IS BACK!
ALINNA

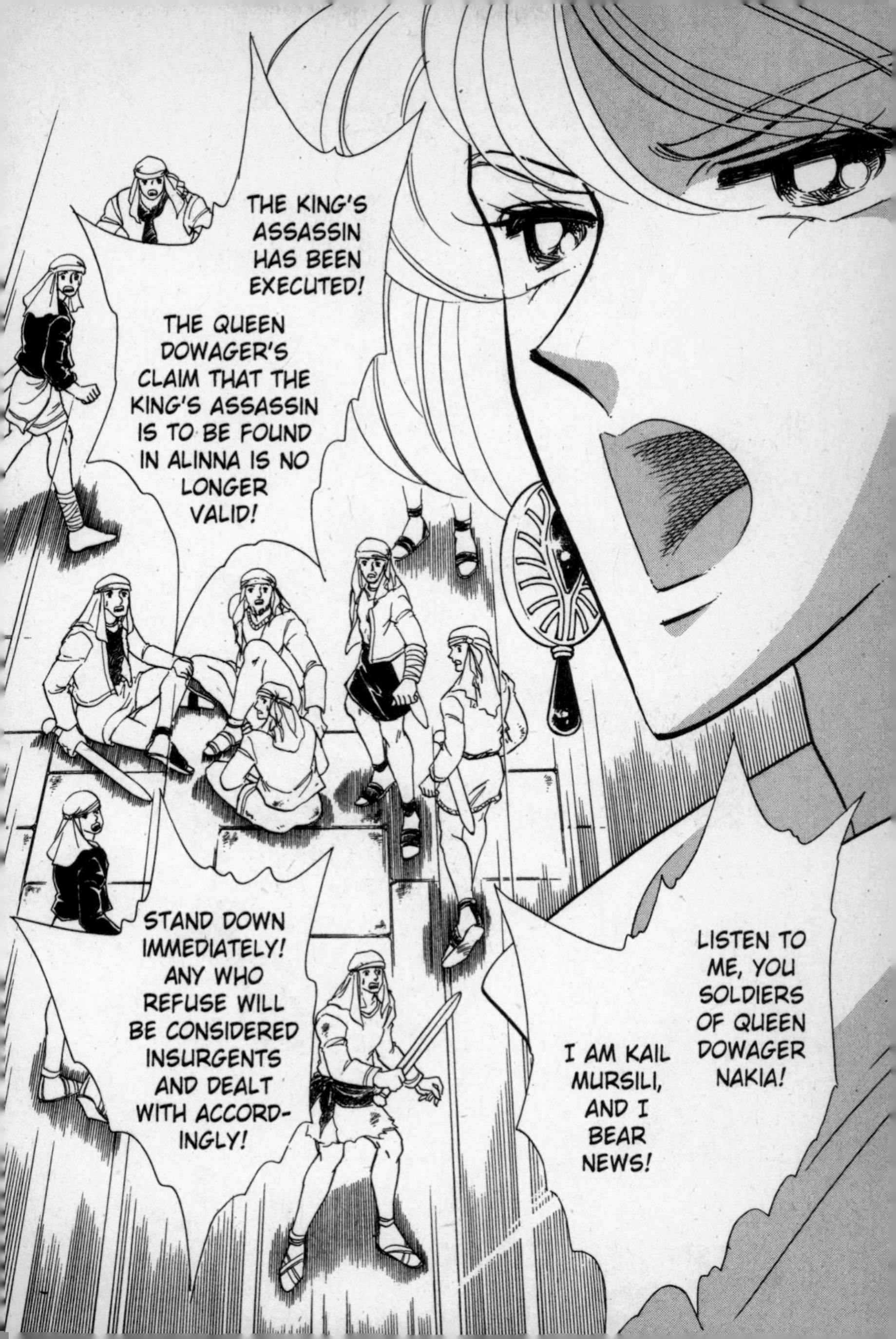
LISTEN TO ME, YOU SOLDIERS OF QUEEN DOWAGER NAKIA!
I AM KAIL MURSILI, AND I BEAR NEWS!
THE KING'S ASSASSIN HAS BEEN EXECUTED!
THE QUEEN DOWAGER'S CLAIM THAT THE KING'S ASSASSIN IS TO BE FOUND IN ALINNA IS NO LONGER VALID!
STAND DOWN IMMEDIATELY! ANY WHO REFUSE WILL BE CONSIDERED INSURGENTS AND DEALT WITH ACCORDINGLY!

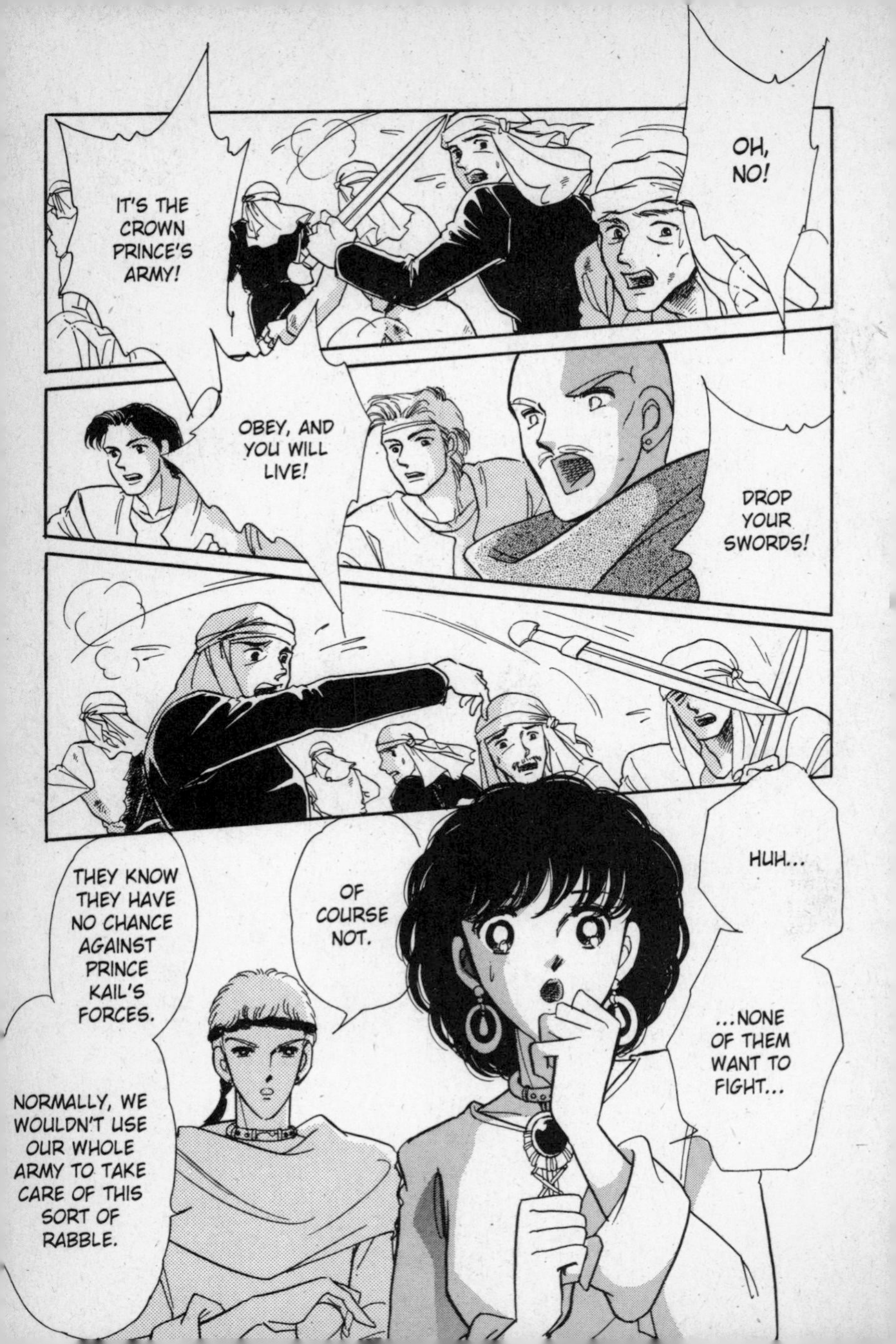
OH, NO!
IT'S THE CROWN PRINCE'S ARMY!
DROP YOUR SWORDS!
OBEY, AND YOU WILL LIVE!
HUH...
...NONE OF THEM WANT TO FIGHT...
OF COURSE NOT.
THEY KNOW THEY HAVE NO CHANCE AGAINST PRINCE KAIL'S FORCES.
NORMALLY, WE WOULDN'T USE OUR WHOLE ARMY TO TAKE CARE OF THIS SORT OF RABBLE.

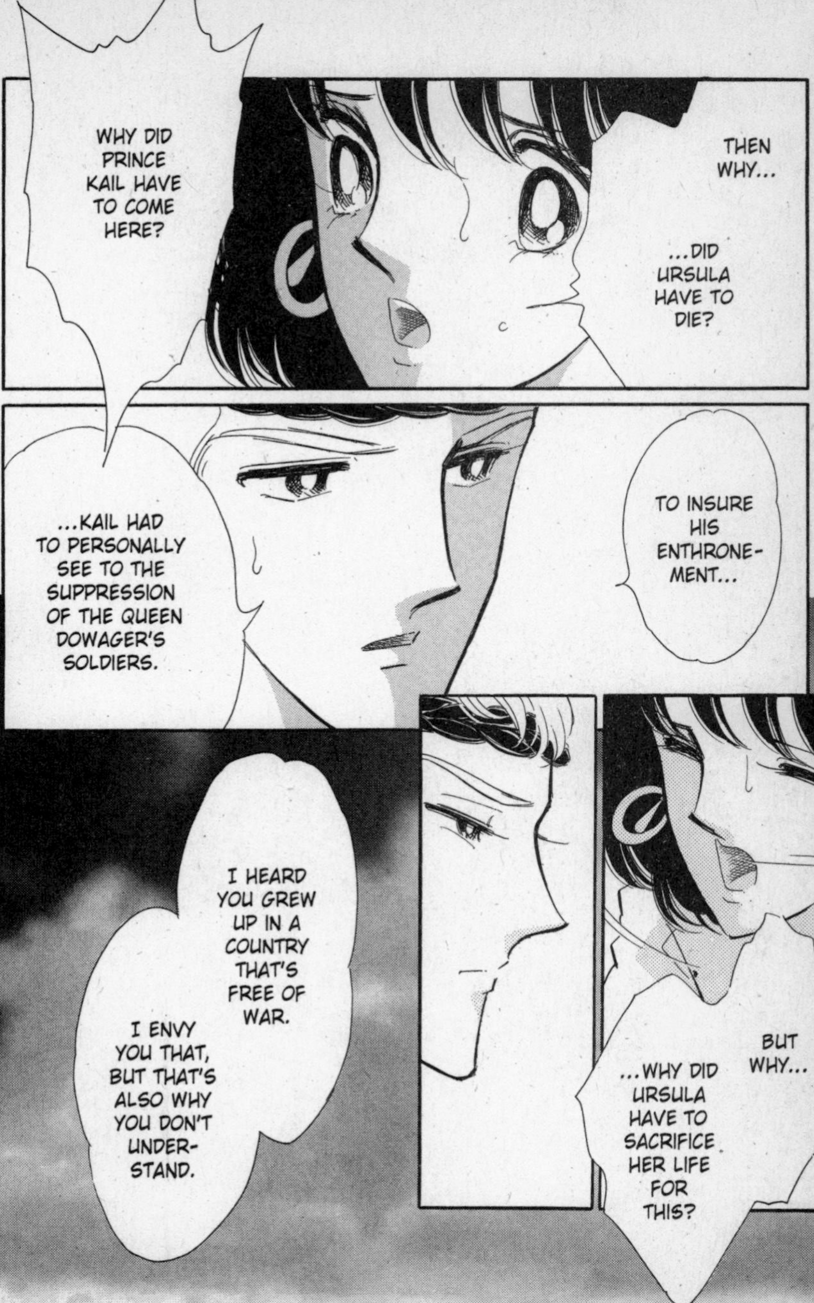
THEN WHY...
...DID URSULA HAVE TO DIE?
WHY DID PRINCE KAIL HAVE TO COME HERE?
TO INSURE HIS ENTHRONEMENT...
...KAIL HAD TO PERSONALLY SEE TO THE SUPPRESSION OF THE QUEEN DOWAGER'S SOLDIERS.
BUT WHY...
...WHY DID URSULA HAVE TO SACRIFICE HER LIFE FOR THIS?
I HEARD YOU GREW UP IN A COUNTRY THAT'S FREE OF WAR.
I ENVY YOU THAT, BUT THAT'S ALSO WHY YOU DON'T UNDERSTAND.

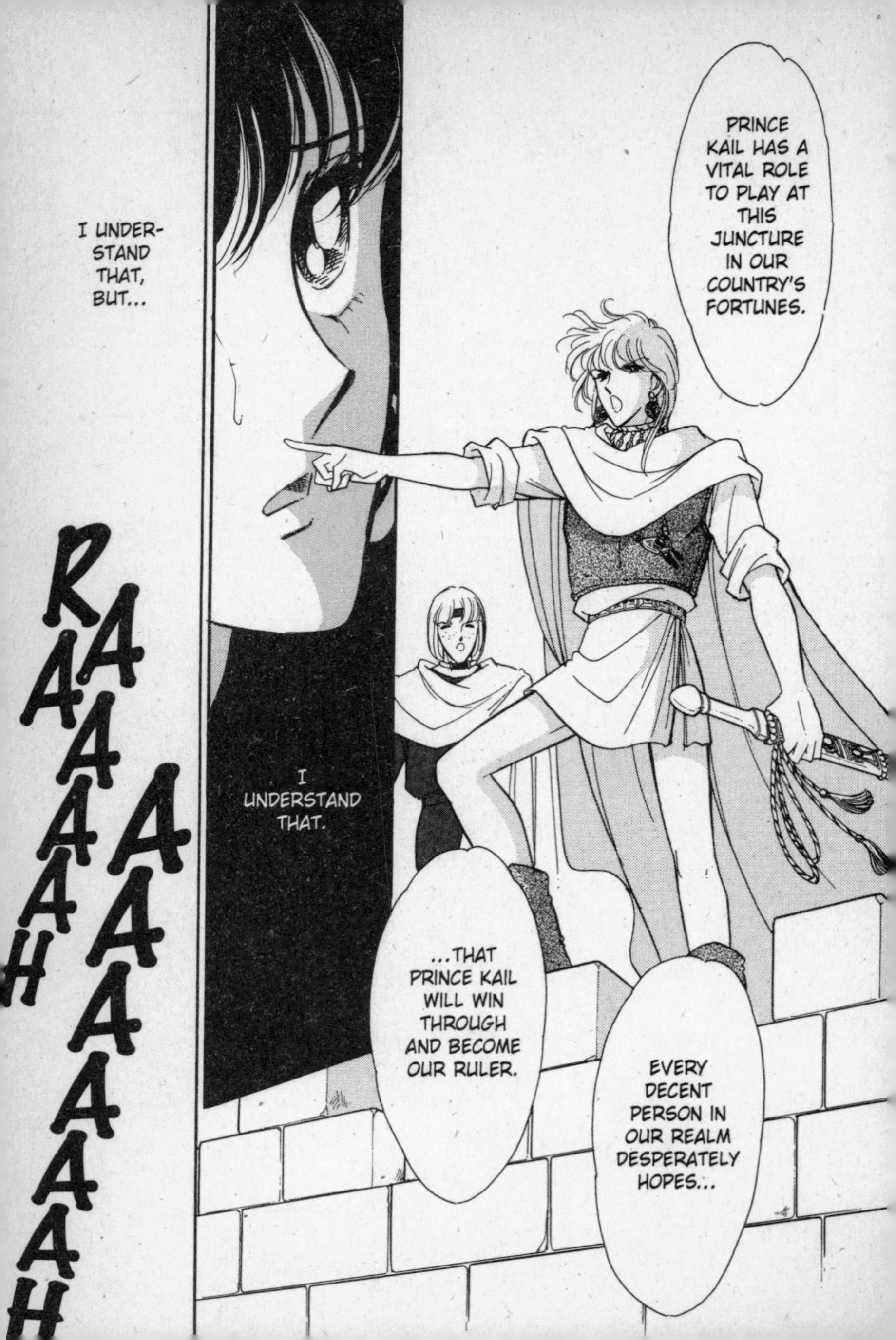
PRINCE KAIL HAS A VITAL ROLE TO PLAY AT THIS JUNCTURE IN OUR COUNTRY'S FORTUNES.
EVERY DECENT PERSON IN OUR REALM DESPERATELY HOPES...
...THAT PRINCE KAIL WILL WIN THROUGH AND BECOME OUR RULER.
I UNDERSTAND THAT.
I UNDER-STAND THAT, BUT...
RAAAAAAAAAAAAAAH

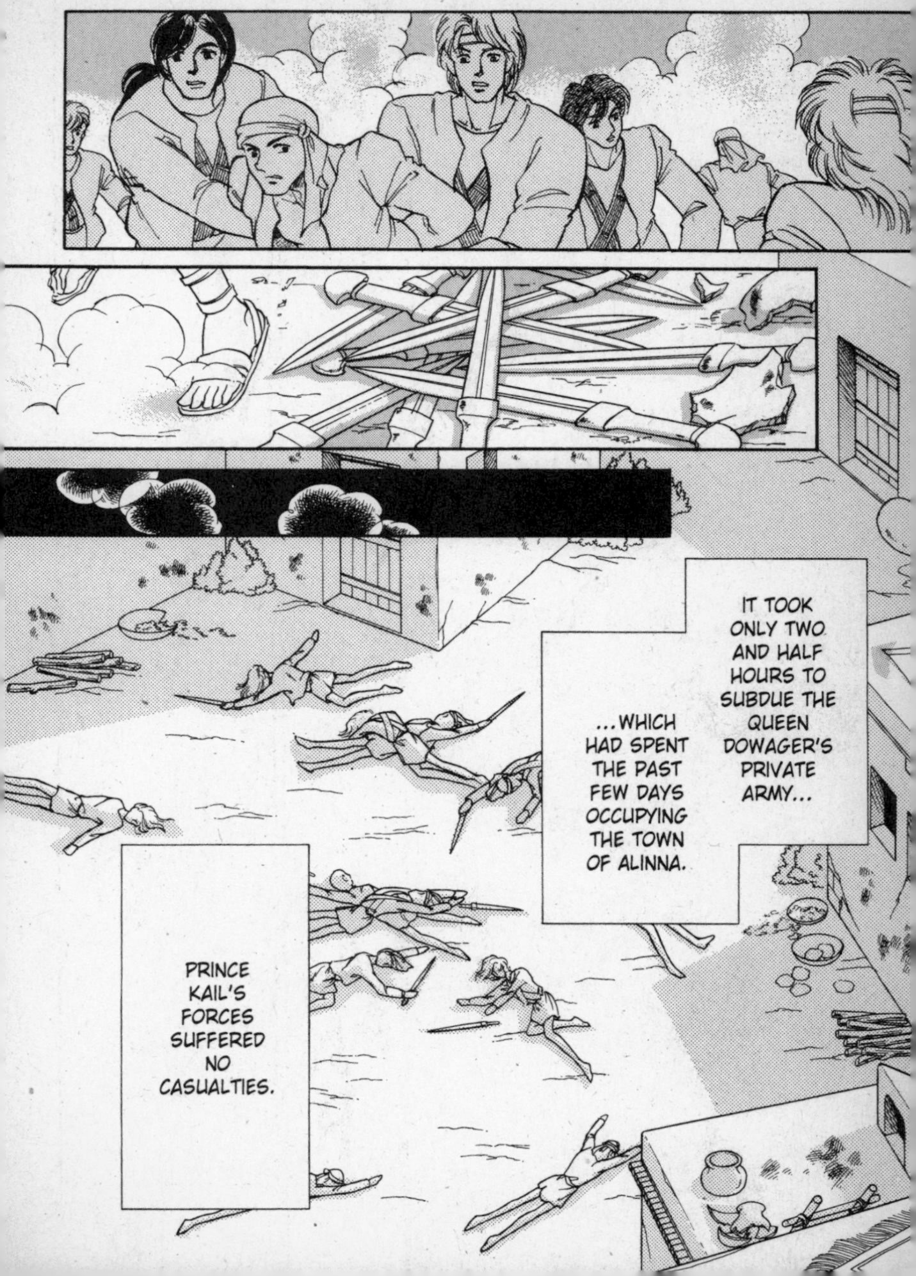
IT TOOK ONLY TWO AND HALF HOURS TO SUBDUE THE QUEEN DOWAGER'S PRIVATE ARMY...
...WHICH HAD SPENT THE PAST FEW DAYS OCCUPYING THE TOWN OF ALINNA.
PRINCE KAIL'S FORCES SUFFERED NO CASUALTIES.

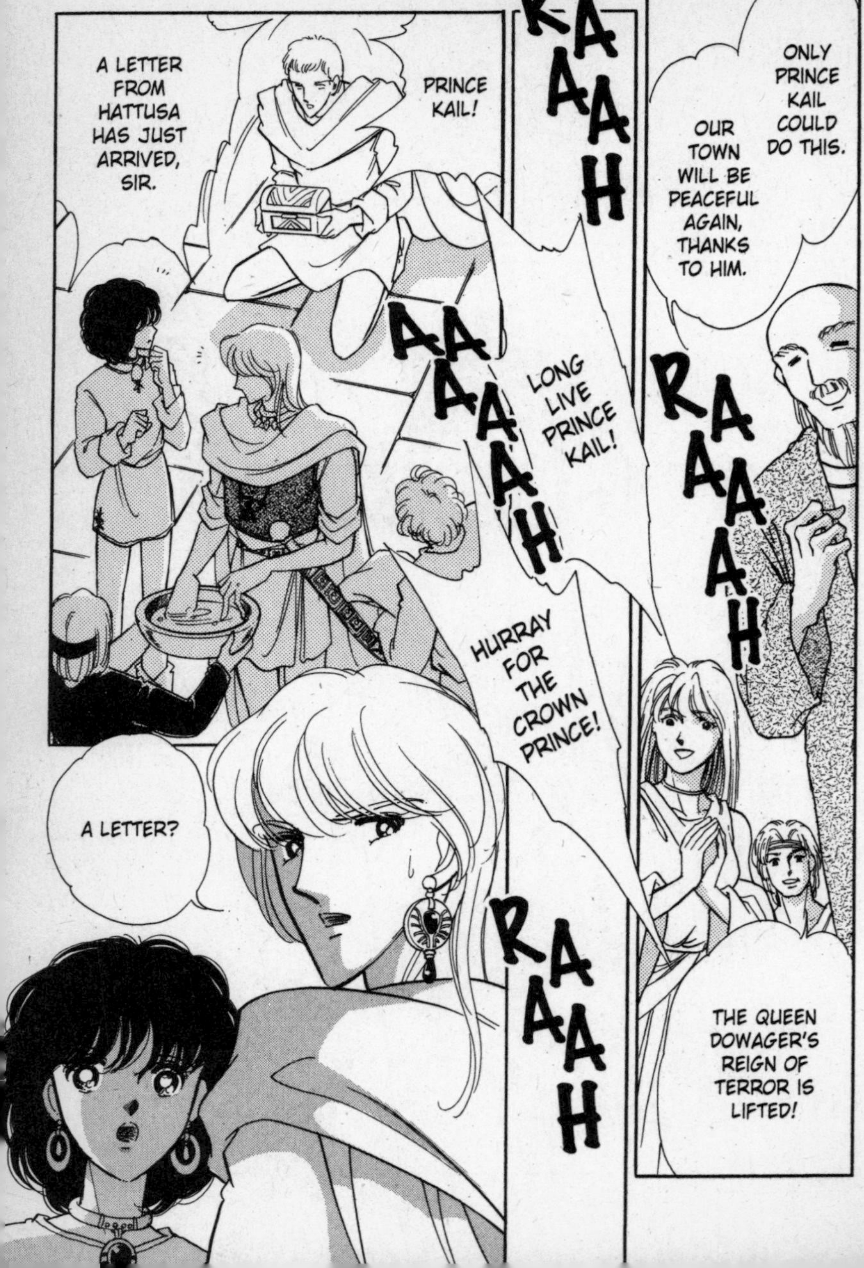
ONLY PRINCE KAIL COULD DO THIS.
OUR TOWN WILL BE PEACEFUL AGAIN, THANKS TO HIM.
RAAAAAH
THE QUEEN DOWAGER'S REIGN OF TERROR IS LIFTED!
RAAAH
AAAAAH
LONG LIVE PRINCE KAIL!
HURRAY FOR THE CROWN PRINCE!
RAAAH
PRINCE KAIL!
A LETTER FROM HATTUSA HAS JUST ARRIVED, SIR.
A LETTER?

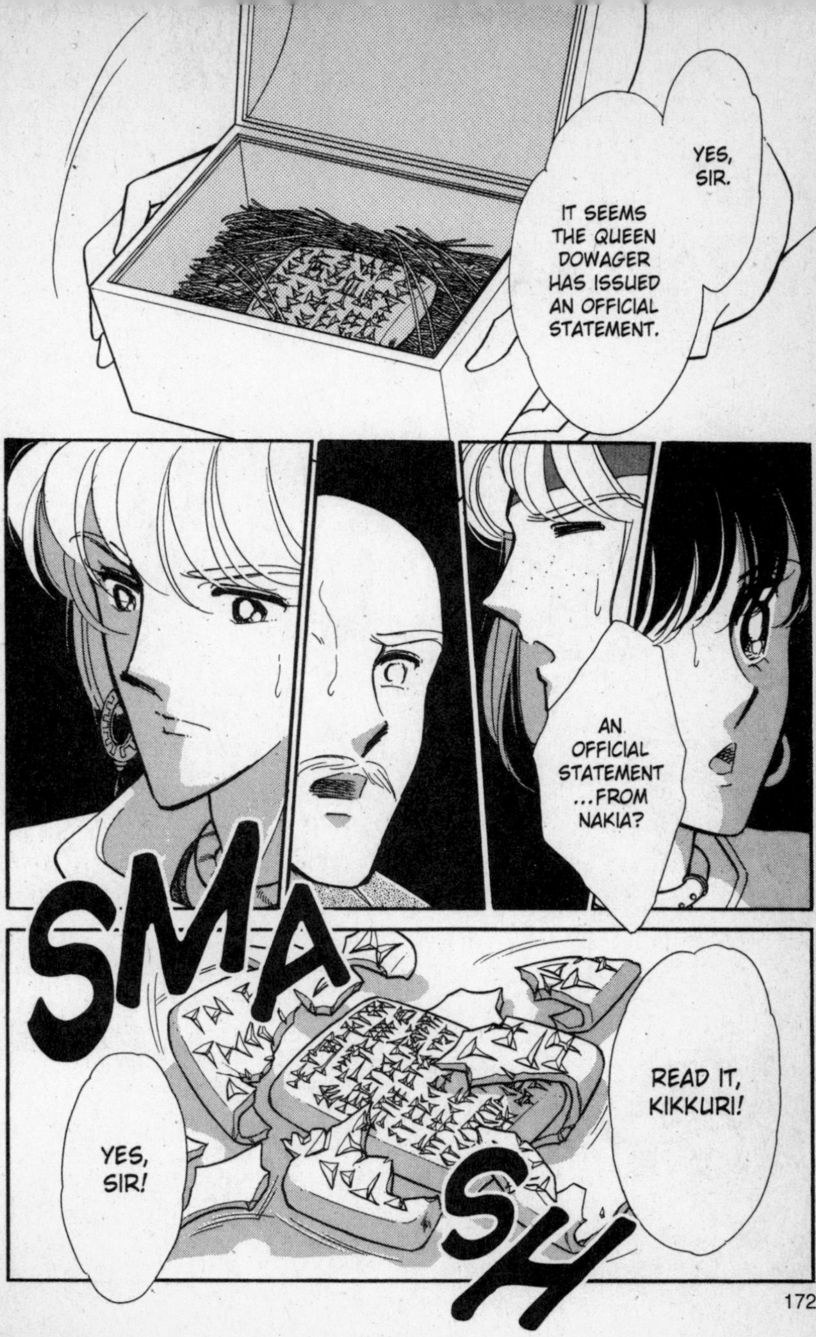
YES, SIR.
IT SEEMS THE QUEEN DOWAGER HAS ISSUED AN OFFICIAL STATEMENT.
AN OFFICIAL STATEMENT ...FROM NAKIA?
READ IT, KIKKURI!
SMASH
YES, SIR!

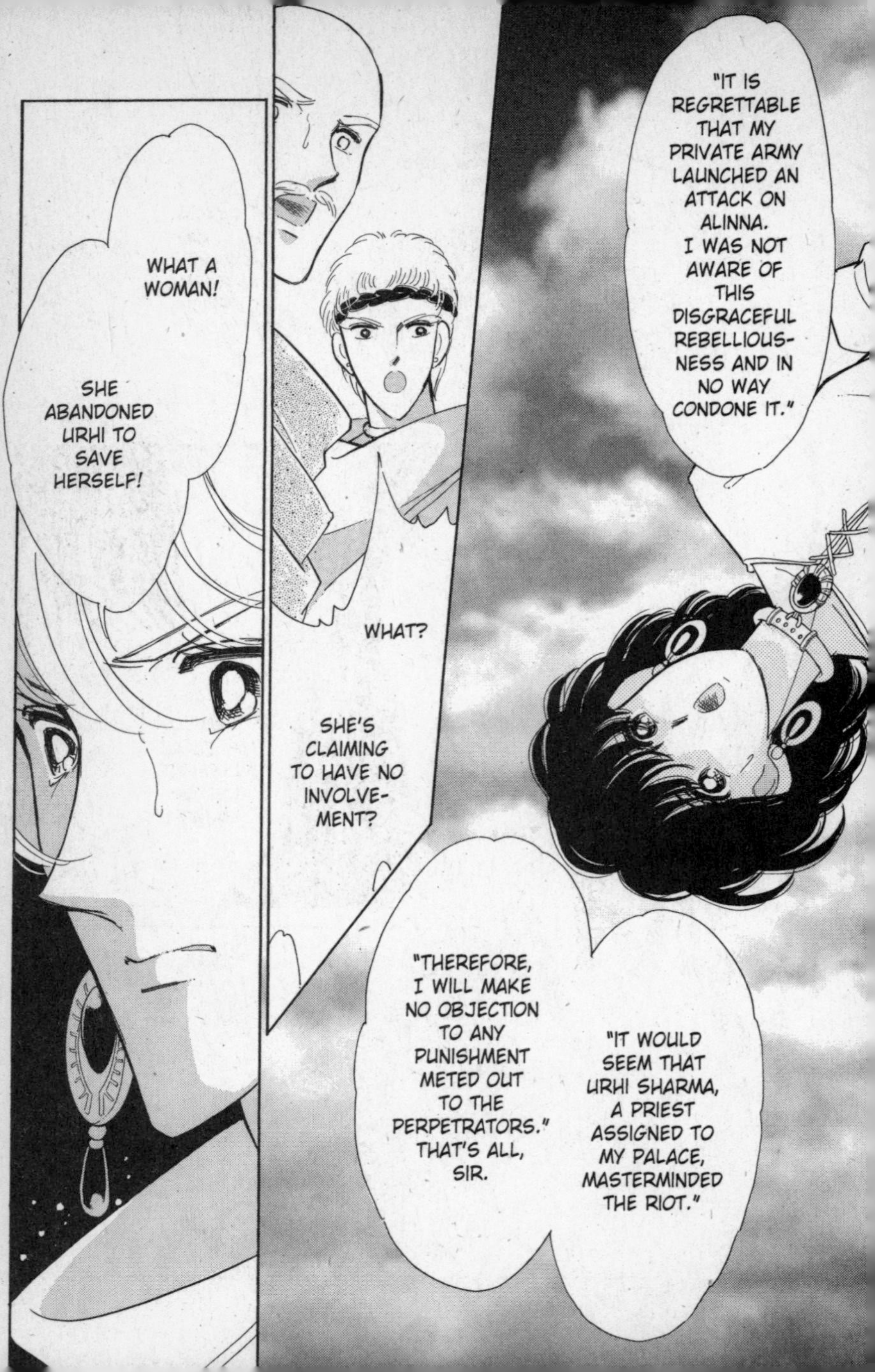
"IT IS REGRETTABLE THAT MY PRIVATE ARMY LAUNCHED AN ATTACK ON ALINNA. I WAS NOT AWARE OF THIS DISGRACEFUL REBELLIOUSNESS AND IN NO WAY CONDONE IT."
"IT WOULD SEEM THAT URHI SHARMA, A PRIEST ASSIGNED TO MY PALACE, MASTERMINDED THE RIOT."
"THEREFORE, I WILL MAKE NO OBJECTION TO ANY PUNISHMENT METED OUT TO THE PERPETRATORS." THAT'S ALL, SIR.
WHAT?
SHE'S CLAIMING TO HAVE NO INVOLVEMENT?
WHAT A WOMAN!
SHE ABANDONED URHI TO SAVE HERSELF!

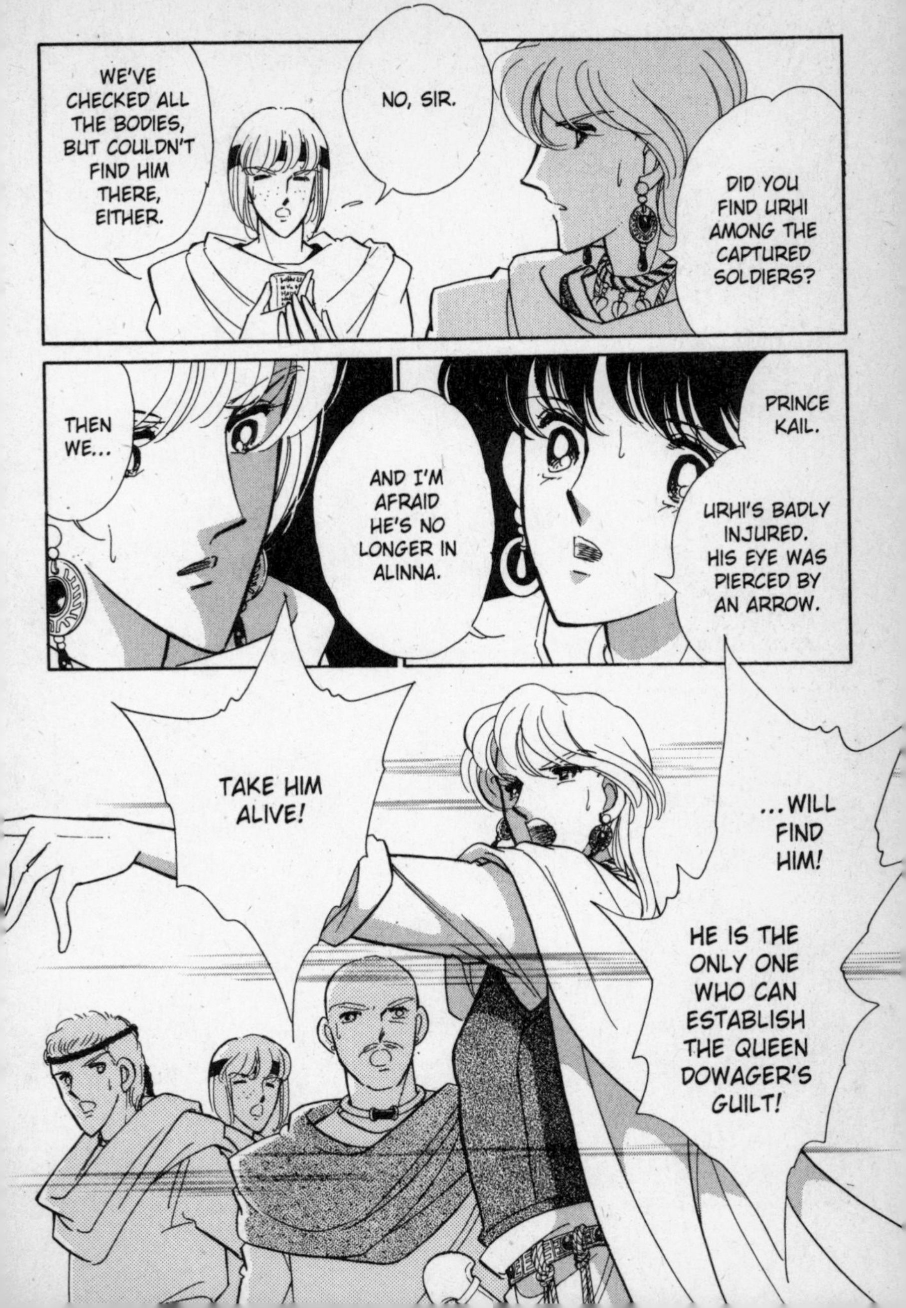
DID YOU FIND URHI AMONG THE CAPTURED SOLDIERS?
NO, SIR.
WE'VE CHECKED ALL THE BODIES, BUT COULDN'T FIND HIM THERE, EITHER.
PRINCE KAIL.
URHI'S BADLY INJURED. HIS EYE WAS PIERCED BY AN ARROW.
AND I'M AFRAID HE'S NO LONGER IN ALINNA.
THEN WE...
...WILL FIND HIM!
HE IS THE ONLY ONE WHO CAN ESTABLISH THE QUEEN DOWAGER'S GUILT!
TAKE HIM ALIVE!

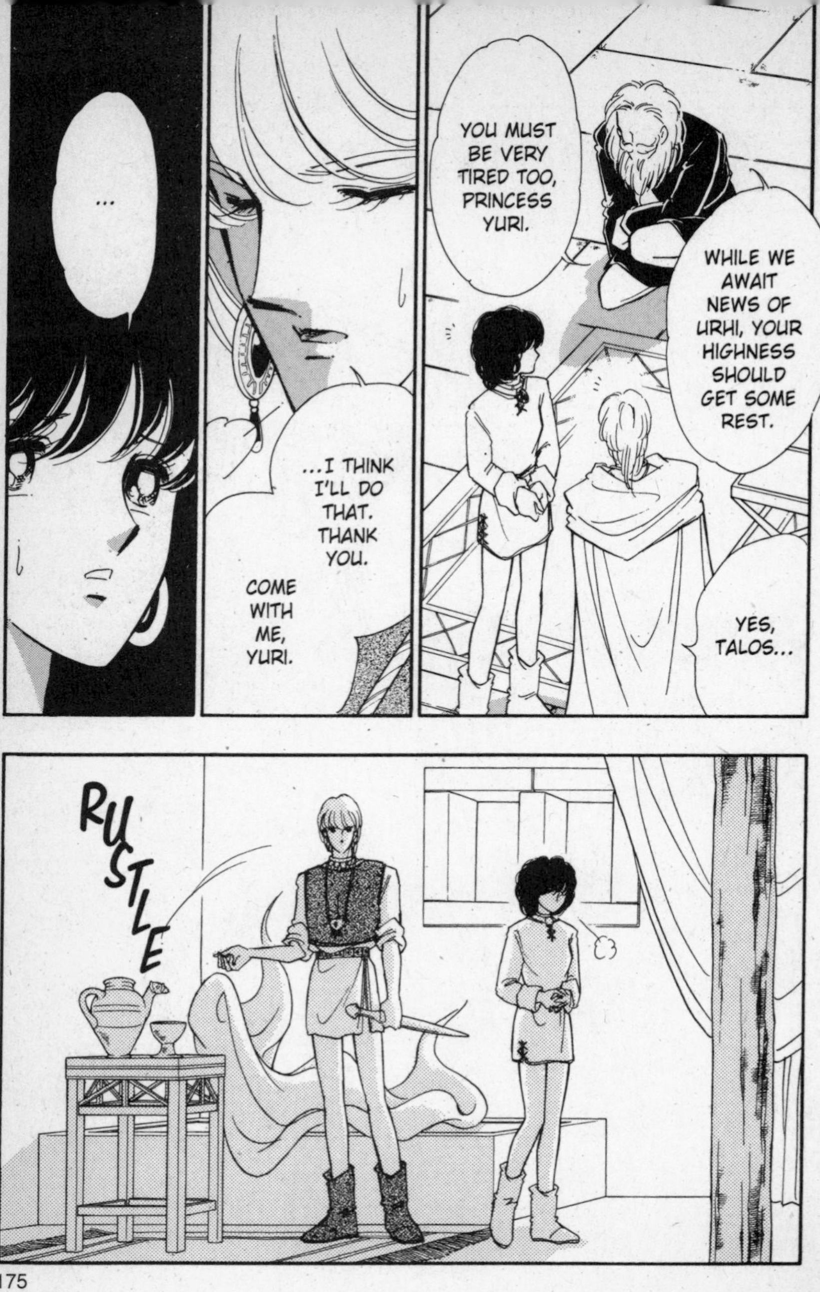
YOU MUST BE VERY TIRED TOO, PRINCESS YURI.
WHILE WE AWAIT NEWS OF URHI, YOUR HIGHNESS SHOULD GET SOME REST.
YES, TALOS...
...I THINK I'LL DO THAT. THANK YOU.
COME WITH ME, YURI.
...
RUSTLE

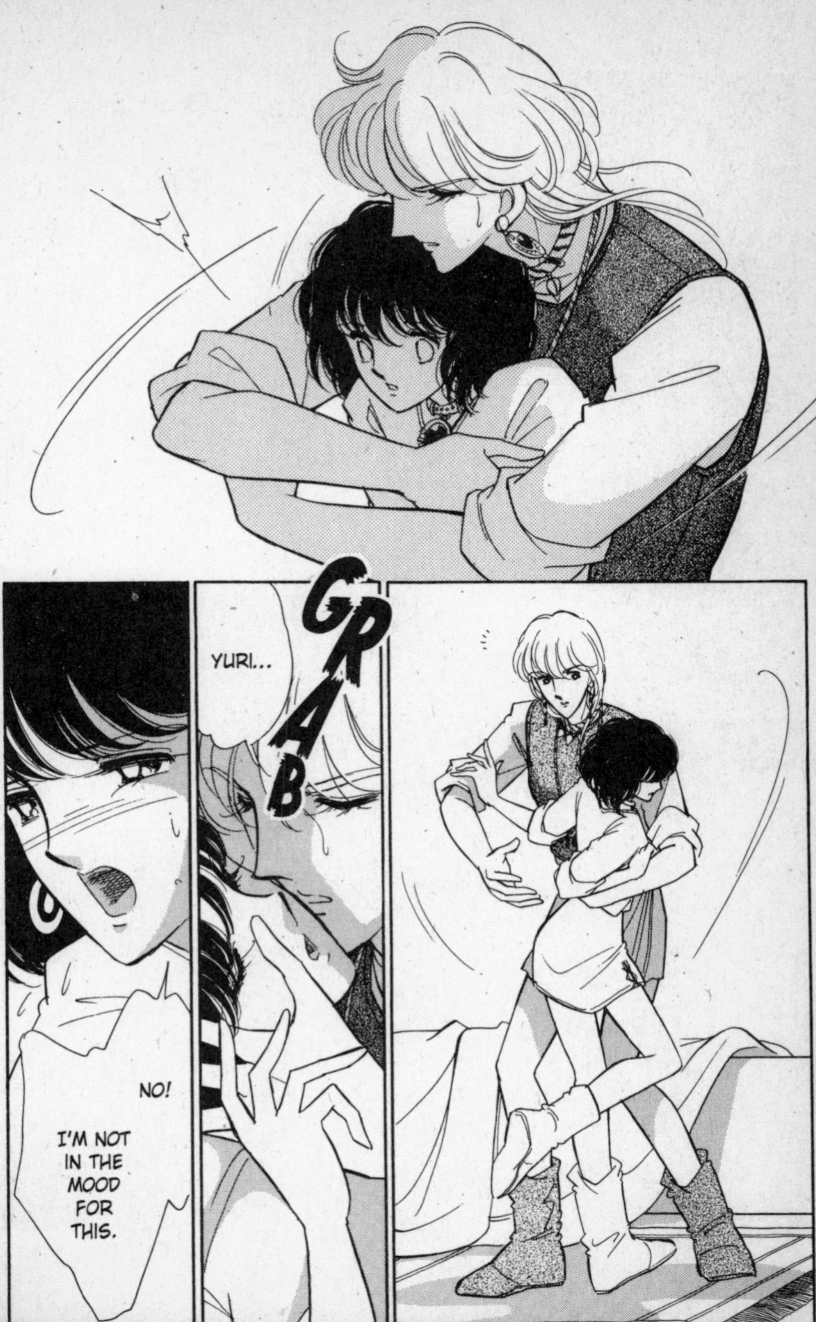
GRAB
YURI...
NO!
I'M NOT IN THE MOOD FOR THIS.

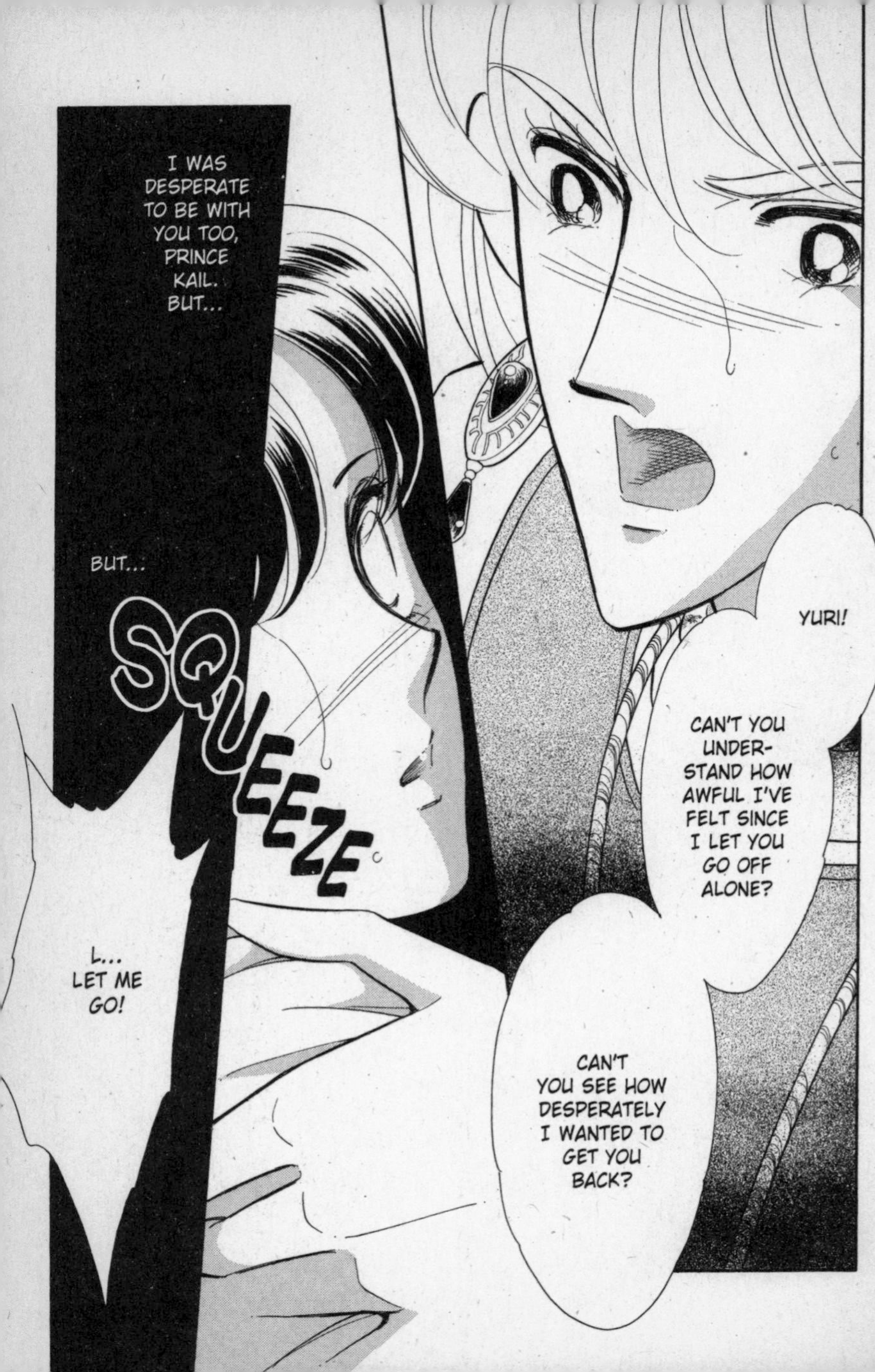
YURI!
CAN'T YOU UNDERSTAND HOW AWFUL I'VE FELT SINCE I LET YOU GO OFF ALONE?
CAN'T YOU SEE HOW DESPERATELY I WANTED TO GET YOU BACK?
I WAS DESPERATE TO BE WITH YOU TOO, PRINCE KAIL. BUT...
BUT...
SQUEEZE
I... LET ME GO!

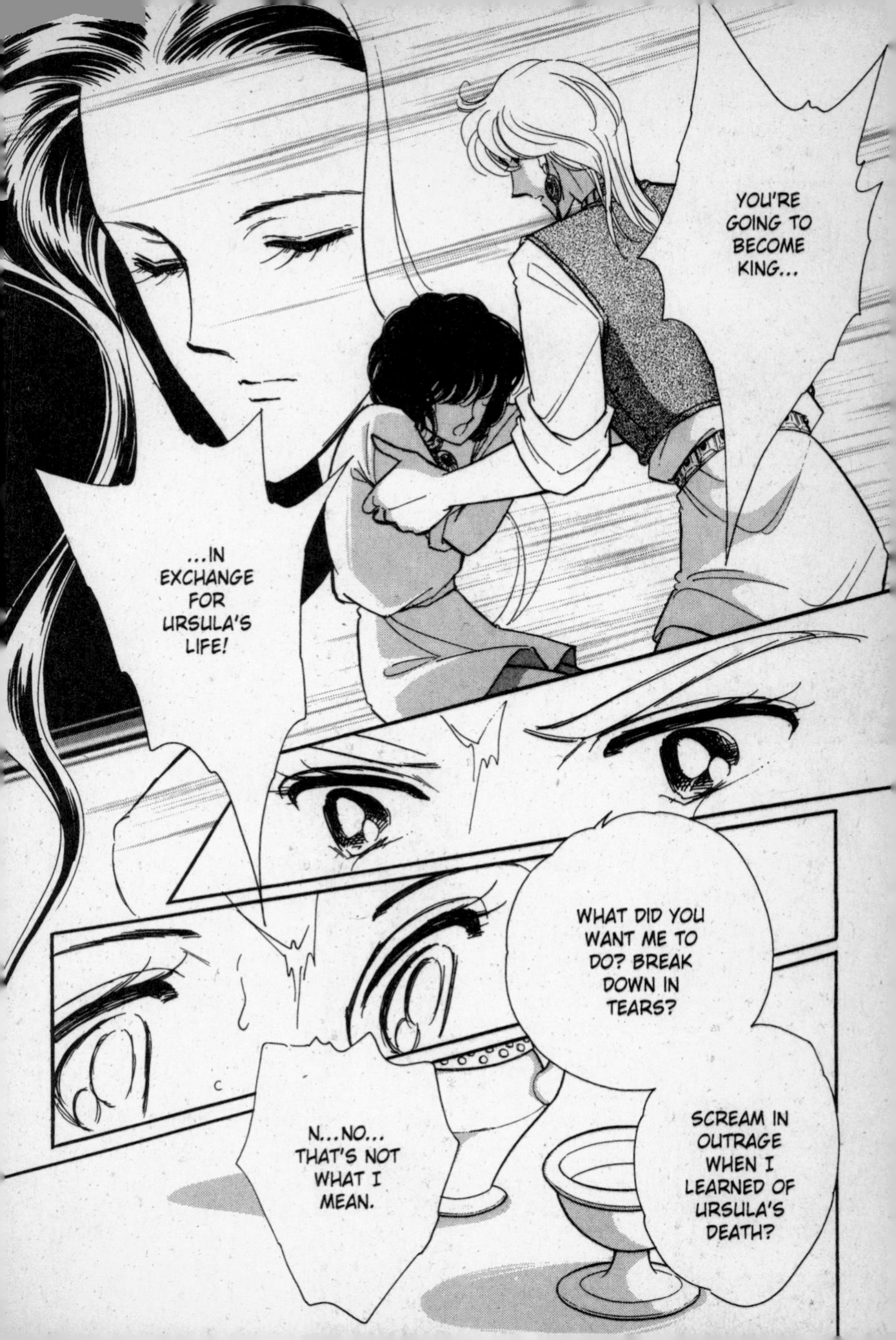
YOU'RE GOING TO BECOME KING...
...IN EXCHANGE FOR URSULA'S LIFE!
WHAT DID YOU WANT ME TO DO? BREAK DOWN IN TEARS?
SCREAM IN OUTRAGE WHEN I LEARNED OF URSULA'S DEATH?
N...NO... THAT'S NOT WHAT I MEAN.

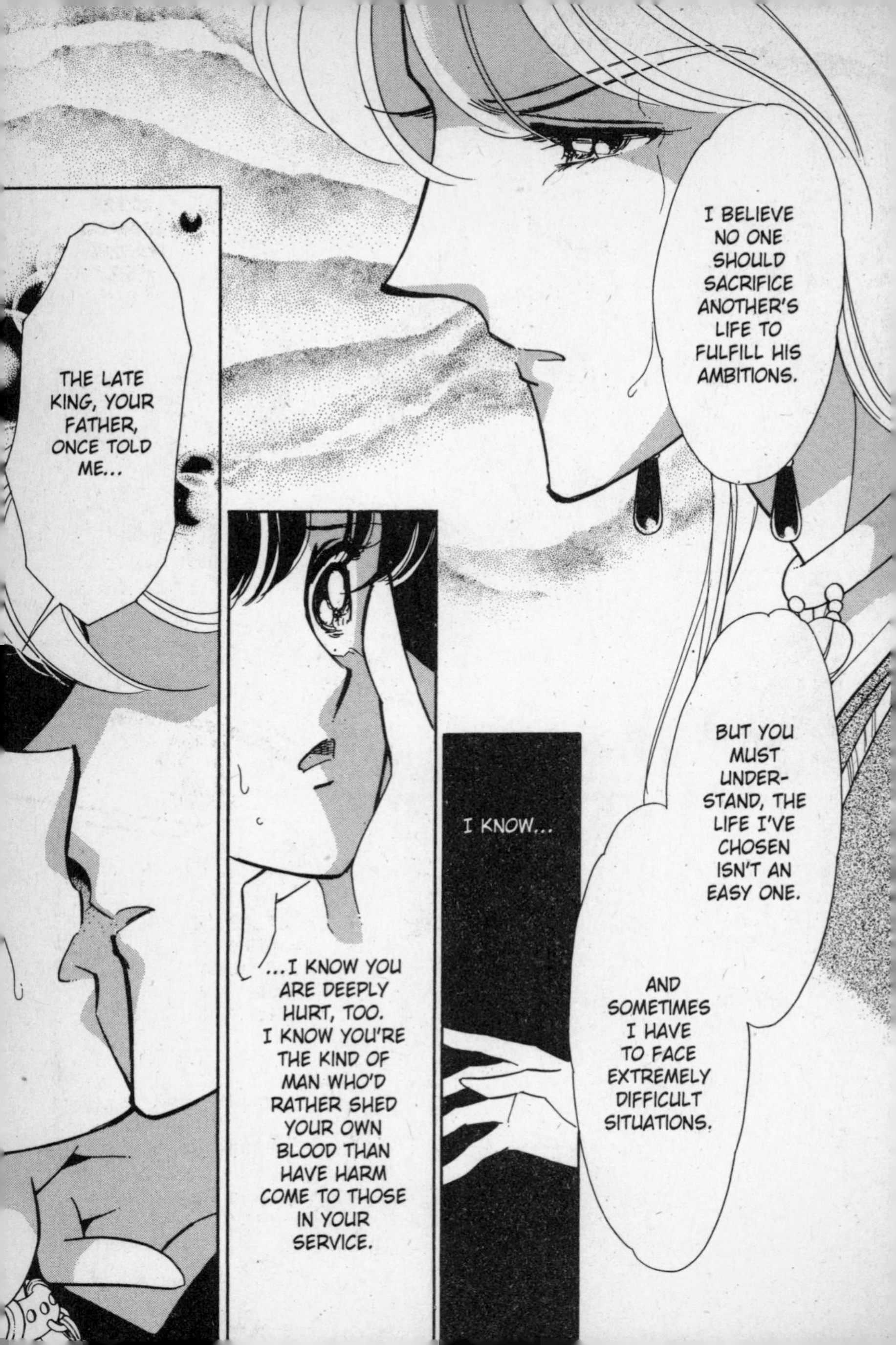
THE LATE KING, YOUR FATHER, ONCE TOLD ME...
I BELIEVE NO ONE SHOULD SACRIFICE ANOTHER'S LIFE TO FULFILL HIS AMBITIONS.
BUT YOU MUST UNDER-STAND, THE LIFE I'VE CHOSEN ISN'T AN EASY ONE.
AND SOMETIMES I HAVE TO FACE EXTREMELY DIFFICULT SITUATIONS.
I KNOW...
...I KNOW YOU ARE DEEPLY HURT, TOO. I KNOW YOU'RE THE KIND OF MAN WHO'D RATHER SHED YOUR OWN BLOOD THAN HAVE HARM COME TO THOSE IN YOUR SERVICE.

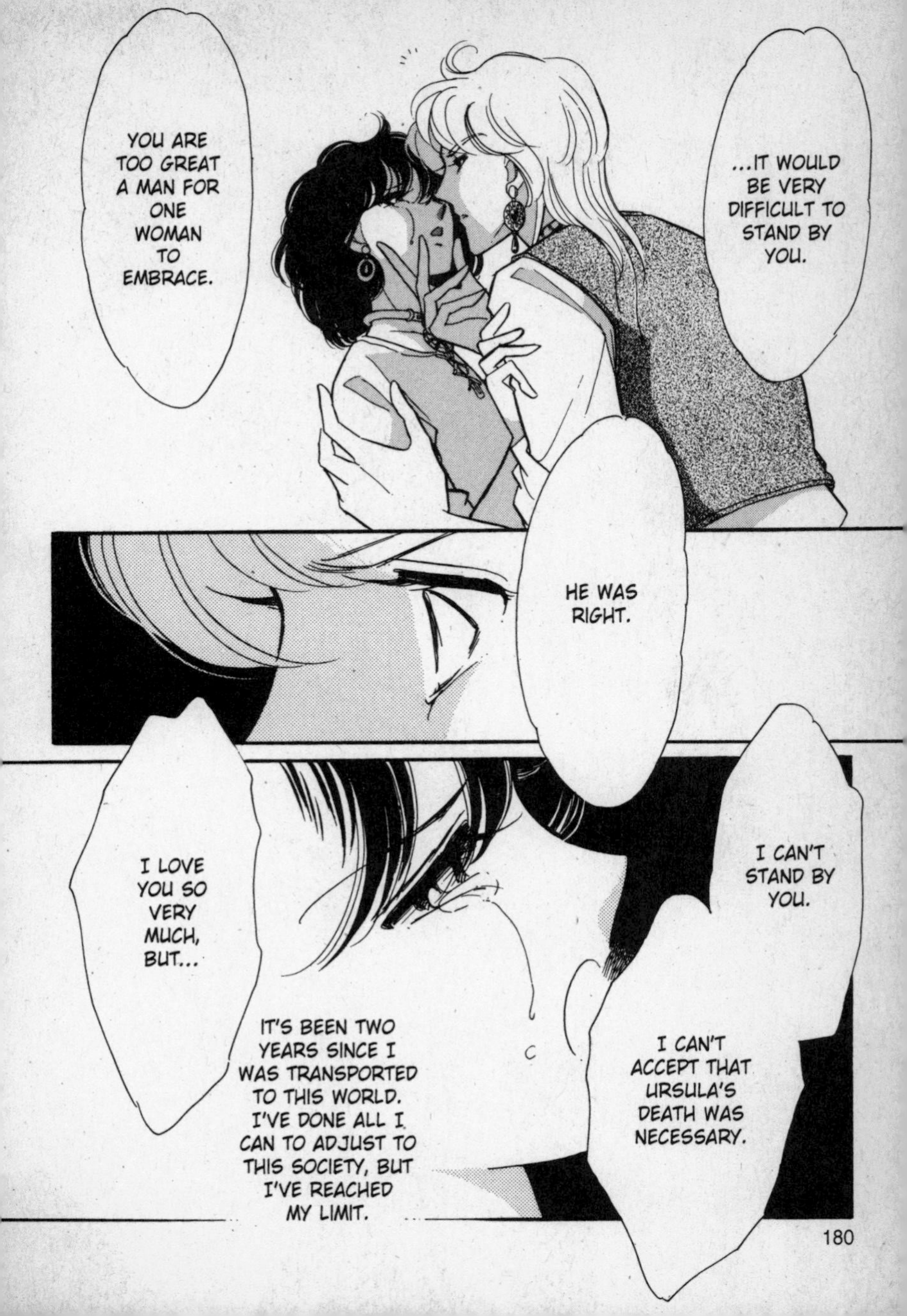
YOU ARE TOO GREAT A MAN FOR ONE WOMAN TO EMBRACE.
...IT WOULD BE VERY DIFFICULT TO STAND BY YOU.
HE WAS RIGHT.
I CAN'T STAND BY YOU.
I LOVE YOU SO VERY MUCH, BUT...
I CAN'T ACCEPT THAT URSULA'S DEATH WAS NECESSARY.
IT'S BEEN TWO YEARS SINCE I WAS TRANSPORTED TO THIS WORLD. I'VE DONE ALL I CAN TO ADJUST TO THIS SOCIETY, BUT I'VE REACHED MY LIMIT.

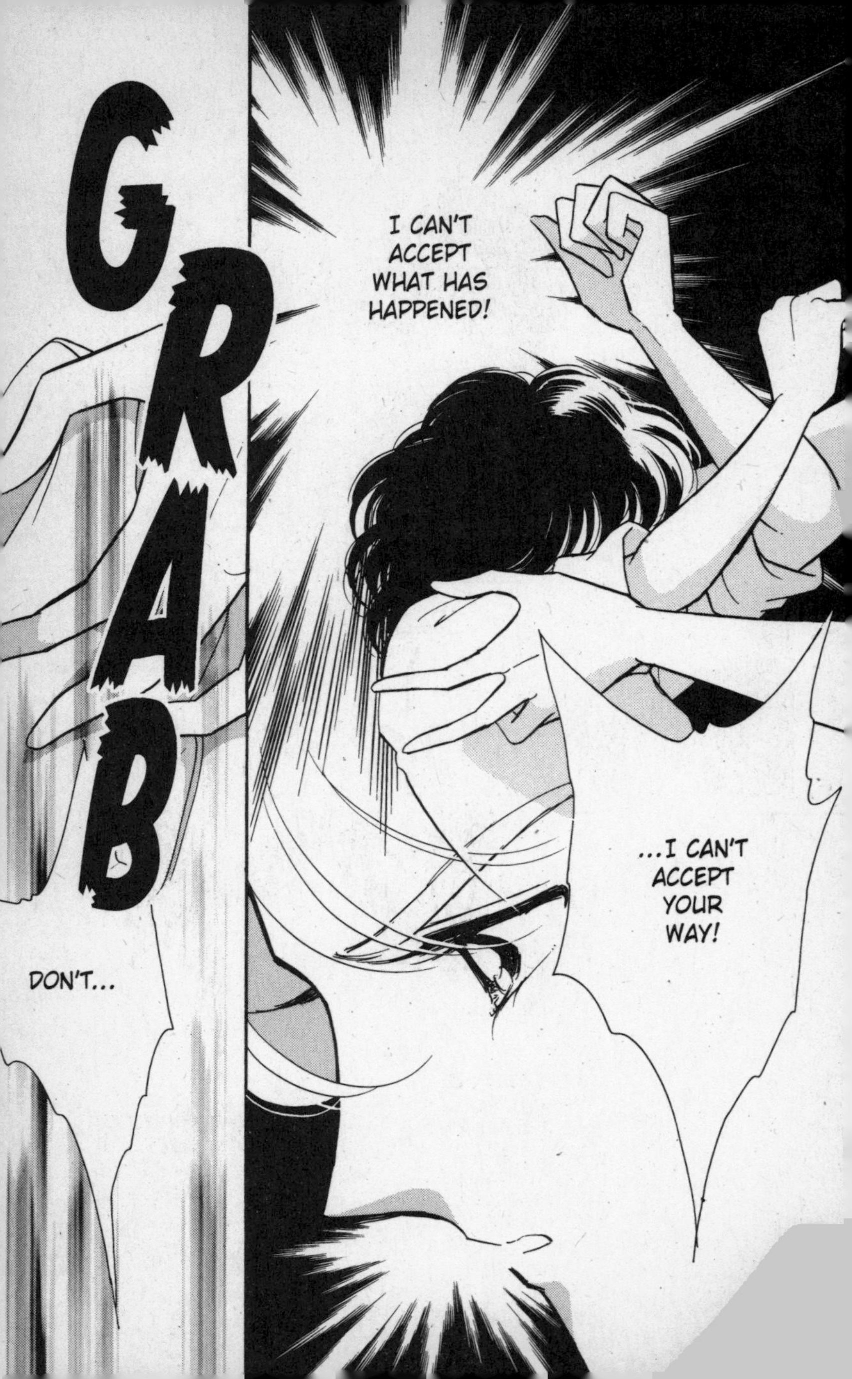
I CAN'T ACCEPT WHAT HAS HAPPENED!
...I CAN'T ACCEPT YOUR WAY!
GRAB
DON'T...

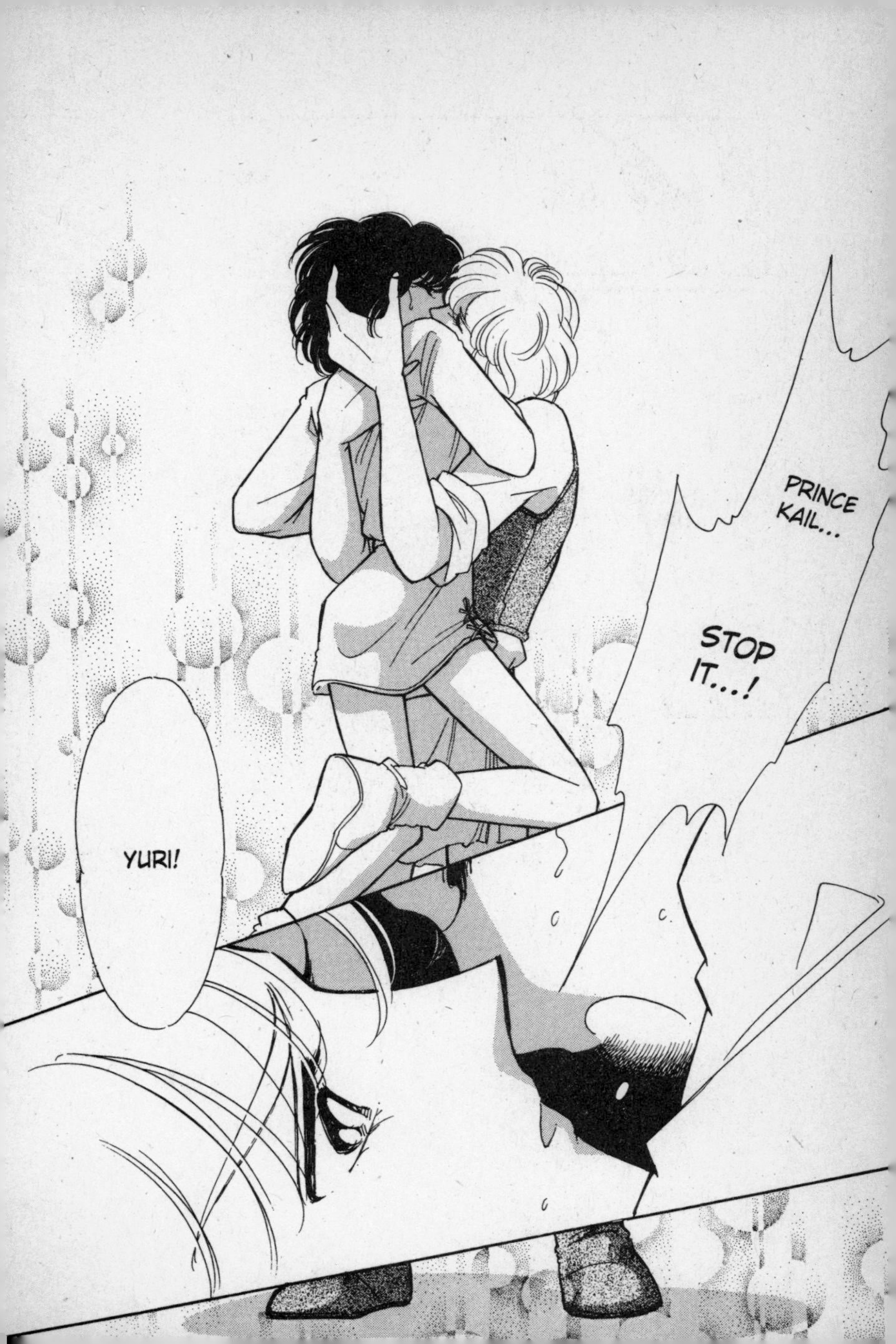
PRINCE KAIL...
STOP IT...!
YURI!

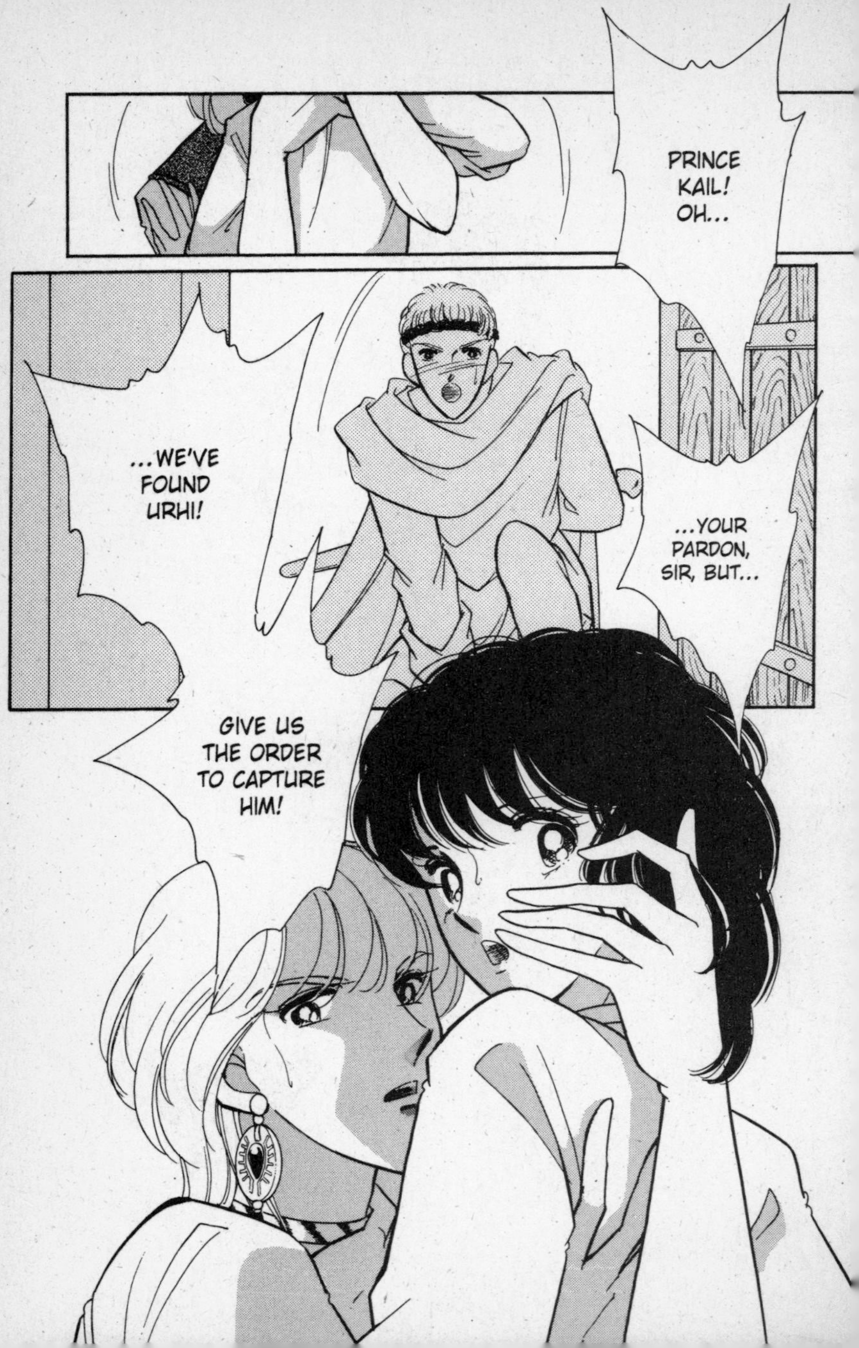
PRINCE KAIL! OH...
...YOUR PARDON, SIR, BUT...
...WE'VE FOUND URHI!
GIVE US THE ORDER TO CAPTURE HIM!

GALLERY ILLUSTRATION

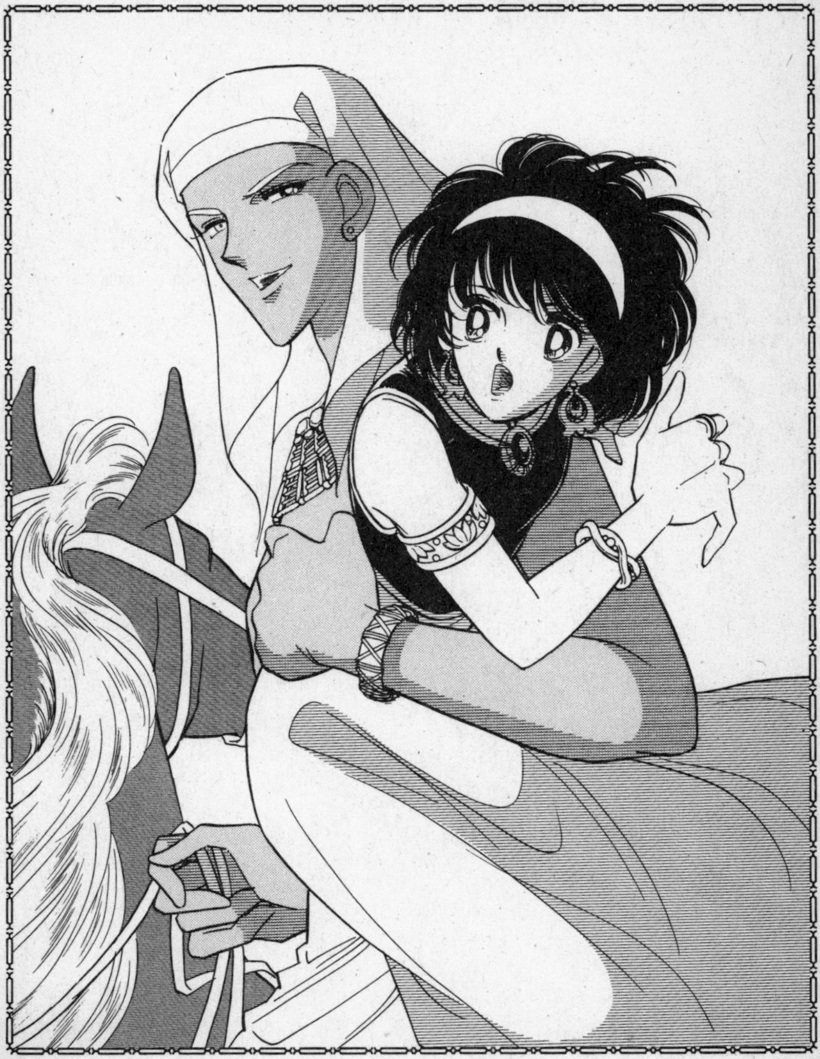

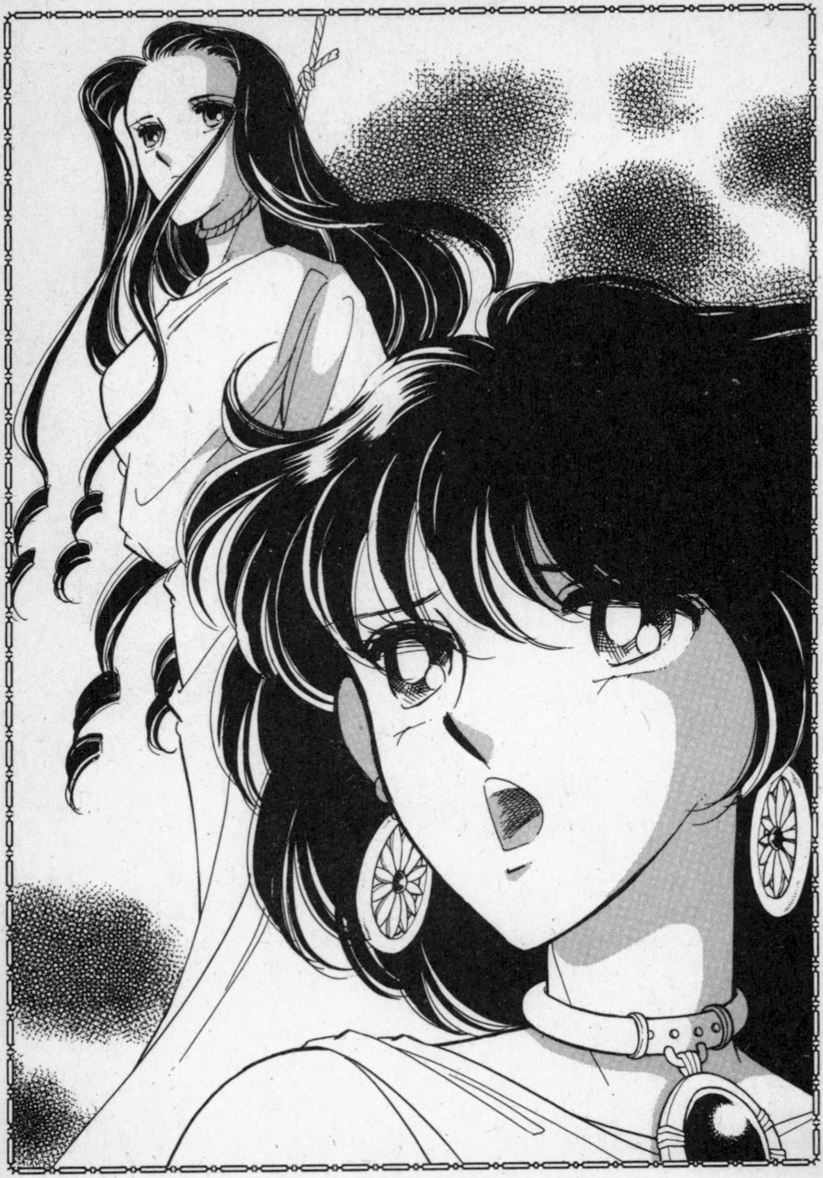

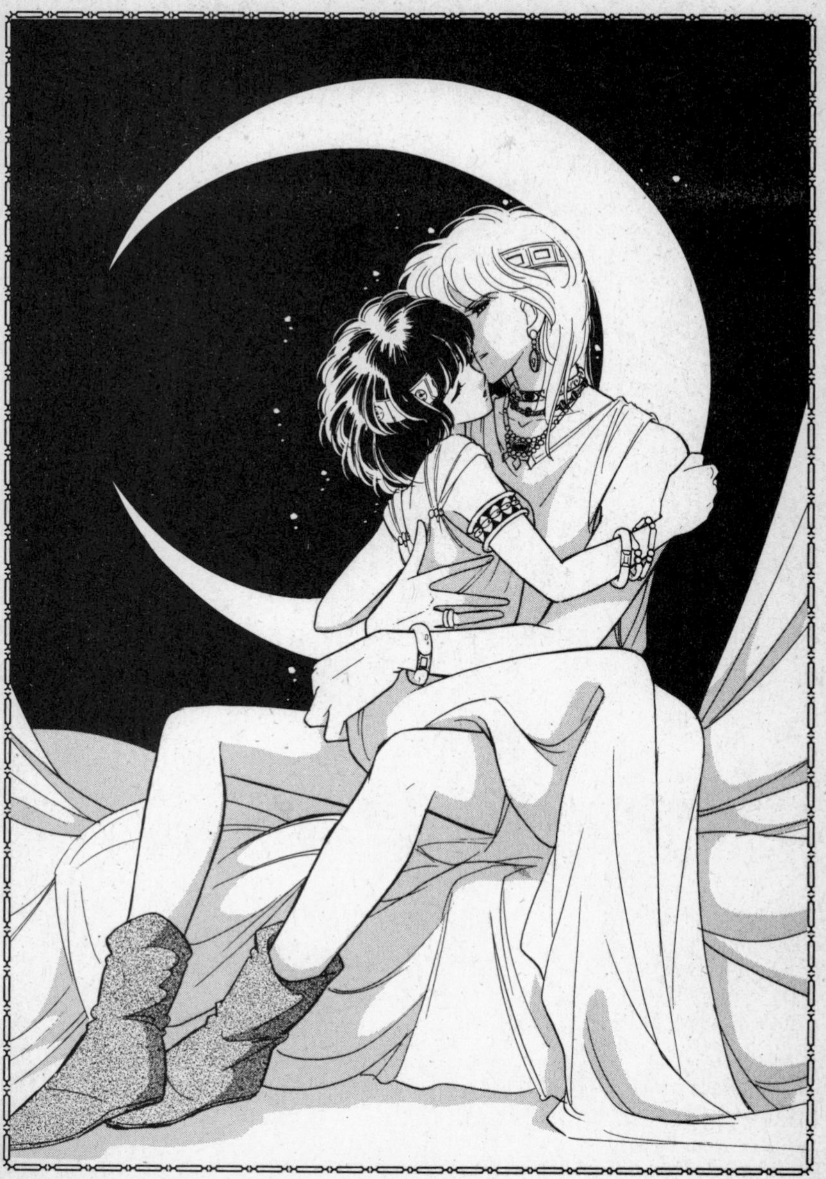

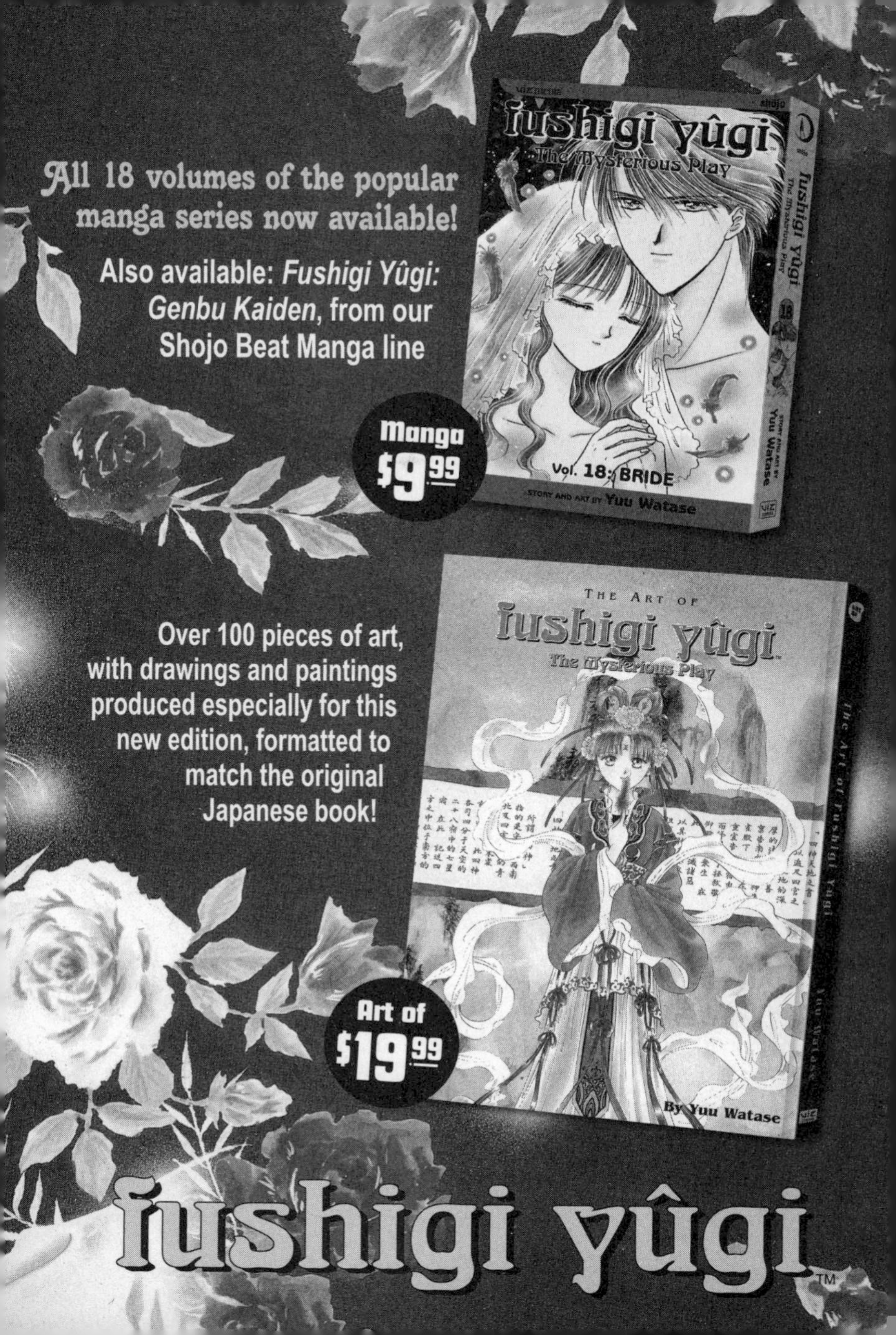
All 18 volumes of the popular manga series now available!
Also available: Fushigi Yûgi: Genbu Kaiden, from our Shojo Beat Manga line
fushigi yûgi
The Mysterious Play
Vol. 18: BRIDE
STORY AND ART BY Yuu Watase
Manga $9.99
Over 100 pieces of art, with drawings and paintings produced especially for this new edition, formatted to match the original Japanese book!
THE ART OF
fushigi yûgi
The Mysterious Play
By Yuu Watase
Art of $19.99
fushigi yûgi™

GET THE COMPLETE
FUSHIGI YÛGI COLLECTION

shôjo

Love Sho

Let us know what you think!

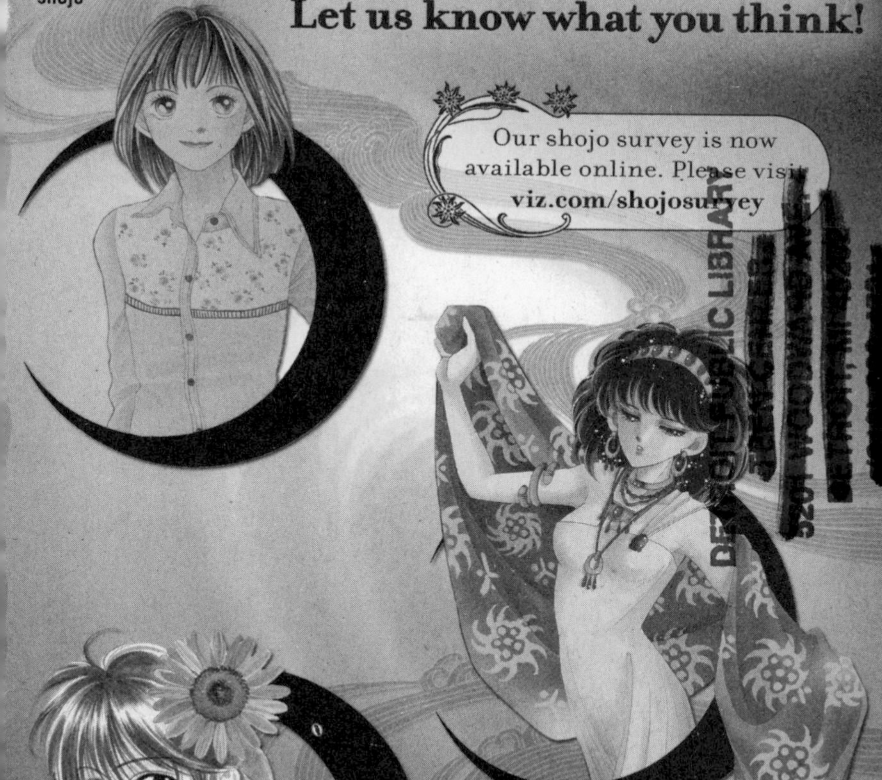
Our shojo survey is now available online. Please visit viz.com/shojosurvey

Help us make the manga you love better!

VIZ media

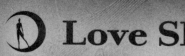

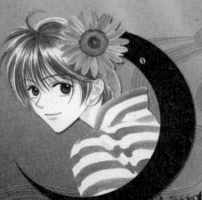